Institutionalization of World-Class University in Global Competition

The Changing Academy – The Changing Academic Profession in International Comparative Perspective 6

Scope of the series

As the landscape of higher education has in recent years undergone significant changes, so correspondingly have the backgrounds, specializations, expectations and work roles of academic staff. The Academy is expected to be more professional in teaching, more productive in research and more entrepreneurial in everything. Some of the changes involved have raised questions about the attractiveness of an academic career for today's graduates. At the same time, knowledge has come to be identified as the most vital resource of contemporary societies.

The Changing Academy series examines the nature and extent of the changes experienced by the academic profession in recent years. It explores both the reasons for and the consequences of these changes. It considers the implications of the changes for the attractiveness of the academic profession as a career and for the ability of the academic community to contribute to the further development of knowledge societies and the attainment of national goals. It makes comparisons on these matters between different national higher education systems, institutional types, disciplines and generations of academics, drawing initially on available data-sets and qualitative research studies with special emphasis on the recent twenty nation survey of the Changing Academic Profession. Among the themes featured will be:

1. Relevance of the Academy's Work
2. Internationalization of the Academy
3. Current Governance and Management, particularly as perceived by the Academy
4. Commitment of the Academy

The audience includes researchers in higher education, sociology of education and political science studies; university managers and administrators; national and institutional policymakers; officials and staff at governments and organizations, e.g. the World Bank.

For further volumes:
http://www.springer.com/series/8668

Jung Cheol Shin • Barbara M. Kehm
Editors

Institutionalization of World-Class University in Global Competition

Springer

Editors
Jung Cheol Shin
Department of Education
Seoul National University
Korea, Republic of (South Korea)

Barbara M. Kehm
University of Kassel
Germany

ISBN 978-94-007-4974-0   ISBN 978-94-007-4975-7 (eBook)
DOI 10.1007/978-94-007-4975-7
Springer Dordrecht Heidelberg New York London

Library of Congress Control Number: 2012953388

Printed on acid-free paper

Springer is part of Springer Science+Business Media (www.springer.com)

Preface

Current discussions on the world-class university (WCU) have focused on national policy development, effectiveness studies of WCU programs in each country, and exploring models for WCUs. For example, in his recent discussions on WCUs, Philip Altbach (2010) in his edited book, *Leadership for World Class University*, focused on WCU leadership in developing countries. Jamil Salmi (2009) in his report *The Challenge of Establishing World Class Universities* compared three models of WCUs and discussed directions for the role of the World Bank as an international agency for economic development. Liu, Wang, and Cheng (2010) also focused on national policy and institutional experience in their edited book *Paths to a World-Class University* (2010). The recent book by Altbach and Salmi (2011) *The Road to Academic Excellence: The Making of World-Class Research Universities* is in the line with these publications.

The policy development approach provides rationales for developing WCUs and provides information on how to build WCUs, particularly in developing countries. This discussion will help policymakers and university administrators in designing and building a research university. On the other hand, in this book, we move the WCU discussions forward from a developmental perspective to a sociological perspective. Our interest is in how WCUs have been institutionalized as social systems as well as culturally in each country, at both the institution and the individual faculty level. Specifically, we focus on how WCUs have been institutionalized as a policy at the governmental level and how the policy is interpreted and adopted by university administrators and individual professors.

This book reviews nine countries: three countries with non-English-speaking advanced systems (Germany, France, and Japan), three non-English-speaking developing systems (Korea, China, and Taiwan), and three English-speaking developing systems (Malaysia, Singapore, and Hong Kong SAR). These countries have set out to build competitive world-class universities. Each contributor discusses their national higher education context and has chosen representative research universities to demonstrate how they institutionalized a WCU at the institutional and individual professor levels. In the case study, authors highlight some unintended side effects of WCUs as well as describe the institutionalizing processes. What is interesting from a sociological point of view is that many researchers are rather skeptical about the idea of WCUs and global rankings.

This book consists of four parts. Part I provides a theoretical and practical grounding for the theme of institutionalization of a world-class university. In Chap. 2, Prof. Shin discusses the world-class university from a conceptual framework of the global, national, and local perspectives. He then proposes dimensions of institutionalization of a world-class university from national policy, university, and individual professor levels. In Chap. 3, Prof. Ma describes the development of a world-class university from her long involvement in WCU discussions. She uses the term global "research" university because a world-class university focuses on research, and she tries to compare global research universities with traditional research universities. She also discusses how American research universities are functioning as global teaching universities through branch campuses and cooperative programs in other countries, such as in the Middle East and China.

In Chap. 4, Prof. Heyneman expands the academic discussions from Jamil Salmi's discussion to the issues of sector-wide requirements for world-class university. Professor Heyneman proposes ten requirements for a world-class university, and he evaluates the extent to which the requirements are satisfied in eight OECD countries. In Chap. 5, Prof. Marginson discusses the growing competition from East Asian countries in the global rankings. He pays attention to the Confucian tradition in the region and compares the Confucian model with the US and the Westminster model (UK, Australia, and New Zealand). Finally, he develops his discussion of a world-class university in relation to national, cultural, and educational issues within a framework of comparative and global higher education.

Part II of the book introduces the institutionalization of world-class universities in selected non-English-speaking advanced countries (Germany, Japan, and France). The strong government initiatives for a world-class university in the region may be related to the governments taking a lead in the sociocultural structure of these countries. In Chap. 6, Prof. Kehm describes the policy development for a world-class university in Germany where horizontal diversity has been longstanding. She shows how the initiative has been approached by individual universities and academic units and evaluates whether the policy initiative has accomplished its primary goals. According to her, there are both positive and negative outcomes from the excellence initiatives. In Chap. 7, Cremonini, Benneworth, Dauncey, and Westerheijden focus on France where its universities are not ranked highly globally although its higher education has a long history as a model of the modern university. They explain how the French government has approached excellence initiatives through its contract with universities and the impact of its contract-based approach. In Chap. 8, Prof. Yonezawa discusses how Japan established a world-class university in the 2000s and how policy initiatives have been influenced by political changes and the recession. Special focus is given to how the governance changes of incorporation of national universities affect the world-class university initiatives among leading Japanese universities including Tokyo University and Nagoya University.

Part III introduces the institutionalization of a world-class university in selected non-English-speaking developing Asian countries (Korea, China, and Taiwan). In

Chap. 9, Prof. Shin and Jang focus on how perspectives about a world-class university differ by government, universities, and professors. In the chapter, they conclude that governments are proactive, universities are responsive, and professors procrastinate. To demonstrate this, they selected Seoul National University as a case study. In Chap. 10, Prof. Luo discusses a brief history of the Chinese government's policy efforts to build knowledge centers in the global economy since the early 1990s. Professor Luo selected Tsinghua University as a representative Chinese university demonstrating the institutionalization of a world-class university. The Tsinghua's case is impressive in terms of its progress in the global rankings. Luo shows, however, how the rapid growth in research productivity has impacted the academic profession there. In Chap. 11, Prof. Chang discusses how *Plan to Develop World-Class Universities and Top-level Research Centers* which was launched in 2005 has impacted Taiwanese higher education. His main focuses are on how the project changed the institutional mission, governance, administration systems, faculty personnel policy, resource allocation, and faculty workloads in different campuses. In addition, he examines the impact of the WCUs project on Taiwanese higher education at the national and institutional levels.

Part IV introduces the institutionalization of a world-class university in selected English-speaking developing Asian countries (Malaysia, Singapore, and Hong Kong SAR). In Chap. 12, Prof. Sirat introduces the Malaysian government's recent initiatives—the *National Higher Education Strategic Plan 2020*—to build a world-class research university. Professor Sirat focuses on how each individual university interprets the government initiative from their own perspective and how they respond to the initiative. The Malaysian case shows that each university interprets the initiative differently based on their own contexts and has developed their individual strategy. The top-ranked Malaysian universities focus on research, while the other universities focus on teaching or their relationship with industries. In Chap. 13, Prof. Ho discusses the Singapore case which is quite different from that of other countries. As a global city country, Singapore aggressively attracted international scholars and students to do better manpower development as well as to enhance research capacity. In addition, Singaporean scholars and students are actively engaged in international collaboration. In Chap. 14, Prof. Postiglione and Jung introduce world-class university initiatives in Hong Kong, China. They highlight the Hong Kong University of Science and Technology (HKUST) as a case study of how to build a world-class university through establishing a new research university. This strategy is quite different from other countries where the government has strengthened the research capacity of traditional national flagship universities. Interestingly enough, it took only 20 years for the Hong Kong University of Science and Technology to become a top-ranked Asian university following its establishment in 1991. They discuss what different strategy the HKUST applied to build a world-class university and how its academic culture, governance, and funding are different from other universities.

Chapters 15 and 16 are the concluding sections of this book. In Chap. 15, Prof. Ramirez and Meyer analyze and interpret the cases of nine countries from a sociological perspective and extract implications from the world-class university initiatives at a government policy, university, and professor level. This chapter sums up the cases through a theoretical lens focusing on how the world-class university has been disseminated and institutionalized in the world. In Chap. 16, the concluding chapter, Prof. Shin and Kehm highlight the similarities and differences between countries or between historical and cultural traditions in their approaches toward a global competition for a world-class university. They then expand their discussion to the challenges that a world-class university confronts.

We thank Hoon Ho Kim and Yangsun Kim, Ph.D. students at Seoul National University, for their contribution to the editorial works. We could not have completed our editing in a timely manner without their help.

Editors:

(Seoul National University, South Korea)   Jung Cheol Shin
(Kassel University, Germany)   Barbara M. Kehm

Acknowledgement

This work was supported by the National Research Foundation of Korea Grant funded by the Korean Government (NRF-2010-330-B00232).

Contents

Part III   WCUs in Non-English Speaking Developing Systems

Part IV   WCUs in English Speaking Developing Systems

Part V   Conclusion

Chapter 1
The World-Class University in Different Systems and Contexts

Jung Cheol Shin and Barbara M. Kehm

1.1 Global Competition and the World-Class University

The world-class University is a dimension of global competition which is based on a market economy in the knowledge society. The market competition based on neoliberalism has been widely applied in the education sector since the 1990s. This approach was adopted in the late 1970s during the time Margaret Thatcher held political power in the UK and Reagan Administration in the USA. During these two neoliberal administrations, education reforms based on neoliberalism were implemented widely including school vouchers, performance-based accountability, and new public management. The neoliberal approach has been adopted in other countries following the onset of rapid globalization during the 1990s.

In the global society, universities compete with each other to bring external resources as well as talented students and professors into their institutions. This competition between universities is not a recent phenomenon but can in fact be traced back to the medieval period when the University of Paris, for example, competed with Italian universities, Oxford, Cambridge, etc. (Shin and Toutkoushian 2011). However, recent competition differs quantitatively and qualitatively from earlier periods. First, recent competition is primarily global rather than regional competition. Second, the main focus of the current competition is on economic benefits rather than quality enhancement itself. Third, recent competition focuses more on research productivity than on education in general. Fourth, the competitiveness of universities is measured by ranking schemes, especially global rankings.

J.C. Shin (✉)
Department of Education, Seoul National University, Seoul, Republic of (South Korea)
e-mail: jcs6205@snu.ac.kr

B.M. Kehm
International Centre for Higher Education Research, Kassel University, Kassel, Germany
e-mail: kehm@incher.uni-kassel.de

J.C. Shin and B.M. Kehm (eds.), *Institutionalization of World-Class University in Global Competition*, The Changing Academy – The Changing Academic Profession in International Comparative Perspective 6, DOI 10.1007/978-94-007-4975-7_1,
© Springer Science+Business Media Dordrecht 2013

A small change in a university affects its ranking status, causing universities to move upward or downward as a result of small changes. While domestic ranking may not be affected much by a small change, the current global ranking scheme is sensitive to such small changes. A well-known story is that of the University of Malaya, where the university president was dismissed because of the decreased global ranking. In this context, universities became more sensitive about their ranking status because their ranking affects external resources, and the quality of their incoming students largely depends on their rankings. The "winner takes all" society is pervading higher education sector (Johnstone and Marcucci 2011). The rich becomes richer and poor becomes poorer.

In this educational climate, universities are responding strategically to the global competitions. They tend to focus on ranking indicators and selectively invest their resources in order to enhance their ranking status (Longden 2011). By this, global ranking indicators have predictive power in university resource allocations because governments began to consider these indicators in their policy priority and their resource allocation. As a result, ranking indicators became the index of resource allocation at a government level as well as at the university level. The main ranking indicators consist of research productivity such as publications and citations (Toutkoushian and Webber 2011). The outcome of this trend is global competition between universities for publishing papers and receiving citations.

In the knowledge society, the number of top ranking universities (e.g., top 100 universities) is considered a measure of national competitiveness. According to ranking studies (e.g., Shin and Harman 2009; Van Raan et al. 2011), Anglo-American countries are overrepresented in the global rankings. This is because research productivity is mainly measured by publication in English-language journals. Also, the research productivity indexing service—Web of Science—which is the database for global rankings was developed in the USA. Because of this, initiatives to build a world-class university have been adopted in non-Anglo-American countries, and the policy of building a world-class university is a hot issue in the non-Anglo-American world.

The world-class university is an issue in Germany and France where modern higher education systems were developed earlier than the Anglo-American systems. Asian and Latin-American countries are also actively involved in building world-class universities (Altbach and Balan 2007). The policy initiatives are significant in the fast-growing economies of the East Asian countries because these countries are struggling to establish a knowledge-based sustainable economy. This book focuses on Germany, France, and Japan as examples of the advanced higher education systems and on six fast-growing economies (Korea, China, Taiwan, Malaysia, Singapore, and Hong Kong SAR) in the East Asian countries.

1.2 Higher Education Systems and World-Class University

The strategy for building a world-class university may differ according to the development of each higher education system. First of all, policy initiatives in the advanced systems may differ from those in developing higher education systems where it is less easy to build a world-class university. The advanced systems have an established research base and well-grounded management and governance systems and are well networked with other countries. The developed systems, on the other hand, may have difficulty in transforming current systems already in place.

In discussing the differences in the strategic approaches of the advanced and developing systems, one practical question is to determine which systems are "advanced" and which are "developing." One criterion is whether a system was established early and has impacted other developing higher education systems. According to this criterion, the German and French systems are advanced systems. Japanese higher education systems could also be included in the advanced category. Although Japanese higher education systems were modeled on the German systems, they were established in the mid-1800s and had a significant impact on higher education systems in the Northeastern Asian higher education (Altbach 1989). According to the criteria, the nine countries in the case studies can be categorized as either advanced or developing systems. Three countries (Germany, France, and Japan) are in the advanced systems, and the remaining six countries are in the developing systems (Korea, China, Taiwan, Malaysia, Singapore, and Hong Kong SAR).

A second consideration in discussing world-class universities is whether a system uses English as the main language in their teaching and research activities. The use of English is one of main considerations in counting research productivity, in measuring internationalization, etc. English became the global language in academia as a medium of knowledge production and dissemination. The Anglo-American academics and their business partners developed indexing service such as Thomson Reuters (e.g., Science Citation Index, Social Science Citation Index, and Arts and Humanities Citation Index) to evaluate journals and to provide quantified bibliometric data. The indexing systems enabled Anglo-American systems and the English language to become the global language in academia.

In addition, English became a global language through global business, led by Anglo-American companies. With the strong economic power of US-based global companies, English emerged as the dominant global language, and the use of English became essential in working in global companies. The use of English in teaching is therefore a measure of university competitiveness and also a means to attract international students. In global higher education, English has become the dominant teaching language.

Strategies for building world-class universities differ by whether or not a country uses English as their main language. Among the nine countries in the case studies,

Table 1.1 Types of countries by higher education systems and use of language

Higher education systems/language	English speaking	Non-English speaking
Advanced systems	USA	Germany
	UK	France
	Australia	Japan
Developing systems	Malaysia	Korea
	Singapore	China
	Hong Kong SAR	Taiwan

Notes: The three Anglo-American systems are not included in the book, but presented in the table as an example of English-speaking advanced systems

three countries are classified in English speaking (or semi-English speaking) through British colonization, and the remaining six countries are considered non-English-speaking countries. According to the two criteria, the nine countries are classified into three categories as shown in Table 1.1. The first category is the non-English-speaking advanced systems, the second category is the non-English-speaking developing higher education systems, and the third category is English-speaking developing systems. These country groupings may differ in their approach to developing world-class universities.

1.2.1 Non-English-Speaking Advanced Systems

Universities in Germany, France, and Japan are rated lower in global rankings because of the language they use. Most of the research published in their own language is not counted in their global rankings. These advanced systems have initiated systematic changes to enhance their global ranking status. The German university system differs from the French system. The German universities combined research and teaching in a university and are therefore in a better position than the teaching-focused French universities. However, the German university system has strong belief that all universities are "equally" research universities. This perception is rooted in the historical ideals of German universities, but this does not match with the concept of world-class universities, which emphasize competition between universities. As the case of the US systems shows, mission differentiations between universities are critical in the global competition because all the universities cannot be a world-class university. In response to this, German government set out in 2006 to abolish the equal university concept through the excellence initiative (for details of German systems, see Chap. 6).

France has well-developed research base in their research institutes and technology base in the Grande Ecole. The French systems are based on their long-established systems, where there is a division of labor between the university and the Grande Ecole and between the higher education sector and the research institutes (for details of French systems, see Chap. 7). However, the research and technology base does not affect their global rankings because only university-based research is counted. The French government has attempted to merge teaching-focused French universities with research institutes, which would enable French universities to improve their status in the global rankings.

Many Japanese universities are highly ranked in the global rankings. Japanese universities are in better situation than the French and German universities in terms of the global rankings. Because their higher education systems have integrated teaching and research, Japanese universities have a strong hierarchy between universities which puts them in the better position than their German or French peers. Nevertheless, Japanese universities are motivated by their neighbor countries, for example, Korea, China, and Taiwan, whose higher education has grown faster than any other countries in the world. The Japanese government corporatized their national university in 2004 to provide better flexibility and also initiated the Center of Excellence project in 2002, modeled after initiatives in Korea and China (for details of Japanese systems, see Chap. 8).

These advanced higher education systems have also undertaken proactive efforts to challenge the current ranking based on the Anglo-American schemes. The German Center for Higher Education developed a customer-oriented ranking scheme where the ranking used institutional data and customers can rank universities based on their selection of weighted ranking indicators (Shin and Toutkoushian 2011). A new academic indexing service, SCOPUS, was established in the Netherlands to replace and compete with the Anglo-American indexing service Thompson Reuter.

1.2.2 Non-English-Speaking Developing Systems

The non-English-speaking developing countries (Korea, China, and Taiwan) are confronted with two challenges: establishing a research base and adopting English as their main academic language. The research base of these countries is relatively weaker than the advanced non-English-speaking countries. These three countries have adopted various policies to overcome these challenges. First of all, they have established special funding projects to build world-class universities in their territory. For example, China adopted the 211 Project in 1994 and the 985 Project in 1998, in order to build a world-class university. Similarly, the Korean government initiated the Brain Korea 21 Project in 1999. Taiwan adopted the Academic Excellence Project in 1998 to support research and build world-class research centers.

At the same time, these countries are actively internationalizing their teaching and research activities. The internationalization means that English is used in the classroom and research is published in English. To that end, they encourage universities to bring English-speaking professors from the English-speaking countries and provide incentives for those professors whose publications are in English and mainly indexed in Thomson Reuters indexed journals. These projects have been accompanied by a policy of internationalization (e.g., Study Korea Project in Korea) or as a part of research support policy (e.g., World-Class University Project in Korea). Many universities in these countries require publications in Thomson Reuters indexed journals, and some require a given number of publications in the Thomson Reuters indexed journals as a precondition for hiring or promotion.

1.2.3   English-Speaking Developing Systems

The English-speaking developing systems experience relatively little stress in relation to using English as their main language because their universities (or some of universities) use English as the main academic language for teaching and publication. However, their research base lags behind the three non-English-speaking advanced systems, and so they face the challenge of building a world-class research base. Because these countries use English as a means to build their research bases through attracting talented international scholars and graduate students, their strategy for building world-class universities differs from that in the non-English-speaking countries.

In the English-speaking countries, special research funding projects are not widely adopted. As shown in the case studies in Chaps. 13 and 14, the small economies—Singapore and Hong Kong—did not establish special research funding projects, but both countries used a policy of supporting research activities and attracting talented foreign professors to build world-class universities. This strategy was undertaken because as small countries, it is relatively easy to accomplish the goal by bringing internationally well-regarded scholars.

1.3   World-Class Universities in Different Contexts

Understanding policy contexts is important in discussing the policy initiatives in each country. The nine countries discussed in this book differ in their socioeconomic and educational contexts. This chapter pays attention to economic contexts and internationalization of professors in the nine countries. First, the economic context is closely related to the development of a world-class university. The recently developed economies are seeking to catch up with the advanced economies, and at the same time, they are pursued by the growing economies. Because of these "pursuing" and "pursued" economic competition between countries, these three types of countries are competing with each other to develop their knowledge base. Second, internationalization of the academics is critical in building a world-class university. For example, when academics are internationalized, their government and universities may aggressively adopt an internationalization policy to enhance global rankings. The details of the economic, education, and internationalization contexts are presented in Table 1.2.

Table 1.2 Economic, education, and internationalization contexts

Country	GDP per capita (2010)	Tertiary enrollment rate (%) (2008)	R&D exp. in GDP (%) (2009)	International degree (%)	Degree from an E.S.C. (%)
Germany	40,152	47.2	2.82	8.7	2.0
France	39,460	54.6	2.23	–	–
Japan	42,831	58.0	3.45	4.9	2.2
Korea	20,757	98.1	3.36	44.9	31.1
China	4,428	22.7	1.47	6.5	1.6
Taiwan	–	87.0	2.63	–	–
Malaysia	8,373	32.1	0.63	63.3	53.0
Singapore	41,112	–	2.66	–	–
Hong Kong	31,758	55.6	0.79	74.3	65.5
Australia	42,131	77	2.35	26.5	90.4
UK	36,144	57.4	1.87	14.9	92.5
USA	47,199	82.9	2.90	5.6	99.9

Data sources: World Bank (GDP per capita and Tertiary enrollment), UNESCO (the share of R&D exp. in GDP), Web of Science (SCI publication), and CAP (the % of international degree and % of degree from an ESC)

Notes: (a) GDP per capita of Australia is in 2009. (b) Australia tertiary enrollment is (the total tertiary enrollment)/(total tertiary age population). (c) R&D expenditure in GDP is (the total R&D investment)/(total GDP). Japan is in 2008, Korea is in 2008, China is in 2008, Malaysia is in 2006, and Australia is in 2008. (d) SCI publication is the total number of published articles in the journals indexed in Science Citation Index, Social Science Citation Index, and Arts and Humanities Citation Index. (e) International degree is ratio of the total number of professors who earned a doctoral degree from a foreign university in CAP data. (f) Degree from an E.S.C is the ratio of the total number of professors who earned a doctoral degree from one of USA, UK, Australia, or Canada in CAP data

1.3.1 Economic Contexts

The advanced economies (Germany, France, and Japan) invest their resources in research and development (R&D) in order to maintain their economic status in the global economy. The economically developed countries invest over 2.0% of their GDP into R&D. However, the advanced countries are quite slow in expanding access to higher education. Their tertiary enrollment rate is approximately 50% or greater which is high, but the tertiary enrollment rates in growing economies such as Korea, Taiwan, and Hong Kong are higher. In addition, a greater share of knowledge production in the global market is being sought by the recently developed economies.

Recently developed economies (Korea, Taiwan, Singapore, and Hong Kong SAR) have enough resources to invest in R&D and Korea and Singapore in particular aggressively invest in R&D. The share of R&D in the GDP (3.5%) in Korea is the highest among the OECD countries, and Taiwan and Singapore are rapidly increasing its share in GDP. The exception is Hong Kong where R&D is allocated to the universities as part of the operational budget, and so the R&D statistics do not accurately represent the reality of R&D investment in their universities. Based on these aggressive investments, these countries show remarkable growth in the global knowledge production market particularly in science and engineering (Cheng and Liu 2006).

The developing countries (China and Malaysia) are economically less developed, and thus, their tertiary enrollment rates and share of R&D in GDP are lower than advanced or recently developed economies. However, the growth of the tertiary enrollment rates and their R&D investment should not be underestimated. For example, China's share in global knowledge production is the second highest after the USA. In addition, the R&D investment of China (1.49% in 2007) should be interpreted in a different light than other countries. Malaysia, another country classified as a developing economy, is still low in R&D investment, and its growth is relatively slower than the other cases included in this book.

1.3.2 Internationalization of Academics

Internationalization is directly reflected in global ranking indicators (e.g., the Times ranking) or is strongly related to research productivity indicators such as publications and citations. For example, international collaboration with internationally reputed colleagues is a critical factor in conducting high quality research and publishing in highly reputed journals (e.g., Shin and Cummings 2010). In addition, citations also depend on academic networks with well-known international colleagues.

In the contexts, internationalization is directly and or indirectly related to the status of each university through global rankings. This means that how much their academics are internationalized is critical in strategic decision-making for a world-class university. As a proxy measure of internationalization, Table 1.2 shows the proportion of doctoral degree holders who earned their degree from a foreign country or from an English-speaking country (e.g., the USA, the UK, Canada, or Australia). Although the two indexes have limitations in measuring the dimensions of internationalization, both indicators are a proxy for measuring how much academics in a country are familiar with international culture as well as the English language.

According to the indicators, the economically advanced countries (Germany, France, and Japan) are relatively weak in their levels of internationalization compared to recently developed economies. The ratio of academics with a doctoral degree from a foreign country is noticeably lower in these countries. This makes sense because academic research in these advanced economies is well recognized globally, and these countries have trained their academics in their own universities. However, this may not be a good sign in terms of internationalization, for example, for international collaborative research. It suggests that the advanced economies may not be aggressively pursuing internationalization of their academics.

On the other hand, the four recently developed countries (Korea, Taiwan, Singapore, and Hong Kong SAR) have an advantage in internationalization compared to the three advanced economies. As shown in Table 1.2, a large proportion of professors in these four countries earned their doctoral degree in a foreign country and most of them in an English-speaking country. This situation is related to the historical development of higher education in these three countries. Singapore and Hong Kong have been influenced by the UK, and many of their professors received their degree from a UK or US university. Korea and Taiwan have had a strong connection with the US higher education since their independence from the Japan. This tie with the UK and US higher education has enabled these countries to collaborate with the US or UK universities and to import advanced research systems from them.

Although China has a relatively smaller share of foreign degree holders among its academics, one should be careful in interpreting this fact for two reasons. First, the total number of foreign degree holders in China is considerably larger than in other countries. Second, the foreign degree holders are mainly teaching in very competitive research universities. Because of these two reasons, China is in a better position to adopt an internationalization strategy for a world-class university than other non-English-speaking countries. In terms of internationalization of their academics, Malaysia is in a superior position than countries with an advanced economy because over 60% of their professors earned their doctoral degree from a foreign country, and most of them received their degree from an English-speaking country.

1.3.3   Strategies in Different Contexts

The decision to build a world-class university may differ according to the contexts. The developed economy may invest their resources in R&D to build competitive research universities; similarly, the recently developed economies are able to invest in R&D. In reality, the latter are more aggressive in investing in R&D in their efforts to catch up with the developed economies. Of the two developing economies, China has huge resources to invest in R&D because the total domestic gross product is the second highest in the world. In terms of internationalization, Korea, Taiwan, Malaysia, Singapore, and Hong Kong SAR are in a better position than other countries because most of their academics have been trained in a foreign country, in many cases in English-speaking Universities. China is favorably positioned for internationalization because most of its foreign degree holders (which is a large number) are in competitive research-focused universities.

Based on their contexts, the nine countries might adopt different policies depending on their strengths or weakness. First, the countries that are economically developed but less internationalized may be inclined to an R&D-focused strategy. Germany, France, and Japan are in this category. Second, a country with a relatively weak economy but a better internationalization context may choose an internationalization-focused policy. Malaysia fits in this category. The third group, which has a good resource base and favors internationalization, may choose a dual policy of R&D and internationalization to build globally competitive research universities. Korea, Taiwan, Singapore, and Hong Kong SAR fall into this category. China may use both R&D investment and internationalization. Countries that combine both R&D and internationalization initiatives might emerge as global competitors in the global ranking competitions.

1.4   Strategy for Building WCU in Different Systems and Contexts

The strategy for building a world-class university differs in terms of the features of their higher education systems, the use of English as an instructional language, and their contexts (economic contexts and internationalization of their academics). In addition, the size of their economy is related to their choice of strategy. Smaller economies such as Singapore and Hong Kong SAR find it relatively easy to enhance their research productivity through importing talented international scholars and graduate students. On the other hand, the large economies such as Japan and Korea adopt a "selection and concentration" strategy for an efficient use of limited resources to build a world-class university. Table 1.3 outlines the strategy chosen by different systems, language use, and contexts.

Table 1.3 Strategy for WCU in different systems and contexts

HE systems/ English speaking	Country	Contexts		Strategy for WCU	
		Economic development	Internation- alization of academics	Enhancing research productivity	Selection and concentration strategy
Advanced/ non-English speaking	Germany	High	Low	Capacity upgrading	Applied
	France	High	Low	Capacity upgrading	Applied
	Japan	High	Low	Capacity upgrading	Applied
Developing non-English speaking	Korea	High	High	Capacity incubation	Applied
	China	Hi/mid	Hi/mid	Capacity incubation Attracting foreign academics	Applied
	Taiwan	High	High	Capacity incubation	Applied
Developing/ English speaking	Malaysia	Mid	High	Attracting foreign academics/ research is relatively less weighted than teaching	Applied
	Singapore	High	High	Attracting foreign academics	Not Applied
	HK, SAR	High	High	Attracting foreign academics	Not applied

The primary concern of the world-class university initiatives is improving the research productivity of the university. One approach for enhancing research productivity is upgrading research capacity through providing resources. This approach is based on the assumption that their academics will be research productive if they are sufficiently funded. This approach is mainly found in the countries that have advanced higher education systems with research capable academics. Of the nine case studies, six countries (Germany, France, Japan, Korea, Taiwan, Malaysia) have adopted a research support project to enhance research productivity. These countries have trained academics in their own universities (e.g., Germany, France, and Japan) or in developed western countries (Korea, Taiwan, and Malaysia), especially in the USA. For these countries, research funding is the main issue in enhancing research productivity of their academics.

On the other hand, some countries prefer to attract highly reputed researchers in order to borrow research experiences from established systems and to network with the established systems. This strategy is mainly adopted by countries that are smaller in size and which use English as their main academic language. Of the nine cases, two countries (Singapore and Hong Kong SAR) fall in this category. The two countries (Singapore and Hong Kong) are small but with a well-developed economy. They aggressively attract research-productive foreign academics to enhance their research productivity and could accomplish world-class university status in a short time through their policy of attracting talented researchers from abroad.

China is a special case. China has adopted a dual strategy—adopting research support as well as attracting internationally competitive scholars. Although China invests a small share of her resources in R&D (1.49% of the total GDP), this amount is the highest in the world because of the size of the Chinese economy. In addition, China can attract Chinese-born scholars with an international reputation from around the world, especially from the USA. In adopting the dual policy, China's accomplishments on building world-class universities has been remarkable, as seen in the global rankings.

The second concern is whether a country adopts "selection and concentration" as a resource allocation strategy. The R&D investment is effective when it is concentrated on a limited number of institutions (e.g., Shin 2009). This is seen in the practice of establishing innovation parks in the USA, Europe, and Asian countries. The world-class university status is only possible for a limited number of universities even though most universities want to be a world-class university. However, there is often a political controversy over the investment of resources in such a small number of institutions. The controversy is quite significant in the countries influenced by German university where academics believe that all universities should be equally considered research universities.

Many countries including Germany, Japan, Korea, Taiwan, and France have adopted a strategy of project-based competition to build a world-class university. The project-based strategy provides an equal chance to most universities to apply for the project funding, but only a limited number of universities are selected for resource investment. The exceptions are countries with a small economy. These countries are not faced with having to select a small number of universities to build into world-class universities because they have only a small number of research universities in their territory. The selection and concentration strategy leads academics to competitiveness, and as a result, a meritocracy can become embedded at the level of national and institutional management.

As well as selecting and supporting a small number of universities of the existing group of universities, another strategy is to build a brand-new university targeting it as a world-class university (Salmi 2009). In some respects, this is relatively easier than reforming an existing university because reform initiatives often lead to conflict with faculty. This strategy was behind the establishment of POSTECH in Korea and of the Hong Kong University of Science and Technology (Postiglione 2011; Rhee 2011). Both initiatives have been quite successful. However, their success has required enormous investment of resources. Whether selecting few universities to develop as world-class universities, or establishing a brand-new world-class university, the issue is how to obtain the needed resources to invest in this global "arms races."

1.5   Concluding Remarks

Although we use the term "world-class university" in this book, it remains an ambiguous term, as Shin, Ma, and Marginson have discussed in Chaps. 2, 3, and 4, respectively. In addition, government and universities tend to interpret the term differently depending on their contexts. This chapter has discussed the strategy that each country could adopt or has already adopted for building a world-class university in their territory. Special attention has been paid to how each country has approached the issue of a world-class university in different higher education contexts. The historical and contextualized approach helps readers understand why and how each country has adopted different strategies depending on their own contexts.

Readers might also wish to compare those strategies that are relatively successful in improving their global status with those that are relatively less so. It is important to pay attention to the similarities across countries even though each country has adopted its initiatives for different reasons. The world-class university initiative is a good example of how policies are borrowed in higher education. These phenomena are led by many international consulting groups and publications, often supported by international organizations such as the World Bank. Although it is quite premature to evaluate the impacts of these efforts, readers, especially academics, may have some insights on what the global competition for a world-class university brings to academia.

In concluding this chapter, we propose that the critical question to consider is "Do we really need a world-class university in my country?" "If yes, for what purpose?" We may need to establish competitive world-class universities in our country to provide knowledge base for economic development in the knowledge economy. At the same time, we should commence a serious discussion on "the ideals" of the university before it is too late. Once most universities are influenced by global rankings and the desire to be a world-class university, we may lose sight of the true reason for the university. At this point, we need thoughtful consideration of the ideals of the university.

References

Altbach, P. G. (1989). Twisted roots: Western impact on Asian higher education. *Higher Education, 18*, 9–29.

Altbach, P. G., & Balan, J. (2007). *World class worldwide: Transforming research universities in Asia and Latin America*. Baltimore: The Johns Hopkins University Press.

Cheng, Y., & Liu, N. C. (2006). A first approach to the classification of the top 500 world universities by their disciplinary characteristics using scientometrics. *Scientometrics, 68*(1), 135–150.

Johnstone, D. B., & Marcucci, P. N. (2011). *Financing higher education worldwide: Who pays? Who should pay?* Baltimore: The Johns Hopkins University Press.

Longden, B. (2011). Ranking indicators and weights. In J. C. Shin, R. K. Toutkoushian, & U. Teichler (Eds.), *University ranking: Theoretical basis, methodology and impacts on global higher education* (pp. 73–104). Dordrecht: Springer.

Postiglione, G. (2011). The rise of research universities: The Hong Kong University of Science and Technology. In P. G. Altbach & J. Salmi (Eds.), *The road to academic excellence: The making of world-class research universities* (pp. 63–100). Washington, DC: The World Bank.

Rhee, B. S. (2011). A world-class research university on the periphery: The Pohang University of Science and Technology, the Republic of Korea. In P. G. Altbach & J. Salmi (Eds.), *The road to academic excellence: The making of world-class research universities* (pp. 101–128). Washington, DC: The World Bank.

Salmi, J. (2009). *The challenge of establishing world-class universities*. Washington, DC: The World Bank.

Shin, J. (2009). Building world-class research university: The Brain Korea 21 project. *Higher Education, 58*, 669–688.

Shin, J., & Cummings, W. (2010). Multilevel analysis of academic publishing across disciplines: Research preference, collaboration, and time on research. *Scientometrics, 85*(2), 581–594.

Shin, J., & Harman, G. (2009). New challenges for higher education: Asia-Pacific and global perspectives. *Asia Pacific Education Review, 10*(1), 1–13.

Shin, J., & Toutkoushian, R. (2011). The past, present, and future of university rankings. In J. Shin, R. Toutkoushian, & U. Teichler (Eds.), *University ranking: Theoretical basis, methodology, and impacts on global higher education*. Dordrecht: Springer.

Toutkoushian, R. K., & Webber, K. (2011). Measuring the research performance of postsecondary institutions. In J. C. Shin, R. K. Toutkoushian, & U. Teichler (Eds.), *University ranking: Theoretical basis, methodology and impacts on global higher education*. Dordrecht: Springer.

Van Raan, A. F. J., Van Leeuwen, T. N., & Visser, M. S. (2011). Severe language effect in university rankings: Particularly Germany and France are wronged in citation-based rankings. *Scientometrics, 88*(2), 495–498.

Part I
Background of WCU Worldwide

Chapter 2
The World-Class University: Concept and Policy Initiatives

Jung Cheol Shin

2.1 What Is World-Class University?

2.1.1 Conceptual Approach

Does *world-class* university mean top-ranked universities or does it mean the university that contributes to humankind globally? There have been pioneering efforts in the attempt to define the term world-class university. For example, Altbach (2009) proposed excellence in research, academic freedom, flexible governance, adequate facilities, and adequate funding as characteristics of a world-class university. Salmi (2009) discussed three core elements of a world-class university: a high concentration of talented professors and students, enough financial support for teaching and research, and a favorable and flexible governance structure. Mohrman et al. (2008) also proposed eight elements of a world-class university. In their *Emerging Global Model*, core elements are global mission, research intensity, new roles for professors, diversified funding, worldwide recruitment, increasing complexity, new relationships with government and industry, and global collaboration. These efforts define a world-class university from a conceptual perspective.

In the business sector, we use the term *global* rather than *world-class* to describe a company. A global company is one running a business globally and targeting global customers and whose production systems are often globally linked. A similar approach can be applied to defining a world-class university. The world-class university *globally* attracts talented students and faculty, the knowledge they produce is *globally* influential, they educate *global* leaders, they serve *global*

J.C. Shin (✉)
Department of Education, Seoul National University, Seoul, Republic of (South Korea)
e-mail: jcs6205@snu.ac.kr

J.C. Shin and B.M. Kehm (eds.), *Institutionalization of World-Class University in Global Competition*, The Changing Academy – The Changing Academic Profession in International Comparative Perspective 6, DOI 10.1007/978-94-007-4975-7_2, © Springer Science+Business Media Dordrecht 2013

human as well as national development, and finally these activities are *globally* recognized by academics and people in general. From this perspective, a world-class university is defined by the three primary components of global competiveness, value orientation for humanity, and the organization's primary goal of teaching and research.

First, global competitiveness is conceptualized in terms of attracting talented human resources and funding support and excellence in the quality of teaching and research:

- Competitiveness in attracting talented professors and students
- Competitiveness in attracting funding for education and research
- Competitiveness in research productivity
- Competitiveness in student learning outcomes

Second, a world-class university has a human value orientation that goes beyond the university and its country although the value orientation of a world-class university is rarely discussed in academic circles. Unfortunately, most top-ranking universities tend to focus on *national* development rather than on humankind in general. One may argue that a national orientation may also bring value for humankind or that no university can contribute to humankind without focusing on national development. However, a university without a human value orientation cannot be called a world-class university but rather a *globally competitive* research university. This is the type of university most countries have.

Third, a world-class university differs in its primary goal of teaching and research from *globally competitive* research universities. Universities tend to focus on either the benefits to their own institution through their teaching and research activities or they focus more generally on the greater good for humankind. Most current top-ranking universities tend to adopt the former focus, bringing in funding to provide better facilities and higher salaries for their staff. In addition, they tend to focus more on applied research that is more likely to generate funding. This is apparent in the countries where the national government has set out to establish a world-class university to develop the economy and a knowledge society. The differences between a world-class university and others are discussed in the following Subsection 2.2.

The WCU recognized by global rankings is competitive in terms of research performance (we do not know how much of the research contributes to society however); most of them attract considerable funding from public and private sectors (but we do not know how cost-effective they are); they generate benefits; and their main goal is to satisfy the demands of their own society. According to the criteria proposed in this chapter, there are few world-class universities. Most of the current top-ranking universities fail to satisfy these criteria. While there are many universities whose research is globally recognized, those universities should be referred to as globally competitive research universities, but not necessarily as *world-class universities*. Such universities may represent the government's efforts to establish a globally competitive and nationally focused university, but not a world-class university.

Table 2.1 Language, economic, and regional distribution of WCUs (2010)

Characteristics	ARWU Num. of univ.	%	THE Num. of univ.	%	Leiden (Orange) Num. of univ.	%	MINES Paris Tech Num. of univ.	%
English speaking	124	62	121	61	116	58	90	44
OECD member	192	96	182	91	190	95	173	85
Region								
Europe	74	37	82	41	79	40	80	39
North America	97	49	81	41	91	46	72	35
South America	3	2	0	0	2	1	3	2
Asia	15	8	25	13	19	10	45	22
Oceania	7	4	8	4	6	3	3	2
Africa	0	0	2	1	0	0	1	1
Mideast	4	2	2	1	3	2	0	0
Total	200	100	200	100	200	100	204	100

Data sources: Ranking data are from each ranker in 2010. The ranking data are available from:
ARWU (http://www.arwu.org/)
THE (http://www.timeshighereducation.co.uk/)
Leiden (http://www.socialsciences.leiden.edu/cwts/products-services/leiden-ranking-2010-cwts.html)
MINES Paris Tech (http://www.mines-paristech.fr/Actualites/PR/Ranking2011EN-Fortune2010.html)

2.1.2 Common Features of World-Class University

Another approach to define a world-class university is to identify the common features of the current top-ranking universities to provide some insights into the institutionalization of a world-class university. As many academics have said, a world-class university is recognized by global rankings. In practice, many universities tend to model themselves after the top-ranking universities to position their university as a world-class university. Global rankings are currently a measure of a world-class university although there are many theoretical and methodological issues involved in the ranking process (Shin et al. 2011).

What features do world-class universities share? For further elaboration, we chose 200 universities based on the four global rankings. Considering that the main ranking indicators are research productivity related, these universities are highly research productive in terms of publications and citations. In addition, these universities attract internationally renowned professors and talented students. As well as these observable features, however, there are cultural and economic factors, such as language and economic development that are not explicitly included in the ranking indicators.

As shown in Table 2.1, over 50% of these 200 universities are in English-speaking countries. This language barrier is quite a serious hurdle even for German- and French-speaking countries in ranking competitions (Van Raan et al. 2011). The exception is Japan, where eight Japanese universities are listed the 200 universities in 2010 by *The Academic Ranking of World Universities* even though they do not speak English as their main language. The top-ranking universities are not geographically distributed equally—most are located in the USA and the UK. In addition, over 90% of them are in economically advanced countries.

In their efforts to develop a world-class university, policymakers and institutional leaders pay attention to the three factors (research productivity, research funding, and international faculty and students), but the three other factors (English speaking, geographical location, and economic development) are also important. English-speaking countries perform well in the global rankings because the ranking counts only international journal publications, most of which are written in English. In addition, the location of a university is critical because researchers who are geographically close are more likely to engage in collaborative efforts (Kyvik 1995). Third, economic development is also a critical factor in the development of a world-class university because it provides the support for costly research in these countries.

Nevertheless, even a globally competitive university is an ambiguous concept. As Leydesdorff and many other researchers (e.g., Leydesdorff and Shin 2011) have pointed out, global ranking is quite arbitrary, depending upon which criteria are applied. Leydesdorff and Shin (2011) showed how much the ranking can shift by applying different measures, e.g., by total or per capita measure of publications and citations and by integer or fractional counting of publications and citations. Some academics (e.g., Abramo et al. 2010; Tijssen et al. 2009) have applied a collaboration index to measure how much the research contributes to society in the ranking universities. As these initiatives and academic research show, ranking indicators and their weighting systems are quite unstable and their validity questionable (Longden 2011).

2.2 Institutions Called "World-Class" University

The conceptual approach to a WCU proposed the three components of competitiveness, value for humanity, and a primary goal of teaching and research. According to this, most current top-ranked universities do not meet the criteria. Many top-ranked universities, especially the emerging global research universities, emphasize benefit generation and have national development goals. Their research focus is applied research, and their education focuses on educating students in narrow fields. In this regard, it is difficult for current benefit-generating universities to become a world-class university even though they are highly reputed and top ranked, attracting talented scholars and students and attracting a lot of funding from external sources.

Current universities can be classified by their primary goals—as a world-class, national-class, or local-class university. Conceptually, a world-class university differs from national-class and local-class universities in its research focus, teaching, and social services. Although this typology is simple and abstract, it provides one way to conceptualize a world-class university. These three types of universities can be interlinked as systems. For example, a world-class university produces fundamental knowledge, which is then developed as subject knowledge by a national-class university, and a local-class university in turn applies the knowledge to solve local problems. The world-class university educates its students to be global leaders, the national-class university to be subject specialists, and the local-class university to serve their community. A similar logic can be applied in service activities.

2.2.1 Research

1. The world-class university puts more weight on long-term and fundamental research than short-term and applied research. In addition, the research topics may cover broader global issues (e.g., global warming, environment, human health such as HIV and cancer and clean energy). Because of the nature of the research, funding should be long term and supported by public funding. In this way, a world-class university can produce foundational and interdisciplinary knowledge which provides the basis for applied research.
2. By comparison, a national university focuses on applied and pure research, both long and short term, and attracts funding from private as well as public sources. The national-class university produces subject-specific disciplinary knowledge and is more interested in establishing, maintaining, and developing subject-specific areas.
3. The local university is more interested in local issues that require applied and short-term research. The funding for this research is supported mainly by local government as well as by private companies. Through their research, local universities can contribute to local community development.

2.2.2 Teaching

1. The educational goal of a world-class university is to educate global leaders in the sciences, business, politics, nongovernment organizations (NGOs), public organizations (such as supra international organizations), and government leadership. In the education process, a world-class university views creativity as being more critical than simply transmitting established knowledge.
2. The national-class university puts more emphasis on educating national leaders rather than global or local leaders and stresses subject-specific knowledge as well as the liberal arts because these universities are more competitive in subject knowledge than a world-class university or a local-class university. In the education process, these universities emphasize both creativity and understanding of subject knowledge.
3. The local-class university emphasizes educating local leaders, using the liberal arts as well as subject knowledge and focuses more on knowledge transmission than creativity.

2.2.3   Service Activity

1. The world-class university contributes to human society by addressing global issues. Its primary goals in their activities are not to generate benefits for themselves, but for humankind in general. In most of its service activities, the university is not directly involved in social issues; rather, it provides knowledge and the education to contribute to society.
2. The national-class university pays more attention to national issues than to global or local issues. The national-class university is involved both directly and indirectly in service activities to contribute to their society and may seek to generate benefits through these involvements.
3. The local-class university is more interested in local issues than national or global issues and tends to focus on social issues which may also generate benefits back to the university.

According to this typology, only a small number of top-ranked universities fall into the WCU category. The universities that emphasize application, production of subject knowledge, generating benefits, and direct social involvement are not in the world-class category even though they are top ranked on the global rankings. Most of newly emerged top-ranking universities are in the national-class university category because these universities have enhanced their rankings through short-term application of predeveloped knowledge rather than long-term fundamental research. Universities in the countries that have many emerging top-ranking universities are national-class universities according to this typology. On the other hand, universities with a longer history and that have consistently focused on fundamental research are in the world-class university category regardless of their global rankings and their research productivity.

This does not mean that a world-class university is superior to a national- or local-class university. It is not advisable that most of the universities in a national higher education system seek to be world-class and none seek to be a local-class university. An individual university may seek to be a world-class, national-class, or local-class university depending on its vision and strategy. Ideally, these three types would coexist in a national higher education system and emphasize different dimensions of institutional mission (Table 2.2).

2.3   Initiatives to Build World-Class University

Governments and universities benchmark top-ranking universities to establish strategic plans to accomplish their goal of becoming a world-class university. These efforts lead many universities in developing countries to seek to become top-ranking universities in the global rankings. As a result, universities in developing countries copy the university model of developed countries, especially US universities. This isomorphism has happened even in European countries with the emergence of the

Table 2.2 Comparison of world-class, national-class, and local-class university

Functions	World-class university	National-class university	Local-class university
Research	Global issue > national issue > local issue	National issue > global issue > local issue	Local issue > national issue > global issue
	Basic/pure > applied	Pure and applied	Pure < applied
	Long-term research > short term	Long and short term	Long term < short term
	Foundation and interdisciplinary knowledge	Disciplinary subject knowledge and knowledge for national development	Knowledge for civic and community development
	By public fund	By public and private fund	Public and private fund
Teaching	Global leaders	National leaders	Local leaders
	Creativity > knowledge transmission	Creativity and knowledge transmission	Creativity < knowledge transmission
	Liberal arts > disciplinary knowledge	Liberal arts < disciplinary knowledge	Liberal arts and subject knowledge
Service	Global issue > national issue > local issue	National issue > global issue > local issue	Local issue > national issue > global issue
	Nonprofit generating	For profit and nonprofit	For profit and nonprofits
	Direct and indirect service	Direct and indirect service	Direct service
Examples	Established research universities	Emerging research universities	Most teaching focused and liberal arts colleges and universities
	Research productive and pure/fundamental research oriented	Research productive but applied research oriented	Teaching oriented and applied research oriented

Bologna Process of 1999 and the Lisbon strategy of 2000. The Bologna Process Americanizes the education systems, and the Lisbon strategy does the same for the research systems. This isomorphism has been happening at the institution level as well as at the basic academic unit and individual faculty level. The institutionalization process can be addressed from different perspectives—government policy, institution level, and basic academic unit and individual professor level.

2.3.1   Government Policy Level

In many developing countries, national policy is focused on the development of a world-class university. Even governments in advanced countries such as Germany, France, the UK, the Netherlands, and others are also actively involved in building a world-class university through policy initiatives. These government initiatives differ according to their cultural traditions and their governance systems. Governmental initiatives are also quite strong in Asian countries in the Confucian tradition (Marginson 2011) while less so in the Anglo-American tradition.

The government initiatives may start with mission differentiation between universities because current top-ranking universities are all research focused. The government may then allow greater autonomy to a research-focused university by deregulation in order to enhance their productivity through flexible management. A flexible government and deregulation is a core component in Salmi's (2009) three components of world-class university. The third policy initiative may establish or reshape research-funding systems to support these universities and their researchers. Finally, the government may adopt a merit-based personnel and incentive system to enhance academic research productivity.

2.3.1.1   Mission Differentiation

Countries without a world-class university begin by selecting universities that have world-class university potential. To that end, governments begin to differentiate universities one from the other (for details, see Altbach and Balán 2007) in terms of mission difference and focus. The well-known mission classification is the Carnegie Classification in the USA. The Carnegie Foundation developed classification criteria and classified US higher education institutions beginning in 1971. The US mission classification can be traced back to California's Master Plan of 1960 when the state of California reclassified its higher education institutions as the University of California (UC), California State University, and California Community College systems.

This systematic classification is not found only in the USA. Most of the other countries have legal classification systems. For example, the UK and Australia used to have a legal classification although they eliminated the typology in 1988 in Australia and in 1992 in the UK. Legal typology was eliminated in many countries during the neoliberal period, especially during the 1990s. Under neoliberal policies which force higher education institutions to compete against each other, the high performer survives regardless of its former legal status.

In this context, policymakers began to pay attention to mission classification between higher education institutions. The policy concern is how to select a potential world-class university from the pool of universities which had increased under neoliberal policy. The initiatives were successful in China where the government is strong and higher education is relatively less developed. The Chinese government selected 100 universities in its 211 project and 38 universities in its 985 project (Ma 2007). However, a similar approach failed in South Korea and Germany where higher education systems were already in place. Both South Korea and Germany tried to select a limited number of universities as research universities, but they revised their original plan when confronted with political objections from universities and expanded the number selected.

An alternative strategy was the program-based approach in some countries, e.g., Brain Korea 21 in Korea, Center of Excellence in Japan, and the Excellence Initiatives in Germany. Presumably, developed countries have difficulty in adopting an institution-wide approach in mission differentiation. Some disciplines are research competitive, whereas others are not even though they are in the same university. Because of the controversy around selecting a limited number of universities for a world-class university, these countries developed a *voluntary* and *proposal-based* approach to the selection process. Currently, *program-based* (vs. institution-based) and *proposal-based* (vs. government designation-based) approaches are favored. On the other hand, institution-based and government designation-based approaches may be more efficient in emerging higher education systems.

2.3.1.2   Deregulation of Governance

As Salmi (2009) argued, a world-class university needs flexible and autonomous governance to compete with other global universities. For that, governments need to give special consideration to selected research-focused universities. Most governments that have begun a world-class university project deregulate the selected universities and tend to adopt indirect intervention mechanisms such as quality assurance and evaluation-based budget allocation. These changes in the relationship between the state and the university are critical for a world-class university. Without autonomous institutional management, the university may not be able to compete with its peers worldwide.

In considering a world-class university, the quality of teaching and research is a fundamental component. In many countries, the quality assurance systems were developed in the 1990s when neoliberalism was widely adopted. In addition, governments attempted to link quality assurance with budget allocation by adopting performance-based budgeting to enhance institutional performance (Harman 2011). As well as these quality assurance and performance evaluation mechanisms, governments provide performance data of individual universities to the public, enabling parents and students to take into account the institutional performance in their college choices. These policy initiatives have dual purposes: one dimension allows autonomy and the other dimension assures the quality of higher education.

The quality assurance and performance-based accountability have been developed in the USA and the UK, and the approach was adopted by many countries in the 1990s (Shin 2010). Although deregulation and performance-based accountability are not directly related to a world-class university, these policy efforts in the 1990s became the basis of a world-class university in the early 2000s. A world-class university cannot be developed without allowing institutional autonomy through governance changes. The governance reforms are noticeable in European countries, and the changes are impressive in Chinese research universities where the government and communist party used to be deeply involved in higher education governance.

As well as these general national governance changes, governments also make fundamental changes in their relationships with their universities. A representative case is the shift in legal status of the university. The university used to be a national entity, and thus, its legal status was part of government in many Europe and Asian countries. In both regions, many governments are transforming their universities' legal status into a corporate entity. For example, Japan transformed their national university's legal status to a corporate entity in 2004. The Korean government decided to incorporate Seoul National University, the representative national university in Korea, in 2010. The same thing happened in China in 1998, Taiwan in 2008, Malaysia in 1996, and Singapore in 2006. These changes gave their universities more autonomy in their budgeting, faculty and staff matters, and in their administration. Although there are disagreements on the issue of a national university as a corporate entity, these governance reforms may provide more autonomy.

2.3.1.3   Research Supporting Systems

As well as reforms in governance systems, research supporting systems are funda-mental to building a world-class university. One unique feature of a world-class university compared with other universities is its research productivity. In the knowledge society, knowledge is considered as a core element of the economy along with land, labor, and capital. The world-class university is a collection of research-productive professors and talented students. From the government perspective, one issue is how to attract research-productive professors and how to support them to be highly productive.

The government may establish a research-funding agency or reshuffle current research-funding systems to be more efficient. For example, in 2009, the Korean government merged two national research-funding agencies into one entity, the National Research Foundation of Korea. The main goal was the integration of funding supports between the funding agency for soft disciplines (Korea Research Foundation) and that for hard disciplines (Korea Science Foundation). As well as organizational changes, the government may develop various sources of research funding. Governments in many Asian countries and even in European countries es-tablish special funding projects to support research and to build world-class research universities. The special funding approach has been adopted in China, Korea, Japan, Taiwan, Malaysia, Singapore, and even in Germany and other European countries (e.g., Spain, Italy). These special funding efforts have contributed significantly to research productivity.

As well as funding policy, the government has been trying to integrate research with economic development in the knowledge society. The government does not simply set out to build a world-class university for only top-ranking universities; instead, the government desires their universities to provide knowledge and a technology base to enhance their national competitiveness. As a result, these funding efforts are related to national innovation systems. The special funding projects have a research focus that is highly related to their industrial development (Shin et al. 2012).

Finally, governments may develop research evaluation systems to measure how much their universities are close to their benchmarked world-class university and to promote competition between their universities. As a policy effort, Taiwan developed a global ranking system that focuses only on research performance (Hou 2011). Further, governments began to develop domestic journal indexing systems to support and classify journals by their academic quality to evaluate and classify the research productivity of their academics. These policy efforts have led to competition between universities and between researchers to obtain more resources and enhance their reputations through their research competitiveness.

2.3.1.4 Faculty Personnel and Incentive Systems

Attracting research-productive faculty is a critical factor for the success of a world-class university because it is based mostly on research-productive professors. As Altbach (2009) mentions, faculty hiring and promotion systems should be based on meritocracy. However, the academic culture in many countries, especially those with less-developed higher education systems, is not based on their performance. More recently, many Asian governments have adopted merit-based faculty hiring and promotion systems. Faculty evaluation of teaching and research is an initial step for a merit-based personnel system.

Evaluation of teaching was not common in many Asian and European universities until recently, but it has become the norm for most higher education institutions. Research performance is regularly evaluated in most universities. In many Asian countries where the hierarchy within universities is rigid, universities began to hire their academics on the basis of their research performance. These universities used to hire their graduates, and thus, "inbreeding" can become an issue because most of the top-ranking universities tend to hire their own graduates (Horta et al. 2010). Although there is disagreement on whether inbred faculty are less productive than noninbred faculty, inbreeding is not advisable in a university that is seeking to be a world-class university. In Japan and Korea, government initiatives aim to lessen the rate of inbreeding in order to enhance institutional performance (Horta et al. 2010; Shin and Lee 2010).

As well as these policy initiatives, governments pay special attention to faculty incentive systems to enhance their academic productivity. Faculty salary used to be decided on the basis of years of teaching in European and Asian countries. In this environment, there is little incentive to work hard, and the current incentive systems may not attract talented faculty. Governments began to adopt merit-based salary and incentive systems to attract more productive faculty. In addition, faculty contract systems have been established in some countries where previously faculty would teach until they reached retirement age. For example, China adopted a tenure system and Taiwan created a new faculty rank to motivate their faculty to be more productive (Tien 2007).

The countries with an active world-class university policy encourage their universities to hire international professors, especially highly productive professors. To attract star faculty, salary and incentive systems have been changing in these countries. An aggressive policy effort to employ international professors has been applied by the Korean government since 2008 (Shin 2011a). A similar strategy has been adopted in China, Singapore, and many Middle Eastern countries. A high ratio of international to national professors is related to enhanced research productivity. International faculty may also bring a new approach to classroom teaching and impact the academic culture of their host university.

2.3.2   University and Individual Professor Level

Higher education institutions are required to realign their missions to become a world-class university. A university that wishes to be a world-class university is required to focus more on research than teaching and service. In addition, the universities are expected to strategically select some academic fields to support as a global leader. These changes may align with government policy in some countries or be the institutional choice. These efforts lead to mission differentiations between universities and between disciplines within a university. In making these changes, universities adopt a long-term strategic plan because such changes require long time to establish and conflicts between academics need to be overcome.

The universities aiming to be a world-class university establish merit-based faculty hire, promotion, and incentive systems. In Eastern and Western European systems, meritocracy is not an easy task because most of these countries have a tradition of strong faculty influence, the faculty hierarchy is rigid, and faculty evaluation is not easily institutionalized. However, universities in the countries with a strong centralized power and with new public management and evaluation policies, such as quality assurance, have begun to establish performance-based personnel systems. As a result, meritocracy is getting established in many universities.

Universities tend to emphasize teaching in English because internationalization is measured by international students and international scholars are highly rated by global rankings (e.g., Times) (Byun et al. 2011). Universities are aggressively attracting international students because internationalization is considered an important indicator of a world-class university with faculty research productivity. In addition, universities tend to engage in international exchange programs which provide a way to enhance their international reputation and an opportunity to exchange faculty and students which in turn may enhance their ranking status. However, internationalization requires considerable resources because international students need more help from university than domestic students and may be a reason why tuition is increasing in many universities (Shin 2011a).

As well as these efforts, universities have begun to hire more international scholars to provide courses in English in order to enhance their research productivity. The emphasis on English courses has changed many universities' attitude toward PhDs. For example, a university might require a presentation in English during their faculty hiring process. In this situation, faculty who earned their PhD from an English-speaking country are regarded more favorably than a domestic degree holder. In addition, a postdoc from a foreign university is generally required even in the social sciences and humanities (Shin and Cummings 2010). In addition, universities

Table 2.3 Faculty time budget between teaching and research across countries

Country	Teaching	Research	Admin.	Service	Others	Total	% of research
United States	21.23	12.36	4.63	7.66	2.81	48.69	25
Canada	19.98	15.89	8.07	3.83	2.85	50.62	31
United Kingdom	18.27	12.07	9.65	1.63	3.21	44.83	27
Germany	15.55	15.61	4.64	6.05	2.92	44.77	35
Netherlands	19.87	9.89	4.46	2.16	2.87	39.25	25
Australia	17.59	13.91	8.84	2.93	2.91	46.18	30
Japan	20.29	16.71	7.25	3.91	2.87	51.03	33
Korea	21.08	18.11	6.00	4.68	3.34	53.21	34
China	19.23	13.46	5.05	1.86	1.61	41.21	33
Hong Kong SAR, China	19.78	14.78	7.88	3.68	3.35	49.47	30
Malaysia	17.63	7.28	6.48	2.61	2.39	36.39	20

Data sources: Changing Academic Profession (2008)
Notes: faculty time budget is based on during semester

seeking to become a world-class university tend to require their faculty to publish a certain number of journal articles in international journals (e.g., SCI, SSCI, A&HCI journals) because these are counted by global rankings (Shin 2011b). These requirements may or may not be mandatory, but merit-based incentive systems for international journal publications are in place in many Asian and Middle Eastern countries (e.g., China, Korea, Taiwan, Malaysia, Turkey etc.)

The changing higher education environment has had a major impact on academics. Changes at the national and institutional level have a strong influence on their hiring, promotion, and salary. As a result, many faculty opt to reduce their time in teaching and service to devote more time and energy to research. This has been reported by an international comparative study, *Changing Academic Profession* (CAP), focusing in particular on Asian countries where the academics lean toward research (Table 2.3). This shift may lead to a reduced teaching quality in such universities.

In addition, they actively collaborate with each other both domestically and internationally to publish papers in international journals. Individual professors attend international conferences and present their research, to get feedback from their peers and to network with them. These collaborative efforts enhance their research capability and thus their publication opportunities. Recently, research publications in those countries with a world-class university project have increased significantly. In particular, the growth of research publications by academics in East Asian countries is noticeable. However, this may be at the expense of their students (e.g., less teaching and counseling). The Asian academics have also begun to host international conferences and publish international journals to disseminate their research and to communicate with their international peers (Fig. 2.1).

As a result, Asian academics have begun to appear as influential researchers in the international academic world. However, these changes may have negative

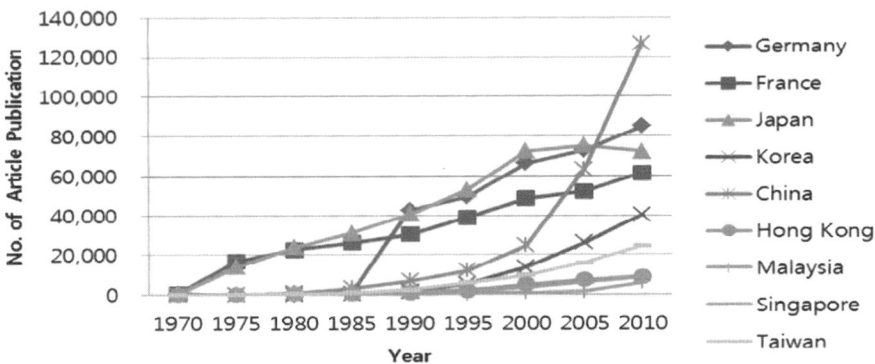

Fig. 2.1 Publish in international journals (Source: Institute of Science Information database. Notes: The number of publication includes only journal articles)

impacts on the balance between the various dimensions of academic scholarship, e.g., teaching, discovery, application, and synthesis. In addition, a growing number of academics view their academic job as stressful (Locke et al. 2011). There may also be a generational gap between senior and junior faculty in adjusting to this new environment. Junior faculty tend to more actively embrace these changes, while more senior academics are not so inclined. Senior professors are more teaching oriented and tend to publish less in international journals, preferring to publish books rather than journal articles, while junior academics publish journal articles rather than books (Shin 2011b). These differences may eventually lead to conflicting values between junior and senior academics.

2.4   Concluding Remarks

It is difficult to define a world-class university even though many universities desire to be one. This chapter developed an idealistic definition based on the conceptual and practical definitions of a world-class university. The world-class university differs in its research, teaching, and service functions from national-class and local-class universities. Its status is not achieved by research productivity alone, but by the quality of research and its contribution to human kind. As well as the research, their classroom teaching should be of a higher standard than national- or local-class universities. Most of the rapidly developing research-productive universities in developing higher education systems do not satisfy the world-class university criteria. The world-class criteria is not just about the level of competitiveness of the university, but about the contributions of the university to society.

This chapter also discussed policy initiatives designed to build a competitive world-class university, reviewing them from a national policy level to the institutional and individual professor levels. In most countries, world-class university initiatives are generally occurring at national policy levels including advanced higher education systems. These national level policy initiatives include mission differentiation, deregulation of governance, research supporting systems, and faculty personnel and incentive systems. However, these policy initiatives differ depending on their higher education development and the context of each case. Some address most of these policy initiatives, while others pay attention to only some of the policy dimensions. Readers of this book should pay attention to why and how each case differs from the others. The similarity and differences between systems will provide informative insights on higher education from a broader perspective.

The readers of this book are encouraged to pay attention to the fact that higher education development, use of language, and their contexts are related to their adoption of world-class university strategies. In addition, the readers should consider whether the ideals of a world-class university that this chapter has laid out are reflected in the various world-class university initiatives in each country or in each case study covered in this book. As a simple answer, very few of the current top-ranked universities are in the "world-class" university category. If most universities in the top rankings are seeking to be a world-class university, I have no objection to it. However, if most top-ranked universities are seeking to be national-class universities, the future of the contemporary university is worrisome. If the latter is the case, higher education researchers should begin to discuss the ideals of the university as many higher education reformers have done in the past.

References

Abramo, G., D'Angelo, C. A., & Solazzi, M. (2010). Assessing public-private research collaboration: Is it possible to compare university performance? *Scientometrics, 84*, 173–197.

Altbach, P. G. (2009). Peripheries and centers: Research universities in developing countries. *Asia Pacific Education Review, 10*(1), 15–27.

Altbach, P. G., & Balán, J. (2007). *World class worldwide: Transforming research universities in Asia and Latin America*. Baltimore: Johns Hopkins University Press.

Byun, K., Chu, H., Kim, M., Park, I., Kim, S., & Jung, J. (2011). English-medium teaching in Korean higher education: Policy debates and reality. *Higher Education, 62*(4), 431–449.

Harman, G. (2011). Competitors of rankings: New directions in quality assurance and accountability. In J. C. Shin, R. K. Toutkoushian, & U. Teichler (Eds.), *University ranking: Theoretical basis, methodology and impacts on global higher education* (pp. 35–53). Dordrecht: Springer. doi:10.1007/978-94-007-1116-7_3.

Horta, H., Sato, M., & Yonezawa, A. (2010). Academic inbreeding: Exploring its characteristics and rationale in Japanese universities using a qualitative perspective. *Asia Pacific Education Review, 12*(1), 35–44.

Hou, A. Y. (2011). Impact of excellence programs on Taiwan higher education in terms of quality assurance and academic excellence, examining the conflicting role of Taiwan's accrediting agencies. *Asia Pacific Education Review*. doi:10.1007/s12564-011-9181-x.

Kyvik, S. (1995). Are big university department better than small ones? *Higher Education, 30*(3), 295–304.

Leydesdorff, L., & Shin, J. C. (2011). How to evaluate universities in terms of their relative citation impacts: Fractional counting of citations and the normalization of differences among disciplines. *Journal of the American Society for Information Science and Technology, 62*(6), 1146–1151. `

Locke, W., Cummings, W., & Fisher, D. (2011). *Governance and management in higher education: The perspectives of the academy.* Dordrecht: Springer.

Longden, B. (2011). Ranking indicators and weights. In J. C. Shin, R. K. Toutkoushian, & U. Teichler (Eds.), *University ranking: Theoretical basis, methodology and impacts on global higher education* (pp. 73–104). Dordrecht: Springer.

Ma, W. (2007). The "flagship" university and China's economic reform. In P. G. Altbach & J. Balán (Eds.), *World class worldwide: Transforming research universities in Asia and Latin America* (pp. 31–53). Baltimore: Johns Hopkins University Press.

Marginson, S. (2011). Higher education in East Asia and Singapore: Rise of the Confucian model. *Higher Education, 61*(5), 587–611.

Mohrman, K., Ma, W., & Baker, D. (2008). The research university in transition: The emerging global model. *Higher Education Policy, 21*(1), 29–48.

Salmi, J. (2009). *The challenge of establishing world-class universities.* Washington, DC: The World Bank.

Shin, J. C. (2010). Impacts of performance-based accountability on institutional performance in the US. *Higher Education, 60*(1), 47–68.

Shin, J. C. (2011a). *The costs of world-class university: Who pays?* The paper presented at 24th conference of consortium for higher education researchers, Iceland, June, 2011.

Shin, J. C. (2011b). Teaching and research nexuses in a research university in South Korea. *Studies in Higher Education, 36*(5), 485–503.

Shin, J. C., & Cummings, W. (2010). Multilevel analysis of academic publishing across disciplines: Research preference, collaboration, and time on research. *Scientometrics, 85*(2), 581–594.

Shin, J. C., & Lee, S. J. (2010). *Faculty perception, performance, activity, and job satisfaction by their doctoral degree training and inbreeding.* The paper was presented at the international conference on changing academic profession, Mexico City, October 2010.

Shin, J. C., Toutkoushian, R., & Teichler, U. (2011). *University ranking: Theoretical basis, methodology and impacts on global higher education.* Dordrecht: Springer.

Shin, J. C., Lee, S., & Kim, Y. (2012). Knowledge-based innovation and collaboration: A triple-helix approach in Saudi Arabia. *Scientometrics, 90*(1), 311–326.

Tien, F. F. (2007). Faculty research behavior and career incentives: The case of Taiwan. *International Journal of Educational Development, 27*, 4–17.

Tijssen, R. J. W., Van Leeuwen, T. N., & Van Wijk, E. (2009). Benchmarking university-industry research collaboration worldwide: Performance measurements and indicators based on co-authorship data for the world's largest universities. *Research Evaluation, 18*(1), 13–24.

Van Raan, A. F. J., van Leeuwen, T. N., & Visser, M. S. (2011). Severe language effect in university rankings: Particularly Germany and France are wronged in citation-based rankings. *Scientometrics, 88*(2), 495–498.

Chapter 3
The Global Research and the "World-Class" Universities

Wanhua Ma

3.1 Introduction

At the beginning of the twenty-first century, the terms global university, global research university, world-class university, and flagship university are frequently used to indicate the new development of current research universities either in the most developed countries or in emerging nations like China, Russia, and India. In a knowledge-intensive society, many people have realized that the global research university is the key institution for social and economic development. Because of the focus on the discovery of new knowledge, the development of next generation leadership and the global partnership or cooperation in research make it possible for research universities to solve the problems confronting the current world.

Serious research on the concept of the global research university began in 2005, when a group of Fulbright New Century Scholars conducted research on the new developmental trend of research universities. As a key member of that research group, the author suggested to look at the developmental characteristics of the American research university. After a year of discussion, the group identified a series of changes for research universities and then coined the term "emerging global model" (EGM) of research universities. At that time, we were still uncertain about the new model, so the term "emerging" was used to indicate the developmental phenomenon, although the term "global university" was frequently mentioned then. Meanwhile, in Economist on September 10, 2005, a survey article about higher education change observed that "a most significant development in higher education is the emergence of a super league of global universities," which is so "revolutionary

W. Ma (✉)
Graduate School of Education, Peking University, Beijing, China
e-mail: hma@pku.edu.cn

J.C. Shin and B.M. Kehm (eds.), *Institutionalization of World-Class University in Global Competition*, The Changing Academy – The Changing Academic Profession in International Comparative Perspective 6, DOI 10.1007/978-94-007-4975-7_3,
© Springer Science+Business Media Dordrecht 2013

in the sense that these institutions regard the whole world as their stage, but also evolutionary in that they are still wedded to the ideal of a community of scholars who combine teaching with research" (p. 4).

Five years later, the "global research university" is considered "a force for globalization" (Marginson 2010). The capacity to go global for those research universities reflects in many aspects. In the last two decades, many powerful research universities have been trying to distinguish themselves in various ways. Mohrman et al. (2007) specified the characteristics that defines them by examining different aspects of the research universities, but the most important characteristic lies in their capacity to go beyond the boundaries of the traditional nation-state by advancing the frontiers of knowledge, diversifying the country background of international students, and tapping financial resources globally. Consequently, the global research university is highly internationalized in many respects.

3.2   The Institutionalization of the Global Research University

Global reach in research and in the development of next generation leadership is the core mission of the global research university. This core mission is well articulated on Yale's university's webpage where Yale President Richard Levin states: "[O]ur goal is to become a truly global university—educating leaders and advancing the frontiers of knowledge not simply for the United States, but for the entire world." Levin's ambition can also be observed in Harvard University President Drew Faust's speech: "We are an American university, but we have a global reach and a global responsibility" (Smith 2010). In carrying out the global mission and taking the responsibility to go global, many research universities have reorganized their administrative structure. Even the University of Colorado-Boulder, hardly considered as a highly research university in the USA, has organized a task force to review the university's international strength and weakness and to reform the university administration for the purpose of better participation in the economic globalization process (Moritz 2007).

In addition, within the global research university, the mode of knowledge production has changed from faculty's independent patterns of inquiry to the current form of "collegialization" (Kleinman and Vallas 2001). According to them, "collegialization" means that like-minded scientists go beyond the traditional concept of research within their own universities and form international alliances or global research teams. In this case, the global research universities act like international buffer agencies in supporting faculty international collaborations. In supporting the global reach of faculties, Harvard university recently establishes another Harvard-backed AIDS research lab in Durban, South Africa. In addition, the recent established Harvard Business School offices in Hong Kong and Shanghai, China, provide more opportunities for faculties in business. While Harvard university president acts like a diplomat, frequently flying around the world. This is indicative of the changing role of the university president who requires the ability not only to operate but also to negotiate and to lead in complex internal and external academic environments.

About the institutionalization of global research universities, on March 18, 2010, the Boston Globe published an article by J. Smith entitled "Students, Faculty Give Harvard a Global Reach." In the article, several things are worth noting about Harvard university. Smith first points out that more Harvard students take part in the study abroad program. In 2009 alone, 1,678 undergraduates studied abroad, which is approximately 25% of the undergraduate student body, while there is a steady growth of international students on Harvard campus too. What is even more impressive is the country coverage of the international students; the 4,131of international students on campus in 2009 came from 140 countries. Clearly, the diversity of international students speaks to the global influence of the university. The second point that needs to be mention here is that the research interests of its faculty are more globalized and diverse than before. Now, there are more than 191 Harvard faculty members who involved their research with China (http://www.boston.com/news/education/higher/articles/2010/03/18/students_faculty_give_harvard_a_global_reach/?page=1). In order to undertake such a global reach, the university has always been able to locate some private funding for support. This is unique to American public or private research universities. As shown in the article in the Boston Globe, in 2008 alone, Harvard pledged $100 million to broaden its international reach, and more individuals made additional donations to support the university's global efforts.

Why should a research university go global? There have been many debates and discussions. The question can be answered at both the macro and micro levels. At the macro level, there are two dynamic forces—the knowledge economy and economic globalization. With the knowledge economy, as Lundvall and Johnson (1994) analyze in their work, there is a shift underway from the economics of the production function to the socioeconomic processes of the contemporary innovation system with the advent of "learning economy." Universities have become part of a new knowledge infrastructure in the national economic development. This was apparent in the United States, after the Second World War, when research universities became part of the national research and development (R&D) system.

Regarding the role of university R&D in the "knowledge infrastructure," Etzkowitz and Leydesdorff (2000) believe that within the context of today's knowledge-based innovation and the associated role played by knowledge-based networking, the model of the university center as a vehicle for technology transfer has become organizationally and institutionally more complex, acting as a conduit through which knowledge exchange and exploitation is made more effective.

In defining the knowledge economy, Toffler (1990) states that "the most important economic development of our lifetime has been the rise of a new system for creating wealth, based no longer on muscle but on mind" (p. 9). The World Bank Report (2003) phrased it similarly: "A knowledge-based economy relies primarily on the use of ideas rather than physical abilities and on the application of technology. ... Equipping people to deal with these demands requires a new model of education and training" (p. xvii). What Toffler and the World Bank Report suggested for the new model of education and training is well reflected in the global research universities. Internationalization of the university curriculum, sending students abroad for multicultural knowledge, and having faculty develop cooperative research projects across nations are some of the strategies explored by the global research university. Going global is the reaction of those universities to the new form of economy.

In the 1990s, the world experienced a considerable change politically, economically, and socially after the fall of the Berlin Wall and the collapse of the former Soviet Union. While politicians from different parts of the world have an interest in debating the new world order, the large multinational firms or international enterprises focused on the establishment of global markets or global systems of production. Higher education or, more specially, some research universities that had been involved with national R&D and had also been involved in national foreign aid programs now began to work with institutions in other countries and were well-prepared to go global.

In 1994, at the General Agreement on Trade in Services (GATS) discussion, education became an important subject in relation to the international economy, because changing trade patterns influence the productive possibilities of the economy and thereby change the demand for education. Economic globalization, according to Held et al. (1999), is the intensification of worldwide social relations which link distant localities in a way that local happenings are shaped by events occurring many miles away and vice versa. The mass movements of goods, information, and labor by modern technology create new demand for higher education. Over commercial exchange, higher education or more specifically the research university becomes one of the major actors in the process. As Ruby (2005) puts it, "universities are creators and disseminators of knowledge; they shape globalization as much as they are shaped by it" (p. 233).

At the micro level, higher education has become increasingly more expensive and less supported by public funding or national governments. Fifty years ago, it was rare for research universities to have an annual operational budget of over one billion dollars, but now it has become the norm, and this figure is barely enough. The virtual research labs, electronic libraries, and world web internet services are all new requirements that universities must provide. Since no government can fully cover those expenses, universities are forced to tap other resources. This situation can be observed elsewhere in universities. In the United States, Michigan University, which moved from a public-supported to a public-aid university, is a good example. In China, Peking University is a government-supported university, which also receives special funding for its world-class building, but it has had to look for additional funding too. Financial constraint forces universities to seek other sources of support, typically from international corporations and organizations. The result, on the one hand, is that universities are very strategic in getting national governments to provide initial financing opportunities and facilitate the transfer of

Table 3.1 Regional
distribution of global research
universities

Ranking	America	Europe	Asian/Pacific	Africa
Top 10	8	2	0	0
Top 50	37	11	2	0
Top 100	68	33	8	1

technologies developed, while on the other hand, they are ready to commercialize their services. The current "privatization" of public research universities therefore becomes a global phenomenon.

Where are the global research universities? The recent development of worldwide university rankings has created such a chaos that university presidents are so much troubled if they are put at the lower end of the lists. Though the university rankings have been questioned and criticized, they at least could provide some insights on where the most advanced scientific knowledge are produced. Upon a careful review of those rankings, one can find some similarities among the universities listed at the top. The following Table 3.1 shows the regional distribution of those universities based on the Shanghai Rankings in 2011.

From the table, one can note that most global research universities are still located in North America and Europe. They grew out of the traditional research universities, but they differ from the traditional ones in many respects.

3.3 The Global and the Traditional Research University

In discussing the global research university, higher education historians review the development of the university from the medieval period through to modern society. However, the origin of the current global research university is quite recent. The concept of the traditional research university began in Germany in the early nineteenth century, developed with Humboldt's vision of a new form of knowledge production through higher education. But Humboldt's idea of research was quite different from the current concept of university research. The concept "universitas litterarum," as Humboldt proposed it, was to achieve a unity of teaching and research for students with an all-round education. Humboldt's Berlin University then pioneered the research-intensive model of university throughout the western world. The establishment of Johns Hopkins University in the USA during the late nineteenth century is a good example of how Humboldt influenced universities in North America. At the time, Daniel Colt Gilman, first university president of Johns Hopkins University, still viewed the research university based on the German model: namely, to promote research for the training of talents. But the mission of establishing universities in the USA is quite different from Humboldt's idea. The basic idea of the Land Grant Act in 1862 was to authorize states to use public property to establish colleges and universities in helping local governments and people to help regional economic development and to solve the daily life problems of local communities.

When the American model of research university took shape, the philosophy behind it was the tradition of American pragmatism, of which is quite different from Humboldt's research university. Especially after World War II, when university research was recognized as important for national security, and when the American federal government started to involve research universities into the country's R&D system, many American research universities experienced a transformation. If Humboldt's vision of the research university is considered as the traditional type that continued for about two centuries in Germany, the current global research university originated from the concept of national capacity building in the United States after World War II. As Geiger (1986) states, the impetus for the global research university is the concept of national development planning and the concomitant expansion of science as a broad authority and economic asset in society.

The great difference between the traditional research university and the current global one is in their approaches to knowledge production and the commercial activity in which the university is engaged. Since the mid-twentieth century, scientific research has been focused not only on the development and acquisition of new knowledge but also on the transmission of this knowledge leading to productivity, whereas a focus on individual scholarship, which was once dominant in traditional research universities, has been transformed into large-scale scientific research with the "big science" as Galison and Hevly (1992) described.

The terms "dual integration" and "entrepreneurial science" are frequently used to describe the difference between the traditional system of creating knowledge and the new knowledge production priority. Currently, scientists and researchers are not only required to produce knowledge but they are also expected to commercialize the knowledge they produced (Ma 2009). According to the current concept of research, the global research university incorporates a belief that new knowledge leads to a better world, though the belief itself has to be testified. A good example of this "entrepreneurial science and international collegialization" is the announcement by Ford Motors that 12 universities have been awarded the company's 13 University Research Programs (URP). Those 12 universities are from different countries around the globe including Wayne State University in Detroit; Stanford University in Palo Alto, California, USA; RWTH Aachen University in Aachen, Germany; and Tsinghua University in Beijing, China. The research mainly deals with testing the properties of thermoplastics modified with nano materials, developing an in-vehicle safety alert system for diabetic drivers, and studying the environmental and economic impact of batteries for electric vehicles.

This international cooperation is indicative of the level of industry and university collaboration. Here, global reach in research universities is mostly in the service of international enterprises, as one of the senior staff at Ford put it: "Research collaborations are a driving force behind the innovations bringing consumers to Ford – and will be crucial to keep them coming back.[1]" The benefit to Ford is quite

---

[1] http://media.ford.com/article_display.cfm?article_id=33090.

clear, but what is the benefit to the universities and what is the benefit to those societies the universities represented? The current debate on the rises of knowledge workers (Kleinman and Vallas 2001) and academic capitalism (Slaughter and Leslie 1997) and public good and private benefits (Tilak 2009) in higher education are all closely linked with the entrepreneurship of the global research universities in scientific knowledge production.

3.4 The Global Reach of Research and Teaching Universities

As mentioned above, the birth of American research universities can be traced back to the end of the nineteenth century, but the real classification began in 1970, when the Carnegie Foundation published its criteria for different categories of universities in the USA. Although there have been several revisions of that classification, the basic definition of a research university is still based on the amount of research grant money from the federal government, the number of PhDs conferred each year, and the numbers of PhD programs a university provides. It has been taken for granted that those universities which can not meet the criteria are teaching universities. Currently, worldwide university rankings, driven by the growing number of international students, have neglected the function of teaching in universities and favored excellence in scientific research. It is commonly believed that teaching in the research university does not count for much in the academic reward systems in these institutions. Criticisms of research universities mostly focus on the faculty neglecting students in favor of spending more time on research. At the same time, the research university is becoming more and more entrepreneurial.

In the current financial crisis, competition for resources has pushed many universities, both teaching and research universities, going global. The term "transnational higher education" not only applies to global research universities but to the global teaching universities also. Research finds that the top US research universities such as Harvard, Cornell, Northwestern, Carnegie Mellon, Georgetown, and Georgia Institute of Technology have established research centers or branch campuses in other parts of the world. They can be found in the Middle East, Southeast Asia, and other areas. The trend of branching out can be found in community colleges and teaching universities too. For instance, Franklin (Ohio) University has developed global programs in Eastern Europe, India, and China. Arizona State University opened an office for international initiatives in the last few years and tried to develop joint degree programs with universities in China and other countries. Teaching universities include many categories in the United States. For example, they include community colleges, public state universities, liberal arts colleges, and technical colleges and universities. Statistics show that United States accounts for 50% of the branch campuses abroad, Australia accounts for 12%, and the UK for 5%. Almost 60% of campuses abroad offer both bachelor and master's degrees (Marilyn 2009). Most of these branch campus activities are commercial ventures of teaching universities in other countries.

There are many reasons for the global reach of teaching universities. An important one is the global demand to prepare a labor force for economic globalization. But in teaching universities, the strength of going global lies not in research, but in vocational education and professional skills. Unlike the global teaching university, global research universities measure global reach by giving special attention to international PhD students and seeking the best minds worldwide to contribute to the university's research agenda. In addition, global research universities develop partnerships with the top institutions abroad, often in research rather than teaching, to expand their influence and intellectual capital in other countries.

Both Yale and Stanford have cooperative teaching programs in Peking University. Instead of establishing branch campuses, these universities created course programs for their undergraduate students on Peking University campus. By so doing they can make the best use of Peking university's resources to teach Yale and Stanford students. Here, internationalization of higher education has a different connotation for global research universities compared with global teaching universities. As discussed previously, the global research university focuses mostly on knowledge production and leadership training, while global teaching universities provide more access for international students in vocational training and skill acquisition. In relation, both research and teaching universities are strategic: the global research university focuses on excellence in research and knowledge production, while community colleges and teaching universities take the path of vocationalism and commercialism (Levin 2001).

3.5 The "World-Class Worldwide"

What is a world-class university? Many researchers tried to define it but still seems to be unclear. The concept actually called attention in 1998, when policymakers in China come up with the decision to build "world-class" universities. To implement that policy, Chinese national government set up a special grant for the two leading universities, increasing it to nine later, and now for 39 universities. The purpose is to increase research capacity of Chinese higher education. This in turn resulted in similar actions in many other countries. In 1999, South Korea adopted a policy called "Brain Korea 21," which focused on the development of the creative and high-quality human resources necessary for a knowledge-based society. For this project, the national government in South Korea allocated a special fund to the graduate schools of leading universities. In 2002, Japan adopted a policy through a process of "legalization of public universities," to make pubic universities largely independent of the national government in terms of their governance. The purpose was to increase efficiency and global competitiveness in Japanese public universities.

Now, South Korea's BK21 Project entered its second phase, and in China, the "985 Program" (a world-class building project) entered its third phrase. European countries also feel the urgency to increase their global competitiveness. In Germany, "the Excellence Initiative" was launched in 2005, aiming to promote top-level research and to enhance the quality of German universities and research institutions. "The Initiative will make Germany a more attractive research location, more competitive internationally and will focus attention on the outstanding achievements of German universities and the German scientific community," as it was described at the website. (http://www.germaninnovation.org/research-and-innovation/higher-education-in-germany/excellence-initiative). In order to understand the phenomena in Asia and Latin America, Altbach and Balan (2007) used the term "world-class worldwide" to indicate that elsewhere in the world, there are many new initiatives to build world-class universities.

In reading the descriptions of these projects initiatives, one can easily find that the core concern is to increase global economic competitiveness and capacity building for nation states through higher education. Though after a decade, there are still problems in defining "world-class," a term first used in China but now recognized worldwide. If a research university is to be considered a category of self-defined universities, world class may refer to a class of educational institutions that have been recognized by the general public. From this understanding, a world-class university is equivalent to a global research university, which means a world-recognized global research university or world-class global research university. The popularity of worldwide university rankings shows the effect of the global classification of higher education. College rankings originated in the United States when the US News and World Report published its ranking list to provide information for high school students in selecting colleges, and the Carnegie classification was used to distinguish American universities. The current worldwide university rankings, which are mostly based on scientific research and global influence in research, serve a much wider audience. Policymakers, university presidents, and students all use the rankings as a point of reference for different purposes.

On how to build a world-class university, independent researchers, international organizations, and university presidents all seem to have their own ideas. In the case of China, Yale University president, Richard Levin (2010), through QS Asia Websites, proposed with three prerequisites, based on his experience in leading an American research university and on his understanding of Chinese higher education. He listed the adequacy of resources, the fair allocation of the resources, and the capacity to cultivate independent and critical thinking.

In relation to the first prerequisite, Levin believes that sufficient funding enables the university to offer competitive salaries to attract scholars and scientists of the highest quality. In the sciences, first-class research facilities and adequate funding to support research are the primary necessities. In the United States, this problem was solved in the 1940s by Vannevar Bush who drafted the paper "Science: The Endless Frontier" in March 1945. In the paper, he put up the proposal to the Federal government to allocate more research funding to basic research in universities. In addition, industry and society contribute billions of US dollars to American higher education, and much of this funding and the research contracts go to research universities later on. In China and other Asian countries, government funding for university research is relatively a new phenomenon. China has included university research in the national R&D system for approximately 20 years only. In most cases, higher education in China lacks social and industry supports, because of the traditional distance between university and society in general. It is only in the recent decade, after mass higher education, some Chinese universities started to respond to social and economic development needs.

The second prerequisite refers to the building of research capacity by equitable use of limited resources. According to Levin, it is one thing to have the resource but altogether another to allocate the resource properly. He points out that a university needs extensive resources and that these must be allocated on the basis of scholarly and scientific merit, rather than on the basis of seniority or political influence. Drawing on his understanding of the Chinese academic culture, Levin points out the problems in resource use in Chinese universities. Chinese culture, in advocating blind obedience and order, creates an academic environment of seniority and academic favoritism both of which are unhelpful forces in world-class university building. In Chinese universities, seniority and academic favoritism comes in many forms, including administrative positions, academic titles, academic connections, and academic rank, to name a few. In point of fact, academic capacity is the least considered element in resource allocations.

To cultivate independent and critical thinking, Levin suggests that Chinese world-class universities must broaden their curricula and change their teaching pedagogy. In the United States, these problems were addressed many years ago through general education, elective curricula, and the teaching of problem-solving. In China, there is curriculum reform occurring, and the American model of general education has been used as a reference for that reform, but the original purposes and practices of general education changed once implemented on the Chinese campuses (Ma 2008). In other words, once a concept is transplanted from one culture to another, the meaning changes because of difference in understanding and the process of adaptation.

One may ask why developing countries should build "world-class" universities. Altbach (2007) points out that research universities generate growing enthusiasm worldwide, because many countries considered such institutions are the key to gaining entry into the knowledge economy of the twenty-first century. But given the social and cultural differences, can the American global research university model be transplanted to other cultures? The answer is yes, if the model is localized into the culture successfully, or no, if the model is directly implanted. Many researchers have responded to the world-class universities in the developing world to at least balance local growth with international appeal and to avoid blindly following the others.

3.6   The Global Reach of World-Class Universities

The recent financial crisis has brought many changes for global research universities. This is especially the case for public research universities in the USA and many other countries. Since they are public, they have to find a balance between elite research and mass access. That is one reason why, in the world rankings of universities, private institutions are always listed at the top. Relatively speaking, a private research university has more academic autonomy in deciding its activities, especially in its global reach, and is more responsive and quicker in taking action. Public research universities by comparison have more obligations to the national government and local communities.

Meanwhile, "world-class" universities are not exempted from challenges or tensions either. Simon Marginson (2010) presents his observations concerning the issues; he pointed out five tensions. They are the tension between national perspectives and global perspectives; tension between elite research and mass teaching; tension between the sameness and diversity; tension inside the hierarchy of the most competitive global research universities; and tension between inside the hierarchy and outside the hierarchy. Marginson's observation is mostly based on Australian higher education and on the US model, which put more emphasis on free competition in the global marketplace. It indicates that being a global research university does not only mean resources, prestige, and status but also more responsibilities and obligations. Many "world-class" universities in the developing countries are mostly public, so they have to show their concerns to equity and access, while fulfilling national development objectives (Ma 2011).

Developing knowledge and strengthening nations have been core concerns of many countries and regions for higher education reform or "world-class" university building. Recently, the Chinese government published "Outline of mid and long term education development plan (2010–2020)," which contains a clear message to the "world-class" universities in China regarding research capacity building and internationalization. Even the "world-class" universities themselves in China start to make their strategic planning to integrate different resources for capacity building and global reach. But one needs to keep in mind that global research universities are not trouble-free as Marginson summarized above; the tensions should be properly addressed and carefully managed. Especially for the "world-class" universities in China, in their capacity building for global reach, they have to be strategic in establishing the university' goals and mission and acting accordingly.

References

Altbach, P. (2007). Empires of knowledge and development. In P. Altbach & J. Balan (Eds.), *World class worldwide – Transforming research universities in Asia and Latin American* (p. 2). Baltimore: The Johns Hopkins University Press.

Altbach, P., & Balan J. (2007). *World class world: Transforming research universities in Asia and Latin America*: The Johns Hopkins University Press.

Etzkowitz, H., & Leydesdorff, L. (2000). The future of the university and the university of the future: Evolution of ivory tower to entrepreneurial paradigm. *Research Policy, 29*(2), 313–330.

Fordincreases investment in university research; more than $60 million awarded over last 20 years. http://media.ford.com/article_display.cfm?article_id=33090

Galison, P., & Hevly, B. (Eds.). (1992). *Big science: The growth of large-scale research*. Stanford: Stanford University Press.

Geiger, R. (1986). *To advance knowledge*. New York: Oxford University Press.

Held, D., McGrew, A., Goldblatt, D., & Perraton, J. (1999). *Global transformations: Politics, economics and culture.* Stanford: Stanford University Press.

Kleinman, D., & Vallas, S. (2001). Science, capitalism, and the rise of the knowledge workers: The changing structure of knowledge production in the United States. *Theory and Society, 30*(4), 451–492.

Levin, J. (2001). *Globalizing the community colleges: Strategies for change in the twenty-first century.* New York: Palgrave.

Levin, R. (2010). The Rise of Asia universities, *Speech at the royal society,* London, England. http://communications.yale.edu/president/speeches/2010/01/31/rise-asia-s-universities

Lundvall, B., & Johnson, B. (1994). The learning economy. *The Journal of Industry Studies, 1*(2), 23–42.

Ma, W. (2008). The University of California at Berkeley: An emerging global research university. *Higher Education Policy, 21*(1), 65–81.

Ma, W. (2009). The prospects and dilemmas in Americanizing Chinese higher education. *Asia Pacific Education Review, 10,* 117–124.

Ma, W. (2011). Why the rural poors get few opportunities to the leading research universities in China. *Asia Pacific Education Review,* pp. 263–271.

Marginson, S. (2010). *GLOBAL: Research: A force for globalization.* http://www.universityworldnews.com/article.php?story=20100326113121559&mode=print

Marilyn, G. (2009). *Colleges going global by establishing campuses abroad.* http://findarticles.com/p/articles/mi_hb3184/is_200906/ai_n32208102

Mohrman, K., Ma, W., & Baker, D. (2007). The research university in transition: The emerging global model. *Higher Education Policy, 21*(1), 5–27.

Moritz, M. J. (2007). *CU-Boulder: A global research university. Report of the task force on international education.* www.colorado.edu/.../IntlGradEdReport_053007.pdf

Ruby, A. (2005). Reshaping the university in an era of globalization. *The Phi Delta Kappan, 87*(3), 233–235.

Slaughter, S., & Leslie, L. (1997). *Academic capitalism: Politics, policies and the entrepreneurial universities.* Baltimore: Johns Hopkins Press.

Smith, J. (2010). *Students, faculty give Harvard a global reach.* From http://www.boston.com/news/education/higher/articles/2010/03/18/students_faculty_give_harvard_a_global_reach/

Tilak, J. (2009). Higher education: A public good or a commodity for trade? Commitment to higher education or commitment of higher education to trade. *Prospect, 38*(4), 449–466.

Toffler, A. (1990). *Powershift: Knowledge, wealth and violence at the edge of the 21st century* (p. 9). New York: Bantam Books.

Wooldridge, A. (2005, September). The Brain business: A survey of higher education. Special report of *The Economist,* 4.

World Bank Report. (2003). *Lifelong learning in the global knowledge economy: Challenges for developing countries.* Washington, DC: The World Bank.

Chapter 4
World-Class Universities: The Sector Requirements

Stephen P. Heyneman and Jeongwoo Lee

4.1 Background

Over the past decades, there have been some significant changes in higher education globally. First of all, entry rates in higher education in the OECD countries were approximately 10% around 1960 (OECD 2003), but by 2008, the enrollment rate in many OECD countries had expanded to over one half of the relevant university age group. In Germany, for example, the enrollment rate had reached 46%; in the United Kingdom, it was 57%; in Australia, it was 77%; and in Korea, it was 98% (UIS 2011). Accordingly, the portion of the adult working population in OECD countries with university degrees expanded in the 30 years between the 1960s and the 1990s from 10% to approximately 30% (OECD 2001). For instance, the rate of college-educated people in the work force in 1960 was 13% for Germany and 8.7% for Japan (Perkins 1991); in 1999, it was 26% for Germany, 33% for Japan, and 39% for the United States in 1999 (OECD 2001).

Second, in many cases, the expansion depended largely on the nongovernmental sector. For instance, approximately 28% of the higher education student population in the USA is enrolled in private universities (OECD 2010). In Poland and Mexico, private universities account for approximately one student in three; in Korea, it is eight out of ten (Shin and Harman 2009). Third, in the OECD countries except for Korea, Turkey, and Switzerland, over half of the student population is now female – a segment once traditionally underrepresented. Both the UK and the US females

S.P. Heyneman (✉)
Peabody College of Education, Vanderbilt University, Tennessee, USA
e-mail: s.heyneman@Vanderbilt.edu

J. Lee
International Education Policy and Management, Peabody College,
Vanderbilt University, Tennessee, USA
e-mail: Jeongwoo.lee@vanderbilt.edu

J.C. Shin and B.M. Kehm (eds.), *Institutionalization of World-Class University in Global Competition*, The Changing Academy – The Changing Academic Profession in International Comparative Perspective 6, DOI 10.1007/978-94-007-4975-7_4, © Springer Science+Business Media Dordrecht 2013

accounted for 57 and 56% in Australia in 2009 (UIS 2011). Their overrepresentation now extends to many professional programs including medical and law schools, engineering, and even computer sciences.

Fourth, higher education is no longer available only to traditional college-age students who enroll full-time right after high school. In both the UK and the USA, 39% of the students attended part-time in 2008 and overage enrollment rate was 6% in Australia and 7% in the USA in 2008 (UIS 2011). Fifth, in the 1990s, higher education finance had not kept pace with the expansion of students. Per-student expenditures declined in such countries as France, Ireland, Spain, the USA, Switzerland, Italy, and Japan. However, by 2006, this trend had reversed. Per-student expenditures increased in every OECD country with the exception of Germany, Greece, Ireland, and Norway (OECD 2010). Once again, the source of expenditure was not always public. The portion of higher education expenditures from public sources declined in the USA from 34% in 2000 to 31.6% in 2007, in Japan from 45 to 32.5%, in Australia from 51 to 44.3%, and even in Germany expenditures from public sources declined from 92 to 84.7% (OECD 2003, 2010). By the end of the first decade of the twenty-first century, many higher education problems remained, but considering these changes in higher education, for the first time in history, the quantity of access to higher education was not among them.

With the publication of the first cross-national assessment of university ranking in quality known as the Academic Ranking of World Universities (ARWU), undertaken annually by the Shanghai Jiao Tong University in China since 2003, what had been suspected was made explicit. Though highly ranked world-class universities were located in 16 countries, one country (the USA) accounted for 53% of the top 100 according the ARWU in 2011. And though many additional sources of cross-national university ranking emerged including the US News and World Report, Washington Monthly, Forbes, Kiplinger, and the Times Higher Education Supplement, each emphasizing different criteria,[1] all ranking systems identified world-class universities in the same few countries such as the USA, the UK, Japan, and Canada, leaving many countries without many or in some cases even one world-class university.

Attention has turned to the quality indicators of world-class universities. One of the first characteristics to be noted was the salaries of university presidents. The president of Harvard University, for instance, earns $US 800,000 a year (Hechinger and Lauerman 2010), although that salary is lower than the presidents of some public universities. The president of the University of Virginia earned over $US 800,000, and the president of Ohio State University earned almost $US 1.4 million in the 2007–2008 school year (Gibson 2009). However, there does not appear to be a correlation between the ranking of universities and the salary of their presidents. The salaries of researchers are also among the characteristics of note. But in terms of

---

[1] In measuring the quality of higher education institutions, these raters choose different, in some cases overlapping, measures from a total of 30 measures. See Richards and Coddington (2010) for more information.

country averages, researcher salaries are of little help. Whether measured in euros or purchasing power parity (PPP), the typical salaries of researchers in the USA, Australia, Japan, Germany, and Austria are approximately the same and do not explain the large national differences in the number of world-class universities in those countries. In this context, the salaries of university presidents and researchers have limited value as indicators of the quality of world-class universities. Then what are appropriate indicators of the quality of world-class universities? We will address this question in the next section.

The remainder of this chapter is organized as follows. In the first section, world-class universities will be defined, focusing on three categories. In the second section, ten sector requirements for world-class universities will be discussed. Finally, a cross-national assessment of public policies that are necessary for world-class universities will be presented.

4.2 Definition of World-Class Universities

World-class universities are thought to build a productive human capital base and elevate national development. Many have pointed out the characteristics they have in common (e.g., Altbach 2004; Levin et al. 2006; Niland 2007; Salmi 2009). These characteristics fall into three categories. First is the concentration of talent in students and faculty researchers. For instance, the student acceptance rate at Harvard University in 1940 was 85%. By the 1970s, this had dropped to 20%, and in 2010, it was 6%. At three other top-ranked universities, Columbia, Yale, and Stanford University, the acceptance rate was less than 8% in 2010 (Menand 2011). This trend is also true in some of the top universities in Britain. For instance, at Oxford University, the acceptance rate was 18%, and at Cambridge University, it was 21% in 2010 (Menand 2011). This suggests that student demand to enter high-quality universities has increased in spite of the increasing private cost. It also implies that a world-class university has an extraordinary amount of choice in those applying to study there. Faculty are similar to students. Instead of hiring its own graduates,[2] a world-class university will consider the world as its source of faculty. That is, world-class universities globally compete for high-quality faculty in professional labor markets beyond national borders. To illustrate, the proportion of foreign born faculty positions in all science and engineering at universities in the USA was 21% in 2001, with even larger percentages, about 39% in computer science and 35% in engineering (National Science Board 2004).

Similarly, a student body at a world-class university is valued not because it comes from wealthy and privileged backgrounds but for its diversity of background

---

[2]Universities in the former Soviet Union, the Middle East, and North African regions often hire only from their own graduates, thus ensuring lower quality.

since world-class universities are expected to prepare students to work and live effectively and cooperatively with people who differ from themselves (Smith and Schonfeld 2000). For the purpose of illustrating diversity in universities in the USA, two dimensions are briefly included here. First, foreign students who are enrolled in universities in the USA accounted for about 3.5% of total US higher education enrollment in the 2008–2009 school year (NCES 2010). More specifically, ten universities in the USA hosted more than 5,000 foreign students in the 2009–2010 school year. The top three universities enrolling foreign students were the University of Southern California (7,987 students, which amounts to about 21.6% of its total students enrolled), the University of Illinois (Urbana-Champaign) (7,287 students, about 17.6%), and New York University (7,276 students, about 16.8%)[3] (IIE 2010). The second dimension is the high percentage of undergraduates receiving need-based financial aid, which is a proxy for the percentage of lower middle and working class students in an institution. The portion of the student population coming from lower income backgrounds is pronounced in such institutions as the University of Southern California (66%), the University of Illinois (Urbana-Champaign) (72%), and New York University (53%) (The Princeton Review 2011). Another good indicator of diversity is the percentage of enrolled undergraduate students who receive Pell grants that are given to low-income students with family income under $20,000 (Morse 2009). The University of California (Los Angeles) (33%) appeared to best serve low-income students, followed by the University of California (Berkeley) (32%), the University of Southern California (17%), and Columbia University (16%). These are indicative of the efforts made by these universities to promote social and economic diversity by attracting talented students from a variety of backgrounds.

The second category of factors concerns resources. They are abundant and come from a wide variety of sources. On average, a university in the USA annually spends over $20,000 per student for educational services, about twice the average for OECD countries (OECD 2010). However, the absolute level of resources spent, although it provides the groundwork for a rich learning environment, is but one indication of potential excellence. Another is the diversity of resources which may stem from public taxes (government budget funding), private gifts, an endowment, tuition, and rewards for research contracts from both public organizations and private firms. For instance, Vanderbilt University, which is private, earns 31% of its income from its investments, 11% from private gifts and contracts, 3% from cost recovery for use of its facilities, and 8% for room and board charges. Although the tuition is $45,000 a year, this provides only 20% of its income (Vanderbilt University 2010). For Vanderbilt and other world-class universities, there is little incentive to increase enrollment because 80% of its income comes from sources other than enrollment. This means the enrollment at world-class universities will likely be

---

[3]These numbers and percentages include both undergraduate and graduate students.

maintained at current levels, which in turn will help increase demand and assure the level of quality indefinitely. Public universities also have a similar diversity of resources. The University of Tennessee is an example. Only 25% of its annual budget stems from appropriations from the state. Seventy-five percent derives from other sources including tuition, gifts, research contracts, and the like (University of Tennessee 2010). The declining portion of a university budget which originates from state appropriations is observed in many other countries as well. At universities in China, the proportion from nongovernment sources in the total revenue was about 25% in 1997, but it increased by about 26–51% in 2002 (Yingjie 2011). In 2010, about 70%[4] of the annual budget (800 million euros) of Aarhus University in Denmark came from state appropriations[5] and 28% came from competitive research grants (300 million euros) which included public resources, the European Union sources, private gifts, and other foreign sources (Holm-Nielsen 2011). The endowment at Aarhus was 500 million euros in 2008 (Holm-Nielsen 2008). In sum, the availability of rich and diversified sources of resources enables higher education institutions to constantly attract even more high-quality faculty and researchers (Salmi 2009), which in turn likely leads to the concentration of the best students in these institutions.

The third category of factors is related to governance structures, that is, the enabling university governance, its internal supporting regulations, autonomy from government, the maintenance of academic freedom, and its management by professional staff. These factors are conducive for higher education institutions to make decisions and to administer resources to effectively and quickly respond to the demand for high-quality higher education, without being unduly impeded by governmental bureaucracy (Salmi 2009). For this reason, higher education institutions have attempted to move toward enhancing favorable governance. For instance, public universities in Europe are moving toward more financial autonomy. In 1995, there were 12 countries with low levels of financial autonomy; by 2008, this had been reduced to four countries. By contrast, in 1995, 12 countries were described as having a high degree of financial autonomy, but by 2008, this had increased to 14 (see Table 4.1 below).

Financial autonomy, professional management, supporting internal regulations, and the other characteristics in this category overlap with the sector requirements discussed below. The reason they are discussed separately is that in many instances, universities cannot create an enabling governance internally because the national policies will not allow it. It is those national policies to which we now turn.

---

[4]Public funding Aarhus University receives from the government (70%) is approximately 10% smaller than other Danish universities where state grants account for about 80% of all income. See Rogers (2009) for more information.

[5]State appropriation includes degree programs, core research funding, and government contract. It also includes competitive research grants from public sources, which means that there is some overlap between 70 and 28%. About 60% of competitive research grants come from public sources.

Table 4.1 Financial autonomy of European public universities ($N = 32$)

Level	1995	2008
Low	Austria, Cyprus, France, Germany, Greece, Hungary, Lithuania, Norway, Romania, Slovakia, Switzerland, Turkey (12)	Cyprus, Greece, Lithuania, Turkey (4)
Medium	Croatia, Denmark, Finland, Malta, Poland, Portugal, Slovenia, Sweden (8)	Denmark, Finland, France, Germany, Hungary, Latvia, Luxembourg, Malta, Poland, Portugal, Romania, Slovakia, Sweden, Switzerland (14)
High	Belgium, Bulgaria, Czech Republic, Estonia, Iceland, Ireland, Italy, Latvia, Netherlands, Spain, UK (12)	Austria, Belgium, Bulgaria, Croatia, Czech Republic, Estonia, Iceland, Ireland, Italy, Netherlands, Norway, Slovenia, Spain, UK (14)

Notes: (a) Legend: categorization based on a multiple index with average scores/country based on internal allocation of funds, borrowing on capital markets, building up reserves, and spending of operational grants. (b) Source: Jongbloed et al. (2008, Table 3.2, p. 42)

4.3 Sector Requirements for World-Class Universities

There are potentially many sector requirements that will enable the development of world-class universities, but we propose the following ten as being the most important.

4.3.1 A High Percentage of Public Income Awarded Not on the Basis of Regular Annual Institutional Allocations but Through Competition for Excellence in Performance

Linking university financing to performance as a funding method is related to improving quality assurance. As stated above, only a small percentage of income at the University of Tennessee is received from the state through annual allocations – the portion of income from public sources is considerably larger. These funds are awarded on the basis of competition in strategic planning and innovation and through proposals for research.

4.3.2 A High Percentage of Income from Nonstate Sources

In general, the wider the variety of income sources, the more likely it is that an institution can develop and translate its long-term strategic plans and visions on its own without depending on government allocations and without depending on tuition for financial security. There are two underlying rationales for this argument.

First, the diversification of income sources is of particular importance to higher education institutions, especially when governments suffer economic and financial crisis, which means that direct public funding is truly limited. Also, a world-class university incurs huge costs to operate and maintain its academic missions and roles. For instance, the total operating expenses of Harvard University in fiscal 2009 were about $3.73 billion (Harvard University 2010), which is equivalent to GDP at PPP of small, poor countries such as Gambia and Burundi. Thus, broadening the funding base that contributes to strengthening long-term financial sustainability of higher education institutions is required for reaching world-class status.

4.4 A High Degree of Institutional Differentiation

As most countries have transformed from an elite to a mass system of higher education, world-class universities are more likely to thrive when there are a wide variety of other legitimate forms of higher education institutions available. These may include community colleges, technical and professional colleges, small liberal arts colleges, teaching (as opposed to research) universities, private not-for-profit as well as for-profit institutions, institutions which teach from a single base, and others which deliver all courses from a distance. If universities attempt to fulfill all the various higher education functions identically, then the chances of being a world-class university are smaller. This handicap is particularly relevant to those countries where universities are generally public and for the most part are uniform in function. For example, higher education in the USA is characterized by institutions of multiple types. Only 20% of the higher education institutions in the USA are considered selective, and the number considered research institutions is about 6%.[6] Forty percent of the institutions are teaching universities, 15% are liberal arts colleges, and 39% are 2-year community colleges (Snyder and Dillow 2008). Volunteer State Community College in Gallatin, Tennessee, for instance, has an enrollment of 8,000 students and 750 faculty with a budget of $US 7 million. It has 70 different programs spanning the humanities, the social sciences, math, science, and training for the health and business professions. Forty-four percent of the students enrolled are in a program through which they hope to transfer to a local 4-year institution. Thus, a community college helps identify new students capable of completing a 4-year degree in spite of the fact that they were not capable of passing the normal entry requirements during the period in which entry usually occurs. This important "second chance" function played by community colleges frees world-class universities to concentrate on functions in which they have a comparative advantage.

---

[6]Of the 4,294 institutions, only 258 are classified as research universities, 93 of which are private. (US Government, *Digest of Education Statistics*. Washington, DC: National Center for Education Statistics, 2007).

4.4.1 Institutional Autonomy

This characteristic is associated with being public or private. However, there is a range of factors within these terms which determine the essence of what autonomy means. The mission of some institutions may be controlled by public authorities and others by private authorities. Similarly, the control of the ownership of institutions, the source of revenue, fiscal authority, faculty matters, and internal management may be in the hands of public or private authorities. The term "public" or "private" in themselves is not sufficiently meaningful to assess an institution's degree of autonomy. What is necessary to know is whether public policy allows higher education institutions to govern and finance themselves. This implies that they must control their own curriculum, admissions, and salaries. For instance, if public policies prohibit higher education institutions from setting faculty salaries and from determining those salaries on the basis of demand for particular skills and specializations, it is unlikely that they will become world class.[7] World-class status requires policies that allow universities to finance and completely manage their own affairs.

4.4.2 Ownership of Property

A world-class university must own title to its property. This is important because all world-class universities need to develop their own strategic plans, including for construction of new facilities. If a university has to depend on government allocations, their plans are in the hands of those with many other important priorities. World-class universities develop their own private capital sources for construction projects. This includes borrowing. To be eligible for loans, however, they must have adequate collateral. Universities without land ownership cannot borrow, which means they cannot develop and therefore lack competitiveness.

4.4.3 Clear Legal Distinction Between for-Profit and Not-for-Profit Institutions, and Exemption from Taxation for Nonprofit Higher Education Institutions

Nonprofit higher education institutions serve the public interest. They cannot compete in terms of excellence unless they can attract and manage their own resources. These resources are not "profits" but are sources for operating capital

---

[7]In many countries, faculty are treated as civil servants and may not differ in salary within seniority levels. Where this public policy pertains world-class universities are unlikely.

needed to cover expenses in performing their teaching and research functions. Because they put this income into their own operations, they should not be taxed on it. If it is public policy to tax nonprofit higher education institutions, they cannot be expected to attain world-class status.

4.4.4   Open Competition for State-Sponsored Research

Most countries sponsor research in health, pharmaceuticals, defense, social sciences, agriculture, and other fields. In the former Soviet Union and some OECD countries, this research is conducted through networks of specialized research institutions separate from universities. In these cases, university faculty are expected to teach but not be involved in pioneering research, whereas research specialists are not expected to teach. These higher education institutions are not involved in pioneering research and are therefore not competing to be recognized as world-class institutions. On the other hand, there are many countries which sponsor science projects through university competitions. In these instances, universities have the opportunity to be on the cutting edge of science, while students have the opportunity of being trained by faculty at the forefront of their fields. Concerns are raised that the incentives for research are often larger than the incentives for teaching, but it is also true that the university which lacks resources to support the competition for pioneering research is invariably relegated to second class status. In some cases, such as Germany, research monies may be allocated to specific institutions rather than through open competition. In these instances, public policy is antithetical to an enabling environment to support world-class universities. Open competition is important because of the ripple effects of the effort to compete. Even institutions which do not win the research award have learned from competing for it.

4.4.5   Autonomous Agencies of Accreditation and for Licensing of Professionals

If the public sector has a monopoly over institutional accreditation, it tends to favor older public institutions. If the accreditation agency is nongovernmental, there will be less bias against private institutions. An accreditation agency cannot be professional and favor any particular category. The licensing of professionals (law, medicine, architecture, and the like) can be performed by the universities which supply the training or by separate professional associations. If professional licensing is managed by universities, there will be little program innovation on the grounds that the risk to the public would be too great. Curricular and other programmatic innovations which do not work may result in incompetent doctors or lawyers. On the other hand, if the license to practice is acquired separately from the institution which provides the training, this allows all training institutions to innovate without danger to the public. Hence, the curriculum in the law school at the University of Chicago, for instance, can be completely independent from the institution setting the bar examination. This frees a university to base its law curriculum on whatever it considers to be important. This allows for a wide latitude of law school programs and curricula without the risk of incompetent lawyers.

4.4.6 Incentives to Diversity of Students and Faculty

Student bodies which are insular in social background are inferior in terms of intellectual impact. To be competitive, world-class universities must select the brightest and the best from a wide diversity of student backgrounds, citizenships, and academic fields. The best institutions seek students and new faculty from a worldwide market. Public policy can stimulate this diversification and internationalization by providing the incentives to encourage and hasten it. Governments and private foundations can establish rewards such as institutional supplements for increasing the number of students and faculty from outside the country, for instance.

4.4.7 Incentives to Improve Quality

Intelligently designed public policy is an essential ingredient for the development of world-class universities, and there is no policy more important than the incentives to improve quality. These may include the establishment of reward structures through open competition such as the program of the Canada Excellence Research Chairs (CERC)[8] in Canada and the Brain Korea (BK) 21 project[9] in Korea. The role of government is to assist higher education institutions in developing scholarly productivity and institutional innovation.

To illustrate, we have summarized the general pattern across these dimensions in Britain, France, Germany, and the USA (see Table 4.2 below).

In terms of institutional autonomy, one element to consider is the student admission policy. In France, admission is controlled by central public authorities,

---

[8]The CERC is designed to award each of 20 chair holders and their research teams up to CAN$10 million over 7 years in an attempt to support Canadian universities to become world leaders in research and development through innovation. For more information, see http://www.cerc.gc.ca/hp-pa-eng.shtml.

[9]The BK21 project aims to nurture highly qualified human resources and improve the national developmental equilibrium for the twenty-first century knowledge-based society as well as to provide qualified graduate students and the next-generation scholars with financial support. For more information, see http://bnc.krf.or.kr/home/eng/ and http://unpan1.un.org/intradoc/groups/public/documents/apcity/unpan015416.pdf.

Table 4.2 Management and administration in four countries

	France	Germany	Britain	USA
Access	Central government control	State control	University control	University control
Ownership	Public and national	Public and local	Public and national	State government only, one half private
Budget control	Central government rigid	Central government rigid	Central institution managed	University determined loans and aid
Tuition	None with students subsidy	None with students subsidy	Tuition with access to loans	University determined loans and aid
Credit transfer	Rigid tracks	Rigid tracks	Increasing university control	Total university control
Land owned	National government owned	State government owned	National government owned	University owned
Curriculum control	Government approved	State government approved	University control	University control
Faculty control	Civil servants	Civil servants	Common pay, competitive, and scales, no tenure	Market driven
Research	Outside university	In and outside university	Inside university	Inside university
Campus administration	None	None	President as CEO	President as CEO, professional
Relationship with industry	Rare	Rare	Very close	Very close
Endowment	None	None	Beginning	Yes

in Germany by state authorities, and in Britain and the USA by the individual institution. In terms of tuition (one measure of the diversity in resources), it is controlled by public authorities in France and Germany, heavily influenced by public authority in Britain, and established largely by the individual institutions within the USA. Course credit transfer is established through a series of rigid tracks in France and Germany, with increasing university control in Britain, and total university control in the USA. Other patterns can be seen in relation to land ownership, campus administration, endowments, control over faculty salaries, benefits and promotion, and control over curricula.

4.5 Assessment of Public Policy Necessary for World-Class Universities

For purposes of illustration, we have investigated the higher education policies in eight OECD countries: Denmark, Britain, France, Germany, Korea, Canada, the USA, and Japan. Each country has been assessed on the ten components necessary for world-class universities to prosper. We assigned grades ranging between 1 and 10. Components were given equal weight. The total scores represent not the existence of world-class universities, but the potential for world-class universities to develop given the public policy setting in each country.

In terms of the portion of university budgets from nonstate sources, Canada, the USA, and Korea were assigned high grades. Low grades were assigned to Japan, France, and Germany. In terms of the open competition for state-sponsored scientific research, high grades were assigned to Denmark, Britain, Korea, Canada, and the USA, and low grades to Germany and France. In terms of accreditation independence and licensing independence, high grades were assigned only to the USA and Canada. In relation to university property, high grades were assigned to Denmark, Korea, Canada, and the USA.

The grades were then summarized into a single indicator (see Table 4.3 below). High grades were assigned to the USA, Korea, and Canada with lower grades to Britain, Denmark, and Japan, and even lower grades to France and Germany. These summary grades are not indicators of higher education quality but rather of the potential for world-class universities to develop given the local public policies affecting higher education.

Table 4.3 Sector assessment of eight countries

	Denmark	Britain	France	Germany	Korea	Canada	USA	Japan
Nonstate income	6	8	1	1	10	10	10	2
Institutional differentiation	2	4	0	0	8	10	10	5
Institutional autonomy	8	6	1	4	4	10	10	5
University property	9	8	1	5	10	10	10	5
Tax exemption	9	7	8	8	8	10	10	7
Open comp. for science	10	10	0	0	10	10	10	8
Accreditation independence	3	8	0	0	7	10	10	3
Licensing independence	1	7	0	0	7	8	10	3
Diversity incentives	1	1	1	1	7	9	10	4
Quality incentives	10	8	6	8	10	10	10	10
Total	59	67	18	27	81	97	100	53

Note: Range: 1–10

4.6 Summary

All nations believe that high-quality universities are needed to support a competitive economy. This implies that all nations want greater higher education access, equity, and quality. Because no nation can attain all three objectives by utilizing public tax resources alone,[10] all potential world-class universities are competing to diversify resources, improve efficiency, generate greater private resources, and retrench low priority programs and functions. The successful world-class university is the one which succeeds in financing its own strategic objectives and is autonomous from government. Canadian and US universities have traditionally become leaders in this. But all nations have to respond to the same set of managerial dilemmas and challenges. In the future, there will be many rivals to Canada and the USA. This competitiveness is beneficial for higher education as a sector and is in the public good.

The "race" to establish world-class universities depends on the extent to which public policy allows potential world-class universities to compete. These policies include the characteristics discussed above. It is evident that some nations have established public policies that encourage the development of world-class universities. These include Canada, Korea, and the USA. Other countries, such as France and Germany, have yet to revise their public policies to allow world-class universities to prosper. We propose these grading criteria, but additional characteristics will no doubt be identified. The criteria could also be weighted differently. Nevertheless, the development of world-class universities in large part is a function of the public policies which encourage development or alternatively handicap their development.

References

Altbach, P. G. (2004). The costs and benefits of world-class universities. *Academe, 90*(1), 20–23. Retrieved from http://www.aaup.org/AAUP/pubsres/academe/2004/JF/Feat/altb.htm

Gibson, E. (2009). Highest paid university presidents: The top 10 at public and private colleges. *Bloomberg Business Week*. Retrieved from http://images.businessweek.com/ss/09/02/0216_college_pres/1.htm

Harvard University. (2010). *Harvard University financial report: Fiscal year 2010*. Cambridge, MA: Harvard University. Retrieved from http://vpf-web.harvard.edu/annualfinancial/

Hechinger, J., & Lauerman, J. (2010). Executives collect $2 billion running U.S. for-profit colleges. *Bloomberg Business Week*. Retrieved from http://www.bloomberg.com/news/2010-11-10/executives-collect-2-billion-running-for-profit-colleges-on-taxpayer-dime.html

Holm-Nielsen, L. B. (2008, December 6). *Strategies to win the best – A report from Denmark*. Report presented at 2nd forum of AvH International Advisory Board, Berlin.

Holm-Nielsen, L. B. (2011). *Danish university funding model: Aarhus University – An example*. Retrieved from http://www.eua.be/Libraries/Country_Workshop_Austria/Lauritz_Holm-Nielsen_Danish_University_Funding_Model_Final_Presentation.sflb.ashx

---

[10]Exceptions: certain Gulf states and Norway.

Institute of International Education (IIE). (2010). *Open doors 2010 fast facts: International students in the U.S. IIE.* Retrieved from http://www.iie.org/Research-and-Publications/Open-Doors/~/media/Files/Corporate/Open-Doors/Fast-Facts/Fast%20Facts%202010.ashx

Jongbloed, B., Boer, H., Enders, J., & File, J. (2008). *Progress in higher education reform across Europe – Funding reform: Vol. 1. Executive summary and main report.* Enschede-Noord: Center for Higher Education Policy Studies (CHEPS).

Levin, M. H., Jeong, D. W., & Ou, D. (2006, March 16). *What is a world class university?* Paper prepared for the conference of the Comparative and International Education Society (CIES), Honolulu, HI. Retrieved from www.tc.columbia.edu/centers/coce/pdf_files/c12.pdf

Menand, L. (2011). Live and learn: Why we have college. *The New Yorker, 87*(16), 76.

Morse, R. (2009). *New rankings: College economic diversity.* Retrieved from http://www.usnews.com/education/blogs/college-rankings-blog/2009/09/10/new-rankings-college-economic-diversity

The National Center for Education Statistics (NCES). (2010). *Digest of education statistics 2010.* Washington, DC: U.S. Department of Education.

National Science Board. (2004). *Science and engineering indicators 2004* (Vol. 2). Arlington: National Science Foundation.

Niland, J. (2007). The challenge of building world-class universities. In J. Sadlak & N. C. Liu (Eds.), *The world class university and ranking: Aiming beyond status* (pp. 61–71). Bucharest: UNESCO-CEPES.

OECD. (2001). *Education at a glance 2001.* Paris: OECD.

OECD. (2003). *Education at a glance 2003.* Paris: OECD.

OECD. (2010). *Education at a glance 2010.* Paris: OECD.

Perkins, H. (1991). The history of universities. In P. G. Altbach (Ed.), *International higher education: An encyclopedia* (pp. 169–203). New York: Garland.

The Princeton Review. (2011). Retrieved from http://www.princetonreview.com/UniversityofIllinoisatUrbanaChampaign.aspx; http://www.princetonreview.com/newyorkuniversity.aspx; http://www.princetonreview.com/universityofsoutherncalifornia.aspx

Richards, A., & Coddington, R. (2010). *30 ways to rate a college.* Retrieved from http://chronicle.com/article/30-Ways-to-Rate-a-College/124160/

Rogers, T. (2009). *International student policy in Sweden: A comparative study of Denmark.* Retrieved from http://www.si.se/upload/Maf%C3%B6%20utb/Study%20Dest%20Sweden/Arbetsgrupp%203/Comparative%20Fees%20Study%20Denmark%20FINAL%2006-09.pdf

Salmi, J. (2009). *The challenge of establishing world-class universities.* Washington, DC: The World Bank.

Shin, J. C., & Harman, G. (2009). New challenges for higher education: Global and Asia-Pacific perspectives. *Asia Pacific Review, 10*(1), 1–13.

Smith, D. G., & Schonfeld, N. B. (2000). The benefits of diversity: What the research tells us. *About campus, 5*(5), 16–23.

Snyder, T. D., & Dillow, S. A. (2008). *Digest of education statistics 2007.* Washington, DC: National Center for Education Statistics (NCES), Institute of Education Science.

UNESCO Institute for Statistics (UIS). (2011). Retrieved from http://www.uis.unesco.org/Pages/default.aspx. Accessed 21 Apr 2011.

University of Tennessee. (2010). *The University of Tennessee draft 2010 unaudited financial statements.* Knoxville: University of Tennessee. Retrieved from http://bot.tennessee.edu/docs/2010_Unaudited_Finan.pdf

Vanderbilt University. (2010). *Vanderbilt University: 2010 financial report.* Nashville: Vanderbilt University. Retrieved from http://financialreport.vanderbilt.edu/reports/FY2010_Financial_Report.pdf

Yingjie, W. (2011). *Financial restructuring of higher education in China.* [PowerPoint slides]. Retrieved from http://www.oecd.org/dataoecd/29/25/36448504.pdf. Accessed 25 Aug 2011.

Chapter 5
Nation-States, Educational Traditions and the WCU Project

Simon Marginson

5.1 Introduction

This chapter begins with what is common and global in higher education and moves to inquire into, and hypothesize about, that which is different. It is a preliminary study designed to chart a future process of inquiry and research that is as much historical as sociological in character. This chapter acknowledges that there is a worldwide movement towards the 'World Class University' (Liu et al. 2011) or 'Global Research University' (Ma 2008; Marginson 2008) and begins to explore divergences in the pathways to the WCU/GRU. It is interested in what shapes those global divergences, especially the role of the nation-state and of the national traditions in educational culture that are often interpreted by states.

This is a 'glonacal' study (Marginson and Rhoades 2002) that rests on the assumption that each of the global, national and local dimensions of higher education are potent and each can be the leading or dominant dimension at differing moments. Using situated case studies (Deem 2001) of national systems and individual universities to investigate the varying relations, conjunctions and overlaps between these three dimensions—while also paying due regard to the pan-national regional dimension, especially in Europe, Latin America and East Asia—helps us to understand the dynamics of the higher education sector.

This chapter rests also on a second assumption. Although all three dimensions continue to matter and the national dimension is the main source of the resourcing of higher education, in recent years, the global dimension has become qualitatively more important than before in this sector (Marginson 2010; King et al. 2011). We can date the growing role of global referencing, strategy and practices to the rise of

S. Marginson (✉)
Center for the Study of Higher Education, University of Melbourne, Melbourne, Australia
e-mail: s.marginson@unimelb.edu.au

J.C. Shin and B.M. Kehm (eds.), *Institutionalization of World-Class University in Global Competition*, The Changing Academy – The Changing Academic Profession in International Comparative Perspective 6, DOI 10.1007/978-94-007-4975-7_5,
© Springer Science+Business Media Dordrecht 2013

synchronous global communications after 1990 (Castells 2000), which 'thickened' the common relational space. However, the crucial date in higher education is 2003, which saw the publication of the first Shanghai Jiao Tong world university ranking (SJTUGSE 2011). This installed a single template or model of the ideal research university, one that has become common to almost every country. Here the normative logic of globalization is simple. Everyone wants to do well in the world top 500 table (Hazelkorn 2008). To do well, an institution must conform to, and perform well within, the template of the ranking concerned. In the case of the Jiao Tong, it rewards Nobel Prizes, discipline medals and science publication and citation in the leading English language journals in each field of research. Institutions also gain ground by collaborating within each other to circulate their research and lift measured performance and by imitating each other's strengths. The outcome has been not just a worldwide field of comparison that bites deeply into national policy and local practices but a global system of networked and increasingly convergent research universities. Nevertheless, they and their settings remain variant in intriguing ways, which are the subject of this chapter.

The first part of this chapter identifies the elements that comprise the common global template (see also Salimi 2009) and briefly suggests the national and local factors that shape success in global comparison and competition. The second part suggests there are divergent pathways to that success, as noted, and begins the process of identifying and explaining these different pathways. There is also a comparison of the approaches of English-speaking nations and the approaches of Confucian heritage countries in East Asia and Singapore (Marginson 2011). The third section focuses on what is seen as the main driver of this global differentiation of pathways—variations in the character of the nation-state and thus also of state/higher education relations. Reasons for the centrality of the state, and for the neglect of comparative state analysis in higher education studies, are canvassed. The final section begins to identify lines of investigation into the triad of nation/culture/education, in the framework of comparative and global higher education.

Much of what follows is raw theorizing that has moved ahead of systematic empirical investigation. The propositions and conclusions in this chapter should be seen as the starting point of hypotheses for investigation. Unencumbered by much evidence, or even a comprehensive literature review, this chapter is short relative to its ambition and range. Nonetheless, it reflects almost a decade of empirical observation and reading in the area, especially 17 case studies of the global strategies of research universities located in East Asia and the Pacific. The author is confident about the judgments herein (at least until proven otherwise).

5.2 What Is a World-Class University (WCU)?

The term 'world-class university' is an aspirational concept. In itself, the WCU is not fixed in character. Like any assertion of 'quality' or 'excellence' or 'beautiful' or 'best', it is relative and norm referenced. Like all norms, what constitutes a 'world-class university' is in the eye of the beholder. If there are six billion people, there are six billion possible definitions of 'world class'. The very fact of differing rankings shows there is more than one possible definition of the WCU.

However, the dominant role played by comparative research performance measures, and especially the Shanghai Jiao Tong ranking, shows that we can identify a particular concept of WCU that is hegemonic at this time. Here research-related capacities and activities are central but not the whole WCU. Arguably, the objective form that gives substance to the notion of the WCU is the Global Research University or GRU (Ma 2008; Marginson 2008). The GRU has defined characteristics that can be empirically tested and verified. Because it is part of a global system of networked and parallel institutions, its common *global systemic* characteristics, those aspects of its profile that enable comparison and lend themselves to shared activity, are apparent across nations. (We will get to the differences later.) The common features of the GRU include:

– Research capacity sufficient to enable significant output in the sciences ('significant' is open to definition)
– A comprehensive set of academic disciplines and professional training
– Resources sufficient to support globally recognized research and teaching
– Being nested locally and nationally, combined with status and recognition at global level
– Global connectivity through communications, collaboration patterns and people mobility
– Connections to business and industry (extensivity and intensity varies)
– A degree of institutional autonomy ('degree' to be defined) combined with an institutional executive exercising strategic leadership (though there is a tiny handful of exceptions to the requirement about executive supervision, such as Cambridge and Oxford, UK, and also Tokyo)
– A degree of academic freedom in research and scholarship ('degree' to be defined)

Some might want to add to this list the contributions of WC GRUs to the global public good and to the ethical formation of graduates as not just national citizens but globally aware persons. It must be said that at this stage, neither of these qualities is a central part of the common understanding of the WC GRU in many different national systems, which tend to focus more on competitive aspects, despite broad support for collaborative research on global problems.

5.3 What Are the Conditions and Drivers of a WC GRU?

What are the conditions and drivers of a WC GRU? There are economic, political and educational-cultural conditions to meet. The objective characteristics of the WC GRU as listed above require sustained investment and competent performance. The lead time between investment and outcome is long. It takes more than 5 years before the financing of new capacity leads to high levels of research activity, a further delay before this activity turns into published outputs, and up to another decade before outputs translate into stellar citation performance.

Economically, the scale and stability of resources are both important. There must be growth and wealth sufficient to finance the WC GRU on a continuing basis from a combination of public and private sources. It is very difficult for a nation with a per capita income of less than, say, $10,000 USD per annum to sustain a world top 200 university. (China is an exception. Its per capita income is lower than $8000 and it has a university in the Shanghai Jiao Tong University top 200, Tsinghua. In China, regional economies are notably stratified. The nation sustains both advanced concentrations of urban wealth and intensive research and regions at much lower economic levels.) Within institutions, there must be a mix of human resources and physical capacity sufficient to support research, especially, and advanced teaching. There must be locally and globally competent teaching, communications and institutional leadership and organization, including the capacity to manage the national policy settings.

Nations and universities are stronger if they can call on an accumulation of past achievements, especially in producing and using knowledge, consistent with the WC GRU model. It is easier to build on past capacity than to create a WC GRU from nothing, providing that existing institutions can modernize and globalize. Existing leaders in the USA and UK have a considerable first mover advantage.

Politically, it is essential to maintain a mix of nation-state policies, programs and regulations, including investments, that is favourable to—or at least not unfavourable to—the evolution of the GRU. The more enabling and driving is state policy, the more likely it is that WC GRUs can be created. It is important here that the state does not overplay its hand because WC GRUs must have enough autonomy to make good academic decisions, especially about research.

Culturally, government, civil society and industry must sustain an embedded tradition of respect for science, research and scholarship and tolerate the claims of research universities to social status. More specific educational-cultural conditions must also be met. Within the institution, and perhaps the nation-state, there must be desires for institutional prestige and eminence in the form of the WC GRU, extending beyond the university president's office to be shared by academic leaders. To be globally effective, institutions must also have the desire and capacity to connect effectively across borders, work in global English and open themselves to global flows of ideas, knowledge and people.

5.4   Different Pathways to the WC GRU

In worldwide higher education, the most credible single national model of the research university is an idealized version of the comprehensive American doctoral institution. There is no doubt that the American high science university and its

British cousin have been the main influence on the templates used for ranking purposes. Nevertheless, other inherited traditions are also powerful and have shaped distinctive institutional forms and cultures. The more we look at the dynamics of the evolution of WC GRUs, the more we can identify varied paths to the same globally defined goal. National systems and institutions have varying starting points and employ divergent emphases and methods to create WC GRUs.

Without moving now to a full typology, we can tentatively identify certain regional approaches (note that there is variation within some of these models):

1. United States. The USA has a long modern tradition of mass higher education and the research university. The state is less directive than in other traditions, but the growth of higher education has been supported by the partial role of federal government via research funding, the legal framing of intellectual property and the loans-shaped student market. There is also a fecund business/research interface with a strong biomedical industry. A key element is the self-sustaining civil order that grounds the universities locally and in states and cities, while also fostering the Ivy League private sector which is the premier allocator of status through higher education. The USA sector is so strong that its universities can develop often highly effective global activity at their margin without changing their character.

2. The Westminster systems in the UK, Australia, and New Zealand. There are obvious resemblances to the United States, but the dynamics are different, particularly state/civil society/university relations. The Westminster systems came later to mass higher education and are subject to closer central state supervision. These systems are located in finance-sector dominated polities with Treasury-driven government. Civil society is a lesser factor than in the USA. The Westminster systems are organized using a market equity model, with a strong element of interinstitutional competition between formally similar universities. Diversity is not institutionalized via classification as in the USA and China. The national systems of the UK, Australia and New Zealand also run large commercial export sectors.

3. European systems located in polities premised on the social market or social democracy. On the whole, the role of the state is more obvious than in the English-speaking countries—in most European nations, professors are employed, or were previously employed, as state public servants. States, more than internal market competition, are the primary drivers of institutional improvement. States have played the key role in investments designed to create WC GRUs, for example, in Germany and France. However, European higher education is scarcely homogenous, despite a partial convergence in research activities and degree structures via Bologna concords. Some, like Italy, sustain large scale universities with a comprehensive public function but characterized by internal incoherence and fragmentation. Some, like Sweden, give primacy to citizenship equity in higher education and maintaining strong research universities. Some, like Switzerland, veer closer to the Westminster model. Others combine the last two approaches, for example, Germany. Within Europe, there are several roads

to the WC GRU. That particular set of variations will not be explored further in this chapter.

4. The Confucian heritage systems in East Asia and Singapore. These systems exhibit great dynamism in GRU development—Japan in the 1960s and 1970s and Singapore, Korea, Taiwan China, Hong Kong SAR and China in the last 15 years. In these systems, enrolments tend to universal levels, there is strong household investment in schooling, extra tutoring and higher education that is grounded in Confucian values, and the nation-state closely motivates and supervises higher education and research—though as in Europe, many research universities have achieved greater institutional autonomy than before. The state also drives accelerated investments in university research and scholarships for bright students. More is said about Confucian heritage systems in the next section.

5. In the Gulf States and Saudi Arabia, higher education has emerged as quickly, but WC GRU status is not as strongly grounded in local cities and the national economy. Much of the WC GRU development consists of aristocrat-led education theme parks sustained by state oil revenues. This is a very different model, but the nation-state is again a central player.

There are other models that could be discussed, such as the large scale public universities in Latin America such as the national university of Mexico (UNAM) and the University of Buenos Aires in Argentina (UBA), originating in a bonapartist model from France and Italy, and the newer private universities in countries such as Brazil, Argentina, Chile and Japan, though perhaps only the leading Japanese institutions at Keio and Waseda have secure WC GRU status.

5.5 Comparison of English-Speaking Systems and Confucian Heritage Systems

For example, let us compare the established English language systems with the model of the Confucian heritage systems that have now sprung into prominence (Marginson 2011). The distinctive features of the Confucian model are fourfold. First and most important, they are framed, supervised and in many respects powered by a comprehensive and active nation-state. The state exercises a strong direct influence in the leading universities, typically appointing university presidents and often also leading professors, and though there are moves towards greater university autonomy and a managerial executive, it is within the framework of a continued close understanding between government and institution. Second, Confucian systems rest on a 2,000-year-old bedrock of Confucian valuation of self-cultivation via education. This constitutes both an act of familial piety and the way to social preferment. Third, families are locked into educational goals and private investment in educational costs such as private tutoring by one-chance examination systems, inherited from the Confucian tradition, that are the gateway to the most prestige schools and universities in steeply hierarchical systems of institutions. Finally, modern Confucian higher education is characterized by rapidly growing investment in research in science and technology and in scholarships for the brightest students in the leading institutions, which are largely financed by the state.

The state has been at the root of the dynamic economic growth in the Confucian zone where nations do not follow the neo-liberal prescription of letting the market shape the economic trajectory (in reality, Anglo-American countries do not follow that neo-liberal prescription either, but they allow finance rather than state-sponsored industry to call the shots). In higher education as in other sectors, the comprehensive state in the Confucian tradition that dates back to the Ch'in and Han in China (227 BCE to 220 CE) is a common feature of East Asia and Singapore regardless of the political system, whether capitalist or socialist and whether multi-party or one-party. In all these systems, the state encompasses part of the territory of civil society in the liberal West. The role of government is ubiquitous and taken for granted. It is largely unquestioned as the interpreter of the national character, which is continually being constructed by the nation-state in Japan, China and Singapore. There is often debate inside the state institutions—including universities—but dissent is not translated into a challenge to state authority from outside the state except in extreme moments when the objective is wholesale replacement of the regime. There is a tradition of underlying popular scepticism about government but symbolic antigovernment rhetoric in public places, which is an ongoing ritual in the Western countries, especially in the United States, is largely missing in the Confucian zone.

This is not to say that Confucian nations are more conforming than Western or that Western nations are naturally less patriotic. The USA is soaked in national pride, and there is profound voluntary Western conformity to legal, social and economic rules, though often also a broader space for criticism and 'off-the-wall' public aesthetics. Further, there is another long tradition in the Confucian world, that of open statements of the good by learned scholars. Thus, the scholar critic can find a somewhat beleaguered public place, and even whole institutions can gain a certain freedom. In China, Peking University (Beida) seems to have inherited this role within higher education. Beida has been in the forefront of most political movements in the nation since its foundation. The Communist Party was launched there in 1921. The Cultural Revolution began there in 1966. The first 'rightist' to be denounced was the Beida president, but tellingly, he survived the Cultural Revolution in his post. Likewise, the Tiananmen Square movement in 1989 was launched at Beida. Perhaps the WC GRU in China is sometimes less wholly state-driven than is generally assumed; perhaps there is debate within the state.

The English-speaking WC GRUs have emerged in societies with the Western liberal tradition of a liberal state and division of labour between different parts of the state. There is a larger scope for autonomous economic markets and civil societies, and state/market and state/society tensions have long been inherent. State policy, regulation and funding nevertheless frames higher education—more directly and comprehensively in the UK than the USA, though the federal role in research is decisive in the USA. At the same time, institutional autonomy and codified academic freedom are built into the model, and the universities also connect to civil society. In the case of the United States, where the role of the state is also federal with the states sovereign in some areas, they often appear more as civil institutions than as state institutions. (Australia has a formally federal structure, but the states are not as sovereign as in the United States. In higher education, the federal government runs policy and funding.) The tradition of popular commitment to education is not as deep or universal as in the Confucian heritage societies. The modern imaginary of equal opportunity in and through higher education has been a powerful social force in the English-speaking systems, and mass education in these countries has helped to shape its evolution everywhere else. However, in contrast with the Confucian world, the aspiration for education is less likely to be shared by the poorest families, and state funding of tuition is more essential to secure growing participation. Examination and selection systems are more complex than in the Confucian world, with plural routes.

The institutional hierarchy is steep in the United States model, but while all systems are hierarchical and not all universities are WC GRUs, there is a larger element of commonality of mission in the case of the UK, Australia and New Zealand institutions, which sustain a binary between nominally research institutions and vocational institutions, not a multilevel classification. In research, the English-speaking systems, like the Confucian systems, depend on state funding, but state funding and research outputs have never increased with the rapidity of the Confucian systems during their phase of accelerated development, which is still underway in most of East Asia and Singapore. This may be because when the English-speaking systems were building mass levels of participation, government funded a higher proportion of tuition than in the Confucian world, leaving less state resources for building research capacity.

Table 5.1 contrasts the Confucian heritage model with the trajectory of the United States and the Westminster model in UK, Australia and New Zealand. Note that there are important variations and distinctions among the Confucian heritage systems. Nevertheless, they share similar nation-state roles and similar popular educational cultures. For more discussion of the differences, see Marginson (2011).

How do the different pathways translate into a layer of WC GRUs at the top of each system? The American system uses market ideology and federal research funding, and a status hierarchy defined by a classification system and thus protected from destabilizing politicization, to sustain high advancing quality in the leading WC GRUs. The Confucian heritage countries combine examination-mediated competition in the Confucian hierarchy with selective state investment in infrastructure, research and scholarships. This has proven just as successful in demarcating a layer of top universities. In both these kinds of system, there is less tension between merit and status than in the Westminster countries. In the Confucian systems, Confucian values lock in student effort, which is therefore less dependent on individual calculations of the probability of success than the human capital metaphor suggests. In the USA, the popular culture historically saw the USA as the engine of such broad ranging opportunities that there was scope for all to succeed and become rich (even though this was self-evidently impossible),

Table 5.1 Comparison of Confucian heritage and English language country systems

	Confucian heritage systems	United States' system	Westminster systems (UK, Australia, NZ)
Character of nation-state	Comprehensive. Politics commands economy and civil society. State often draws best and brightest	Limited, division of powers, separate from civil society and economy. Federal	Limited, division of powers, separate from civil society and economy. Unitary
National culture in education	Universal and venerable Confucian heritage of family commitment to education: valued in itself and also as instrumental means to social standing	Twentieth century meritocratic ideology of education as common opening to wealth and status, within advancing frontier and prosperity	Post 1945 ideology of state guaranteed equal opportunity through education as path to wealth and status, open to all in society
State role in higher education	State supervises, shapes, drives and selectively funds institutions. Over time part withdrawal from directional role	State regulation fosters hierarchical market via student loans, research grants. Then steps back. Autonomous presidents	State regulation, policy and funding supervises competitive market, shapes certain activities. Autonomous presidents
Financing of higher education	State financing of infrastructure, part of tuition (especially early in model), scholarships, aid. Household tuition and private tutoring, even many poor families	State financing of some infrastructure, tuition subsidies, student loans. Households vary from high tuition to low, poor families more state dependent or drop out	State once financed infrastructure but less now. Tuition loans, some maintenance. Growing household investment but less than other models. Austerity
Hierarchy and social selection	Traditional examination, 'one-chance' universal competition/selection into unquestioned prestige hierarchy of institutions. WC GRUs provide fast track for life	Race to enter prestige institutions mediated by SAAT scores. Some plurality of routes and second chances, mainly public sector. WC GRUs provide fast track for life	Competition into university hierarchy mediated by end school selection with some plurality and second chances. WC GRUs provide strong start
Dynamics of research	Part household funding of tuition plus ideology of WCU, with structure of hierarchy, sustain rapid investment in research at scale. Applied emphasis that reduces over time	Research heavily funded by federal government unburdened by direct tuition. Some industry and civic/philanthropic money. Basic science plus commercial IP	Research stringently funded by government which finances tuition. Less philanthropy and civic money than USA. Basic science, applied growth, IP wannabee
Fostering of World Class Global Research Universities (WC GRUs)	Part of tradition, the universal target of family aspirations, fostered by funding and regulation. Rapid building over time is not much questioned	Entrenched hierarchy of Ivy League and flagship state universities, via research grants, tuition hikes, philanthropy. Source of global pride	Ambivalence about status of top institutions in national temperament and government policy. Private and public funding hit ceilings

and it was and is widely believed that high wealth based on market-earned success is wholly admirable. It might be that this vision is now faltering, as the current generation of Americans is mostly worse off than its predecessors, and there are signs of proletarianization in parts of the middle class amid global competition and faltering US economic management (Brown et al. 2011).

In contrast, the Westminster countries have struggled to centre adequate resources in a layer of WC GRUs. High-status leading universities cut across the post-1945 idea of equality of opportunity, post-1980s neo-liberal ideology of market equity and the policy goal of using lesser status institutions to advance participation. Without the potential for enrichment that has characterized the USA, equal opportunity to compete does not deliver enough benefits to enough families. Over time, social inequality in and through education has become more apparent, though this has not made educational status any more acceptable, for it is part of the social mechanisms whereby inequality is reproduced, an inequality acceptable in the East and the USA but unacceptable in the UK or Australia. However, unlike Australia and New Zealand, the UK is able to deploy the inherited status, old imperial role and accumulated resources of its top universities, especially Oxford and Cambridge that are the British equivalent of Harvard, Tokyo, Peking University and Tsinghua. Even so, Oxford and Cambridge struggle to sustain their material pulling power in the global market for talent. Stellar intellectual cultures lacking money eventually wind down.

5.6   The Role and Nature of the Nation-State

Table 5.1 suggests that the main elements of difference between the cases are (1) the character and role of the nation-state in higher education and (2) the national culture that shapes popular commitment to and investment in higher education. The state must work with and not against this national culture, while also interpreting tradition and often leading its further development. These two conditions, state and culture, are more foundational than higher education itself. We can note that in each of the three cases, the two conditions are synchronized. The state in Confucian heritage societies draws on Confucian tradition to part finance the roll out of participation at advancing levels of quality of provision. The state in the English-speaking nations is locked into the politics of response to growing social demand for educational opportunities while working at the margins to universalize social inclusion in the system.

The role of the state underpins both higher education development and the organization of student learning at school level, in East Asia and Singapore. It shows itself in state-financed investment in university infrastructure, research, student aid and scholarships and selective funding of programs to bring foreign-trained talent back to the country. The state appears to be solidly behind the leading universities as they go global, and it expects them to exhibit an improving world-class performance over time. It appoints the university president and supervises the president on an ongoing basis via the joint system of leadership president and party secretary in China, it supports the selection of the president by a nominal autonomous university council in Singapore but expects the universities to harmonize with the state agenda, and there are other variations in between. The state is also the obvious driver in the accelerated WC GRU investment programs in higher education in Germany, France and some other European countries and in the Gulf States and Saudi Arabia.

As the table suggests, in the English-speaking countries with their liberal ideology and practice of the limited state and with the endemic state/university tensions that are fostered by this ideology, and despite increasing withdrawal of the state from the funding of tuition, the state maintains a shaping power in higher education. Peter Scott's work (1998) emphasizes the central role of the state in modern higher education systems, in which mass higher education and innovation systems are harnessed to nation-building agendas. Even in the outlying case of the United States, where universities appear as more part of civil society than the state sector that contains them in most countries, higher education is historically a product of government and expected to serve national purposes as it does elsewhere. It is a mark of the synchrony between state, university and civil society in the USA that patriotic university boards and presidents voluntarily pursue the national interest.

But is it the same role of the state in each case? Is it the same kind of nation-state? Is it the same kind of relationship between formal education, civil society, economic markets and the household? No it is not, and the differences are important.

In sum, identification of distinctions between system type, and the description of factors that appear to represent the differences, suggests the following hypothesis:

Hypothesis 1. That in comparing national higher education systems, differences between systems—and especially differences between types of higher education system such as those of Confucian heritage and the United States—can be explained in terms of variations in the nature, role and activity of the *nation-state*. This includes the conjunction between national cultures and state policies.

In fact, differences in nation-states, their traditions, resources, strategies and so on, might even help us to explain differences in the effectiveness of systems and individual universities on the pathway to the WC GRU.

Before going on to look at a possible research agenda for investigating this hypothesis, this chapter will remark briefly on why the role and nature of the nation-state has been somewhat neglected in comparative higher education.

5.7 Why Is the State Neglected in Higher Education?

Peter Scott's point that modern higher education is a function of nation-building programs is broadly understood. The field of higher education studies is often closely tied to state-funded research and national policy agendas. It is obvious the WC GRU project is driven by the global competition state around the world as well as by institutional ambition. So the idea that national system differences are closely affected by the differing histories and trajectories of the nation-state is unsurprising.

Yet, we do not talk about those differences much and we do not investigate them comparatively and, especially, historically. We compare policies. But we rarely place those policies in their specific context, preferring instead to abstract comparative policy analysis by comparing policies in what is apparently a neutral analytical vacuum (while de facto, introducing our own specific national policy culture as the implicit frame of reference). We rarely compare states themselves, their traditions and institutions, their ways of working and their political and social cultures, and draw the connection between that analysis and the variations in higher education.

Why is the question of the state neglected in our field? A useful way into this question is a set of readings edited by Evans et al. (1985) and published by Harvard University Press as *Bringing the state back in*. Neglect of the state is a function of the domination of American social science. The focus on the state is more a European perspective than an Anglo liberal perspective. Liberal English-speaking societies have downplayed the role of the state in comparative analysis of modernization. In many respects, the United States is the outlying case in state/society relations—as is the case in higher education—yet the sheer weight of American ideas in a global knowledge system in which the USA has four out of every five leading social science schools (SJTUGSE 2011) means that US perspectives tend to set the framework of thinking. In the 1950s and 1960s, American structural-functionalism and pluralism pushed away consideration of the state. This reflected the American liberal political culture, which emphasized society-driven explanations for states and for higher education also. Where higher education was seen in political terms, it was seen as an arena for contestation between plural social groups. Interestingly, this coincided with the orthodox Marxist emphasis on another set of socioeconomic explanations for states and for higher education, based in classes, capital accumulation and class struggle as the motor of history. There is some truth but not the whole truth in both kinds of explanation. What is missing is the autonomous drive and capacity of states. States are never wholly autonomous from class forces and social groups and from economic markets, but a wide variety of arrangements (more or less autonomy) are possible.

The case of the United States continues to hypnotize much of the analysis in higher education studies. It is perhaps not surprising given the USA has 17 of the top 20 research universities, 53 of the top 100 universities (SJTUGSE 2011), and more than half of the top 1% most cited scientific papers (NSB 2011). For example, it is often argued as a matter of course that a US-style independent research culture is essential for creativity, not just because states that depart from merit make bad decisions about research selection, which is obvious—moments of expert freedom are essential to creative work—but because governed research contradicts what is believed to be the American case. Yet, the research culture in the USA reflects a developed civil society along American lines, within the distinctive US political culture, conditions that cannot be replicated anywhere else, and in many respects, the practice of American research is rather different to what the ideology suggests.

Skopcol (1985) notes that it has been a longstanding habit in the USA to attribute even public programs and institutions such as research universities to the civil society or the market, to talk up contestation in the civil order, and downplay the role of the state bureaucracy. In the USA, the Constitution is sovereign, not the executive. The Constitution did not establish a state machine as such to provide for the public welfare. The public welfare is seen as the aggregate of private benefits and transactions. Politics is defined not as contestation over administrative programs, as in many European nations and the Westminster countries, but as contestation over bills in Congress. In effect, politics is seen as contestation over legislation that defines the meaning of the Constitution, hence the sacred character of freedom of transaction and the need to define higher education as a market—even though as in other polities, higher education is shaped by nation-state regulation and resources. Most American research is fed by directed HSF and NIH funding. The research culture is not so independent after all, nor is the US freedom to criticize and dissent necessarily manifest as nonconformity. The jury is still out on how necessary is an American style research culture in all fields to being a WC GRU and how open creativity can be configured in non-American cultures.

5.8 Openings for Investigation

States are more than the identifiable machinery of 'government' and also more than 'politics', party-centred, electoral or internal to the state. By 'state' is meant the full set of administrative, bureaucratic, coercive, communicative and financial systems and institutions, which overlaps into markets and civil society. Established states exhibit much continuity between specific political regimes. Basic patterns of state organization and of the relationship of the state to social groups and institutions often persist even in major crises. If we assume that higher education is closely affected by the nation-state, then we could expect it to be affected by differences between nation-states in the tradition, identity and national culture and also in:

- The capacity of the machinery of state, including fiscal capacity (a robust tax system is essential) and its power of communications and persuasion
- The capacity of the state to articulate and implement a common ideology of 'the nation', including the desired global trajectory of the nation
- The autonomy of the state and its agencies
- The scope for rapid intervention in which the state moves substantial resources quickly on its own initiative
- The agendas and strategies of the coordinating centre of state
- The capacity of the state in the production and distribution of resources
- The political capacity of the state, in the context of popular traditions and expectations, including its effectiveness in shaping the polity and the political culture and in defining the options for legitimate action
- The modes of intervention used by the state

- The relations between state and civil society and economic market
- In higher education, the machinery and culture of governance, policy and funding that links the state and the institutions

5.9   An Example: State Autonomy

All of these areas are accessible to comparative investigation. Such investigation will identify variation between the different system types in higher education; though more than one interpretation of these variations is possible. For example, consider the issue of state autonomy. Weberian analysts of the state focus on 'strong states', which they define as autonomous states. It is not that simple. State autonomy and state capacity are not identical and do not always go together. Autonomous states are states where the administrative machine cannot be stopped by social forces, while states with capacity are states that can get things done. But while some strong states displace ruling groups, for example, the Meiji Restoration in Japan, building state autonomy in that process, other states flourish when they achieve symbiosis with ruling groups, for example, the role of MITI in Japan after World War Two. Still, other states collaborate with ruling groups as partners, for example, the British state collaborates closely with finance capital in the city of London, through the power of Treasury in the Westminster system. The same comment can be made about WC GRUs. Autonomy in a research university by itself is not enough to generate global potency, though it appears that at least some autonomy is necessary to global effectiveness. This is because states cannot handle global relationships on behalf of universities as well as universities can handle such relationships themselves.

State autonomy (like university autonomy) is always partial and contested. It fluctuates in continuing tugs of war between state and economy, state and leading families, or the state and the army. Likewise, university autonomy is pulled back and forth between university and market, and university and government. Skopcol (1985) remarks that autonomy also can and does change over time. For example, the more effective state programs are in affecting the economy and society, the more the state agencies responsible for implementing those programs become tangled with interest groups, clients and corruption around those programs. The agencies lose autonomy, and the programs lose traction and legitimacy. Capacity becomes negatively correlated to autonomy. This is why the New Deal stalled in the United States. In some countries, like Australia, state building of mass higher education was seen to be followed by producer capture, triggering state disillusionment with its programs. It can also happen to universities—potentially, the more clients they connect with, the more they are inhibited. On the other hand, Treasury power in Westminster systems increases the autonomy of state. The state appears as an independent shaper and arbiter. Yet, this can be at the price of nonintervention. In Australia, Treasury blocks a more active pursuit of building the WC GRU because as in the UK, Treasury opposes any and every proposal to increase government funding.

All states are characteristically concerned with capital accumulation, and some are concerned with income and wealth distribution. Most states want higher education to fulfil the requirements of 'the economy', meaning business and industry, and to contribute to employment. But states vary in extent and type of advice they take from business and industry, whether they mediate the relationship for higher education or set up direct 'market' signal systems, and to what extent they get involved instrumentally in graduate employment issues. This in turn affects state expectations about the WC GRU—whether its connections to industry are a primary policy indicator and whether this is imagined specifically in terms of particular national industries and firms or managed at the level of generic national and global business. WC GRUs vary considerably in the extent to which they are instrumentally tied to nationally based capital though structured innovation systems and funding.

Most states seem to exhibit strong capacity in some areas only and strong autonomy in some areas only. For example, does the USA have a strong state or not? A neo-Weberian would probably say 'no', because the state is not autonomous of business and industry and interest groups and the political trading and coalition-building in Congress. A neo-Marxist would probably say 'yes', because the American state, seen as the servant of American capital, represents a very powerful interest both on the world stage and at home. In reality, the picture is mixed. America the state has both high capacity and high autonomy in the military domain and medium capacity and weak autonomy in the economic domain. In higher education, it has autonomy in research policy but little power to drive the specific strategies of research institutions, unlike the state in the Confucian zone, which often has its hands directly on the presidency and unlike the Westminster state which shapes the detail of research practice with performance measures and specific incentives. To implement policy with effect, in creating the WC GRU and other areas, states need not just autonomy but policy structure and culture. In China and Singapore, the state has autonomy and is also highly focused in delivery.

Hypothesis 2. Nation-states vary in higher education, in the combination of state autonomy and state instrumental power. These variations partly explain differences in the speed and effectiveness of WC GRU development.

5.10 An Example: The Scale and Scope of the State

Another issue for investigation is the scale and scope/range of state responsibilities. The contrast between the Western liberal state and the comprehensive Confucian state has been noted. In the polities of the English-speaking world, what governments can or cannot do is primary and is characteristically unresolved. The debate about higher education continually turns on fractured relations between universities and government. The first instinct of interest groups and public actors in the higher education sector is often to create or play on such tensions. The tensions are also substantial—the main debates often turn on issues of institutions versus government, for example, demands for more funding and opposition to the detail of regulation. These issues are often about where the state/institution boundary is set. Partly because of the tensions around state intervention, liberal states are often reluctant to support and advance objectives other than unquestionable instrumental economic objectives, such as the furthering of economic productivity and growth, or issues of probity in state expenditure where the politics of low taxation dictates surveillance.

National tradition plays a role in determining the extent to which higher education is expected to contribute to the cultural formation of society—and the extent to which it is meant to work for the nonmarket objectives of civil society— and to the ethical and moral formation of students. When the state subsidizes the humanities, it also subsidizes civil society. In the liberal Westminster systems, in which taxpayer populism is a tool for building electoral support, this is often stigmatized as funding an 'elite' or the 'chattering classes'. In the UK in December 2010, the UK government decided that funding the humanities and the social sciences could be sourced entirely from students, without direct public subsidies for teaching. Here civil society is modelled as a spillover from the higher education market. It is inconceivable that Confucian states would be formally indifferent to the question of ethical and moral formation, though they expect parents with Confucian values to foster those values at home and finance much of the educational cost themselves.

Hypothesis 3. The scale and scope of normal state intervention is positively correlated to the speed and effectiveness of systems in advancing the WC GRU, providing that the state is instrumentally effective across its range of responsibilities.

Note that the British funding decision can be interpreted either as a strong British state enforcing its instrumentalist neo-liberal economic view of education or as a weak state that has abstained from using higher education to shape the national culture and (unlike, say, China with the Confucius Institutes) is indifferent to injecting that culture into the global space via the WC GRU. In other words, generalizations solely focused on 'strong' and 'weak' states do not take us far into an understanding of comparative higher education. Even states of similar broad type vary quite markedly in autonomy, capacity and agency freedom and will. Their resources and other circumstances can also vary greatly. The same is true of universities.

States also vary according to where they are placed on one of the curves of WC GRU evolution. Perhaps emerging states have more scope to manoeuvre in higher education because they are less path dependent and there is likely to be internal consensus about the need to improve, but they also have problems not shared by established systems. Apart from the obvious point that capacity is underdeveloped, they must deal from a weaker position with global capital and the neo-imperialism of the Anglo-American powers and are constrained by the Anglo-American dominance in higher education which is continually reinforced by global systems like research publishing and ranking. Emerging states do not control global policy rules in higher education. They can only start to work the global people flows in their favour with strenuous investment and effort. Nevertheless, on their way up, the system managers in Taiwan and Korea did reverse the brain drain and China appears to be following.

5.11   An Example: State-University Relations

If different parts of the state have different levels of autonomy and capacity—and if we consider higher education, including the globally linked research universities, as part of the state, broadly defined—then in most but not all cases, higher education is one of those parts of the state with higher relative autonomy. At the same time, as noted, the general relations between higher education and other parts of the state vary, from direct administration to the idea that even state universities are part of a semiprivate civic and market order. Specific indicators of the state to university relationship include resources and the conditions attached to their use; the state's own relations with civil society and business and industry; the relations between WC GRUs and civil society; the forms of intellectual freedom and also how it is advanced and protected; and universities' capacity to initiate, outside specific or direct regulation, particularly the strategic autonomy and capacity of the executive.

Structures apparently similar between systems can have different means and associations. Consider the new public management reforms in England, Japan, Malaysia, and China. All led to corporatized structures. But all function differently. In England, legal and financial rules are exceptionally tight and political economy of funding drives conformity to the official culture. In Japan, the system still conforms to state preferences while sustaining a conservative culture, and unlike the UK, a uniformly strong university executive is yet to emerge. In Malaysia, autonomy is stymied by direct state control over the appointment of the vice-chancellors and capacity is inhibited by the politicization of the system. In China, corporate universities are tied to state agendas not only by appointment of the leaders but via the system of dual leadership, with president alongside party secretary. Yet in some cases (not all!), the party secretary acts as guardian of presidential autonomy.

One suspects there are no universal laws here. However, there is an analytical question: what are the implications of the mix of state/GRU factors for each different kind of WC GRU project? Can we identify an *optimal* configuration of state-university relations for *each* pathway to the WC GRU? And is there scope for transplanting models and techniques between traditions to change the potential outcomes? For example, can the Confucian model of state/university relations be transferred to, say, France and achieve a more dynamic evolution of the WC GRU in that national system? What modifications would be needed to replicate a similar dynamism across borders?

Hypothesis 4. Each kind of WC GRU system is characterized by a configuration of the relationship between state and higher education institution that is optimal for *that particular kind* of WC GRU development, all else equal. This optimal configuration can be identified through historical research, case studies and analytical inquiry.

5.12   Conclusion

The next steps are to refine the hypotheses as tools of investigation and to conduct specific research in each different zone in which WC GRU evolutions are occurring.

References

Brown, P., Lauder, H., & Ashton, D. (2011). *The global auction: The broken promises of education, jobs and incomes*. Oxford: Oxford University Press.

Castells, M. (2000). *The rise of the network society: The information age: Economy, society and culture* (Vol. 1). Oxford: Blackwell.

Deem, R. (2001). Globalization, new managerialism, academic capitalism and entrepreneurialism in universities: Is the local dimension still important? *Comparative Education, 37*(1), 7–20.

Evans, P., Rueschemeyer, D., & Skopcol, T. (Eds.). (1985). *Bringing the state back in*. Cambridge: Cambridge University Press.

Hazelkorn, E. (2008). Learning to live with league tables and ranking: The experience of institutional leaders. *Higher Education Policy, 21*, 193–215.

King, R., Marginson, S., & Naidoo, R. (Eds.). (2011). *Handbook of higher education and globalization*. Cheltenham: Edward Elgar.

Liu, N., Ching, Y., & Wang, Q. (Eds.). (2011). *Paths to a world-class university*. Rotterdam: Sense Publishers.

Ma, W. (2008). The University of California at Berkeley: An emerging global research university. *Higher Education Policy, 21*, 65–81.

Marginson, S. (2008, December 10–11). *Ideas of a university for the global era*. Paper for seminar on 'Positioning university in the globalized world: Changing governance and coping strategies in Asia', Centre of Asian Studies, The University of Hong Kong; Central Policy Unit, HKSAR Government; and The Hong Kong Institute of Education, The University of Hong Kong. http://www.cshe.unimelb.edu.au/people/staff_pages/Marginson/Marginson.html. Accessed 1 Aug 2011.

Marginson, S. (2010). University. In P. Murphy, M. Peters, & S. Marginson (Eds.), *Imagination: Three models of imagination in the age of the knowledge economy* (pp. 167–223). New York: Peter Lang.

Marginson, S. (2011). Higher education in East Asia and Singapore: Rise of the Confucian model. *Higher Education, 61*(5), 587–611.

Marginson, S., & Rhoades, G. (2002). Beyond national states, markets, and systems of higher education: A glonacal agency heuristic. *Higher Education, 43*(3), 281–309.

National Science Board. (2011). *Science and engineering indicators 2010*. http://www.nsf.gov/statistics/seind10/. Accessed 18 Aug 2011.

Salmi, J. (2009). *The challenge of establishing world-class universities*. Washington, DC: The World Bank.

Scott, P. (1998). Massification, internationalization and globalization. In P. Scott (Ed.), *The globalization of higher education* (pp. 108–129). Buckingham: The Society for Research into Higher Education/Open University Press.

Shanghai Jiao Tong University Graduate School of Education. (2011). *Academic ranking of world universities 2011*.http://www.shanghairanking.com/ARWU2011.html. Accessed 18 Aug 2011.

Skopcol, T. (1985). Bringing the state back in: Strategies of analysis in current research. In P. Evans, D. Rueschemeyer, & T. Skopcol (Eds.), *Bringing the state back in* (pp. 3–43). Cambridge: Cambridge University Press.

Part II
WCUs in Non-English Speaking Advanced Systems

Chapter 6
To Be or Not to Be? The Impacts of the Excellence Initiative on the German System of Higher Education

Barbara M. Kehm

6.1 Introduction: Traditional Characteristics of Higher Education in Germany

Germany is essentially a binary system consisting of 117 universities (including technical universities) and 207 universities of applied sciences. The latter offer professionally oriented higher education programmes and do not carry out basic research. There are also 55 tertiary level institutions for arts and music. In 2010, about 66% of all German students were studying at university, 32% at universities of applied sciences, and the remaining 2% of students at colleges of art and music. In this chapter, only the universities will be referred to. All universities are considered to be research universities. According to the Humboldtian ideal, there is a close relationship between teaching and research, and all professors are supposed to do both; that is, there is no official differentiation into teaching only or research only professorships.

The German higher education system is essentially a public system. There are 240 state institutions and 139 private institutions for higher education, although the latter do not enrol many students. Ninety-five percent of all students study in public, that is, state-funded higher education institutions. Furthermore, until very recently, the German public higher education system did not ask for tuition fees. When the federal government made an attempt to introduce tuition fees in 2008, there were massive student protests. Since Germany is a federal system and the individual states are responsible for the education sector (including universities), some of the

B.M. Kehm (✉)
International Centre for Higher Education Research, Kassel University, Kassel, Germany
e-mail: kehm@incher.uni-kassel.de

J.C. Shin and B.M. Kehm (eds.), *Institutionalization of World-Class University in Global Competition*, The Changing Academy – The Changing Academic Profession in International Comparative Perspective 6, DOI 10.1007/978-94-007-4975-7_6,
© Springer Science+Business Media Dordrecht 2013

states opted out of the introduction of tuition fees from the beginning – especially the East German states – and several states introduced tuition fees but then had a change of government which eventually abolished them. Of the 16 German states, four currently require tuition fees and twelve do not.

Until recently, the German higher education system was also closely state controlled. Government was regarded as the 'guardian angel' of academic freedom on the one hand, but at the same time, it acted as a strong regulatory power on the other.

All universities have the right to award doctoral degrees; in fact, each professor can accept doctoral candidates as part of his or her academic freedom. As a rule, most professorships have one or two positions for research assistants, that is, doctoral candidates, as part of the infrastructure or resources of the chair which are negotiated when receiving the call or being offered a professorial position. These research assistant positions are fixed term (4–6 years) and part-time (50%) positions in the framework of which the assistants are expected to support the professor's research and teaching activities and also write their PhD thesis. The traditional form of research training is then basically 'on the job'. No formal training or coursework is required. The research assistants are employees in the civil service with a salary and all regular social benefits. As such, they are not considered students. However, ongoing reforms of doctoral education and training in Germany strongly promote the establishment of doctoral programmes or graduate schools to complement training on the job with more systematic training through coursework. Furthermore, for doctoral candidates not employed as junior researchers or assistants, it is the only opportunity to get systematic research and transferable skills training.

Another characteristic of the German higher education system is that until very recently, there was only moderate vertical and horizontal diversity. All institutions of one type were considered to be more or less equal, their treatment by the government was based on legal homogeneity (Neave 1996), and they received funding based on the number of students, the institution's maintenance requirements and the salaries for all staff. Professors were paid according to the same salary scale with only limited differences. Institutions of one type were considered to have more or less the same level of quality. Of course, employers might prefer to recruit graduates from particular universities more than from other institutions, but legally all degrees were considered to have the same value. Finally, universities did not have a tiered structure of studies with undergraduate and graduate degrees, but all degrees (altogether three different ones: professional, academic, state) were master level degrees. There was no bachelor or undergraduate degree.

6.2   Major Areas of Change Since the 1990s

Many things have changed in the German higher education system in the last 15–20 years. A quick overview of the most pertinent reforms can be summarised in the following eight points (Teichler 2009b).

First, there has been state deregulation. That means the state has withdrawn to some extent – although not as much as in other European countries – from close control and granted more institutional autonomy. However, in exchange for more autonomy, higher education institutions have also been held more accountable and now have to report regularly about their performance.

Second, state funding changed from line item budgets to lump-sum budgets, and greater decision-making power was given to the institutional management concerning internal allocation of funds. However, lump-sum budgeting has been linked to budget cuts and performance contracts with the ministries.

Third, both these changes have given more decision-making power to the central level or institutional management leading to a certain degree of professionalisation in this area, but decision-making power has to be shared increasingly with external stakeholders (the state among them) represented in university boards. This has led to a weakening of the traditional collegial bodies of decision-making.

Fourth, there is a strong drive towards further internationalisation and an increased labour market relevance of degrees. The Bologna Process has acted as a catalyst in this respect also leading to far-reaching curricula reform and the introduction of the tiered structure of bachelor and master degrees and programmes.

Fifth, the initiative of the European Commission to establish a European Research Area (Lisbon Strategy), closely linked with the Bologna Process to establish a European Higher Education Area, has led to more expenditure on research. However, there is also a stronger orientation than before towards research contributing to economic growth and technological innovation. There is talk of a new triangle of education, research and innovation (a variation of the 'triple helix' model developed by Etzkowitz and Leydesdorff), but there remain considerable problems to articulate these three elements.

Sixth, there is a growth in evaluation activities. Governmental funding and internal budget allocation within higher education institutions are increasingly based on performance indicators, goal agreements and contract management.

Seventh, there is also an increased monitoring of the teaching and research activities of professors linked to the introduction of performance-related salary components.

Finally, we observe a shift away from horizontal or inter-institutional diversity towards increased vertical diversity.

6.3   The Breaking of a Taboo

In 2004, the then Federal Minister of Education and Research (a Social Democrat) proposed identifying Germany's top-level institutions. That was surprising and also broke a taboo as the Social Democrats had always opposed the idea of elite institutions which in their mind was linked to the political perspective of the Conservative Parties (Kehm 2006; Pasternack 2008). The official reasons given for this proposal (Bulmahn 2007) were as follows:

– Germany needed to identify and support more cutting-edge research to secure its economic future.
– Ongoing demographic changes required the mobilisation of all available talent.
– The role of higher education institutions was becoming more important in the emerging knowledge society.
– The establishment of European higher education and research was leading towards further internationalisation as well as more global competition.
– Cutting-edge research and innovation was becoming more and more interdisciplinary and required additional support.
– There was an increasing demand for advanced research and highly qualified research staff not only within universities but also in the knowledge-intensive sectors of the economy.

Underlying needs identified included:

– A need to strengthen university research in the face of a growing migration of research into extra-university research institutions
– A need to strengthen the international visibility of German universities
– The government's desire to identify 'lighthouses' with the potential to become global players and to put German universities among the top-ranking institutions in international rankings.

Despite widespread criticism of global rankings (Marginson and Rhoades 2002; Zechlin 2006; Kehm and Stensaker 2009), these seem to have a strong appeal to national policymakers. At that point in time, there were only six German universities in the top 100 of the Shanghai Jiao Tong Ranking, although there were 41 in the top 500.

The German states criticised this proposal on the part of the Social Democrats because they insisted that higher education was their responsibility and the federal government was meddling in their affairs. After difficult negotiations, a compromise was reached in June 2004 to invest 1.9 billion euros into what then became known as the Excellence Initiative over the course of 5 years. The federal government contributed approximately 250 euros annually, and the 16 German states between them contributed 130 million euros annually.

In 2005, the Federal Ministry for Education and Research announced that funding would be made available on a competitive basis for:

(a) Forty graduate schools for doctoral training, each to be funded 1 million euros annually
(b) Thirty clusters of excellence for interdisciplinary strategic alliances of partners to carry out cutting-edge research, each to be funded about 8 million euros annually
(c) Ten institutional development concepts with the potential to become top-level universities, each to be funded about 25 million euros annually

Funding was promised for 5 years after which an evaluation would take place and possibly a review which institutions would be awarded further funds. Universities of applied sciences were not allowed to participate.

6.4   Outcomes of the Selection Process

Because of the lengthy negotiations between the federal government and the states, and the complexity of the application and selection process, it was decided to have two rounds of selection, the first in 2006 and the second in 2007. There was also some discussion as to whether this process should be undertaken every 5 years. In the meantime, a third (and probably final) round has commenced. Universities submitted their proposals in the fall of 2010, and candidates on the shortlist were named in March 2011. Final decisions are expected at the end of 2011.

The selection process is based on a two-step procedure. The first step consists of universities submitting an outline of their proposals in each of the categories. Following a preselection, a shortlist of successful proposals is announced. These universities are then asked to develop their full proposals. This is followed by a more rigid evaluation and the final selection which is a complex procedure including a review by international peers.

In January 2006, the results of the first round of applications were announced. For those universities who had submitted an institutional development concept, aiming for the 'elite' status, this was a day of hope and fear because it was publicly known that not all proposals would be accepted. There was concern that a rejection might negatively impact the reputation of the university. The media had been speculating for weeks about which universities might be among the ten chosen to officially become the first German elite universities.

The following table (Table 6.1) provides an overview of the outcomes of the first round when the winners were announced in October 2006.

The ten universities on the shortlist in the institutional development concepts category were the Technical University Aachen, Free University Berlin, University of Bremen, University of Freiburg, University of Heidelberg, Technical University Karlsruhe, University of Munich, Technical University of Munich, University of Tübingen and University of Würzburg. What is remarkable about this list is the fact that the majority of these institutions are located in the southern states of Germany; there is also no institution from any of the East German states. In the final selection, only three were announced as winners in the third category: the University of Munich, the Technical University of Munich and the Technical University of Karlsruhe. Munich is located in Bavaria and Karlsruhe in Baden-Württemberg. Both states are located in the south-west of Germany.

Table 6.1 Outcomes of round 1, German Excellence Initiative (2006)

	Graduate schools	Excellence clusters	Institutional development concepts
Number to be selected	About 20 (out of 40)	About 15 (out of 30)	About 5 (out of 10)
First proposals received	135	157	27
Selected for shortlist (full proposal)	39	39	10
Winners	18	18	3

Source: Fallon (2007:12), adapted by author

Table 6.2 Outcomes of round 2, German Excellence Initiative (2007)

	Graduate schools	Excellence clusters	Institutional development concepts
Number to be selected	About 22	About 12	About 7
New first proposals received	118	123	20
Round 1 proposals carried forward	21	22	7
Selected for shortlist (full proposal)	44	40	8
Winners	21	20	6

Source: Fallon (2007:13), adapted by author

In the two other categories, the distribution of winning institutions is interesting from a geographical as well as a discipline-related perspective. There were 18 winners in the graduate schools category from eight different states, the majority again located in southern Germany with only one in East Germany. The subject distribution shows a majority in engineering and life sciences (9), fewer in mathematics and physics (4) and four in the social sciences and humanities. One graduate school cannot be specified according to subject groupings. In the graduate schools category, it is notable that many of the proposals had a strong interdisciplinary orientation with the others showing close to an equal distribution across disciplines.

The 18 winners of excellence clusters are distributed over seven states, with the majority again in the south-west and only one in East Germany. Similar to the graduate schools category, the majority of the winners come from engineering, informatics and life sciences, with three clusters in mathematics and physics, and only one at the interface of social sciences and humanities.

The results show a clear bias towards hard and applied natural sciences and technical sciences. There was criticism regarding the selection criteria which seemed to favour these subject groups while being less compatible with the humanities and social sciences (DFG/WR 2006).

The outcomes of the second round were announced in October 2007 and are shown in Table 6.2.

The winners of the second round of selections in the institutional development concepts category were the Technical University of Aachen (North Rhine Westphalia), the Free University of Berlin (Berlin) and the Universities of Freiburg (Baden-Württemberg), Göttingen (Lower Saxony), Heidelberg (Baden-Württemberg) and Konstanz (Baden-Württemberg). Four of these six universities (Aachen, Berlin, Heidelberg, Göttingen) had already applied in the institutional development concepts category in the first round but had ultimately been rejected. The two universities rejected in this category in the second round were Humboldt University in Berlin and Bochum University (North Rhine Westphalia). Although the distribution is more varied than in the first round, there is still an over-representation of institutions located in southern Germany.

Table 6.3 Shortlisted new candidates for the third selection round (2011)

	Graduate schools	Excellence clusters	Institutional development concepts
Number to be selected in final decisions	24–60	37–97	12
New proposals	98	107	22
Shortlisted candidates	25	27	7

Taking both selection rounds together, we have four universities with elite status located in Baden-Württemberg and two in Bavaria, accounting for two thirds of the total located in the south of Germany. The winners in the second round of the graduate schools category are more varied. Berlin is strongly represented (4) but so is Baden-Württemberg (5). Two of the winners are in East German states. There is also a stronger representation of the humanities (3) as well as social sciences (3). With eight graduate schools in the life sciences and biology and four in engineering and computer sciences, these two subject groups are well represented, while the hard sciences (mathematics and physics) are represented by three graduate schools.

The winners of the second round in the excellence clusters category are distributed over ten of the German states, although none is located in East Germany. North Rhine Westphalia (4 clusters), Berlin (4 clusters) and Baden-Württemberg again (4 clusters) are strongly represented. The subject distribution is as follows: seven clusters in the fields of life sciences, biology, engineering and computer sciences, five clusters in the humanities and one cluster in physics (DFG-Pressemitteilung 2007).

Two trends which emerged in the first round of selections and confirmed in the second round were an increasing number of interdisciplinary approaches among the winning graduate schools and excellence clusters, and that there was a large number of cooperative projects, either in the form of a university cooperating with an extra-university research institute (as is the case for the Karlsruhe institutional development concept formalising cooperation with a Fraunhofer Institute which won elite status in the first round) or in the form of two universities cooperating within the framework of a graduate school or excellence cluster. The excellence clusters also frequently included the integration of private sector companies. These features were strongly emphasised in the guidelines and selection criteria.

In 2010, a third round of selections was announced for the same three categories and using much the same procedures. Funding was increased from 1.9 billion euros to 2.7 billion euros for the 5-year period from 2012 to 2017. Universities had to submit their proposals by September 2010. At the beginning of March 2011, the candidates on the shortlist for the third selection round were announced. Despite the fact that the final selection has not yet taken place, it is interesting to compare the results with the first two rounds. Table 6.3 provides an overview of the new applications followed by a geographical analysis. Universities which came out as winners in any of the three categories in the first two rounds did not have to submit proposals for continued support but will enter into the competition with the full proposals of the new candidates in September 2011. The final decisions are expected in the summer of 2012.

Altogether 227 proposals were submitted in all three categories. A large number of proposals came from North Rhine Westphalia (51), Baden-Württemberg (36), Bavaria (31) and Berlin (22). These four states were also the most successful ones on the shortlist. Altogether 59 proposals in all three categories were shortlisted of which 16 came from North Rhine Westphalia (31%), 10 from Baden-Württemberg (28%), seven from Bavaria (23%) and eight from Berlin (36%). The most interesting information, however, is which universities will compete in the final selection round together with the existing nine universities to become a member of the 'elite club'. The seven newly applying universities shortlisted for the third category are the Humboldt University in Berlin (formerly East Berlin), the University of Bremen, the Technical University of Dresden (Saxony, formerly in East Germany), the University of Cologne (North Rhine Westphalia), the University of Mainz (Rhineland Palatinate) and the University of Tübingen (Baden-Württemberg). These seven will have to compete with the existing nine universities already supported in the third category. As support will only be given to a total of 12 universities in this category, four will not make it and it is undecided as yet whether they will be from the group of new applicants or whether some universities from the already existing group will lose the support.

Compared to the first two rounds, it is notable that two universities made it on the shortlist for the third category (institutional development concepts) which are located in former East Germany. Furthermore, the shortlisted candidates in all three categories are no longer so clearly concentrated in the south of Germany. Looking at the disciplinary fields of the graduate school and excellence cluster proposals which have been selected for the shortlist, we can observe an increasing number of interdisciplinary graduate schools and excellence clusters. Among the 25 shortlisted graduate schools, there are five in engineering and information technology, 11 in social sciences and humanities, five in life sciences and four in physics and mathematics. Among the 27 shortlisted clusters of excellence, there are five in engineering and information technology, six in social sciences and humanities, ten in life sciences, three in material sciences and three in physics. These results also demonstrate a degree of change insofar as the support for the humanities and social sciences has increased, an issue which was strongly criticised after the decisions of the first two rounds.

6.5   Restructuring the German Higher Education Landscape

6.5.1   The Systems Perspective

What have been the effects of this initiative on German higher education to date? At this point, one can only point to trends rather than identifiable effects because the initiative is so recent (Kehm 2006; Kehm and Pasternack 2009; Fallon 2007; Hinderer 2007; Bloch et al. 2008). However, seven trends can be identified.

First, the Excellence Initiative is not officially regarded as a ranking of German universities but indicates a shift towards a more vertical differentiation of the system as a whole.

Second, while the initiative has triggered more competition among German universities, it is focused on research excellence only. Thus, some of the results are not very surprising. There were more universities among the winners in all three categories located in richer states which have been better able to financially support their universities.

Third, financial incentives have recently been introduced to reward teaching excellence. However, these are often just a onetime incentive and only a fraction of what is awarded in the Excellence Initiative. Consequently, universities continue to establish their credibility through research, while the importance of teaching is downgraded.

Fourth, the fact that no decision was made about the overall structure of the German higher education system was a missed opportunity.

Fifth, the question needs to be asked whether 'steep stratification' (or rankings) is the only solution or whether there are other more appropriate systems. Diversification in mass higher education systems is necessary, but this can also be achieved through intra-institutional differentiation or through functional (horizontal) diversification into different institutional types (Teichler 2009a).

Sixth, another issue to consider is whether there is more than one type of excellence. In both the Excellence Initiative and in university rankings, it is unclear what constitutes the unit of excellence. Is it the individual researcher or a research group; is it the department or faculty, a network of partners or the institution as whole? It is commonly accepted that no university is 'excellent' across the board (Teichler 2007).

Finally, what are the effects of the Excellence Initiative on German higher education as a whole? What about those universities which lost out in the competition, who did not apply because they assumed their chances to be selected were too low, or who did apply but were not selected? It is important to find a credible role for them within the national higher education system and not penalise them by reducing their funding. They too have a role to play. An example of such a role might be to educate the pool of talent from which top-level institutions will recruit future students, doctoral candidates or young researchers.

As Teichler (2009a) has pointed out, there are a number of historical phases in German and European debates on the role of diversification and differentiation of higher education systems. In the higher education expansion of the 1960s and 1970s, diversification was achieved through creating different institutional types (e.g. polytechnics, colleges) and internal (i.e. intra-institutional) differentiation through programme diversity. In recent years, this horizontal differentiation has gradually been replaced by vertical differentiation due to increased international competition and supported by the growing popularity of global and national rankings, particularly among institutional leaders and policymakers. It has become an imperative to have 'elite institutions' or 'world-class universities' in one's own national system. This has led to the view that national higher education systems should be more vertically stratified, that success at the top of the system is important and that the 'top' compares itself with other institutions globally rather than just nationally (Teichler 2009a). This perspective played a major role in the decision to commence the Excellence Initiative in German higher education.

What of the universities and other higher education institutions not in the top group? The first two selection rounds of the Excellence Initiative triggered a sense of being a 'loser', in particular among universities which participated in the competition but lost. The other German universities which did not participate also perceive themselves 'the second league' but seek to counter this by emphasising their difference in function and mission. If in the face of mass and even universal higher education a national system caters exclusively to the 'top league' of institutions, it is likely to lead to imitation of the best to the detriment of the national higher education system as a whole. In response to this possibility, Marginson and Rhoades (2002) argued for a closer relationship between global, national and regional higher education activities in the face of globalisation, which they describe as a 'glonacal' process.

Rarely discussed is the question raised by Teichler (2007) as to how the emergence of a top stratum of elite institutions will influence the rest of the system. We have mentioned the danger of mimetic isomorphism (i.e. imitation). It is doubtful whether the decision to establish the Excellence Initiative was based on a clear understanding of the need for a new structure of the system as a whole. Decision-makers wanted 'Harvards' in Germany as a matter of prestige without being able or willing to provide funding at the required level (Zechlin 2006; Hinderer 2007). The issue of a reconfiguration of the system never came up in the public debates.

Salmi (2011) warned of the dangers in the race to develop world-class universities. German universities not only lacked the three factors necessary to become a world-class university, that is, a concentration of talent, abundant resources and favourable governance, but in terms of policy, it is much more important to support the development of a world-class university system. It is easier for the German higher education system to attain this goal than to develop up to 12 world-class universities as envisioned by the Excellence Initiative.

Overall, the question whether steep stratification will dominate the restructuring of future national higher education systems or whether other forms of differentiation will emerge is unclear. Within Europe, certainly the Bologna reform process will intervene into the trends towards steep stratification because it promotes cooperation and mutual recognition of degrees and credits as equally valid. In addition, those higher education institutions ranked in the middle or lower strata of a vertically stratified system will have to reorient their functions and missions as well as improve the marketing of those elements where they excel.

6.5.2   The Institutional Perspective

At the urging of the Berlin-Brandenburg Academy of Sciences, an interdisciplinary working group was established late 2008 to provide an independent assessment of the positive and negative effects of the Excellence Initiative. Initial findings and suggestions for the next round of competition were published in 2010 (Leibfried 2010).

There is general agreement about the positive effects of the initiative – for example, institutional profiles and structures, the growth in interdisciplinary cooperation and opportunities for young researchers, especially in the post-doc stage (Zürn 2010). However, the interdisciplinary working group also identified four problem areas (Interdisziplinäre Arbeitsgruppe Exzellenzinitiative 2010): institutional governance, human resource development, the impact of priority setting and equal opportunities for disciplines.

(a) *Tensions in institutional governance*
    Recent thinking about institutional governance has emphasised the need to strengthen leadership and management to enable universities to develop an organisational identity. However, the graduate schools and the excellence clusters so generously funded by the initiative are becoming independent players with their own agendas. The clusters and schools are increasingly managed in a professional manner, and this allows them to influence institutional decision-making processes by the deans, the leadership and the boards. Gaethgens (2010) talks about 'islands of competence' and 'parallel entities of authority' for which the usual rules of procedure do not apply, leading to an internal fragmentation of the institution.

(b) *Human resource development*
    The clusters and the graduate schools were able to provide a number of positions for junior researchers and post-docs, but most post-doc positions were filled without having a tenure track because of the 5-year funding time limit. Additionally, most clusters carry out their research in a highly specialised field which may not be offered at other universities. Planning for exit options after the 5-year funding period has been neglected. Where tenured professorships have been filled in the framework of clusters, these must be financed by the university after the end of the funding period through the Excellence Initiative, leading to imbalances in departmental teaching and research portfolios, especially where the departments were not involved in the selection process.

(c) *Impacts of institutional priority setting*
    In universities applying to the Excellence Initiative, careful thought was given to which research groups should be supported in the application on the basis that if successful the clusters and graduate schools were going to be important components of the institutional profile. However, profile building is not about priority setting only. In Germany, universities typically have a rather

broad portfolio of disciplines. The internal structure is based on teaching and the provision of degree programmes. Consequently, those departments which were unsuccessful felt threatened, especially because considerable institutional overhead was provided in support of promising applications and then on the establishment of clusters and graduate schools. The Excellence Initiative can thus unintentionally threaten a balanced portfolio of subjects in favour of priority areas winning the extra support and funding.

(d) *Equal opportunities for disciplines*
The Excellence Initiative has been criticised for preferring certain disciplines or preferring particular research cultures which are not always found in all disciplines. For example, the humanities and social sciences did not win much support in the first round of decisions. By contrast, life sciences, natural sciences and engineering had a much higher success rate. Zürn (2010) discusses the different assessment and reviewer cultures in different disciplines. In those disciplines in which reputation is based on one or two criteria such as number of publications, the reviewing culture tends to make simple yes/no decisions based on a number. In those disciplines with a multidimensional culture of reviewing and assessment, for example, considering publications in the best international journals, societal and theoretical relevance, innovation potential and number of published monographs, it is rare that reviewers come to the same conclusion. This reduces the chances of a successful application.

To date, no published analysis has focused on the impacts of the Excellence Initiative from the perspective of the individual academic. Such research should include the views of winners, losers and nonparticipants.

6.5.3 Excellence in the Making and Its Side Effects

Besides the impact of the Excellence Initiative on the national system and the universities, the selection process has been criticised.

Some have cast doubt on the legitimacy of the procedure itself and whether it is assessing the quality and style of the application, or institutional excellence? In other words, have winners been selected on the basis of their performance promises or past achievements? Only those universities selected for the overall institutional excellence shortlist (i.e. the third category) were actually visited by the reviewers. The divide between 'excellence achieved' and 'excellence in the making' is all the more difficult to determine when it comes to drawing the line between which institution is awarded the final winning place in any of the categories and the very next institution, or even the one equal to it but not selected (Pasternack 2008; Zürn 2007).

A second point of criticism is the inconsistency between the first two categories (graduate schools and excellence clusters) and the third (institutional development concepts). While the first two categories are clearly based on an evaluation of research output and evidence-based strategies designed to increase this output, the third category actually awards institutional management concepts. These may have merited their own Excellence Initiative – like teaching excellence as well – but the relationship between excellent management strategies and excellence in research is not a given. Instead, the Excellence Initiative made eligibility for awards in the third category dependent on winning at least one graduate school and one cluster of excellence, thus excluding universities that could have provided evidence of overall management excellence but did not score in the other two categories. One might argue that it is the combination of excellent research and excellent management which will, with considerable additional funding, enable a university to achieve world-class status. The criticism highlights the fact that the first two award categories (graduate schools and excellence clusters) are of a different nature from the third (institutional development concepts). In addition, the bigger the institution, the more heterogeneous it is likely to be. So the question remains: are the awards in the third category, which are supposed to identify potentially elite institutions, in fact the result of a compromise because there was no trust in the forms of excellence evaluated in the other two categories (Teichler 2009a)?

A third issue concerns the unintended side effects of the Excellence Initiative on the system as a whole. It is not yet possible to determine how the elite institutions will influence the rest and vice versa. It is also unclear whether the competition for excellence status will lead to increased resource concentration among institutions in terms of funding and best talent (Teichler 2007).

Fourth, there is concern about the status and reputation of those universities which were not successful in the competition or did not participate in it. The winners not only gained additional resources, but they have become more attractive partners for top-level institutions abroad and are now recruiting outstanding academics from other universities. On the other hand, those universities which did not win extra funding in the Excellence Initiative have lost out twice which makes their effective participation in the next round all the more difficult. There may be a trend towards a new stratification of the German higher education system, but it also raises the issue as to whether the system will develop more heterogeneity or more homogeneity as all institutions try to achieve the same officially valued goals (Teichler 2007).

Fifth, the winners have complained about a loss of time for research, thanks to the additional time-consuming administration (e.g. establishing the infrastructure, recruiting staff). There has been a trend towards fragmentation in some universities. Graduate school and excellence clusters have started to develop independently in some cases because they are typically outside the departmental structure. This leads to envy from the departments where every day university life and work tends to be less prestigious.

6.5.4 Critical Discussion and Conclusions

In summary, it can be said that the Excellence Initiative was based on a political prognosis of the global competitiveness of the German higher education, research and innovation system which had identified a number of problems. While the solution for the problems in teaching and learning is sought in the implementation of the Bologna reforms, the solution for the problems in research was sought in a steeper stratification of the system by identifying top research universities and providing them with considerable extra funding. The process established in achieving this goal was based on academic selection based on peer review to provide legitimacy. Due to time constraints and some inconsistencies in the selection procedures, in particular when the first and the second rounds of selections are compared with each other, some criticism has been voiced that the procedures lacked sufficient legitimacy (Zürn 2007). To improve the situation, a number of suggestions have been made:

– Repeat the competition for excellence in research every 5 or 6 years.
– Improve the selection procedures.
– Clarify the relationship of the selection criteria to each other.
– Focus on an assessment of the ability to perform.

As Pasternack (2008) recently pointed out in an analysis of the Excellence Initiative as a political programme, the initiative has changed its focus. Formally, it was established as a primarily government-funded higher education support programme. Seen from a content perspective, it turned out to be an open acknowl-edgement of existing differences among universities within the German higher education system and forced the system as a whole to focus more on research. With regard to terminology, it introduced a particular concept of excellence into the public discourse and established the term as code language for 'the highest quality', without clearly defining which functions are central to the definition of excellence. In terms of political and public discourse, tacit knowledge about differences among higher education institutions became visible, and opportunities were offered to the winners to gain more attention and reputation. In the context of higher education policy, it meant the termination of the long-standing fiction of a qualitatively homogeneous higher education system supported by de facto legal homogeneity.

But does that mean that the Excellence Initiative is just a new form of competitive funding or does it imply a paradigmatic shift for German higher education? According to Pasternack, it is possible to conceptualise the initiative in three different ways: (a) as a catalytic funding programme, that is, to achieve critical mass for later unassisted development, (b) as a compact funding programme, that is, long-term additional funding for the winners under conditions of suspended competition for them, or (c) as permanent competition for funding, that is, a succession of calls for tenders in the most important category, the institutional development concepts, possibly with a slightly changing focuses. In the current stage of development, espe-cially when we also look at developments in other European countries, Pasternack concludes that the Excellence Initiative cannot yet be cast as a paradigmatic shift but must be regarded rather as a component of an increasingly competitive culture in the field of higher education. The initiative therefore has a potential catalytic function for the German higher education system. But much will depend on further decisions to continue the competition periodically or not.

What will be its effects on the overall German system of research funding? Will it not only entail decisions about the concept and configuration of the system as a whole but also about its overall forms of funding, and the relationship between organisation and innovation within universities? It is almost certain that the initiative will be an important factor in the establishment of new hierarchies at the national level, within the individual states, within institutions among the subjects and departments or faculties and finally within departments or faculties (e.g. between those being involved in a graduate school or excellence cluster with funding from the initiative and those not funded). Consequently, it is worthwhile to analyse the effects of the Excellence Initiative on the overall system's configuration and to see how the system as a whole actually performs (Teichler 2007).

But there are further conclusions which can already be drawn. First, there is a general trend to integrate research funding within the framework of programmes and projects. The Excellence Initiative is part of this development. In this respect, Germany is a latecomer again as this form of competitive research funding was introduced some years ago in a number of other European countries. Secondly, there is a trend towards increased competition for funding. Many academics currently have to engage in some form of competitive bidding for even minimal resources. This requirement pertains not only to third-party research funding but also to a variety of funding possibilities within their institutions, for example, tutors and research assistants, seed money, contracts for doctoral students and funding for participation in conferences. A growing amount of time is spent on writing applications, submitting reports and the possibility of exposure to further evaluation requirements. In addition, institutional management also expects that academics be involved more than ever before in such competitions, which diminishes the time actually spent on research.

Finally, looking at the use of the term 'excellence' in public and political discourse, we note the inflationary character it has acquired. It is also infiltrating the language of calls for proposals, tenders and applications. Everything has to be 'excellent' in order to justify funding at all. This brings to the fore a tension between performance and status in which it becomes difficult to distinguish between reputation on the one hand and performance on the other. The social construct of excellence based on reputation and the assessment of objective performance become intertwined and raise questions about the validity of peer review. If we cast the Excellence Initiative as a process of differentiation and distribution of reputation, 'objective' measuring and assessment are hardly possible any longer, at least not within the classical forms of peer review led by scholarly and scientific criteria (Hornbostel 2008). Time will tell whether in the future a legitimate balance between attributed status and reputation and objective performance and achievement can be found.

References

Bloch, R., Keller, A., Lottmann, A., & Würmann, C. (2008). *Making Excellence. Grundlagen Praxis und Konsequenzen der Exzellenzinitiative*. Bielefeld: Bertelsmann.

Bulmahn, E. (2007). *Die Exzellenzinitiative: Genese einer bildungspolitischen Idee*. Paper presented at the conference making excellence. Grundlagen, Praxis und Konsequenzen der Exzellenzinitiative, 23–24 November, Institute of Higher Education Research Halle-Wittenberg. Wittenberg: HoF.

DFG/WR. (2006). *Gemeinsame Pressemitteilung von DFG und WR Erste Runde in der Exzellenzinitiative entschieden*. http://idw-online/pages/de/news179792. Accessed 3 Dec 2007.

DFG-Pressemitteilung. (2007). *Zweite Runde in der Exzellenzinitiative entschieden*. http://www.dfg.de/aktuelles_presse/pressemitteilungen2007/presse_2007_65.html. Accessed 3 Dec 2007.

Fallon, D. (2007, March 26–27). *Germany and the United States, then and now: Seeking eminence in the research university*. Paper presented at a symposium organised by the Centre for Studies in Higher Education, University of California at Berkeley.

Gaethgens, P. (2010). Die Dritte Säule der Exzellenzinitiative – eine offene Agenda? In S. Leibfried (Ed.), *Die Exzellenzinitiative. Zwischenbilanz und Perspektiven* (pp. 269–279). Frankfurt a. M./New York: Campus.

Hinderer, W. (2007). *Die deutsche Exzellenzinitiative und die amerikanische Eliteuniversität*. Berlin: Liberal Verlag.

Hornbostel, S. (2008). Evaluation der Exzellenzinitiative. Gibt es objektive Kriterien für Exzellenz? In R. Bloch, A. Keller, A. Lottmann, & C. Würmann (Eds.), *Making Excellence. Grundlagen Praxis und Konsequenzen der Exzellenzinitiative* (pp. 49–63). Bielefeld: Bertelsmann.

Interdisziplinäre Arbeitsgruppe Exzellenzinitiative. (2010). Bedingungen und Folgen der Exzellenzinitiative. In S. Leibfried (Ed.), *Die Exzellenzinitiative. Zwischenbilanz und Perspektiven* (pp. 35–50). Frankfurt a. M./New York: Campus.

Kehm, B. M. (2006). The German "initiative for excellence" and rankings. *International Higher Education, 44*, 20–22.

Kehm, B. M., & Pasternack, P. (2009). The German "excellence initiative" and its role in restructuring the national higher education landscape. In D. Palfreyman & T. Tapper (Eds.), *Structuring mass higher education. The role of elite institutions* (pp. 113–127). New York/London: Routledge.

Kehm, B. M., & Stensaker, B. (2009). *University rankings, diversity, and the new landscape of higher education*. Rotterdam/Taipei: Sense.

Leibfried, S. (2010). *Die Exzellenzinitiative. Zwischenbilanz und Perspektiven*. Frankfurt a. M./New York: Campus.

Marginson, S., & Rhoades, G. (2002). Beyond national states, markets and systems of higher education: A glonacal agency heuristic. *Higher Education, 43*(3), 281–309.

Neave, G. (1996). Homogenization, integration, and convergence: The Cheshire cats of higher education analysis. In V. L. Meek et al. (Eds.), *The mockers and the mocked: Comparative perspectives on differentiation, convergence, and diversity in higher education* (pp. 26–41). Oxford: Pergamon.

Pasternack, P. (2008). Die Exzellenzinitiative als politisches Programm. Fortsetzung der normalen Forschungsförderung oder Paradigmenwechsel. *die hochschule, 17*(1).

Salmi, J. (2011). *Establishing world-class universities*. Keynote speech presented at the International Higher Education Congress: New trends and Issues on 27 May 2011 in Istanbul, Turkey.

Teichler, U. (2007, December). *Exzellenz und Differenzierung: Auf der Suche nach einer neuen Systemlogik*. Paper presented at the conference "Exzellente Wissenschaft im 21. Jahrhundert oder Harvard weltweit in fünf Jahren?", Berlin, Germany.

Teichler, U. (2009a). Between over-diversification and over-homogenization: Five decades of search for a creative fabric of higher education. In B. M. Kehm & B. Stensaker (Eds.), *University rankings, diversity, and the new landscape of higher education* (pp. 155–181). Rotterdam/Taipei: Sense.

Teichler, U. (2009b, April 22). *Innovation in higher education in Germany and the academic profession in comparative perspective*. Presentation at the innovation forum of the German Federal Ministry of Education and Research and the Korean Ministry of Education, Science and Technology, Berlin. Unpublished manuscript.

Zechlin, L. (2006). Im Zeitalter des Wettbewerbs angekommen. *Forschung & Lehre, 8*, 446–448.

Zürn, M. (2007, November 23–24). *Legitimität, Transparenz, Partizipation. Zur Praxis des Begutachtens*. Paper presented at the conference making excellence. Grundlagen, Praxis und Konsequenzen der 'Exzellenzinitiative', Institute of Higher Education Research Halle-Wittenberg. Wittenberg: HoF.

Zürn, M. (2010). Ein Rückblick auf die erste Exzellenzinitiative – Es geht noch besser! In S. Leibfried (Ed.), *Die Exzellenzinitiative. Zwischenbilanz und Perspektiven* (pp. 219–229). Frankfurt a. M./New York: Campus.

Chapter 7
Reconciling Republican 'Egalité' and Global Excellence Values in French Higher Education

Leon Cremonini, Paul Benneworth, Hugh Dauncey, and Don F. Westerheijden

7.1 Introduction

The focus of this volume is on policies to promote world-class higher education and world-class universities. The idea of world-class universities has attracted a great deal of attention from policymakers in government and in the higher education sector (Liu 2006, 2007; DIISR 2009). Many universities have become caught up in the race for world-class status and in particular in the global university rankings published annually (Vught and Westerheijden 2010), and national governments often seek to make their higher education institutions more visible on the world stage through world-class university programmes (WCUPs). But what has been missing to date – with the exception of this volume – is more critical academic interest, seeking to explore the outcomes behind this increasing trend.

Embedded within this movement is the belief that world-class universities are a vital element of a competitive higher education system and that supporting an élite group of universities creates a wider set of societal benefits and returns (Wildavsky 2010). At the same time, there is a growing critique of the notion of world-class universities for being overly focused on a limited range of variables and emulating a particular kind of university – the Anglo-American research-intensive university (the so-called Stepford University as identified by Head 2011) – not necessarily beneficial in every situation. These critiques argue that WCUPs are a drain on,

L. Cremonini (✉) • P. Benneworth • D.F. Westerheijden
Center for Higher Education Policy Studies, University of Twente, Twente, The Netherlands
e-mail: leoncremonini@yahoo.co.uk; p.benneworth@utwente.nl; d.f.westerheijden@utwente.nl

H. Dauncey
Department of French Studies, Newcastle University, Newcastle upon Tyne, UK
e-mail: hugh.dauncey@newcastle.ac.uk

J.C. Shin and B.M. Kehm (eds.), *Institutionalization of World-Class University in Global Competition*, The Changing Academy – The Changing Academic Profession in International Comparative Perspective 6, DOI 10.1007/978-94-007-4975-7_7,
© Springer Science+Business Media Dordrecht 2013

rather than a benefit to, national higher education systems and give a limited number of élite institutions the capacity to withdraw from national arenas into exclusively serving these narrow global positions (Altbach and Balán 2007).

In this chapter, we contribute to a critical academic debate about the meaning and practice of the idea of a 'world-class university'. We start by offering a note of caution to the two normative positions outlined above and arguing that what is necessary is an objective framework by which the public benefits of WCUPs can be understood, and against which the claims by interested parties may be tested. We argue that the benefits of WCUPs are an *emergent* property, which is to say that under certain circumstances they might drive up standards whilst in others they might contribute to a fragmentation of national systems. It is therefore necessary to identify the potential contributions which WCUPs might make to national systems and map the changes resultant from particular policy interventions to better understand how WCUPs redirect national higher education systems.

To test our framework, we explore an interesting example, the case of France, where one would expect the benefits to be clearest, and the problems to be minimised. The French higher education system is strongly rooted in what might be considered Republican values of equality. But at the same time, France has had since pre-Revolutionary times an implicit segmentation in its higher education; the *Grandes Écoles* were created as higher vocational colleges but evolved into finishing schools for the Republican technocratic élite. France has sought to use the idea of a WCUP as part of a decade-long reform programme to address the stagnation in its university sector.

In this chapter, we consider whether these reforms have shown signs of improving the situation in France. We firstly set out our framework for understanding the public benefits potentially offered by universities and set out the criteria by which the public benefit of a WCUP can be tested. We then present the French case study, which we split into three elements, a first historical element looking at the divisions in the system to which reforms were a proposed solution, secondly setting out the reforms themselves, and then examining the extent to which these reforms created public value in the university system. On this basis, we outline some preliminary findings about the characteristics upon which the public value of WCUPs might depend and suggest future research directions.

7.2   Higher Education Systems and the Public Value of a WCUP

In this chapter, we seek to contribute to an increasingly important strand of debate seeking to refocus higher education's research attention onto the importance of understanding how higher education institutions (HEIs) function within national and international systems. At a recent public lecture, the Executive Director of the OECD's Centre for Education Research and Innovation (CERI),

Dirk van Damme (2011), called for higher education research to move beyond its narrow focus on new public management towards a concern with managing higher level systems. His argument was that attempts to assume that competition between universities would produce socially optimal outcomes had reached a practical limit and that a more pressing problem was the need for increased collaboration between universities to collective societal ends than encouraging efficiency in quasi-markets.

In a recent book, Professor Ellen Hazelkorn (2011) has also pointed to the inadvertent and unintended consequences of an obsession with league tables for higher education performance. She argues that there are three problems with the idea of world-class universities: they promote a neo-liberal model based on concentrating resources in a few good universities, a misapprehension that more world-class universities raise system performance, and teaching is arguably universities' most important social contribution whilst strangely absent from ranking criteria. It is the second of these points that we believe is most important in meeting Van Damme's challenge: it remains to be empirically proven that creating world-class universities improves a national HE system. Whilst intuitive – more, better universities can only be a good thing for a country – the case of France suggests the opposite. A few élite institutions may dominate public discourse and funding discussions, leading to a neglect of the 'ordinary' universities, which in France became problematic.

7.2.1 The Public Value of a Higher Education System: A Conceptual Framework

In this chapter, we want to explore how a policy intervention – World-Class University Programmes – can create overall public benefits. We situate this in a distinction which economists have made about education as a product dating back to Adam Smith and The Wealth of Nations. The argument is that higher education deserves a public subsidy because it creates public benefits beyond the benefits which accrue to individual recipients. Although higher education does create private benefits, it is the public benefits that justify subsidy (see also Bergan et al. 2009). Universities provide a skilled workforce, create knowledge for businesses and public and voluntary organisations, and have become significant economic sectors in terms of their purchasing power and their salary impacts. Table 7.1 below, taken from Institute for Higher Education Policy (IHEP) (2005), provides a snapshot of higher education's most important private and public benefits.

Building on Van Damme's argument, we think it is important to consider these benefits – public and private, and economic and social – within the system of higher education and understand how the WCUP creates different outcomes by shifting the system. At its most simple level, a higher education system is a process which converts inputs (funding from inter alia governments) through these three processes (education, research, and knowledge exchange) into outputs, which are in part public.

Table 7.1 The array of higher education benefits

	Public	Private
Economic	Increased tax revenues	Higher salaries and benefits
	Greater productivity	Employment
	Increased consumption	Higher saving levels
	Increased workforce flexibility	Improved working conditions
	Decreased reliance on government financial support	Personal/professional mobility
	More research and innovation	*Status/reputation resulting from research outputs*
		Financial benefits resulting from research outputs
Social	Reduced crime rates	Improved health/ life expectancy
	Increased charitable giving/community service	Improved quality of life of offspring
	Increased quality of civic life	Better consumer decision making
	Social cohesion/appreciation of diversity	Increased personal status
	Improved ability to adapt to and use technology	More hobbies leisure activities

Source: IHEP 2005, p. 4 (*benefits in italics added by authors)

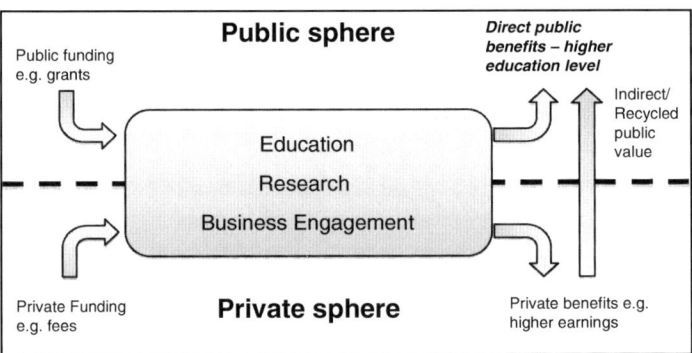

Fig. 7.1 A systems model of investment in the higher education sector

In the absence of public funding, the equilibrium consumption of higher education would be much lower than socially optimal, so through public funding of higher education, higher public returns are produced. Thus, the idea behind any public subsidy for a higher education system is to maximise the public benefits, both directly and indirectly (i.e. public benefits which accrue from recycled private benefits such as increased salaries producing additional taxation) (Fig. 7.1).

There is no necessarily direct value added in a WCUP which simply involves additional expenditure. It is uncontroversial to argue if you spend more money on an activity, you can increase the volume of outcomes. The basic argument underpinning WCUPs is an efficiency one, namely, that resources spent on the sector are better

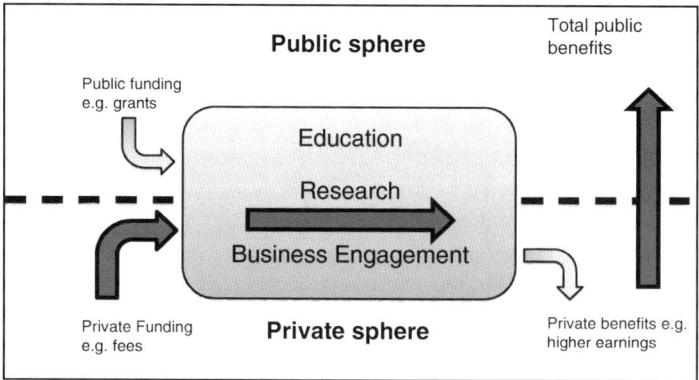

Fig. 7.2 A WCU programme increasing higher education system efficiency

spent on a few world-class universities than across the system. From a system analysis perspective, this involves a normative claim – that public funding means that the same amount of money spent on WCUPs produces a greater public benefit. In Fig. 7.2, we identify how a WCUP might bring system benefits.

A WCUP might improve the functioning of the system as a whole in four ways. Firstly, it might attract more private funding into the system. Secondly, it might lead to individual processes within the system such as the education, the research, and the business engagement, functioning more effectively. Thirdly, these more effective processes might produce greater direct societal benefits. Fourthly, greater private benefits might be recycled into greater public benefits. At this point, we make two caveats. Firstly, this is a conceptual model, and whilst it might make sense to conceptually distinguish greater private inputs from more efficient research, in practice, the four elements will be unrelated. Secondly, this refers to the overall output from the system rather than the performance of individual institutions.

7.2.2   The Systems Effects of a World-Class University Programme

Higher education's public benefits stimulate thinking about whether WCUPs improve public value. Today, universities' research takes place within global knowledge systems in which they are just one node. They may attract foreign companies to co-locate on campus via research and development, bringing external resources into the nation, which create spillover benefits for the economy, but which also create infrastructures and attract talent that flow into other higher education institutions. Globalisation and internationalisation provide new opportunities to reform national higher education systems and acquire more highly educated citizens and more public benefits:

> Every nation wants strong research universities. Every research university wants to lift its reputation. All are focused on policies to lift capacity and performance. (Marginson and Van der Wende 2007, p. 34)

World-class university policies contribute to ensuring that higher education delivers the anticipated public benefits and national socioeconomic growth. Sadlak and Cai (2009) argue:

> Universities, particularly those considered as 'world-class', hold a special place in the chain of innovation. They are [. . .] viewed as the key to realizing significant economic returns.

Such policies are said to:

- Raise investments in research, both public and private, and national and international, leading to more and better public benefits (both social and economic)
- Increase research outputs, measured, for example, by bibliometrics and citation studies and further boosted by cross national research flows (another global externality; see Marginson and van der Wende 2007)
- Create a better educated workforce, in large part by attracting bright students and staff within and beyond national borders. World-class universities are assumed to effectively advance the overall educational attainment of a country's labour force (IHEP 2005).
- Promote knowledge transfer, that is, the processes by which knowledge, expertise, and skills transfer between the research base and its user communities to contribute to economic competitiveness, effectiveness of public services and policy, and quality of life (DIUS 2003; DELNI 2010)

Taking our systems perspective outlined above, we characterise these benefits of WCUPs for university systems into five classes:

1. *Increased exogenous resources*: The attraction of additional staff, students, and research funding from outside the country/higher education system which spill over to other higher education institutions.
2. *Increased private endogenous resources*: Greater private resources that would have either not been spent in the country's universities or gone to other universities go into the sector, which spill over to other higher education institutions.
3. *Systemic improvements*: The presence of a world-class university improves the functioning of the higher education system and produces more efficient use of public resources.
4. *New products*: By creating new globally competitive higher education products (such as graduate school trajectories), the sector is more competitive in export terms, attracting more students as a whole.
5. *Reputational benefits*: All national universities benefit from a higher external awareness/reputation from the presence of one or more world-class institutions in the system.

7.2.3 The Tensions of World-Class University Programmes: From Individual to Systems Benefits

In the above characterisation, there is an implicit assumption that the benefits must automatically be positive (or zero). This is tied to the normative belief that WCUPs are intuitively a sensible approach with the capacity to greatly improve national higher education systems. We argue that this benefit remains to be empirically proven. The imminence and urgency associated with the rise of league tables have precipitated premature reactions from policymakers primarily concerned with reputational benefit. Nevertheless, our contention is not that WCUPs are a bad idea but that the empirical evidence underpinning claims they are always beneficial is thin.

Based on the 'systems benefits' schematic, WCUP advocates must demonstrate WCUP's aggregate public benefit if they are to become a tool used by public investment. There have been cases of private funding seeking to create world-class institutions, such as the private endowment which came with the merger to create Finland's Aalto University (Aalto University Foundation 2008). But because these privately funded mergers do not involve public subsidies, the evidence that they function to the overall benefit of the system is less compelling.

Playing devil's advocate, one could envisage situations for each of the five variables outlined above where the 'world-class' institutions get stronger but the system as a whole is weakened. As well as creating linkages, world-class university policies could create barriers between the 'haves' and the 'have-nots'. Rather than acting as an entrepôt to the 'world' for the rest of the universities, they may act as a kind of enclave for global actors exploiting the best of the country's resources, whilst restricting the benefits that can be created. There might also be a beggar-thy-neighbour effect, where the benefits to one national system come at the expense of another. This would mean that WCUPs were effectively a state aid distorting the trade of educational services (an issue that lies beyond the scope of this chapter).

A hypothetical example might be a research department at a world-class university which signs an exclusive confidentiality agreement with a leading firm located in its science park which in turn has a no-compete clause for its employees. Millions of Euros may be spent on the research without any public benefit. In such a case, the public resources invested in making that department world-class and attracting the private investment are spent on benefits which are exclusively private.

Clearly the public benefit of WCUPs is an emergent question that remains to be empirically delivered rather than proven conceptually. In this chapter, we therefore seek to establish the conditions under which a WCUP might produce the greatest public benefit. Do WCUPs offer public value for money at a time of fiscal austerity? We operationalise that concern into our research question of 'can world-class university programmes produce clear public benefits to national higher systems?'

To address that question, we look how one WCUP attempted to solve a systemic problem in French higher education, namely, the segmentation between the élite Grandes Écoles and the mass university system, in a country whose universities have performed sluggishly in the league tables (Ritzen 2010). This segmentation was specifically blamed by Valérie Pécresse, the French Minister for Higher Education, for this poor performance. Thus, a decade of reforms culminating in *Opération Campus* appears to use a WCUP to address an identified system problem. France therefore offers an interesting case to explore this issue of WCUPs.

The case study also offers an interesting set of tensions and contradictions. There is a strong culture of Republican égalité – or equality – in French public life, and although the elitism of the *Grandes Écoles* is accepted, there is a sense that the universities are mass, rather than élite, institutions. Encouraging competitive improvement runs directly counter to these Republican values which are a critical and central guiding feature of French education. Even those activities which have been successful, such as attempts by one of these *Grandes Écoles* (Sciences Po) to improve its recruitment from less wealthy areas, have been criticised for running counter to French Republican values (Grove 2011).

We present this case study and analysis at three levels. We firstly present an overview of the idea of Republican values in French education. We then consider the last decade of reforms which have set the context for the French WCUP which we define as *Opération Campus*. We then present the French WCUP and in particular the new kind of global managerialist discourse it has introduced into French higher education. This provides the basis for the identification and analysis of the public value embodied in the WCUP as outlined in our conclusions.

7.2.4   *Republican Values as the Guiding Principles of French Higher Education*

The French higher education system is classically described as a 'dual' system, in which the publicly funded universities and the state- or privately managed *Grandes Écoles* coexist. Within this system of two competing but complementary sectors of education and training after the *Baccalauréat*, young French citizens are equipped with the knowledge and skills necessary to make them effective contributors to French society and the French economy.

Since its considerable expansion in recent decades, the university sector, which is unselective, has been viewed as catering for the mass of French students, whereas the highly selective *Grandes Écoles* sector, despite the 'massification' of the universities, has continued to cater for an élite minority. In order to discuss the university and *Grandes Écoles* components of the French higher education, we provide an overview of the system and how it is structured (Toulemonde et al. 2006; Chapoulie et al. 2010).

7.3 The French Higher Education System

7.3.1 An Overview

The public university sector comprises a large number of *Universités* (otherwise described as *'facultés'*), *Instituts universitaires de technologie* (IUT), and other institutions (Kaiser 2007). There are currently some 80 universities and 120 IUTs, organised and named 'geographically' reflecting the strong linkages between the traditional universities and their cities and regions as well as the tendency for French students to attend their local university.

Following the Faure reform of the organisation of the university sector implemented in late 1968 in reaction to the student and social protests of May-June 1968, 'traditional' universities were separated into their constituent elements (science, law and social sciences, arts and humanities, medicine). Bordeaux University, originally founded in 1441, was split in 1970 into the universities of Bordeaux I (science), Bordeaux II (law, social sciences), and Bordeaux III (arts and humanities). An earlier reform of the university sector in the 1960s – the Fouchet reform – had added one or more IUTs to the majority of the traditional universities from 1966. Using the example of Bordeaux again, the reform resulted in IUT Bordeaux I (1966) and IUT Bordeaux III (1966).

Many universities have adopted names reflecting their disciplinary specialisations and their regionalism. Thus, although Bordeaux I retains its descriptive title 'Sciences et technologie', the arts and humanities university is Bordeaux III – Université Michel de Montaigne, and law and social sciences university Grenoble II is the Université Pierre Mendès-France. Within each university, still often referred to as 'facultés', different groupings of individual or related subjects/disciplines, known as *Unités de formation et de recherche*, provide the teaching and research supervision for undergraduate and postgraduate students.

The *Baccalauréat* (created in 1808) has traditionally been considered the first qualification of the higher education system, conferring the right to pursue tertiary education in a university. Degree programmes generally last 3 years after the *Baccalauréat* ('Bac +3'), resulting in the obtaining of a 'Licence'. Postgraduate courses take 2 years of study after the Licence, resulting in a Master ('Bac +5'), with PhD students undertaking research for a further 3 years ('Bac +8'). Taken together, these three qualifications represent the Licence-Master-Doctorat (LMD) reform, part of the European Bologna process. Until 2007, an intermediate qualification rewarding 2 years of successful study, called the *Diplôme d'études universitaires générales* (DEUG), also existed for students unable to complete a *Licence*. This LMD system replaced a slightly more confusing system of DEUG, *Licence*, *Maîtrise*, DEA, and *doctorat* during the mid-2000s with the current 3:5:8 progression. IUTs deliver 2-year courses leading to the *Diplôme universitaire de technologie* (DUT), generally regarded as a worthwhile and respected 'more vocational' qualification than a *Licence*.

The *Grandes Écoles* sit outside the university system. The original rationale behind the *Grandes Écoles* system was that France required a highly trained élite able to drive development through all sectors of the economy and society. The *Ancien Régime* and the Revolutionary periods saw the creation of institutions for the training of engineers of all kinds. The *École des ponts et chaussées* was set up in 1747, the *École des mines de Paris* was created in 1783, and the *École polytechnique* and *Conservatoire national des arts et métiers* was created in 1794. These have always been highly selective, and the rigorous selection of entrants is still common to the *Grandes Écoles*. Whereas universities are 'mass' institutions for all those possessing the *Baccalauréat*, *Grandes Écoles* use highly competitive examinations known as 'concours' to select students. The preparation for such examinations may take a number of years of intensive coaching in specialised schools.

7.3.2   The Mass-Élite Split in French Higher Education

During the French Third Republic (1870–1940), there was an increase in the number of state universities as well as private *Grandes Écoles*. This was linked to the increasing need for more highly educated individuals in an albeit slowly modernising economy, along with the will of Republicans both to consolidate the Republic and to link socioeconomic progress to Republican values via the medium of education. As far as the *Grandes Écoles* were concerned, the introduction of compulsory primary education and widening access to secondary schooling should have given, at least in theory, access to a wider range of French citizens. Throughout this period, the driving principle was the creation of an '*élite républicaine*' through meritocratic selection.

Universal secondary education was introduced in France in 1958, creating the opportunity for mass higher education. In 1929, 5% of the population completed the Bac. By 1958, this had risen to 23% and by 1985 67%. As secondary education has been massified and democratised in France beginning in the early 1960s with a greater proportion of each age group sitting and passing the Bac, the university system has been progressively squeezed by the democratically mandated right to higher education at age 18. The minimal annual fees paid by students (€177–€372, depending on level of study) are set to encourage participation, but help little with universities' funding needs.

The French university system, with the occasional exception of IUTs, has been continually criticised for poor infrastructures and an inability to deal satisfactorily with the large and increasing numbers of students. Despite the best efforts of teachers and administrators, these mass universities have acquired the nickname of 'la Fac poubelle' (or 'rubbish-bin university'). Beginning with the socialist governments of the 1980s, there have been calls for a target of 80% of age groups to obtain the Baccalauréat. The overall success rate for the diploma seems to be stabilising at around 85%, but the percentage of young people who actually obtain the qualification is failing to rise above 65–70%.

Occasional government attempts to introduce university selection have met with violent opposition from secondary pupils and university students alike. Nonselective entry to public courses leads to overcrowding, lack of individualised attention, and a subsequent weeding out of weaker students through academic failure. At each stage of university education, this 'sélection par l'échec' can reach 50% (Beaupère and Boudesseul 2009). Although IUTs generally select their intake, study at university is a massified experience where only the 'fittest' reach the higher levels of *Master* and *Doctorat*, at which point group sizes and resources are better and there can be high-quality teaching informed by research. Increasingly, universities have tried to create prestigious and market-facing 'professional' *Licences* and *Masters* in order to bolster the attractiveness of university qualifications to employers, but traditionally it has been higher education in the *Grandes Écoles* sector which has provided the most prestigious diplomas.

The dual system of mass higher education in universities and élite training in *Grandes Écoles* that has developed in France since the 1960s has been matched by a similarly dualistic system of research activity. The French research effort has traditionally been led by state organisations specialised in specific fields and collaborating with universities, *Grandes Écoles*, and other partners through shared research teams, research groupings, thematic programmes, and other mechanisms.

The *Centre national de la recherche scientifique* (CNRS) has played a central role in coordinating pure research in all fields through joint research projects and teams organised with universities, *Grandes Écoles*, and other state organisations and industry. There are many other organisations who are significant research funders, including:

- The *Commissariat à l'énergie* atomique (CEA), which directs nuclear research (pure and applied)
- The *Centre national d'études spatiales* (CNES) in the area of space research
- The *Institut français de recherche pour l'exploitation de la mer* (IFREMER) in the marine science field

Grandes Écoles were thus essentially 'vocational', training experts for work in industry, commerce, administration, technology, and engineering, rather than academia. In the schools devoted to the arts and humanities as well as the sciences, such as the *Écoles normales,* training teachers and lecturers, teaching and research intermingled. But research was principally undertaken in the universities, and therefore research and theoretical teaching were perhaps surprisingly associated with mass institutions, whereas sectoral training in particular technocratic fields was an élite activity.

7.3.3 The Long-Term Effects of a Mass-Élite Split

The defining characteristic of French universities has been the notion of 'merit', crucial to the organisation of the system of élite tertiary education. In the years before the massification and democratisation of the 'Bac' and before proper sociological understandings of the workings of social and cultural capital, the contribution to social mobility made by the *Grandes Écoles'* meritocratic selection was minimal. Iconic examples of 'grand mérite' (humble origins transformed into high Republican service), such as Edouard Herriot or Jean Jaurès, were few. Most social mobility was limited to the 'petit mérite' of underprivileged children obtaining junior posts in the civil service (Borne 2007).

This reflected the reality that the *Grandes Écoles* were not about equality, but rather about providing a technocratic French élite able to manage its progressive modernisation. An example of this principle was the creation in 1946 of the most celebrated of France's *Grandes Écoles*, the *École nationale d'administration*, charged with producing the senior civil servants needed to restore French grandeur. In the private *Grandes Écoles*, especially the business schools, high-quality intensive teaching is provided to children of privileged socio-professional groups in exchange for substantial annual registration fees.

Both *Grandes Écoles* and universities were traditionally aware of the need for social inclusivity, albeit interpreted in a minimalist fashion because of the tension between Republican attachment to 'egalitarian' treatment of all and problems associated with the favouring of some on the basis of 'need'. There was therefore a system of scholarships and fee waivers, but awareness of social inequalities reflected in educational attainment increased throughout the later decades of the twentieth century (Bourdieu and Passeron 1979). The underrepresentation of lower socio-professional groups in *Grandes Écoles* and the higher levels of university (*Licences* and *Masters*) increasingly came to be seen as morally and socially unacceptable and wasteful of France's human capital.

In the 1980s, the socialist administration was concerned about the strength and competitiveness of French science, technology, and industry, prompting the *Assises nationales de la recherche* in 1982. During the 1990s, the French state recognised the need to 'modernise', by improving teaching in the university and *grande école* sectors in parallel with their contribution to France's overall research efforts.

In the early 2000s, France undertook a series of wide-ranging reforms of its higher education. These reforms were intended to make universities and *Grandes Écoles* more fit-for-purpose in terms of efficiency, equality, and their contribution to French competitiveness. Towards the end of the 2000s, concern about the continued need for modernisation of the tertiary education sector and its associated research activities was translated into the world-class university programme.

7.3.4 Reviving the Mediocre Mass Higher Education System

The post-2001 French HE reforms have had two foci. First, they have sought to improve the sector's financial efficiency and productivity, along with boosting France's human capital through enhancing 'democratisation' of access to higher education. Old-fashioned and restrictive interpretations of the concept of 'sélection méritocratique' have been tempered by studies demonstrating the socially narrow recruitment to *Grandes Écoles* and higher levels of university study/research. In response, 'egalitarian' approaches have been replaced by attempts to make education 'equitable'. This concept of 'equity' emerged in the mid-1990s through – amongst other *fora* – the study commission led by Alain Minc on the future state of France in the year 2000. Undertaken within a wider survey of 'the state of France', it recommended renovating the university sector as part of a synthesis of Republican values and neo-liberal economic efficiency in French society more generally (Minc 1994).

7.3.5 A Decade of Reforms in French Higher Education

Measures supporting a broadened uptake of élite higher education gained support in the late 1990s and early 2000s. These were often equated to US initiatives of positive discrimination which is controversial in France. The highest profile initiative was implemented by the Institut d'études politiques de Paris ('Sciences Po.') from 2001. In 2001, the prestigious École supérieure des études économiques et commerciales (ESSEC) likewise implemented a similar mechanism aiming to combat social inequality in recruitment.

Sciences Po., an innovative initiative in favour of widening participation, started in Paris in September 2001 with the *Conventions Éducation Prioritaire* (CEP). Talented Baccalauréat-level students were identified in seven lycées participating in the scheme and given prioritised institution entry. By 2011, 85 lycées were involved in *conventions* with Sciences Po., 850 students had been recruited via the scheme, and six cohorts had graduated from the 5-year (including Masters-level) course. By 2011, the CEP scheme was well established despite ongoing criticisms from inside and outside the institution. Sciences Po. undertook an assessment of the on-course performance and employment history of the 172 students who graduated 2006–2011.

This study demonstrated the project's success, contradicting negative press claims that the students from 'non-traditional' catchment areas given special admission via the CEPs were weaker in performance and employability than 'normal' students recruited via competitive selection from 'privileged' backgrounds (Tiberj 2011). In terms of on-course success, CEP students reported finding the first year of study more challenging than other entrants, with a larger proportion being required to retake the first year before continuing with progression towards graduation after year 5. The initial difficulty of adapting to expectations and ways of studying experienced by CEP students was not surprising. Despite the fears of some, it did not lead to ongoing poor performance or failure for the candidates, and equally positively for Sciences Po. itself, the institution has been able to adapt to the needs of a more diverse student body.

Tiberj's study also demonstrates how the scheme has contributed to the social diversification of the institution itself, in response to concerns in previous years about its role in the social reproduction of French and Parisian élites. A decade of CEP recruitment has attenuated the overrepresentation of privileged socio-professional categories at Sciences Po. Although the institution is now more 'open' than other *Grandes Écoles*, it remains significantly less representative of French society overall than the state university sector student population. A key indicator is the percentage of scholarship students (the government target since 2007 is 30%) in selective higher education, and the 27% of 'boursiers' at Sciences Po. in 2009/2010 compares favourably with other *Grandes Écoles* such as Polytechnique (11%) or HEC (12%) (*ibid.*).

Since 2007, French governments have sought to diversify recruitment to *Grandes Écoles* through a target of 30% of students on state scholarships entering the 'preparatory' schools which coach young people for the *concours* (competitive entry exams for *Grandes Écoles*). Universities progressively realised that alongside 'formal equality' of standardised admission, teaching, and assessment, some students required extra support and tutoring of various kinds to achieve their real 'merit' in a mass system long characterised by a sink-or-swim institutional approach. Existing systems of (small) grants and subsidies for university study have been simplified and extended, to facilitate access to higher education by underprivileged students.

During the 2000s, French governments attempted to modernise the university sector to better align it with perceived 'international' models whilst encouraging a neo-liberal efficiency compatible with Republican values. In parallel with the reform of the public management approach (aligning neo-liberalism with traditional technocracy) came the so-called LMD reform of degree structures. This package coincided with the adoption of various measures inspired by the Bologna Agreement (1999) and was intended to internationalise the system from 2002 by fitting France's higher education into the increasingly 'Anglo-Saxon'-dominated European qualification structures.

Perhaps more challenging to the universities were the reforms implemented from late 2007 by conservative governments under President Sarkozy. The first of these was the August 2007 law on the freedoms and responsibilities of universities (hereafter LRU). The LRU reform was presented by the government as a way of creating a 'New University' culture at the service of 'equal opportunities for all'. But underneath the apparently traditional Republican values of *égalité* lay a shift which mirrored the general shift in administrative culture. These equal opportunities for all were to be delivered by a fairly traditional programme of marketisation and competitiveness in the sector, freeing universities from the control of central government and making them compete for their public funding on the basis of outputs. There was considerable resistance to the removal of universities' perceived privileges as state organisations and to the loss of security which these new freedoms would bring, particularly with the attempts to cut staff salary costs as part of the reform programme.

7.4 From Widening Participation to World-Class Institutions

7.4.1 Regional Collaboration Initiatives (PRES)

The LRU clarified a trend already under way for a number of years. The story of WCUPs in France cannot be told without understanding the crisis of 2003, in which French higher education engaged in soul-searching as a result of French institution's markedly poor performance in the 2003 Shanghai Ranking (Academic Ranking of World Universities, ARWU). In response to this crisis, a new policy of research concentrating and profiling was introduced in the mid-2000s (Harfi and Mathieu 2006). The *Pôles de recherche et d'enseignement supérieur* (PRES, see following section) and the announcement of the Opération Campus schemes contributing to France's overall world-class university programme, which paralleled the LRU, were a direct result of the crisis.

In 2006, the Pacte sur la recherche implemented an initiative to create what were termed Pôles de recherche et d'enseignement supérieur (PRES), regionally grouping together the activities of a variety of actors and stakeholders (Aust et al. 2008). This creation process was strongly steered by the national ministry, from the appointment of project managers to the retention by the ministry of the final approval process, and there are suggestions that this was influenced by strong political pressure (IGAENR 2007). By 2011, 21PRESs involved almost 60 universities, engineering Grandes Écoles, Instituts d'études politiques, private business schools, public research institutes, and other bodies, alongside research and teaching hospitals. The complete list of the PRESs, although not their participating members, is given in the Table 7.2.

Administratively and legally, the PRES groupings have been set up as *établissements publics de coopération scientifique* (ECPS), seen by government as the most appropriate for the collaborative management of research and teaching. The ECPS is the only legal status which allows the universities working together in a PRES to award degrees and other qualifications. This 'common' identity is further underlined by the requirement that all research work published by PRES members carry the name of the PRES itself, in an attempt to further raise the visibility of France's major centres of research activity. Although research and higher education Minister Valérie Pécresse stated that her motivation was not simply 'big is beautiful', the PRES programme is also described as an 'accelerator' of mergers between universities.

7.4.2 Opération Campus and the Saclay Super-Campus

The second part of the reform came in addressing the decades of underinvestment without having to completely rebuild the campus estate. *Opération Campus* was launched in early 2008, promising an infrastructural renovation of a number of

Table 7.2 Pôles de recherche et d'enseignement supérieur (PRES), France, 2011

Aix-Marseille Université
Université de Bordeaux
PRES Bourgogne Franche-Comté (ESTH-Innovation Université)
Université européenne de Bretagne
Centre – Val de Loire Université
Clermont Université
Université de Grenoble
HESAM (Hautes Etudes-Sorbonne-Arts et Métiers)
Université Lille Nord de France
PRES Limousin Poitou-Charentes
PRES de l'Université de Lorraine
Université de Lyon
Université Montpellier Sud de France
Université Nantes Angers Le Mans
Université de Toulouse
ParisTech (Institut des Sciences et Technologies de Paris)
Université Paris Cité
Université Paris Est
Paris Sciences et Lettres – Quartier latin
Sorbonne Universités
UniverSud Paris

Table 7.3 Opération Campus: campuses selected for improvement, France, 2011

Campus	Funding (million €)
Saclay	850
Paris	700
Lyon	575
Aix-Marseille	500
Bordeaux	475
Campus Condorcet (Paris-Aubervilliers)	450
Grenoble	400
Strasbourg	375
Montpellier	325
Toulouse	350
Lorraine	190
Lille	110

France's university campuses. Based on the admission that 30% of campuses were run down and dilapidated, government funding was made available in a competition amongst universities to be one of the dozen or so 'winners' of the programme. As of late 2011, the 12 campuses selected for improvement are listed in Table 7.3.

More than the simple improvement of the nationwide poor university infrastructures that had spawned the nickname of '*la Fac poubelle*', Opération Campus represented a narrowly focused project which sought to transform a limited number of campuses (and a larger number of universities, as some campuses are shared by more than one institution) into internationally visible 'shop windows' of French higher education and research excellence. These '*Campus d'excellence*' have been

Table 7.4 IDEX shortlisted for final round of competition, France, 2011

Region	Acronym	Nom	Project leader
Rhône-Alpes	GUIPLUS	Grenoble-Alpes Université de l'Innovation	Grenoble-Alpes Université de l'Innovation
Aquitaine	IDEX Bordeaux	Initiative d'excellence de l'université de Bordeaux	Université de Bordeaux
Rhône-Alpes	IDEX Lyon Saint-Etienne	Université de Lyon, imagine: Lyon/Saint Etienne, métropole d'innovation et de création	Université de Lyon
Ile de France	PSLetoile	Paris Sciences et Lettres étoile: rendons possible le nécessaire	Paris Sciences et Lettres
Ile de France	SUPER	Sorbonne Universités à Paris pour l'Enseignement et la Recherche	Sorbonne Universités
Midi-Pyrénées	Toulouse IDEX	Toulouse initiative d'excellence	Université de Toulouse
Alsace	UNISTRA	Université de Strasbourg: par delà les frontières, l'université de Strasbourg	Université de Strasbourg

criticised for the way in which they deflected attention from the ongoing difficulties experienced by smaller institutions.

In late 2010, the Ministry of Higher Education and Research announced another programme intended to make French universities more visible on the world stage. This was the '*initiatives d'excellence*' (IDEX) scheme, part of the wider *Investissements d'avenir* ('investing for the future') programme. In March 2011, seven 'initiatives d'excellence' were shortlisted for the final round of competition, judged on the criteria of excellence in research, the robustness of their management plans, and the intensity of linkages between the public and private sectors (Table 7.4).

By July 2011, the first tranche of three projects was announced. These three '*initiatives d'excellence*' were planned to be the first of some 5–10 '*pôles d'excellence*' to be funded with a war chest of €7.7bn:

- Idex Bordeaux led by the Bordeaux University PRES (four universities, the Institut polytechnique de Bordeaux and Sciences Po. Bordeaux)
- Unistra led by the University of Strasbourg (formed in 2009 by merger of the universités Louis Pasteur, Marc Bloch et Robert Schumann)
- Paris Sciences et Lettres (PSL) led by a Fondation de coopération scientifique (13 participants including the Collège de France, École normale supérieure, Université Paris-Dauphine, ESPCI ParisTech, Chimie ParisTech, Observatoire de Paris, Institut Curie, and Institut Louis Bachelier)

Perhaps the best-known case study of France's overall policy to create world-class universities is Saclay Campus development in the Parisian *Île de France* region. Saclay was favoured by President Sarkozy, who regarded the Saclay project, grouping universities, public-sector research organisations, private-sector high-tech businesses, and large research infrastructures, as an iconic example of France's global research strength. At the same time, the initiative was widely criticised as exemplifying the many difficulties of the overall plan to create excellence in the university sector.

Sarkozy's view was ascribed to a desire to mobilise a group of over 20 stakeholders in the project, thereby creating synergies in innovation and creativity. By centralising the management of Saclay's multiple and disparate activities, the intention was to create economies of scale and foster efficiency. But the head of the CNRS voiced concerns that neither the area's geography, the number of actors involved, nor the proposed governance of the grouping seemed propitious for realising its ambitious and multidimensional goals (Huet 2011). As with the earlier reforms of higher education and research implemented in the 2000s, lecturers and researchers have reacted adversely to perceived threats to their working conditions.

One of the driving principles underlying the ambition to create world-class universities is the 'critical mass' of institutions. The idea of WCUs has therefore become bound up with a move towards mergers and collaboration between universities, research organisations and other bodies. However, in the case of France, which is characterised by an already complex ecology of different HE/research institutions, the creation of this critical mass through new initiatives is actually adding layers of administration, rather than clarifying and simplifying administrative structures. The question is (a) whether this will reinvigorate French higher education fortunes and its global research reputation and (b) what the wider public benefits of the decade of reforms, and the recent plethora of programmes by which France has attempted to address its perceived world-class university gap, are.

7.4.3 Formative Evaluation: France's WCUP and the Five Public Benefits

In the overview of the theory of WCUPs, we characterised five kinds of public benefits which could be produced by WCUPs. These were not private benefits to individuals or to particular institutions but benefits which accrued at the level of the higher education system. In order to bring the French reforms and WCUPs into perspective, we consider the reforms' contribution over the last decade along each variable.

The first variable was the attraction of increased exogenous resources. There has been an increase in the internationalisation of France's higher education system since the late 1990s with numbers of French students studying abroad as well as a marked increase in the number of foreign students hosted in France (Vincent-Lancrin 2009), and France representing both one of the major hosts and one of the sources of foreign students. In that sense, the reforms, both those with a national logic and those driven by the Bologna process, have come some way in creating public value, bringing new students into the French system as well as providing French students with access to higher education abroad. Although Vincent-Lancrin (2009) points out that other countries have come much further than France (notably China) in terms of both outgoing and inbound market share, France performs well and has improved its performance, which suggests that some level of improvement has been delivered in the system.

The second variable was increased private resources from France that would not have been spent in the HE sector on research. The French WCUP – through IDEX and the PRESs – has formed part of Le Grand Emprunt in which the French state is investing an additional €18.5bn through L'Agence nationale de la recherche (ANR), a research council created in 2005 to award research funding to universities through direct competition (Davesne 2007). These additional resources were not created by the WCUP, but it can be argued that the reforms created an environment where the government was willing to invest greater sums in research, believing it offered promising returns.

The third variable was whether the emphasis upon world-class universities has improved the functioning of the higher education system and produced a more efficient use of public resources. Clearly, the PRESs have the potential to do this, because the biggest challenge for French higher education is enriching the quality of the education that higher education students in publicly funded universities receive. The reforms led to the creation of AERES the Evaluation Agency for Research and Higher Education and in their synthetic evaluation of French research in 2010 were keen to conclude the reforms including Opération Campus and the Grand Emprunt had succeeded. This report presented the results of a comprehensive, four-wave review of all French universities, which ranked all research into four categories. They argued that the pressure to collaborate had led to the creation of a critical mass and raised the quality of higher level training. However, in the absence of a convincing baseline, it is impossible to evaluate this claim.

The fourth variable is related to the creation of new products which increased the overall attractiveness of France as a location for study, including, for example, the creation of graduate schools. As part of the 2010 AERES evaluation, data was presented for universities and their students with foreign diplomas (i.e. non-Bac students); in the 5-year period 2004–2005 to 2009–2010, there was a 7% increase in the number of these foreign students (covering the 82 universities that returned data and excluding the Grandes Écoles) increasing from 153,000 to 164,000 foreign students. Vincent-Lacrin points out that this increase is relatively small but from a relatively high base. How much of this can be attributed to the WCUP is debatable, but it has taken place at a time of increasing institutionalisation.

The fifth area of public value is in terms of improving the public profile for all universities. It is difficult to directly measure this and can only be hinted at with increasing numbers of foreign students. But any thought of an improvement in the prestige of French universities should be tempered by the failure of the reforms to increase French universities' performance in the Academic Ranking of World

Table 7.5 French universities in each of the top ranks 2003–2011

	Top 20	Top 100	Top 200	Top 300	Top 400	Top 500
2011	–	3	7	13	18	22
2003	–	2	8	12	17	22

Source: www.arwu.org

Universities. The Table 7.5 below shows the performance from 2003 (the date of the original crisis which created French policy interest in WCUPs) and the most recent data (2011).

What is notable about this is that the distribution is similar to that in 2003. There are the same number of universities in the top 500 (namely 22), and although there is one more in the top 300, there is one less in the top 200. Despite the efforts to reverse the situation, these changes have not improved French performance. With the funding for improvements only now beginning, and rather more slowly than intended, French universities may improve their position in the future. But this question of the longer-term effects of the reforms is salient, and in order to better understand the perceived public values of this reform, we now turn to the longer-term public value of a decade of reforms seeking to produce competitive, dynamic universities in France.

7.4.4 The Langue Durée of French Higher Education Reform

The French political culture is one in which considerable legitimacy derives from administrative competence French higher education administration faced a crisis in the early 2000s in response to a perception that France's universities were increasingly out of step with international trends, as demonstrated by Bologna; student mobility; and university league tables. France's interest in world-class universities was restricted therefore to improving resource efficiency but also their symbolical deployment to legitimate French higher education policy on the domestic stage. From this perspective, it becomes possible to frame these reforms as an attempt to reinvigorate higher education through the neo-liberal mechanisms of market-based reforms, competition, and selectivity.

Overall, policy initiatives undertaken in France in the 2000s to improve French universities have moved steadily towards a free-market vision of institutions made autonomous from centralised state control and competing in a global environment of knowledge and research. The Sarkozy administration appeared to have adapted, through a form of 'policy transfer', some of the managerialist/commercial value sets that France has previously opposed in other fields, such as culture, or language. Although the value sets at the heart of the policies may be novel for the French state, the often semi-dirigiste nature of the initiatives subsequently employed to effect change suggest that old habits die hard for government.

France's current readiness to espouse what might be called 'managerialist' policy choices in higher education and research as attempts to improve France's knowledge competitiveness in the globalised economy is a clear example of 'policy transfer'. In effect, the French state is adopting attitudes and behaviour it has hitherto strongly resisted in defence of 'French exceptionalism' (Hoareau 2011). It seems that the Sarkozy administration is more ready to move away from French traditions of centralised, public sector-led models of higher education and research. Framed in this perspective, globalisation has been seen as an opportunity rather than a threat.

At the same time, traditional attitudes have remained, evident in both a mix of 'Republican' rhetoric (e.g. around 'Egalité des chances') and semi-dirigiste government initiatives to encourage change in the university sector. One might speculate that élite French administrators feel, analogous to university staff, that their professions are being destroyed by the introduction of foreign values. The frequent attempts by the state to enlist traditional Republican values such as 'Egalité des chances' in support of change to the universities driven by international competition (arguably an anathema to those values) reflects the clear tension and problems in attempting to introduce these new values into French HE.

A major criticism of the French state's current effort to reform higher education and research in general, and simultaneously to improve the visibility and competitiveness of French universities and research worldwide, is that there are too many initiatives creating confusion in the sector (Soulé 2011). It therefore seems that the government runs the risk of fragmentation, with its drive for competition and a plethora of policy initiatives which run counter to the real public value, namely, making French universities more attractive to the world, and providing a more effective higher level education for the French labour market.

7.5   Conclusions

It is clear that the last decade of reform in France has constituted a substantive effort to overhaul the higher education system and in particular to use a world-class university programme to drive a set of changes. Yet, there is a sense that these changes are not producing the desired results. There has been a resistance from university staff and students, in particular, to the highly controversial law for the reform of universities.

The most interesting lesson to be drawn from France is about the more general use of WCUPs as a means of transforming, modernising, and dynamising French higher education. The WCUP was part of a wider transformation process in French public governance and inevitably was influenced by the progress of that broader change. The ideas behind a WCUP were in line with the cultural changes that the French government wished to achieve, creating dynamic and competitive university leadership. But there was a cultural clash between traditions of top-down management and balance, and unleashing the dynamism of competition.

The ARWU crisis was clearly a moment which allowed the government to advance a new administrative paradigm into the French higher education sector. At the same time, having raised expectations of transformation, the ministry found itself pulled towards WCUPs (and indeed much higher funding for the sector) as part of an attempt to complete that transformation. It is therefore important not to interpret the changes in France purely as the rational implementation of a policy. Rather, there were a range of problems which policymakers regarded as important to address, and when particular solutions were implemented, new problems emerged. It is likely that later interventions have sought to undo or remedy some of the higher education system problems.

In this chapter, we have been arguing for the importance of taking a systems perspective in understanding the impacts of WCUPs and in particular to not assume that WCUPs automatically produce positive benefits. There were some hints that the overall transformation process through which French higher education had progressed had indeed made some systems improvements, including widening participation, increasing internationalisation, and justifying increased investments in the system. But the role of the WCUP in that process has not been straightforward, only really emerging towards the end of a wider shift, which itself did not proceed without considerable opposition from key stakeholders.

The challenge for France is the revitalisation of its university sector and, in particular, reconciling the tension between the resource-rich *Grandes Écoles* and the university sector where chronic underfunding has led to a hands-off approach to education and low performances at the undergraduate level. The CEP at Sciences Po. provides very few students for French universities, and the key systems improvements must come through improving the student experience in a mass university system which differs markedly from the Anglo-American university model. In short, the French experience does not demonstrate that WCUPs provide greater value in improving systems than other approaches, beyond that brought by the additional resources.

In the case of France, where one would have expected considerable benefits, we have been unable to identify any intrinsic advantages from the WCUP approach. Advantages have come where WCUP activities have played to existing strengths in the system, or concentrated resources on achieving difficult changes. The French government should be commended for resisting the urge to concentrate resources on the *Grandes Écoles* to simply increase the numbers of French universities in the rankings. Instead, there appears to have been a sincere effort to address the systems problems, and WCUPs have been one element of those efforts.

We therefore call for caution regarding the value of WCUPs. WCUPs have been useful in persuading governments of the value of investing in higher education and for governments seeking to profile their nations more aggressively internationally. This is not to say that the approach has no value but that it has value under particular circumstances, and it is therefore necessary to be much more circumspect about the claims that are made regarding their utility. In particular, we highlight three areas which could potentially benefit from a much greater nuance if national Education Ministries are to improve the quality and performance of their higher education systems as a whole.

The first is the definition of WCUP and in particular in the view that being world-class means being like Harvard or MIT. In understanding the idea of a world-class university, we add to Salmi's (2009) criteria of excellence in teaching, research, and facilities, excellence in national impact. Secondly, we suggest that governments in their use of rankings should understand what matters about higher education, corroborating Hazelkorn's claims that rankings methodologies need to take greater account of outcome rather than volume and resource metrics. Thirdly, there is a need for a much more nuanced understanding of national higher education system conditions to enable governments to nuance their policy choices to achieve what is really desirable rather than simply achieving apparently valuable but ultimately meaningless improvements in league table rankings.

Higher education research is coming to terms with a sense that the paradigm that has dominated the previous quarter century, namely, of driving efficiency improvement competition, has reached the limits of its success and that new approaches are necessary to ensure efficiency of public investments in higher education. A new conceptual framework is necessary for effective coordination between institutions without restricting their freedom to innovate and improve their service delivery. Perhaps the most valuable message to take away from the French experience is the depth of change in the way that the problem is framed within public service that is necessary if this broader change is to be achieved. World-class university programmes must therefore be understood as the first step on a longer journey towards world-class university systems, and this end point will require considerable focus and application to successfully achieve.

References

Aalto University Foundation. (2008, June 25). Charter of foundation. At: http://www.minedu. fi/export/sites/default/OPM/Koulutus/artikkelit/Innovaatioyliopistohanke/Liitteet/Charter_of_ Foundation_Aalto_University_Foundation.pdf. Accessed 15 Oct 2011.

AERES. (2010). *Analyses régionales des évaluations réalisées entre 2007 et 2010*. Paris: Agence d'évaluation de la recherche et de l'enseignement supérieur.

Altbach, P. G., & Balán, J. (Eds.). (2007). *World class worldwide. Transforming research universities in Asia and Latin America*. Baltimore: Johns Hopkins University Press.

Aust, J., Crespy, C., Manifet, C., Musselin, C., & Soldano, C. (2008). *Rapprocher, integrer, differencier. Elements sur la mise en place de poles de recherche et d'enseignement superieur* [Bringing closer, integrating, differentiating. Elements on the establishment of centers of research and higher education]. Paris: Inter-Ministry Delegation.

Beaupère, N., & Boudesseul, G. (2009). *Sortir sans diplôme de l'Université: Comprendre les parcours d'étudiants "décrocheurs"*. Ouvrage réalisé à l'initiative de l'Observatoire de la Vie étudiante (OVE), Paris: La documentation Française.

Bergan, S., Guarga, R., Polak, E. E., Sobrinho, J. D., Tandon, R., & Tilak, J. B. G. (2009). *Public responsibility for higher education*. Paris: UNESCO. http://unesdoc.unesco.org/images/0018/ 001832/183238e.pdf. Accessed 15 Oct 2011.

Borne, D. (2007). 'Le Mérite' special number of *Les Cahiers français* on 'Les 'Valeurs de la République', *336*(January–February), 70–76.

Bourdieu, P., & Passeron, C. (1979). *The inheritors: French students and their relation to culture*. Chicago: University of Chicago Press.

Chapoulie, J. M., Fridenson, P., & Prost, A. (2010). Jalons pour une histoire sociale de la science et des établissements d'enseignement supérieur en France depuis 1945. *Le Mouvement Social, 233*(4), 3–12.

Damme, D. V. (2011, March 11). *Autonomy and connectedness: New challenges for higher education governance.* Paper presented at CHEPS 25th Lustrum conference.

Davesne, S. (2007). L'Etat vend 3 % d'EDF pour construire des campus [The state sells 3% of EDF to build campuses]. *L'Usine nouvelle, 30*(November). http://www.usinenouvelle.com/article/l-etat-vend-3-d-edf-pour-construire-des-campus.124440. Accessed 15 Oct 2011.

Department for Innovation, University and Skills (DIUS). (2003). *The future of higher education.* http://www.dius.gov.uk/assets/biscore/corporate/migratedd/publications/f/future_of_he.pdf. Accessed 15 Oct 2011.

Department of Employment and Learning of Northern Ireland (DELNI). (2010). Website. http://www.delni.gov.uk/index/further-and-higher-education/higher-education/role-structure-he-division/knowledge-transfer.htm. Accessed 15 Oct 2011.

Department of Innovation, Industry, Science and Research of Australia (DIISR). (2009). *Powering ideas. An innovation agenda for the 21st century.* http://www.innovation.gov.au/innovationreview/Documents/PoweringIdeas_fullreport.pdf. Accessed 15 Oct 2011.

Grove, J. (2011, September 15). Science Po proves critics of priority scheme wrong. *Times Higher Education.* http://www.timeshighereducation.co.uk/story.asp?sectioncode=26&storycode=417405&c=1. Accessed 15 Oct 2011.

Harfi, M., & Mathieu, C. (2006). Classement de Shanghai et image internationale des universités: quels enjeux pour la France? *Horizons stratégiques, 2*, 1–16.

Hazelkorn, E. (2011). *Rankings and the reshaping of higher education: The battle for world-class excellence.* London: Palgrave Macmillan.

Head, S. K. (2011, September 25). Conference looks at 'Stepford Universities'. *University World News.* http://www.universityworldnews.com/article.php?story=20110923213109807. Accessed 15 Oct 2011.

Hoareau, C. (2011). *Globalisation and dual modes of higher education policymaking in France: je t'aime moi non plus.* CSHE University of California, Berkeley Research and occasional paper series CSHE 2.11. http://cshe.berkeley.edu/publications/publications.php?id=376. Accessed 15 Oct 2011.

Huet, S. (2011, January 31). Saclay, le plateau de la discorde [Saclay, the plateau of discord]. *Libération.* http://www.liberation.fr/societe/01012316920-saclay-le-plateau-de-la-discorde. Accessed 15 Oct 2011.

IGAENR (2007*). La mise en place des pôles de recherche et d'enseignement supérieur (PRES)* (Report No. 79/ 2007). Paris: Inspection générale de l'administration de l'Éducation nationale et de la Recherche.

Institute for Higher Education Policy (IHEP). (2005). *The investment payoff. A 50-state analysis of the public and private benefits of higher education.* Washington, DC. http://www.ihep.org/assets/files/publications/g-l/InvestmentPayoff.pdf. Accessed 15 Oct 2011.

Kaiser F. (2007). *Higher education in France.* Country report. International Higher Education Monitor. Enschede: CHEPS.

Liu, N. C. (2006). *Academic Ranking of World Universities (ARWU).* Presentation at Leiden University, 16 February 2006. http://www.authorstream.com/Presentation/FunnyGuy-19604-presentation-prof-liu-Outline-Dream-Chinese-WCU-Extra-Funding-985-Project-2001-2003-Goals-Top-Universities-Quest-as-Entertainment-ppt-powerpoint/. Accessed 15 Oct 2011.

Liu, N. C. (2007). The differentiation, classification, and future world-class status. In P. G. Altbach & J. Balán (Eds.), *World-class world-wide. Transforming research universities in Asia and Latin America* (pp. 54–69). Maryland: Johns Hopkins University Press.

Marginson, S., & van der Wende, M. (2007). *Globalization and higher education* (Education Working Paper No. 8). Paris: OECD.

Minc, A. (Ed.). (1994). *La France de l'an 2000. Rapport au Premier ministre.* Paris: Odile Jacob/Documentation française.

Ritzen, J. (2010). *A chance for European universities?* Amsterdam: Amsterdam University Press.

Sadlak, J., & Cai, L. N. (Eds.). (2009). *The world-class university as part of a new higher education paradigm: From institutional qualities to systemic excellence.* Bucharest: UNESCO-CEPES.

Salmi, J. (2009). *The challenge of establishing world-class universities.* Washington, DC: The World Bank.

Soulé, V. (2011, January 31). On rajoute des strates, sans en supprimer [We add layers, without removing]. *Libération.* http://www.liberation.fr/societe/01012316921-on-rajoute-des-strates-sans-en-supprimer. Accessed 15 Oct 2011.

Tiberj, V. (2011). *Sciences Po, dix ans après les Conventions Education Prioritaire.* Paris: Science Po (Centre d'Etudes Européennes). www.sciencespo.fr/sites/default/files/CEP_Etude_VTiberj_final.pdf. Accessed 15 Oct 2011.

Toulemonde, B., Post, A., Geoffroy, J., & Cyterman, J.-R. (2006). *Le système éducatif en France.* Paris: Documentation Française.

Vincent-Lancrin, S. (2009). Cross-border higher education: trends and perspectives. In Centre for Education Research and Innovation (Eds.), *Higher education to 2030. Vol. 2: Globalisation.* Paris: OECD/ CERI.

Vught, F., & Westerheijden, D. (2010). Multidimensional ranking: A new transparency tool for higher education and research. *Higher Education Management and Policy, 22*(3), 1–26.

Wildavsky, B. (2010). *The great brain race – How global universities are reshaping the world.* Princeton: Princeton University Press.

Chapter 8
Challenges for Top Japanese Universities When Establishing a New Global Identity: Seeking a New Paradigm After "World Class"

Akiyoshi Yonezawa

8.1 Introduction

Establishing the world leading position in higher education has been the ambition of both the government and top universities in Japan in the last decade (Yonezawa 2003, 2007). However, the context in which they are situated is quite different from those of emerging economies in Asia. The top Japanese universities had already been recognized as being among the top universities in Asia by the end of the 1990s. In the Asian University Rankings published by *Asiaweek* in the latter half of the 1990s, the top positions were dominated by Japanese universities. At the same time, in every major world ranking since the mid-2000s, the top 10 positions in the world have been monopolized by two English speaking countries, namely, the United States and the United Kingdom. Therefore, the ambition shared by the Japanese government and the universities has been to elevate one or more Japanese universities to the top 10 and increase the number of Japanese universities with world-class status.

On the other hand, for the last 10–20 years, the socioeconomic environment surrounding the top universities in Japan has not been accommodating. Firstly, demographic change has produced strong pressure for universities to maintain the quality and quantity of higher education learners. For instance, Japan's population of 18-year-olds dropped from 2.05 million in 1992 to 1.19 million in 2011. At the same time, the academic achievement among secondary school students, especially those of a lower socioeconomic status, deteriorated. Secondly, public or private institutions of higher education have failed to become more affordable. The cumulative national debt increased from 76.7% of GDP in 1997 to 183.5% of GDP in 2009, which is the worst among member countries of the Organisation for

A. Yonezawa (✉)
Graduate School of International Development, Nagoya University, Nagoya, Japan
e-mail: yonezawa@gsid.nagoya-u.ac.jp

J.C. Shin and B.M. Kehm (eds.), *Institutionalization of World-Class University in Global Competition*, The Changing Academy – The Changing Academic Profession in International Comparative Perspective 6, DOI 10.1007/978-94-007-4975-7_8,
© Springer Science+Business Media Dordrecht 2013

Economic Co-operation and Development (OECD). On the other hand, the GDP per capita in constant price (reference year 2000) and constant purchasing power parities (PPPs) have stagnated from 25,608 USD in 2000 to 26,309 USD in 2009. Thirdly, the development of postgraduate education has been slow, mainly because of Japan's long-standing reliance on in-house training and promotion through its highly developed internal labor market. The OECD reviewed Japanese higher education and pointed out its ongoing changes—namely, the increase in non-regular and temporary workers as well as the changes in employment that are experienced by new university graduates (Newby et al. 2009). However, the graduates of top universities generally have better access to the shrinking number of careers in the government and in large, established enterprises. Lastly, the earthquakes and tsunami on March 11, 2011, and the subsequent accident at the Fukushima Daiichi Nuclear Power Plant may have significantly damaged the attractiveness of Japanese higher education for international students, at least in the short term.

Although Japanese universities and researchers have confidence in their research performance in science and technology, the risk that Japan might be caught up or surpassed by new, emerging economies has been widely stated within the last 20 years. World-class university policies implemented in Korea and China in particular have been noted by the policy makers, researchers, and higher education managers in Japan.

In 2001, the official plan for fostering world-class universities was revealed in a short memo submitted to the Economic Finance Committee of the Koizumi Cabinet by Atsuko Toyama, at that time the Minster of Education, Culture, Sports, Science, and Technology (MEXT). He outlined the government's intention to foster around 30 world-class universities, although the definition of "world class" and a concrete agenda were not explained. This "Toyama Plan" was submitted under strong pressure from Prime Minister Koizumi in order to bring attention to the role of higher education in national development. The world-class university plan was presented by the government on short notice and then announced to university leaders after its submission.

In sum, the challenge of creating world-class universities in Japan began partly because of Japan's ambition to take a top position globally and partly as a response to the decisive policies of Japan's two neighboring countries, Korea and China. This chapter will examine the ideas and actual implementation of the world-class university policy in Japan at both the national policy level and the university level.

8.2 National Policy Level

8.2.1 Historical Background

Salmi (2009) defines the three factors necessary for establishing a world-class university as (a) a concentration of talents, (b) abundant resources, and (c) appropriate governance. The history of modern universities in Japan begins with the ambition to establish world-class universities. Thus far, the top universities in the nation's public sector have satisfied all three criteria.

After the establishment in 1877 of Japan's first national public university, the University of Tokyo, the Japanese government established a limited number of "imperial universities" as a distinct category, one that remained separate from other universities and colleges until the end of World War II. After the war, the official distinction of those imperial universities was abolished. Currently, according to the School Education Act, enacted in 1947, all of Japan's 778 universities (86 national, 95 local public, and 597 private, in 2010) share the same status.

The top universities, especially the national public ones, have continued to show potential for becoming world-class universities. With the highest concentration of the country's talent, the top universities in Japan have succeeded in attracting the domestic elites by means of highly selective entrance examinations. At the same time, a high level of academic autonomy at prestigious universities has been maintained, especially at the school or faculty level (Terasaki 1970, 1992).

Public funding for higher education has been highly concentrated toward top national public universities. Firstly, there is a clear distinction in the national budgetary allocation between national and local public and private schools. In the 2011 fiscal year, the budgetary allocation for national universities was 1,202 billion Japanese yen, while the national budgetary support for private universities remained at 321 billion yen, in total. Essentially, local universities rely on public funds from their municipal governments. For almost all private universities, the main source of financial revenue is tuition fees, though it is not uncommon for private universities to also receive financial support from municipal governments.

Secondly, although all national universities share the same legal status, there have always been some mechanisms for adjusting the allocation of funds among national universities. At the beginning of the postwar higher-education system, the organizational structure of faculties within former imperial universities adopted the "chair" system, while other institutions implemented the "department" system. The chair system, an integration of the education and research functions based on the traditional Continental European system, was set only for a limited number of universities that had research-oriented graduate schools. For such institutions, the budgetary allocation per faculty member was more than double than for those with the department system.

In the 1960s and 1970s, the argument for creating a distinct category for research universities appeared in the policy reports of the Central Council for Education of the Ministry of Education (Central Council for Education 1963, 1971). However, an officially distinct category for research universities was not defined, even though national universities established after World War II had developed their graduate schools in the 1970s. In the 1980s, the basic operational budget for national universities did not increase as a result of financial stringency, though specially itemized project funds were created and allocated mainly to prestigious research universities (Amano 2008). In the beginning of the 1990s, the chair system was transformed into a new system such that almost all the professors became postgraduate professors (Ogawa 2002). This transformation occurred mainly within the top national universities, and was, at least at first, linked to better budgetary treatment.

Thirdly, the addition of a new science and technology policy, via enactment of the Science and Technology Basic Act in 1995, has also functioned as a tool for varying the allocation of national funds among universities. This act requires that the government establish a Science and Technology Plan every 5 years and that it make efforts to secure the necessary funds for realizing the plan. The various competition-based funding projects for research, including Grant-in-Aid (a government scientific-research fund), have increased in number since the 1980s (Asonuma 2003). In turn, Japan's top research universities have benefited significantly from such progress in science and technology policy.

Governmental policy proposals in the 1990s pointed out the necessity for a more decisive policy that would foster world-class research and education through performance assessment (University Council 1998; National Commission on Educational Reform 2000). However, implementation of an official world-class university policy had not been realized by 2000. On the other hand, China and Korea had already started to implement their own world-class university policies. China started to establish around 100 research universities in 1994 (the 211 project); in May 1995, the official declaration for establishing world-class universities was made by the Chinese government (the 985 project) (Ma 2007). Korea's Brain Korea 21 (BK21) project, which aimed to support world-class research units, began in 1999, with its second cycle starting in 2007 and a world-class university project launching in 2008. Details of these projects in neighboring countries have since been presented to Japanese higher-education experts and policy makers (see, for example, Umakoshi 1999, 2010).

8.2.2   The Toyama Plan and Incorporation of National Universities

In June 2001, Astuko Toyama, the Minister of Education, Science, Sports, Culture, and Technology at the time, published a memo entitled "Guidelines for restructuring the (national) university system (Toyama Plan)." In it, the idea was put forward to foster around 30 world-class universities through competitive funding and performance budgeting.

Based on a proposal of the Toyama Plan, "Introduction of the principle of competition by third-party (external) evaluation," the establishment of project funds for key research units was introduced under the name Twenty-First Century Centers of Excellence (COE21) project (Yonezawa 2003). Most of the 274 Centers of Excellence (COEs) selected between 2002 and 2004 came from widely known top universities. However, the impact of COE21 on university finances was rather limited. For example, in 2004, the University of Tokyo received 4.2 billion Japanese yen, 12.4% of the total budget for the COE21 project. This amount was only 2% of the university's total revenue (206.7 billion yen).

The Toyama Plan also proposed "the reorganization and integration of national universities" and the "introduction of private sector managerial methods to the national universities." Based on these guidelines, some mergers of small national universities were implemented, and the number of national universities was reduced from 100 in 2003 to 87 in 2004. In 2004, all national universities became incorporated. To incorporate all national or public universities in one country is unique from a comparative point of view. Some countries, such as Indonesia and Malaysia, implemented incorporation beginning with a limited number of top universities, in order to give them autonomy regarding their institutional management (Lee 2004). Japan's incorporation scheme, the National University Corporation Act, also respected the special nature of academic activities. At the same time, the incorporation was implemented as part of a nationwide scheme to divorce many public service organizations from the government under the concept of new public management. A report regarding the 6-year medium-term goals and plans for prospective national universities was published in 2004, and a performance assessment of the operations of national university incorporation against those purposes and plans was linked to financial allocations in the second cycle of medium-term goals and plans from 2010.

As to the basic operational budget and the property given from the government to the national university corporation, the diversity among universities remained even after the incorporation (Shima 2009; Amano 2008). Adding to this, every year from 2004 until 2009, all national universities experienced a 1% cut in the government's subsidy of their operational budgets.

8.2.3   Diversification Through Autonomous Choice and Competitive Funding

In order to set up a system for Japan's higher education after incorporation, the Central Council of Education (CCE), the advisory council of educational policy for the MEXT, published a report in June 2005 entitled "The Future of Higher Education in Japan." Reflecting on the long-term prospects for Japan's mature economy and society as well as on demographic changes as a front-runner of aging societies, the report argued for a paradigm shift based on "incrementalism" in terms of both making budgetary decisions and the higher-education population.

The report proposed establishing functional differentiation among universities. It defined seven functions of higher education: that it should (1) be a key base for world-class research and education, (2) foster highly skilled professionals, (3) have a wide range of vocational and professional training, (4) have general and liberal arts education, (5) consist of specific areas of education and research (e.g., arts, sports), (6) be a local base for lifelong learning, and (7) offer social contributions (e.g., contributions to a local community, have a link with industries and government, encourage international exchange, etc.). The report indicated that prospective universities should try to achieve one or more of these functions based on their own mission, and the government should provide competitive-based funds for promoting prospective functions.

Amano (2008) points out that this report symbolizes a renouncement of the government's official categorization of universities in that it allows a university to function as "a key base for world-class research and education" (Central Council for Education 2005, p. 14), with the government providing funds based on an assessment of its function. The report clarifies that the government will contribute to the "building of a multifaceted funding system tailored to the diverse functions of each institution" (Central Council for Education 2005). This means that the government will not intervene in setting the mission of prospective universities but may guide them through functionally differentiated sets of funding projects.

The official categorization of a world-class university was not implemented after the publication of the Toyama Plan and incorporation of national universities. Instead, providing project-based finances to research units in order to foster world-class research, as well as the training of globally competitive young researchers, was implemented with COE21. The universities competed among each other for the limited number of COE positions and earning such a title reflected a hierarchical positioning of historical prestige (Kitagawa and Oba 2010).

In 2007, the Twenty-First Century COE scheme was replaced by the Global Centers of Excellence (GCOE) scheme. In this new scheme, the number of selected universities was reduced to about half, and the funds per unit were significantly raised. In 2007, the World Premier International Research Center Initiative (WPI) program was started in order to support cutting-edge research institutes for a period of 10–15 years. The WPI aimed to attract globally distinguished researchers, and the use of the English language for both research and administration was stressed. Of the six research institutes selected for the WPI, five were universities, namely, Tohoku University, the University of Tokyo, Kyoto University, Osaka University, and Kyushu University. Thus far, the investment of project funds has been concentrated toward a limited number of research universities. Shima (2009) points out that an increased share of competitive funds in the governmental budget for universities had diversified the sources of financial revenue among national universities. However, partly because the top national universities had already received huge operational budgets, the financial impact of these project funds toward already-established research universities has been rather limited.

8.2.4   Internationalization and Privatization

After the Koizumi Cabinet, from 2001 to 2006, the Japanese government was ruled by the Liberal Democratic Party and Komeito, and encountered increased instability. Facing severe competition with emerging Asian neighbors such as China, Korea, Taiwan, and Singapore, Japanese higher-education institutions and society as a whole were forced to reconsider their role in Asia and in the world. Under the Abe Cabinet (from 2006 to 2007), the government published a report entitled "Asian Gateway Initiative" in May 2007 in order to promote national development by means of an equal partnership with emerging Asian economies. This report required

Japanese universities to open up to the world, and it introduced competitive funds and assessments in order to encourage their internationalization. At the same time, the report recommended strengthening the policy in order to attract international students, in turn making Japan the hub of Asia's human resource network. Following this, in July 2008, the Fukuda Cabinet (from 2007 to 2008) set up a plan to invite 300,000 international students by 2020.

Within this plan, the government commenced a project whose goal was to select 30 universities as "Core Universities for Internationalization" (Global 30). Although the number 30 is the same as that in the Toyama Plan's proposal for fostering 30 world-class universities, these two schemes are not directly linked. Nevertheless, the indicators utilized for selecting the first round of universities in 2009 (e.g., by looking at the number of research grants, international faculty, international students) closely resembled the typical indicators adopted by the World University Rankings. Under the Aso Cabinet (from 2008 to 2009), the first 13 universities (seven national—Tohoku University, Tsukuba University, the University of Tokyo, Nagoya University, Kyoto University, Osaka University, and Kyushu University— and six private—Meiji University, Sophia University, Keio University, Waseda University, Doshisha University, and Ritsumeikan University) were selected. Except for Tsukuba University, every national university selected had formerly been an imperial university, and all the private universities were located either in Tokyo or Kyoto. The Global 30 project was meant to support educational activities related to internationalization. Therefore, the size of the fund was greatly limited (between 100 and 400 million yen per university annually), and the universities had to provide matching funds in order to implement the project.

Because it was an easy, accessible tool for categorizing universities, the Global 30 project was sometimes recognized as a proxy categorization for world-class universities. In the second year of selection, there was a discussion about selecting other types of universities with strong international characteristics, such as small liberal arts colleges that taught English. However, the change in Japan's ruling party in 2009 from the Liberal Democratic Party (LDP) to the Democratic Party of Japan (DPJ) led to the suspension of university selection for this scheme, and the scheme itself was changed in 2011 into a project that became oriented more toward international networking.

Science and technology policy under the Aso Cabinet was advantageous for top research universities. Adding to the abovementioned Global COE and WPI projects, the Funding Program for World-Leading Innovative R&D on Science and Technology (FIRST) was launched in 2009 as one of the projects aiming to revitalize the Japanese economy after the economic crisis of 2008. Originally, it was meant to provide a total of 270 billion yen for 30 research projects. In 2010, the 30 research projects were selected, and 150 billion yen was granted after budgetary reconsideration. Out of the 30 projects, 11 were given to project leaders at the University of Tokyo.

The booming of world-class rankings (Hazelkorn 2011; Shin et al. 2011) had another impact on thinking about the public status of national universities. Heizo Takenaka, a professor at Keio University and minister of Internal Affairs and

Communication at the time, proposed privatizing the University of Tokyo by means of abolishing the public budgeting allocated to operational costs. His idea was based on the fact that the world's top 10 universities were private US universities. Although this was a clear misinterpretation of the financial structure of those private US universities, this idea was proposed as policy by the LDP. Because the LDP strongly supports fostering world-class universities, this idea appeared in their manifesto in both the 2009 and 2010 elections. Support for Takenaka's idea symbolized the widespread concern about Japan's significant government debt and the steadily increasing social cost of Japan's aging population.

8.3 University Level

8.3.1 Historical Background

Although top universities in Japan, especially the oldest national universities such as the University of Tokyo and Kyoto University, were established from the beginning to become world-class universities, their histories have not always shown them to be successful in this regard. For instance, the campuses of almost all of the top national and private universities were severely damaged during World War II. In the 1960s and 1970s, almost all of the prestigious universities were flooded with radical student movements. Many of the universities' campuses were occupied by student activists, and the universities' education and research activities were significantly disrupted. By the mid-1970s, the rapid increase in the number of students interested in higher education had raised concerns about the quality of education, especially among private universities. Most of the top private universities, such as Keio University and Waseda University, were faced with financial difficulties, and the rise of tuition fees became one of the main targets of student activists.

Nevertheless, the academic performance of the top universities in Japan was high enough to consider the higher-education system as being world class. Looking at the number of publications in the field of physics, for example, Arima (1989) points out that top Japanese universities have produced a comparable number to that of the top US universities since the mid-1970s. At the same time, Arima also admits that the performance of Japanese universities, when weighted by citation impact, tends to be lower than that of US universities. However, the academic performance of those top Japanese universities improved significantly from the mid-1970s to the mid-1980s. For example, the number of publications in physics at the University of Tokyo was 763 (558.71 if weighted by impact factors) in 1976, and 1,015 (1015.92) in 1986, while the number at MIT was 557 (729.184) in 1976, and 689 (843.804) in 1986.

Asonuma (2010) argues that the prominence of Japanese universities as key research bases started to drop in the 1960s with the development of national research institutes and R&D divisions that were part of private enterprises. In the 1980s, the curtailed national budget established a strict ceiling on the operational budget of national universities, so the universities started to seek endowment- and contract-based research funds from private enterprises. Nevertheless, international recognition of the research done by Japanese universities increased, partly because Japanese researchers started to submit papers to international journals instead of only domestic journals (Nakayama et al. 1999). Reviewing the literature about universities and science, Asonuma (2010) concludes that Japan's research began to be noticed in the mid-1980s and that in many fields, Japan caught up with European countries, occupying the second-place position just after the USA, at that time.

Also in the 1980s, top Japanese universities started to pay attention to their ranked positioning in the world. Akito Arima (1989), the president of the University of Tokyo from 1989 to 1993 argued that the positioning of his university, 67th in the *Gourman Report* (an international university ranking published in 1989) was too low. In order to improve the reputation of research in Japanese universities, Arima and other presidents of national universities campaigned for drastic changes to university finances. This movement led to policies promoting science and technology in the 1990s. By the end of the 1990s, the top universities in Japan dominated the top positions in *Asiaweek*'s Asian university rankings, and by the end of the 1990s, Japanese universities had established their world-class status, or at least top positions in Asia.

8.3.2 Incorporation of National Universities

In 2004, all national universities were incorporated, including the top ones. From the beginning, both the Ministry of Education, Science and Culture (Monbusho)[1] and the Japan Association of National Universities (JANU) were opposed to incorporation. However, Akito Arima, the minister of Education, Science, and Culture (and formerly president of the University of Tokyo) decided in favor of in-corporating all national universities, doing so under strong political pressure to shift various governmental service functions to independent administrative institutions. In negotiations with other cabinet members, Arima and Monbusho succeeded in creating a special status for national universities, calling them "national university corporations" in order to respect the special characteristics of their research and education activities. He also clarified his intention to develop world-class education and research through incorporation (Osaki 2011). Minoru Matsuo, at the time the president of Nagoya University, formerly one of the imperial universities, and other leaders of national universities were actively involved in the design process for the national university incorporation scheme. At the same time, many universities prepared for incorporation by means of governance reform, strategic planning, financial reforms, etc.

---

[1]Monbusho was reorganized into Ministry of Education, Culture, Sports, Science and Technology (MEXT) from 2001.

8.3.3   Governance Reform

Japanese national universities, especially the top ones, had a highly decentralized institutional power structure. However, in the transition period before incorporation, Takeshi Sasaki, the president of the University of Tokyo, requested that his university's senate transfer its power to the president in order to successfully implement incorporation (Uesugi 2009). In order to adapt to the new environment during and after incorporation, many national universities, including top ones, faced the need for governance reforms in order to strengthen their management capacity.

Firstly, the nomination process for university presidents was reexamined. The presidents and deans of national universities had been elected by a vote from faculty members, and each faculty had a great deal of autonomy in terms of recruiting new faculty members and allocating funds. As part of the new national university corporation scheme, each national university set up a committee for selecting the president, so that, in theory, the committee did not have to include the faculty in voting. After incorporation, Tohoku University, a former imperial university, officially abolished the faculty voting system in its process for selecting a president, although it does allow the faculty to present their preference via representatives. Although other top universities also set up selection committees for choosing their presidents, they continued to respect the results of faculty voting. Waseda University and Keio University, top private universities recognized as world-class universities, also implement voting for presidents and faculty deans by faculty members. At the same time, the university presidents who were nominated were cautious enough to avoid overemphasizing their leadership.

Secondly, the vice president system came to be used to substantially strengthen the decision-making capacity of universities. Even before incorporation, most leading Japanese universities had vice presidents appointed by presidents. Before incorporation, however, national universities also had another strong instrument in administration, that is, the administrative bureau. Because these universities were government organizations, the head and senior staff of the administrative bureau of a national university were rotated among national universities and others under the control of the Ministry of Education, Science, Sports, Culture and Technology (MEXT) (Yamamoto 2002; Uesugi 2009). During incorporation, many universities, especially leading ones, abolished the position of head of the administrative bureau (Osaki 2011), while other universities (Nagoya University, for example) retained that position. As a result, the number of vice presidents increased in most the universities, with some of them becoming governing board members (executive vice presidents). It became typical for presidents to assign specific tasks (e.g., research, international affairs) to prospective vice presidents, and the vice president would implement them with the assistance of related directorates and divisions of the administrative bureau.

Today, most vice presidents are appointed from among academics. However, it is common that at least one vice president or executive vice president is appointed from among nonacademics as part of a "personnel exchange" with the MEXT, and typically, they are in charge of general affairs. The vice president and executive vice presidents are important positions upon which a university president can have a direct influence under the condition that faculty and school deans are still elected by means of voting. At the same time, effective coordination among various initiatives by prospective vice presidents has become another challenge for many universities, especially for the top comprehensive universities. Tohoku University developed the office of president position and appointed one vice president to the position of director of the office of president (this can be understood as a position similar to that of a provost). The University of Tokyo established its office of president in the 1970s and has appointed middle-aged professors and associate professors to assist in the university's governance. These presidential offices also function as platforms for fostering future university leaders.

8.3.4 Strategic Planning

The incorporation of national universities in 2004 forced national universities to implement planned operations. It required them to set medium-term goals and plans every 6 years. The National University Corporation Evaluation Committee, under the MEXT, assesses their achievement against these medium-term goals and plans. Under this scheme, national universities are expected to examine their mission and purposes, set their operational plans, implement a self-assessment, and develop a plan for the next period. Previously, the introduction of the concept of the management cycle (plan-do-check-action) had emerged much earlier in some universities. In fact, the University of Tokyo issued its first self-evaluation report in 1991, examining its mission and purposes based on its history since 1877 and on the contemporary environment.

Adding to the medium-term goals and plans submitted to the government, the University of Tokyo released, in 2005, its original Tokyo University Action Plan 2005–2008, under the presidency of Hiroshi Komiyama, and then released its Action Scenario FOREST 2015, under the presidency of Junichi Hamada, in 2010. Komiyama's action plan was the first attempt to clarify the vision and plan of the president, with the subtitle being "Aiming at the pinnacle of global knowledge." It itemized the concrete actions to be taken by the institution. The university was now annually publishing the results of its assessment. Hamada's action scenario included the subtitle "Moving the forest," portraying its university as "a heavily wooded forest" with "the great breadth and diversity of intellectual activity." The link between a medium-term plan that is submitted to the government and the university action plan is explained as follows:

FOREST 2015 builds on principles set out in earlier programs established by my esteemed predecessors and is firmly rooted in the culture of the University. Prior to our reorganization as a national university corporation in 2004, the Charter of the University of Tokyo was established under then President Takeshi Sasaki, laying forth basic principles for the

University's long-term management. Thereafter, a wide range of independent initiatives were carried out under its First Medium-Term Goals and Plans, and under Action Plan 2005–2008, mapped out by President Sasaki's successor, President Hiroshi Komiyama. Beginning in our 2010 academic year, the University of Tokyo will begin to implement our Second Medium-Term Goals and Plans, paving the way for the realization of FOREST 2015. With these parallel undertakings, we will present to society our basic approach to the management of the University of Tokyo. (The University of Tokyo 2010, p 1)

The action scenario stresses the vision of having a public and international profile for this flagship university, the leading university supported by Japanese society and the government. The university set up the following nine priority areas: (1) to ensure academic diversity and pursue excellence, (2) to build a truly global campus, (3) to further develop collaboration with society—from "contributing knowledge to society" to "joint creation of knowledge with society," (4) to develop Todai (University of Tokyo) students with intellectual toughness and personal resilience, (5) to enhance the faculty's educational skills and sustain academic vigor, (6) to train administrative staff as professionals, (7) to build a close-knit network with alumni, (8) to enhance the agility of management and reinforce the university's foundations, and (9) to reinforce governance and compliance (The University of Tokyo 2010).

Developing a comprehensive action plan as an institution is not an easy task, especially for a large, comprehensive university that supports world-class researchers. Faculties, schools, and research institutes have their own opinions and beliefs, and yet a high degree of autonomy is presumed.

Such was the case with Hamada's action scenario, in which prospective schools and research institutes were meant to publish their own scenarios modeled after university-level action scenarios. Other top universities also published action plans, typically under the name of their presidents. Tohoku University released its action plan under President Akihisa Inoue in 2007 and declared its ambition to be a global leading university ranked around 30 in the world. Nagoya University issued its action plan under President Michinari Hamaguchi, aiming to improve its international recognition. Hokkaido University set up a long-term plan of contributing to sustainable development.

8.3.5 Diversification of Financial Resources

Under the incorporation scheme, the governmental subsidy toward the operational expenditure of national universities was cut 1% every year from 2005 to 2009. Top universities aiming to be world-class universities were not exempted. As a result, the top research universities had to initiate fundraising campaigns for additional income by means of contract-based research for industry, collecting donations, etc. So far, they have successfully increased their total revenues, though the majority of the national universities have not been as successful as the top universities (Fig. 8.1).

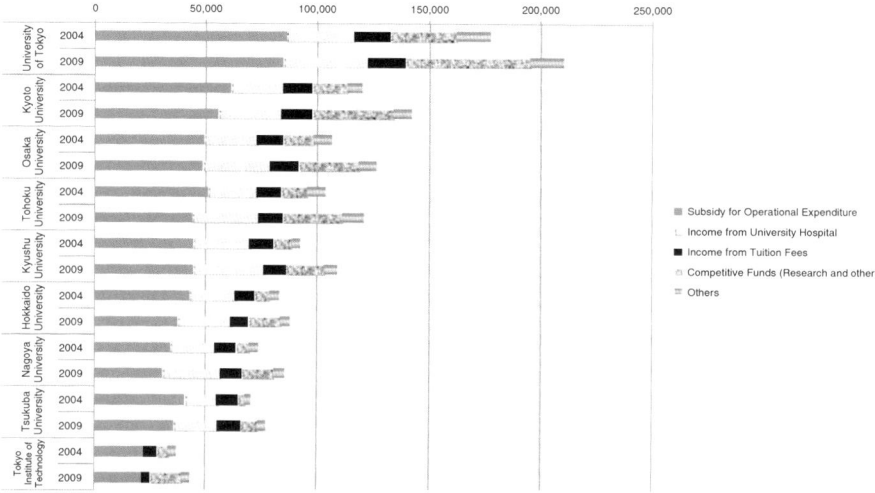

Fig. 8.1 Diversification of financial resources among top national universities (2004–2009) (Source: Annual financial report of prospective universities)

8.3.6 Internationalization

As referred to briefly earlier, the most serious current challenge for top Japanese universities trying to achieve distinguished global recognition is their internationalization. Based on the reputation survey conducted by *Times Higher Education*, the University of Tokyo was ranked eighth in the world in 2010. However, its international profile, which includes factors such as its share of international students and faculty members, is still low compared with top US and UK universities. Partly because of its relatively large faculty size, top Japanese national universities tend to be ranked higher in terms of their publication numbers, while the publication numbers per faculty are much more moderate. Moreover, regarding the impact of their publications, there is room for further improvement through the establishment of closer ties with the international research community (Kobayashi et al. 2007).

As a result of receiving incentive funds, such as from Global COE and Global 30, the top universities in Japan have tried to strengthen their international profiles, both in research and education, by setting targets to claim a certain share of international teachers and students. Providing attractive working conditions in Japan for world-renowned researchers is a big challenge, especially for universities located in mid-sized cities. Even so, Tohoku University, for example, continues its efforts to provide a world-renowned research environment, a competitive salary, and a good educational environment for the families of international professors. The University of Tokyo provides various academic positions under a differentiated salary scale for those working on projects for WPI or the endowment chairs.

   Attracting international students both at the undergraduate and graduate levels is even more important and challenging. For a country whose national language is not shared with other countries, at least historically, quite a few international academics enter the Japanese academic world as students, at least when starting out. Faced with a decrease in Japan's youth population and with globalization, it is crucial to encourage the next generation of researchers to be internationally competitive. Most of the top universities now provide postgraduate degree programs that are taught in English and covering a wide range of fields, including the humanities and social sciences.

   Providing a more international learning environment for undergraduate programs is also important both for improving international communication skills among Japanese students and for fostering in international students a deeper understanding of Japanese society. Waseda University, a top private university, set up the School of International Liberal Arts Studies in 2004 and offers an undergraduate liberal arts program both in English and Japanese in which Japanese and international students are taught together. Under the Global 30 scheme, the member universities are required to provide degree programs in English both at the undergraduate and graduate levels. For all national universities selected for the Global 30 scheme, the introduction of full-scale degree programs in English at the undergraduate level was a new experience. Starting with worldwide student recruitment and hiring international teaching staff to provide high-quality undergraduate classes, top Japanese universities are currently learning to operate internationally competitive education programs in the English language. On the other hand, such universities urgently need to improve the English communication skills of their students, the majority of whom mainly attend classes in Japanese. The Graduate School of Engineering of the University of Tokyo provides special English language lessons in collaboration with a language school. As well, it has developed a web-based self-learning system called SNOWBALLS for improving English among students (The University of Tokyo 2011). To improve the English-language teaching skills among faculty members, Tohoku University and Nagoya University organize training programs and send their faculty and graduate students to teacher training programs at universities in the USA and Australia.

   At the same time, top Japanese universities have made efforts to exchange students and researchers with other leading universities in the world. The University of Tokyo began the Four East Asian University Forum (BESETOHA) in 1999 together with Peking University, Seoul National University, and Vietnam National University, Hanoi, and its College of Arts and Sciences formed the East Asia Liberal Arts Initiative (ELAI) with them. The University of Tokyo also set up a program for exchanging researchers of Japanese studies with Yale University. Tohoku University and Tokyo Institute of Technology set up double-degree programs at the graduate level with Tsinghua University. Keio University, a top private university, set up double-degree programs with Fudan University in China and Yonsei University in Korea.

   Top Japanese universities also participate in university consortiums made up of leading universities in the world. The University of Tokyo, Kyoto University,

Tohoku University, Keio University, and Waseda University belong to the Association of Pacific Rim Universities (APRU). Waseda University is the only Japanese member of Universitas 21, and Nagoya University has a secretarial role in Academic Consortium 21. These consortiums are used as platforms for student and faculty exchanges.

8.4 A Change in the Ruling Party and the Consequences

8.4.1 Policy Revision by the Democratic Party of Japan

In September 2009, the Democratic Party of Japan (DPJ) replaced the government ruled by the Liberal Democratic Party (LDP) in a ruling position almost continuously since 1955. The emergence of the DPJ government, at least at the beginning, was expected to bring fundamental changes. The new government started its educational reform by focusing on secondary education rather than on higher education, increasing its financial support for families with children under the age of 18 years. At the same time, in the DPJ's manifesto, the party promised to cancel the annual 1% cut in the subsidy for the national universities' operational expenditures. The total subsidy for the operational expenditures of national universities was still cut by 0.94% in 2010.

In order for the DPJ to carry out the key policies listed in its manifesto while at the same time dealing with the government's debt, the new government actively utilized the budget screening reviews for the existing budgetary items. The review process was made public through the website and became one of the most popular policies of the new government.

The review started in November 2009 and has occasionally been used to analyze various budgetary items. Eventually, a review was conducted regarding the subsidy for the operational expenditures of national universities and the budget for various projects related to universities, science, and technology. The review advised that the subsidy be reconsidered and undergo a drastic budget cut.

In June 2010, Naoto Kan of the DPJ became the prime minister and set up the New Growth Strategy, which included new science and technology policies focused on investing in environment and life sciences innovations. Again, in order to carry out the new strategy and policies, all ministries were required to cut 10% of the budgetary request to the Ministry of Finance (MOF) in 2011. The government then implemented a "policy contest" requiring prospective ministries to bid on project proposals for revitalizing Japanese society. The MEXT requested a budgetary increase in education, science, and technology, declaring that an investment in human resources, science, and technology should be at the core of revitalization. In the policy contest, 71,474 public comments, the largest number of comments, were made in support of increasing university-related expenditures. Based on the result of the policy contest, the subsidy for the operational budgets for national universities was maintained at almost the same amount, and in 2011, the overall budget concerning universities was increased by 3%.

On March 11, 2011, the east side of Japan was hit by a series of disasters: a magnitude-9.0 earthquake, the resulting tsunami, and the accident at the Fukushima Daiichi nuclear power plant that followed. Among the top universities, Tohoku University and Tsukuba University suffered substantial damage to their facilities and laboratory equipment. The universities around Tokyo also bore some damage. As a result, many universities postponed the start of the spring term by about 1 month. Electrical power shortages occurred immediately after the earthquake and in the following summer because nuclear power plants all over Japan were disabled in order to reexamine their security in the event of another catastrophic earthquake and tsunami. Universities, as well as Japan's industrial sector, were asked to conserve electricity. Top research universities in particular had to refrain from laboratory work that required huge amounts of electricity. Some academics had to temporarily move to other universities in Japan and abroad to continue their research. However, within 3 months, most of them had returned to their own campuses and had resumed their education and research activities. The government is planning to provide a special budget in order to restore the facilities and equipment of those damaged universities. At the same time, it is examining the possibility of another drastic cut to the subsidy for operational expenditures for national universities in 2012.

8.4.2 Alliances Among Top Universities

With the increasing pressure from the dwindling public spending on the universities as well as science and technology, Japan's top universities strengthened their collaboration. In Japan, there are four major university associations, namely, Japan Association of National Universities (JANU), which is made up of all national universities; Japan Association of Public Universities (JAPU), which includes around 85% of the local public universities; Japan Association of Private Universities and Colleges (JAPUC), which includes around 20% of the relatively old, private universities; and Association of Private University of Japan (APUJ), which includes around 65% of private universities. Top national and private universities have been responsible for leading and representing prospective university associations as a whole. At the same time, these research universities share the common interest of needing support from the government, society, and industry in order to sustain their internationally competitive academic activities.

Facing the first budget spending review in November 2009, the presidents of former imperial (national) universities (Hokkaido University, Tohoku University, the University of Tokyo, Nagoya University, Kyoto University, Osaka University, and Kyushu University) and of two top private universities (Keio University and Waseda University) released a joint statement showing concern for the future of academia and the research capacity of Japanese universities. In August 2010, Tsukuba University and Tokyo Institute of Technology joined their consortium, which began to call itself Research University 11 (RU11). In August 2011, RU11 launched its official website and published its mission of getting Japan's research universities ready to face fierce global competition. The website reveals their intention to set up a "grand design" of the future perspective for research universities in Japan and increase the group's collaboration with industry.

Concerning the budgetary spending reviews, other groups, such as the member universities of the Global 30 scheme and Nobel Prize winners, also released a public statement advocating for investment in universities, science, and technology. In January 2011, the CCE of the MEXT published its Interim Report by the University Council of Japan, outlining a new grand design of higher education system of Japan that follows from the 2005 report. In it, mission diversification among universities was stressed, as was the promotion of partnerships between universities.

RU11 is also taking collaborative action to deal with the issue of world university rankings. In the summer of 2011, RU11 sent an official request for a revision of the *Times Higher Education*'s ranking methodology. The statement argues that the newly introduced "regional modification" of citation scores that gives different modification to different countries leads to large discrepancies in the ranking results of Japanese universities. RU11 also requested an increase in the Times Higher Education's information disclosure as well as transparency concerning its ranking processes.

After the disasters of March 2011, RU11 also took a leading role in stimulating discussion about a vision for the reconstruction. It did so by means of presidential statements and a series of symposiums. Tohoku University offered to take responsibility for advanced world research based on experiences from the disaster.

8.5 Conclusion

After establishing its world-class status during the 1990s, Japan pursued an official policy of fostering world-class universities in the first decade of the twenty-first century. Faced with the budgetary constraints of government debt, further improving its ranking position in the world became, in reality, a difficult task. However, the Japanese government and Japan's universities have made efforts toward that goal and have succeeded in maintaining the international reputation of its top universities, amid strong competition from both existing and emerging opponents.

The institutionalization of world-class university policy has progressed at the levels of national policy and university policy. At the national policy level, the government has encouraged universities to voluntarily choose different functions, including conducting world-class education and research. Toward this end, the government developed various project funds for promoting top-level research. The funds related to world-class research and education were awarded primarily to a limited number of comprehensive research universities, which compensated for the budgetary cut in the operational expenditure subsidy for national universities. The government also implemented the incorporation of all national universities but tried to maintain the existing structure of financial allocation, in which research universities have some advantages. At the same time, the government provided funds for supporting internationalization projects among universities, which would then represent the country.

At the university level, the top universities, especially national universities, implemented governance reforms during the incorporation process. At the same time, they developed their own management structures by establishing original and distinct action plans. Although the government subsidies for their operational budgets had decreased, even among top universities, they succeeded in increasing their total revenue by diversifying their income sources. They also tried to improve their international profiles in order to improve their international image.

The change in Japan's ruling party led to a reexamination of government educational policies. The funds related to supporting world-class universities were scrutinized in the budgetary spending reviews. The top universities collaborated with each other to underscore the importance of university education and research and set up a consortium comprised of research universities. At the same time, the new government began to emphasize the importance of science, technology, and innovation, and public support for investing in universities was promoted through a campaign led by leaders in universities and the science world. After the disasters in March 2011, the top universities actively committed themselves to the reconstruction process.

Faced with rapid changes in the internal and external environments, both the government and universities have undergone a major reexamination of why public funds should support the development of world-class universities in Japan. It would seem that the world-class university policies, through dialogue and discussion, have become deeply embedded in both national policy and the university management system in Japan.

References

Amano, I. (2008). *Daigaku Hojin Ka no Yukue* [Direction of incorporation of national universities]. Tokyo: Toshindo. [in Japanese].

Arima, A. (1989). *Kokuritsu Daigaku no Kiki* [Crisis in national universities]. *IDE* 307, 11–24. [in Japanese].

Asonuma, A. (2003). *Sengo Kokuritsu Daigaku niokeru Keijohi Hojo* [Subsidy for operational expenditure of national universities in post-war Japan]. Tokyo: Taga Press. [in Japanese].

Asonuma, A. (2010). *Daigaku to Gakumon* [University and academism]. Tokyo: Tamagawa University Press. [in Japanese].

Central Council for Education. (1963). *Daigaku Kyoiku no Kaizen ni tsuite* [University education reform]. Tokyo: Monbusho. [in Japanese].

Central Council for Education. (1971). *Kongo ni okeru Gakko Kyoiku no Sogo teki na Kakuju Seibi no tameno Kihonteki Shisaku ni tsuite* [Basic policy for total expansion of school education in the future]. Tokyo: Monbusho. [in Japanese].

Central Council for Education. (2005). *Wagakuni no Koto Kyoiku no Shoraizo* [The future of higher education in Japan]. Tokyo: MEXT. [in Japanese].

Hazelkorn, E. (2011). *Rankings and the reshaping of higher education: The battle for world-class excellence*. Hampshire: Palgrave Macmillan.

Kitagawa, F., & Oba, J. (2010). Managing differentiation of higher education system in Japan: Connecting excellence and diversity. *Higher Education, 59*(4), 507–524.

Kobayashi, M., Cao, Y., & Shi, P. (2007). *Comparison of global university rankings*. Tokyo: Center for Research and Development of Higher Education, University of Tokyo.

Lee, M. (2004). Global trends, national policies and institutional responses: Restructuring higher education in Malaysia. *Educational Research for Policy and Practices, 3*(1), 31–46.

Ma, W. (2007). The flagship university and China's economic reform. In P. G. Altbach & J. Balan (Eds.), *World class worldwide: Transforming research universities in Asia and Latin America* (pp. 31–53). Baltimore: Johns Hopkins University Press.

Nakayama, S., Goto, K., & Yoshioka, S. (Eds.). (1999). *Tsushi Nihon no Kagaku Gijutsu* [History of Japanese Science and Technology] 5(1). Tokyo: Gakuyo Shobo. [in Japanese].

National Commission on Educational Reform. (2000). *Kyoiku Kaikaku Kokumin Kaigi Hokoku* [Report of National Council on Educational Reform]. Tokyo: Prime Minister of Japan and his Cabinet.

Newby, H., Weko, T., Breneman, D., Johanneson, T., & Maassen, P. (2009). *OECD review of higher education: Japan*. Paris: OECD.

Ogawa, Y. (2002). Challenging the traditional organization of Japanese universities. *Higher Education, 43*(1), 85–108.

Osaki, H. (2011). *Kokuritsu Daigaku Hojin no Keisei* [Forming National University Corporation]. Tokyo: Toshindo.

Salmi, J. (2009). *The challenge of establishing world-class universities*. Washington, DC: The World Bank.

Shima, K. (2009). *Kyoso teki Shikin ni Chakumoku Shita Kokuritu Daigaku kan nai Shikin Haibun no Jittai* [Status of financial allocation within and among national universities: Focusing on competitive funds]. In Japan Educational Administration Society (Eds.), *Gakko to Daigaku no Governance Kaikaku* [Governance reform of schools and universities]. Tokyo: Research Institute for Educational Development. [in Japanese].

Shin, J., Toutkoushian, R. K., & Teichler, U. (Eds.). (2011). *University rankings: Theoretical basis, methodology and impacts on global higher education*. Dordrecht: Springer.

Terasaki, M. (1970). *Sengo no Daigaku Ron* [On Universities after World War II]. Tokyo: Hyoronsha. [in Japanese].

Terasaki, M. (1992). *Promenade Tokyo Daigaku Shi* [Promenade: History of the University of Tokyo]. Tokyo: Tokyo University Press. [in Japanese].

Uesugi, M. (2009). *Daigaku Shokuin ha Kawaru* [Changing university administrators]. Tokyo. Gakko Keiri Kenkyukai. [in Japanese].

Umakoshi, T. (1999). Kakkyo wo teisuru Ugoki ha Nihon wo Shinogu [Korea exceeds Japan in activeness in higher education]. *College Management, 17*(4), 21–23. [in Japanese].

Umakoshi, T. (2010). *Kankoku Daigaku Kaikaku no Dynamism* [Dynamism in Korean University Reform]. Tokyo: Toshindo. [in Japanese].

University Council. (1998). *21 Seiki no Daigaku Zo to Kongo no Kaikaku Hosaku ni tsuite* [Image of university in 21st century and reform policy in the future]. Tokyo: Monbusho. [in Japanese].

The University of Tokyo. (2010). *Action scenario: Forest 2015*. Tokyo: University of Tokyo.

The University of Tokyo. (2011). *Regional and interregional cooperation of universities*. Tokyo: University of Tokyo.

Yamamoto, S. (2002). Daigaku no Soshiki Keiei to Sore wo Sasaeru Jinzai [Organization and management of universities and the human resources]. *Journal of Higher Education Research, 5*, 87–107. [in Japanese].

Yonezawa, A. (2003). Making 'world-class universities': Japan's experiment. *Higher Education Management and Policy, 15*(2), 9–23.

Yonezawa, A. (2007). Japanese flagship universities at a crossroads. *Higher Education, 54*(4), 483–499.

Part III
WCUs in Non-English Speaking Developing Systems

Chapter 9
World-Class University in Korea: Proactive Government, Responsive University, and Procrastinating Academics

Jung Cheol Shin and Yong Suk Jang

9.1 Introduction

Competitiveness in knowledge production is critical to the Korean economy because the Korean economy entered into a knowledge-based economy in the late 1990s. The Korean economy is globally competitive in the semiconductor, electronics, mobile phone, ship building, and automobile industries. These industries rely heavily upon technological developments. Government policy prioritizes how to educate competitive manpower to support and lead international competition through producing leading-edge technology. At present, the knowledge base for these industries has been built through studying abroad in advanced countries and industry-based research institutes within Korea. In the mid-1990s the Korean government began to invest in the establishment of a knowledge base through competitive universities in Korea (Shin 2009a).

In the late 1990s, the Korean government began to aggressively invest in research and development (R&D) expenditure to support the national research capability. The share of R&D expenditure was 0.37% in 1970, 0.56% in 1980, 1.72% in 1990, 2.3% in 2000, and 3.47% in 2007 (Korean Ministry of Education, Science, and Technology 2010). Currently, Korea's share of R&D investment is the highest among the OECD countries. As part of the effort, the government began to develop a project to support university-based research. A well-known project is the Brain Korea 21 (BK 21) project which was launched in 1999. The project was designed to support the next generation of academics by supporting research funding.

J.C. Shin (✉)
Department of Education, Seoul National University, Seoul, Republic of (South Korea)
e-mail: jcs6205@snu.ac.kr

Y.S. Jang
Public Administration, Yonsei University, Seoul, South Korea
e-mail: yongsuk68@gmail.com

J.C. Shin and B.M. Kehm (eds.), *Institutionalization of World-Class University in Global Competition*, The Changing Academy – The Changing Academic Profession in International Comparative Perspective 6, DOI 10.1007/978-94-007-4975-7_9, © Springer Science+Business Media Dordrecht 2013

The project entered the second phase in 2006 and will be terminated in 2012. As well as the BK 21, the Korean government launched similar research projects. Recently, the Korean government began to support the humanities and social sciences research that used to be isolated from research funding. For example, Humanity Korea (HK) project was designed to support humanities and the Social Science Korea (SSK) project to support social science research.

With the technology-based industrial development and national investment in R&D, building a world-class university (WCU) became a hot issue among policymakers and academic leaders in the mid-2000s when the global rankings emerged. In response, the Korean government launched a funding project called *World-class University* in 2008. The world-class university has been a continuing issue in Asian society where hierarchy between universities is rigid and the hierarchy has been socially embedded in many aspects of society including the job market (Teichler 2011). With the emergence of world-class university and global rankings, many competitive Korean research universities began to establish their strategies for becoming a world-class university. These universities benchmarked the top-ranked international universities and the ranking indicators to enhance their ranking status by strategic efforts.

These strategic efforts have had a huge impact on many other Korean universities as well as their leading universities because the low-ranked universities benchmark the leading universities. For this chapter, we selected three representative research universities in Korea to explain and discuss how a WCU has been institutionalized in the representative Korean universities though we focused on Seoul National University as the case of Korea. Our focus in this chapter is to see how national policy led a WCU through policy initiatives and financial tools, how a university responded to government policy to build a WCU, and finally how professors responded to these governmental and institutional drivers. This approach enables us to understand what happened and how a WCU has become embedded in Korean higher education.

9.2 The Context of Korean Higher Education and the Selected Case

Korean higher education has developed rapidly since the 1980s, and its tertiary enrollment rate reached 98% in 2010. The development has three phases: the first phase in the 1980s, the second phase in the 1990s, and the third phase in the early 2000s. The first phase is represented as quantitative enrollment growth; in the second and the third phases, growth was qualitative as well as quantitative. This growth in Korean higher education is closely related to economic development in Korea. The Korean economy has been changing from a labor intensive economy to a skill and technology-based one since the 1980s and moving toward a knowledge-based economy from the late 1990s. These economic shifts require a knowledge base to support Korea's economic development.

Table 9.1 Research performance and global ranking of Korean universities

University	Publications	Citations	Citations/ Publications	ARWU	Times	QS
POSTECH	2,941	6,715	2.283	301–400	53	98
SNU	12,814	28,709	2.240	102–105	124	42
Yonsei	6,809	13,445	1.975	201–300	226–250	129
Korea	5,911	10,682	1.807	301–400	226–250	190
KAIST	4,776	8,268	1.731	201–300	94	90
SKK	5,239	9,063	1.730	301–400	301–350	259
Hanyang	4,350	6,718	1.544	301–400		314

Notes:
(a) The publication and citation data are adopted from Leydesdorff and Shin (2011)
(b) ARWU is based on the 2012 ranking, Times on 2011/2012, and QS ranking on 2011

As Marginson (2011) pointed out, the Korean government has been deeply involved in planning for national development since the early 1960s. Presidential Commission on Education Reform proposed a research university project in 1995. According to the project and its action plan, the Brain Korea 21 was launched in 1999. These efforts were fruitful in enhancing research productivity (Shin 2009a). In addition, these efforts contributed to the building of competitive research universities. According to Shin (2009b), there are seven research-focused universities in Korea. These universities are Seoul National University (SNU), Yonsei University, Korea University, Sungkyunkwan University, Hanyang University, and two science and technology—focused universities—Korea Advanced Institute of Science and Technology (KAIST) and Pohang University of Science and Technology (POSTECH).

Among the seven universities, SNU is the most prestigious leading national university in Korea. SNU does not have a board of trustees and has a strong tradition of faculty hierarchy between senior and junior professors. The cultural tradition is based on Korean's seniority-oriented culture of Confucian tradition. In addition, the German model, which accords a level of authority to senior professors, has been embedded in SNU through Japanese higher education during the colonial period. Concerning the governance, professors have a strong influence on academic affairs but not in administrative affairs (Shin 2011a). Historically, the Korean government tends not to be deeply involved in academic affairs although the national university is under government control. On the other hand, the Korean government is deeply involved in administrative affairs (e.g., personnel, finance, and administrative organization and management).

As the university rankings show in Table 9.1, SNU is the top university and has the largest graduate programs in Korea. It has been transforming its educational focus from undergraduate education to graduate education since the mid-1990s when globalization and knowledge-based economy emerged in Korea. SNU now emphasizes research productivity in its faculty hiring and promotion processes. Recently, its publications have been highlighted in the international media and in academic journals (e.g., Leydesdorff and Shin 2011). SNU obviously attempts to transform itself to a WCU that is able to compete with the best universities in the world.

9.3   Government Initiatives for a WCU: *Proactive*

The Korean government has been aggressively building a WCU since the mid-1990s. As many developing countries do, the Korean government established a quality assurance system in the early 1990s, launched a special research funding systems for a WCU in the late 1990s, and initiated governance reform in the mid-2000s. The Korean government uses research funding as its main policy tool and systemic changes as a supplementary tool to build a competitive WCU. This is because systemic changes such as mission differentiation and governance reform encounter strong resistance from academics.

9.3.1   Mission Differentiation Initiatives

The Presidential Commission for Education Reform, which was launched in 1985, released its report *Ten Agendas for Education Reform* in 1987 and proposed mission differentiations by identifying Korean universities as teaching-focused or research-focused universities (The Presidential Commission for Education Reform 1987). Since the release of the report, mission differentiation between universities has been continuously discussed by policymakers and the Presidential Committee for Education Reform which was organized in 1993 during the Kim Young-sam administration (The Presidential Commission for Education Reform 1997). However, the approach that the Korean government adopted was not direct involvement in mission differentiation by government initiatives as the *Master Plan* of California did in 1960.

Instead, the Korean government has promoted mission differentiation by providing special research funding for the research-productive universities and their academic units. The Korean government adopted a special research funding policy in 1999. The funding policy was proposed by the Presidential Committee for Education Reform in 1995 (*5.31 Education Reforms*). By the 5.31 Reforms proposal and Kim Dae Jung's administration's (1998–2002) decision, the Korean government adopted the Brain Korea 21 project in 1999 which was designed to build world-class research universities as a hub of knowledge production for the knowledge society (Shin 2009a).

In discussing government policy in Korea, a brief understanding of evaluation-based budget allocation is important because most government policy comes with evaluation-based funding. Evaluation-based funding is in line with neoliberal policy

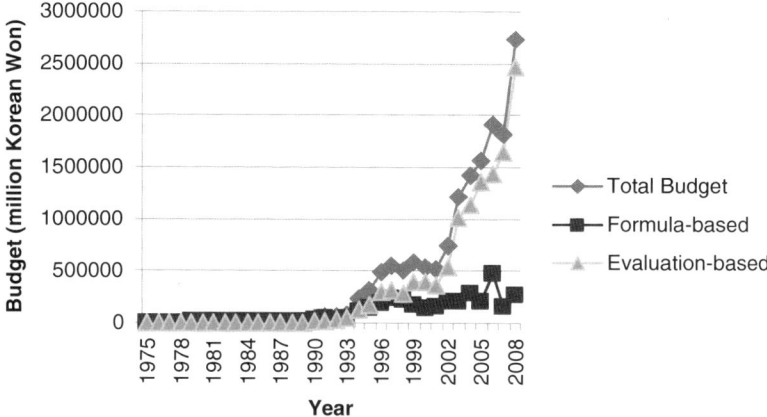

Fig. 9.1 Growth of evaluation-based budget (Data sources: Annual Education Statistics (1975–2008) Notes: The classification of budget by formula-based and evaluation-based budget is based on author's coding. The budget systems have been changed in Lee Myung-Bak administration (2008–2012), but the budget allocation mechanism is quite similar in terms that the budget allocation is based upon evaluation indicators)

which the 5.31 education reform is based upon. In Korea, evaluation-based funding has been increasing since the 1990s and currently most of the special budget is allocated by this evaluation. There are two reasons. The *Korean Ministry of Education* (the name of ministry has often been changed) tried to persuade the *Korean Ministry of Finance and Planning* (the name of ministry has often been changed too) to bring more budgets by applying evaluation-based budget allocation. The proposal was attractive to the Ministry of Finance and Planning because evaluation-based budgeting is in line with neoliberal thought that many in the Ministry of Finance and Planning prefer. Because of the compromise, most of the new budget items have been allocated by evaluation-based budgeting since the 1990s (Fig. 9.1).

The evaluation-based budget allocation has had a huge impact on universities. This is clear when the structure of the higher education budget is considered. The higher education budget consists of an operational budget for the public university and a special budget for both public and private universities. Most of operational budget for public universities consists of salary and building and maintenance costs; the special budget is provided for specific goals and is a policy tool well used by the Korean government because the special fund provides better opportunity for the grantees to advance in the competitive education environment. Because of the strong impact of the evaluation-based budget allocation on higher education, it is important to understand the budget allocation mechanism. The evaluation-based budget allocation has a protocol:

- The government releases project goals and evaluation indicators.
- A university prepares and submits its proposal to the government.

Table 9.2 Government initiatives to support research productivity

	Brain Korea 21		World-Class University	Humanity Korea project	Social Science Korea
	1st stage	2nd stage			
Duration	1999–2005	2006–2012	2008–2012	2008–2015	2010–2019
Total budget (US$)	1.4 billion	2 billion	825 million	400 million	120 million
Num. of project team	247	244	79	56	157

Notes: One US dollar is 1,000 Korean won

- The government evaluates the proposal and allocates budget based on the evaluation results.
- Finally, the government releases an evaluation report at the mid and/or end of the project.

The predetermined indicators have a strong influence on universities. The indicators include the current condition of university (per faculty student ratio, facility, finance, etc.), future plans associated with the proposed project goals, and their institutional performance. The indicators function as a guideline for the university. The evaluation-based budget allocation mechanism may or may not have a positive impact on Korean universities. Because of the strong influence of the indicators, most Korean universities are realigning their institutional policy to the government guidelines regardless of their mission focus, their sectors, their regional location, characteristics of their professors students, etc.

9.3.2 Research Funding Projects

According to the 5.31 Reforms proposal, the Korean government designed and implemented the BK 21 project to build world-class research centers in Korea. The research funding was allocated to a project team, which is an academic unit or multiple units. The project followed the same format as the evaluation-based budget allocation. The project supported 1.4 billion US dollars from 1999 to 2005 and the second project is being implemented from 2006 to 2012. The first project was successful according to an evaluative study by Shin (2009a). The Korean government was encouraged by the first step and launched the second project in 2006.

As well as the BK 21 project, the Korean government launched similar projects to enhance the research productivity of Korean universities. These funding projects are the *World-Class University* project, the *Humanity Korea project*, and the *Social Science Korea projects*. The last two projects (Humanity Korea and Social Science Korea) are focused on supporting academic research in the soft disciplines—humanities and social sciences. Compared with the other projects, the World-Class University project is intending to build a world-class university through inviting distinguished international scholars and supporting Korean academics in conducting research with distinguished scholars (Table 9.2).

As a second step of the World-Class University project, the Korean government is planning to support graduate programs by providing special funding for talented graduate students (the project is called the post-WCU project.) The new initiative is endeavoring to train talented PhD students as the next academic generation. The new initiative is related to the fact that only 60% of Korean academics have been trained by a Korean university (Shin 2012) and that Korean university-trained academics tend to be less preferred by Korean universities.

Therefore, the new initiative sets out to attract talented Korean PhD students in Korean universities and train them as competitive scholars in the global market. To efficiently manage these various projects, the Korean government merged the former Korea National Research Foundation, which was for social sciences and humanities, and the Korea Science and Engineering Foundation, into the National Research Foundation of Korea in 2009 (National Research Foundation of Korea 2011). This organizational change is intended to produce more efficient and better-managed research funding in Korea.

9.3.3 Governance Reforms

As well as mission differentiation and research funding policy, Korean government has initiated a policy to deregulate universities in order to allow more autonomy. The deregulation policy assumes that institutional autonomy will enhance the competitiveness of universities. The Korean Ministry of Education attempted to get rid of university regulation in the 1990s and the 2000s (Shin et al. 2007). Also, the current Lee Myung-Bak administration (2008–2012) has actively applied a deregulation policy. Through the policy initiatives, the Korean government reduced a much of the regulatory intervention in universities. However, it is unclear whether universities feel that they are more autonomous after the government's deregulation because there are perceptual differences between academics and government on the autonomy and regulations (Shin et al. 2007).

The Korean government launched a new quality assurance system in 2008 which gave autonomy to higher education institutions. Under the former system, Korean universities were supposed to receive accreditation from the Korean Council for University Education. Although it was a voluntary accreditation, most Korean universities received accreditation from the Korean Council for University Education (KCUE). Under the new system, established in 2008, Korean universities are required to conduct self-evaluation, and thus, the new system allows more autonomy to higher education institutions. Universities may receive accreditation from a quality assurance agency, but that is up to university to decide.

Going even further, the Korean government set out to transform national universities from national organizations to independent public corporations to allow autonomy in personnel, finance, and management. This governance change was proposed in the late 1980s by the Korean Council for University Education (1989).

However, it was not adopted as an official policy agenda until 2006 because of strong political resistance from universities and professors. After the Korean government initiated the policy in 2006, there was strong resistance from the universities. Currently, one newly established university (Ulsan National Institute of Science and Technology) achieved public corporation status in 2009. The SNU Corporation Law passed in the National Assembly in 2010 and the SNU have public corporation status in 2012. The incorporation of national universities may provide greater autonomy to Korean higher education.

Nevertheless, academics do not perceive that their university is autonomous from the government regulation. Shin and Park (2007) conducted a study to explore where and why the perceptual differences between government and academics occurred. They found that the government has been deeply involved in higher education institutions through various means such as inspection, providing guidelines, and providing official memorandums. In general, however, according to the Changing Academic Profession data which was collected in 2008, Korean academics feel that the Korean government is not deeply involved in academic and procedural areas in the universities. Only 1.3% of academics perceive that the Korean government is involving in university affairs (Shin 2011). These results tend to support the view that the deregulation policy works to some extent.

9.4 University's Response: *Responsive*

In these sociopolitical contexts, Korean universities have adapted themselves to the government policies. Korean universities are responsive to the evaluation indicators proposed by the government because special funding (rather than operational budget) is allocated on the basis of the government's evaluation. As a response to government policy toward a competitive WCU, most of the research-productive universities have aggressively responded though their responses differ by university and their academic unit (college and department) within a university.

9.4.1 University Administration

University administration (university headquarter) is aggressive in adjusting itself to changing environments. SNU prepared a long-term plan to realign its vision and goals with the knowledge society. SNU organized a task force in 2006 to prepare an SNU strategic plan for 2007–2025. According to the plan, SNU is striving to be a top 10 university globally by 2025 (Committee for SNU Strategic Plan 2007). To achieve the goal, the committee proposed an agenda in nine areas (e.g., quality of education, research competitiveness, internationalization, governance, finance, and campus building, and facility).

SNU has prepared action plans to implement the strategic plan. For example, SNU organized a task force to transform its governance from being a government organization to a public corporation in 2009 and proposed a plan that led to the Public Corporation of Seoul National University Act in 2010 (Committee for Public Corporation of SNU 2010). The public corporation act would allow flexibility in administrative organization, personnel (e.g., faculty hiring and promotion), and management. This flexibility in turn would allow SNU to make timely responses to changes in the environment. However, still there is a controversy on the relevance of the policy because professors, especially in soft disciplines, worry that their disciplines have been isolated by the governance changes; administrative staffs are concerned about their job security; and students worry that tuition will be increased.

In addition, in 2008 SNU began to aggressively hire international professors and to attract international students to enhance the internationalization of the university (Shin 2012). Hiring international professors is supported by government policy which has set aside special funding for hiring internationally distinguished professors. The number of international professors hired reached 200 which is approximately 10% of the total professorial body. The number of international students has also increased considerably. The proportion of international students among undergraduates is 7.6% and among graduate students it is 13.9% (SNU Fact Book 2011). These ratios are high when compared with the numbers in 2000, when undergraduate students were at 0.2% and graduate students at 2.5%. To teach international students, SNU encouraged its professor to teach their courses in English by providing funding incentives and by reducing teaching hours. Currently, 558 courses are taught in English (SNU Office of International Affairs 2011).

SNU also began to hire more professors to compete with global universities. SNU is the largest in terms of the number of faculty in Korea, but its total number of professors was less than 2,100 which is quite small compared with many competitive universities elsewhere in the world (Shin 2009b). In point of fact, larger universities benefit in global rankings because the rankings do not take into account the size of the university. Rankers generally count the number of publications and citations without considering the size of the university. Although there is a difference of opinion on the effects of faculty size on research productivity, a small university may have difficulty in increasing the number of publications and citations and thereby improving its ranking.

As well as these changes, SNU upgraded its evaluation criteria. In 2001, the university decided not to allow tenure status for associate professors. Associate professors are now required to publish more papers if they wish to be promoted and tenured at SNU. Since 2011, in addition, SNU now also requires a professor to provide recommendation letters from distinguished scholars in the field to be promoted to full professor. These processes have forced junior professors to internalize the *publish or perish* culture. Currently, SNU is discussing how to improve the quality of publications because the university's research productivity per capita has already reached the top level worldwide (Shin 2012).

These initiatives require new funding sources to support them. To that end, the university began to aggressively search for external funding from public and private

Table 9.3 University development fund and external research fund

University		2007	2008	2009
SNU	Development fund (gift/donation)	53,081	40,299	51,134
	External research funds	351,237	381,673	422,877
Yonsei	Development fund (gift/donation)	62,929	78,338	56,915
	External research funds	196,101	211,594	239,922
Korea	Development fund (gift/donation)	55,001	41,982	53,292
	External research funds	108,892	126,643	153,561

Data source: University Information Providing System (http://www.academyinfo.
go.kr/mainAction.do?process=load)
Notes: Units is million Korean won

sources. One such fund is called a *university development fund*. The development fund is similar to *endowments* and *gifts* in the USA. Endowers may tie their donation to a specified purpose or not. The university development fund is the primary source for investment in capital expenditures (e.g., building a new facility, lab, computer facility) and hiring competitive professors. The university fund has increased during the 2000s when many Korean universities have begun to pursue becoming a WCU (Table 9.3).

Through the institutionalization processes, the influence of the university presidents has increased and shared governance is losing its influence on campus. As Shin (2011b) has discussed, government involvement has decreased during the current decade and the shared governance model is losing its influence within higher education institutions. Planning and evaluation functions have become critical for a WCU if they are to upgrade their competitiveness in the global market. Consequently the university administration has become empowered and is now the strongest actor in higher education governance. The incorporation of a national university in Korea accelerates this trend.

9.4.2 College/Department Level

As well as the university administration, individual colleges began to respond to the changing educational environment. Some colleges are aggressive while others are not. Often, colleges in hard disciplines (engineering, natural science, medicine, etc.) are aggressive while those in the soft disciplines (social sciences, arts, and humanities) are defensive in their response. In the late 1990s, the College of Natural Science has adopted a policy to promote the research productivity of their professors. For example, the college began to discourage their professors from doing service work (e.g., act as an editorial member of a domestic journal, as a board member of a domestic academic association) because these service activities might take away time from research. In addition, the College of Engineering began to upgrade faculty hiring and promotion criteria to enhance its research performance and required their professors to publish in highly regarded international journals.

As well as these efforts, the individual colleges began to attract external research funding to support their professors. Some colleges or departments actively have engaged in national projects such as BK 21, the World-Class University project, the Humanity Korea project, the Social Science Korea projects, or other research funding opportunities from public or private funding sources (see Table 9.3). For example, the Department of Education at the College of Education, SNU is involved in the first and second BK 21 project, and two project teams are funded by the SSK project. An important initiative was proposed and institutionalized in the College of Education at SNU. In the Faculty Personnel Committee discussions of the College of Education in 2006, the committee decided to require a certain number of publications in Science Citation Index, Social Science Citation Index, or Arts and Humanities Citation Index journals in most major areas.

As a result, professors began to focus on research in order to be able to publish more papers in international journals. They also began to apply for external research funding for their research and to hire graduate students as research assistants. With an increase in the number of professors working with their graduate students, both graduate students as well as professors have increased the number of papers published. Some departments (or programs) even require their graduate students to publish a certain number of papers before they can defend their master's thesis or dissertation. For example, in 2007 the *Educational Administration and Policy Studies* program in the Department of Education at SNU began to require master students to publish one paper in an academic journal and PhD students to publish two. This requirement encourages graduate students to team with their professors on research projects. The Department of Education established a committee called a *Committee for Department Development* in 2008 to respond to for the needs to be more competitive. The committee studied and discussed a plan for long- and short-term actions to reshape the department and to strategically respond to this demand. The committee consists of a senior professor, an associate professor, and an assistant professor. The committee reports their ideas to the department whenever there is an issue. Although it takes a long time to produce major changes, these strategic efforts and the new environments are intertwined and are leading to the emergence of a new culture among academics.

9.5   Academics' Responses: Responsive or Counteractive?

The academics' response toward the WCU initiative by the government and their universities ranges from responsive to counteractive. The changes caused by the WCU initiative have huge impacts on academics' campus life. Academics are quite resistant if the changes are related to their job security and working conditions. Their attitude about the changes may differ depending on their age, academic discipline, and general perception, but they do respond in order to survive in the demanding academic environments.

9.5.1 Counteractive Response

Academics are quite resistant to the government initiative and university's responses toward the WCU movement. The resistance occurs when the university tries to change the system of governance, funding systems, personnel systems, etc. For example, academics were quite negative about the proposal to transform public universities to public corporations. Professors object to the governance changes because they are concerned that the changes may isolate them from the campus-wide decision-making process and they may find themselves in an even more competitive culture on campus.

The Korean government and SNU have tried to transform the current seniority-based systems into a meritocracy. The current salary system is based on years of teaching in most universities although some universities including the national university provide incentives based on performance (mainly on research performance). However, even the incentive system does not work as designed because the financial incentive is given to senior professors, proving that the meritocracy does not work among Korean academics. To change these practices, the Korean Ministry of Education decided to adopt an annual salary system in 2010 for implementation in 2011; however, there were objections from professors and finally the government compromised and agreed to apply it to newly hired professor from 2011 and to current professors from 2015.

SNU now has a more rigid faculty evaluation system to enhance its productivity. Before 2002, associate professors were tenured, but SNU decided not to allow tenure status to associate professors unless they demonstrated internationally distinguished performance (Kim 2007). However, this new policy did not apply to current professors at that time. The College of Education also adopted a policy that requires professors (full-time lecturer, assistant professor, and associate professor) to publish a certain number of articles in an international journal in 2006. However, these new requirements have met with strong faculty resistance, and the college compromised by applying the new policy to newly hired faculty only. The fact that the university president and college dean are elected by faculty vote explains why the faculty have such influence (Shin 2011).

As these cases show, most professors, especially established professors, are quite negative about these changes. Interestingly, most academics recognize the problems with the current governance, salary, and personnel systems. However, there have been changing patterns of faculty culture since the emergence of a WCU. Individual professors have begun to reallocate their time to produce more papers. For example, they have assigned more time to research, and reduced their time on teaching and service activities (Shin 2011). However, this has led to conflict between senior and junior professors. In a seniority-based society like Korea and Japan, senior academics tend to assign their service work to the junior academics. Under the pressure to publish, junior professors are in a dilemma: They are required by their senior colleagues to put more time into service activities, but their evaluation criteria also require them to publish more. This tension is becoming serious in the academic units where service activities are critical to their fields.

In the transitional environment, these conflicts are between disciplines, between junior and senior professors, and between professors with different perceptions. The gaps may grow wider in the changing environment and may not be short-term.

- *Disciplinary gaps*: Academics are quite different in their perceptions, their academic epistemology, their way of working with their students, etc. The differences are quite clear between academics in hard and soft disciplines (Biglan 1973). This is evident even in a college such as a College of Education. The college has humanities (literature, philosophy, history etc.), social sciences (policy and administration, economics, political sciences, sociology etc.), natural sciences (physics, biology, chemistry, earth science etc.), and engineering (engineering education).
- *Generational gaps*: There are generation gaps between junior and senior professors. Junior professors may be proactive about the changes and may wish to put more weight on research and in turn reduce teaching and service activities. Because of these different attitudes, there are continuous conflicts between junior and senior professors. Senior professors wish that junior professors would work more on service activities and support senior professors' activities. On the other hand, junior professors wish to conduct more research to meet the newly established evaluation criteria and reduce their service and teaching loads.
- *Perceptional gaps*: Some professors are aggressive in their support of a WCU while the others are neutral or opposed. Some professors may put more weight on the value of preserving the departmental traditions, while the others may favor the new vision and embrace the challenges of the future. Quite often, the different perspectives are in competition in determining how to enhance competitiveness in their own academic units.

Because of the conflicts and rapid changes that relate to the WCU initiative, professors often find their job stressful and their job satisfaction low. The CAP data showed that 76.9% of Korean academics reported their academic job is a source of stress. Surprisingly, however, their job satisfaction (77%) is the second highest among the 19 participating countries (Shin 2011). This finding shows that although Korean academics feel that their job is quite stressful, they are satisfied with their current job. There may therefore be another factor that makes them happy with their academic job.

9.5.2 Responsive Changes

Under this difficult environment, professors have had to find a way to survive and adapt to the changing patterns of faculty culture since the emergence of the WCU model at SNU. Individual professors have begun to reallocate their time to

Table 9.4 Academic performance of the department of education

Publication		2006	2007	2008	2009	2010
Article publication per professor	Domestic journal	1.49	1.97	2.12	1.85	1.82
	International journal	0.20	0.57	0.38	1.07	0.61
Article publication per student	Domestic journal	0.23	0.63	1.46	1.45	0.88
	International journal	0.02	0.04	0.10	0.06	0.04

Data source: *Annual Report of Brain Korea 21 Project Team (2006–2010)*, Academic Leadership Institute for Competence-Based Education, Department of Education, Seoul National University (http://competency.snu.ac.kr/eng/)

produce more papers, assigning more time to research, and reducing their time on teaching and service activities. They have also begun to collaborate with each other to produce more papers. For example, a government guideline indicates that a paper published in a journal by one author is counted as "100%" but that one published with a colleague counts as "70%." Clearly the professor who can publish a paper by himself or herself can add another professor's name to the paper with only a minimum contribution, thus producing a total of 140% rather than 100% (70% × 2 = 140%). Although collaboration is encouraged, the collaboration in this case may not produce better results because while producing more papers, the quality of the research in not improved.

In addition, professors, especially junior professors, have begun to coauthor with their students. This provides an opportunity for graduate students to work with their professors and learn from them. This is also encouraged by national research projects such as BK 21, HK, SSK, and WCU. The number of student publications is regarded highly by the evaluation indicators. Because of these factors, professors are actively engaging in collaborative work with their students and their colleagues. It is unclear whether an increase in collaborative work will produce better results, but government policy and the institutional environment has affected the increase in collaboration and change in academic culture (Table 9.4).

Faculty members have also sought to work with international colleagues on the publication. They frequently attend international conferences, and invite distinguished scholars to SNU to interact with them in their research and share their academic experience. Some departments have hosted international conferences to increase the opportunities for collaboration with international peers and to publish in international journals. Academics' pattern of sabbatical leave is changing too. Many academics used to consider the sabbatical as a period of relaxation after they had served their university; however, academics are now more inclined to consider their sabbatical leave as an opportunity to collaborate with their international colleagues and get published in international journals.

These changes affect the academic culture of the universities reviewed here. These changes are occurring widely although the changes differ by university and academic units. The changes are summarized as follows:

• Meritocracy in academia: A growing number of departments are applying merit criteria (research productivity, course evaluation) in the evaluation. This was formerly based on seniority but is now changing because global standards are being embedded in Korean universities.

- Sharing research performance: Korean academics used to *hide* their research from their colleagues because academics who *take pride in their research* were not welcomed. However, the academic culture has begun to encourage the exchange of research products among academics. The university often provides research products to the media to enhance the university's reputation.
- Division of labor between professors: The division of labor between academics is a hot issue in institutional policy though most academics consider themselves to be efficient both in teaching and research. Professors began to discuss the division of labor between teaching, research, and service, allowing them to engage in higher research productivity and improved teaching quality.

9.6   Concluding Remarks

This chapter described and discussed how the WCU model has been initiated and encouraged by government policy, how Korean universities responded to the policy, and finally how the academics are struggling to adapt to this new environment. In general, the government has been quite aggressive as the initiator of the WCU model, universities have been responsive to the government policy, and academic reactions are varied (active but counteractive at the same time).

Implementing the policy initiatives, the Korean government used financial tools to reform universities in the directions the government wished to pursue. At this point, the policy initiatives appear to have been successful. Korean academics' research productivity is the highest among the 19 CAP countries and the ISI data also show that Korea has the fastest growing academic publication rate among the OECD countries (Shin 2012). The rapid growth of research productivity is reflected in global rankings as seven universities are ranked within the top 400 universities. In addition, Korea is emerging as a strong competitor in international patent registration in the three representative patent offices (the USA, European Union, and Japan) (Park and Leydesdorff 2010).

In responding to the rapidly changing institutional environment, many Korean universities with different backgrounds attempt to conform to the emerging global standard, the WCU model. Korean universities have experienced changes in governance, academic culture, and teaching and research systems. In an effort to adopt more flexible governance, SNU has changed its legal status from government organization to public corporation. In addition, Korean universities began to aggressively secure external research funds from the government and private sectors. These new sources provide better research environments, e.g., experiment lab, computer facility, and new building. In addition, Korean universities began to hire international professors and students. Although in the early stages, Korean universities are paying attention to transforming teaching and research systems in order to enhance research productivity without sacrificing teaching quality. These new initiatives may result in Korean universities being a strong competitor in the global market.

In the face of the changes caused by global competition and the expansion of the WCU model, Korean academics have responded to the demands with some difficulty, with conflict between different disciplines, generations, and personal perspectives. Through various efforts and collaboration, Korean academics have changed their culture and set a new vision and goals. Previously, academic scholarship was imported and established by westerners or indirectly through the scholars who studied abroad, but now Korean academics are emerging as strong competitors in the global knowledge market.

Exploring the institutionalization of the WCU model in Korean higher education, we observe different reactions of the related actors: The government is aggressive, universities are responsive, and academics are struggling to respond to these changes. These changes have resulted in higher stress for Korean academics, but it has also contributed to the growth of knowledge production. What have we gained and what have we lost in the process? How to better shape the future for Korean society needs further discussion. The government initiatives and universities' responses may serve as benchmarks for other countries, but to be benchmarked by other countries, we need to answer the question: "Are we on the right path?"

References

Biglan, A. (1973). The characteristics of subject matter in different academic areas. *Journal of Applied Psychology, 57*(3), 195–203.

Committee for Public Corporation of SNU. (2010). *Proposal for Public Corporation of Seoul National University Act (unpublished report)*. Seoul: Committee for Public Corporation of SNU.

Committee for Seoul National University Strategic Planning. (2007). *SNU strategic plan for 2007–2025*. Seoul: Committee for Seoul National University Strategic Planning.

Kim, K. (2007). A great leap forward to excellence in research at Seoul National University, 1994–2006. *Asia Pacific Education Review, 8*(1), 1–11.

Korean Ministry of Education, Science, and Technology. (2010). *The survey of research and development in science and technology (each year from 1970 to 2010)*. Seoul: Korean Ministry of Education, Science, and Technology.

Leydesdorff, L., & Shin, J. (2011). How to evaluate universities in terms of their relative citation impacts: Fractional counting of citations and the normalization of differences among disciplines. *Journal of the American Society for Information Science and Technology, 62*(6), 1146–1151.

Marginson, S. (2011). Higher education in East Asia and Singapore: Rise of the confucian model. *Higher Education, 61*(5), 587–611.

National Research Foundation of Korea. (2011, June 26). *About National Research Foundation of Korea*. The material is available at: http://www.nrf.re.kr/html/en/about/about_02_01.html

Park, H., & Leydesdorff, L. (2010). Longitudinal trends in networks of university-industry-government relations in South Korea: The role of programmatic incentives. *Research Policy, 39*, 640–649.

Seoul National University. (2011). *Fact book (each year)*. The report is available from: http://www. snu.ac.kr/about/ab0501_list.jsp

Seoul National University Office of International Affairs. (2011). *International programs*. The report is available from: http://oia.snu.ac.kr/

Shin, J. (2009a). Building world-class research university: The Brain Korea 21 project. *Higher Education, 58*, 669–688.

Shin, J. (2009b). Classifying higher education institutions in Korea: A performance-based approach. *Higher Education, 57*(2), 247–266.

Shin, J. (2011). South Korea: Decentralized centralization: Fading shared governance and rising managerialism. In W. Locke, W. Cummings, & D. Fisher (Eds.), *Changing governance and management in higher education: The perspective of the academy* (pp. 321–342). New York: Springer.

Shin, J. (2012). Foreign PhDs and Korean PhDs: How they are different in their academic activity, performance, and culture. In D. Neubauer & K. Koroda (Eds.), *Mobility and migration in Asian Pacific Higher Education*. New York: Palgrave.

Shin, J., & Park, H. (2007). Various types of governmental intervention in higher education. *The Korean Journal of Educational Administration (Korean), 25*(4), 315–339.

Shin, J., Kim, M., & Park, H. (2007). Perceptional differences between government and universities on institutional autonomy. *The Journal of Educational Administration (Korean), 25*(3), 243–269.

Teichler, U. (2011). The social contexts and systemic consequence of university rankings: A meta-analysis of the ranking literature. In J. Shin, R. Toutkoushian, & U. Teichler (Eds.), *University ranking: Theoretical basis, methodology, and social impacts*. New York: Springer.

The Presidential Commission for Education Reform. (1997). *Education reform for the 21st century: To ensure leadership in the information and globalization era*. Seoul: The Presidential Commission for Education Reform.

The Presidential Commission for Education Reform. (1987). *Ten agendas for education reform*. Seoul: The Presidential Commission for Education Reform.

Chapter 10
Building World-Class Universities in China

Yan Luo

10.1 World-Class University: A Century's Dream of China

China has a long history as a great nation. In the first millennium to 1,000 CE, China accounted for about 25% of the world economy. It maintained roughly 23% in the following 500 years. In fact, within this 1,500 year period, the Chinese economy had doubled that of Western Europe, which had been ranked as the second largest economy in the world. However, the early eighteenth century witnessed a reversal. In the missing of the first revolution of technology and science and later becoming a victim of the colonialism of the Western countries, China declined rapidly in the following two centuries. The Chinese national economic gross dropped to 17% of the global total in 1897, 8.9% in 1913, and 4.5% in 1950 (Maddison 2001).

Along with the declining national economy was the disorganization of Chinese social institutions. The year 1911 witnessed the collapse of the political institutions of the empire together with the imperial education and examination systems. Chinese contribution to world knowledge system largely discontinued. Chinese intellectual elites, suffering from self-doubt, started to look to the West. The modern education system, including universities, in China was imported from the West in the nineteenth century. By 1912, China had only 18 universities, 13 of which were church-based universities. Of the remaining five Chinese universities, three were actually under the control of missionaries (Ye 2009). However, the number of Chinese universities grew very fast and outnumbered the church universities in the 1930s.

Despite their growth, Chinese universities were not able to train qualified faculty for their own universities. All PhD holders in China were trained in the West, obtaining their degrees mainly from the United States, Germany, and France.

Y. Luo (✉)
Institute of Education, Tsinghua University, Beijing, China
e-mail: luoy11@mail.tsinghua.edu.cn

J.C. Shin and B.M. Kehm (eds.), *Institutionalization of World-Class University in Global Competition*, The Changing Academy – The Changing Academic Profession in International Comparative Perspective 6, DOI 10.1007/978-94-007-4975-7_10,
© Springer Science+Business Media Dordrecht 2013

Recognizing this as a kind of dependence, Chinese intellectual elites advocated the independence of the Chinese academy should be one of the primary goals of national modernization. Among the prestigious figures, Shi Hu (胡适, 1891–1962) was one of the few who had proposed that China needed a world-class university and what such a world-class university should be like. Hu's formula of four conditions provides the Chinese definition of a WCU if Mohrman's argument is right that the goal of world-class status is clear, though the definition of world-class status is not (Morhman et al. 2008):

1. Chinese universities should be able to provide training on modern (academic) disciplines so that Chinese students do not need to study abroad.
2. Those who are trained in modern disciplines should be able to find a place (in China) so they can research further in the fields they are interested (to generate new knowledge).
3. National needs in health, industry, security, etc., should be addressed by domestic talent and research institutions in China.
4. Chinese domestic talent and research institutions, as part of the global academic community, should collaborate with the research talent and institutions worldwide, contributing to human knowledge and welfare.

Hu named his plan A Ten-Year Plan to Resume (Chinese) Academic Independence (Hu 1998). Because the plan was formulated by Hu in 1940s, it was not implemented because of the Sino-Japanese war and then the civil war between the Communist Party and the Kuomintang (KMT).

However, Hu's idea of seeking national academic independence as a leader of the new culture movement in China was well accepted by Chinese intellectuals including the communists.

10.2 The Initiatives of WCU as a National Policy

The end of the 1940s witnessed the establishment of Communist China. The Chinese communists rejected the Kuomintang (KMT) learning model of the Western approach. They adopted the Soviet model instead. They believed a planned and centralized social system would fit China better because the country was still in the early stages of industrialization.

Therefore, they established a centralized and specialized system in the field of science and higher education. This system was effective in particular of the fields related to national defense. In view of the party reformers in 1980s, however, this system had one great weakness – namely, knowledge production was largely disengaged from the national economy. This was because of, on the one hand, the separation of knowledge production from common production and, on the other, the separation of knowledge production from the training of top talent. By building world-class universities based on research universities, the party reformers believed that they would reconnect knowledge with production and the training of top talent.

10.2.1   Yuasa Law and Zhao's Strategy of "Red Light Effect"

The idea of a world-class university is globally important in the field of higher education, and the research on it in China can be traced back to a well-known study named Yuasa Law in the field of science studies in the mid-twentieth century. Based on the theoretical framing of Bernal (1954), Mintomo Yuasa, a Japanese historian of science, used statistics to illustrate Bernal's theory of the shifting of world science activities center (Yuasa 1962). According to Bernal and Yuasa, world science activities experienced a series of shifts from Italy to the United Kingdom (the first shift), from the United Kingdom to France (the second shift), from France to Germany (the third shift), and from Germany to the United States (the fourth shift). Each stage lasted on average for 80 years.

Hongzhou Zhao (赵红州), a renowned Chinese scholar, using a copy of Great Events in Science, independently uncovered a similar trend in 1974 when he was sent to Henan province during the Cultural Revolution. Unlike Bernal and Yuasa who believed that the Soviet Union would become the next science center of the world, Zhao believed that China would have a chance to lead global knowledge production under the "effect of red light." In other words, that China would eventually surpass developed countries while they waited for a "green light" (Yuan 2005).

Although both Yuasa and Zhao failed in their prediction (since there is no evidence that United States will cease to be the center of global science activities in the near future), the efforts of Zhao and his colleagues provided Chinese policymakers with the ambition of improving the contribution of Chinese science and technology in the world. Zhao was later recruited by the China Academy of Science, on the strong recommendation of Xuesen Qian, the father of Chinese nuclear and space technology. With great efforts, Zhao established a new research field scientometrics in China and became a leading figure in it.

In 1987, China published its first university ranking in the Daily of Science and Technology, an authoritative publication in the field of science and technology. It was a national ranking (of universities) based on scientometric indicators. This was a bold innovation by Zhao and his team. Examining the 1987 ranking, we find that it was different from most of the rankings appearing later. Zhao's was an effort to capture the essence of the competitiveness of knowledge production at an institutional level, rather than functioning mainly as a "consumer guide" for higher education as most rankings do (Luo 2006).

The Academic Ranking of World Universities (ARWU) published by Shanghai Jiaotong University in 2003 and now known worldwide followed the same path. As Niancai Liu, the founder of ARWU, remarked often, "ARWU is an unexpected outcome when we focused on uncovering the distance between us (Chinese elite universities) and the world-renowned universities (according to the scientometric scale of knowledge production competitiveness)."

10.2.2 WCU Legitimized as National Policy

Although it was mainly an ideation of academic elites in the beginning, WCU later became a national policy in China. Inspired by the successful experiences in developing nuclear weapons and space technology in the 1950s–1970s, the party elites believed that science was the field that relied more on the talents and resource projection rather than national gross GDP.

The Party Central jointly together with the State Council promoted an important document entitled *China Education Reform and Development Outline* in 1993 (http://www.moe.edu.cn/publicfiles/business/htmlfiles/moe/moe_177/200407/2484.html). It argued that

> We are living in the world where international politics change rapidly, science and technology develop quickly and the global competitions are fierce. ... the nation that leads education in the 21st century will ultimately obtain a strategic position in the coming global competition.

Therefore,

> Focused resources at both the national and provincial level should be projected to a group of key universities (around 100) and key disciplines and programs, so that a certain number of universities and programs will be upgraded to the world-class level of quality in the sense of teaching, research and governance.

This is the first time when WCU was incorporated into an important document released by the Chinese government. Being a policy cornerstone in the era of party reformers, the outline signaled the new rationality that favors higher education had emerged. This new rationality was continued in the 985 Project and was again consolidated in the *Medium and Long-Term Program for Education Reform and Development 2010–2020*, released in 2010 (Yang and Welch 2011).

As the government's ambition becomes more pronounced, WCU becomes an important theme in the Chinese academy. Figure 10.1 illustrates the number of papers on WCUs published in China during the period 1993–2010, which, in the viewpoints of the authors, indicated the shift in WCU from a vision shared by a handful of elites to the Chinese academic community at large.

This is of great significance. According to the theory of neo-institutionalism, a new rationality (cultural-cognitive meaning system) should be established before new institutions can be set up (Scott 2001).

10.3 Implementing WCU Policy: National Strategies

Apart from the new cultural-cognitive meaning system, strategies are important instruments to accommodate the existed structure of system with a new vision in institutionalization.

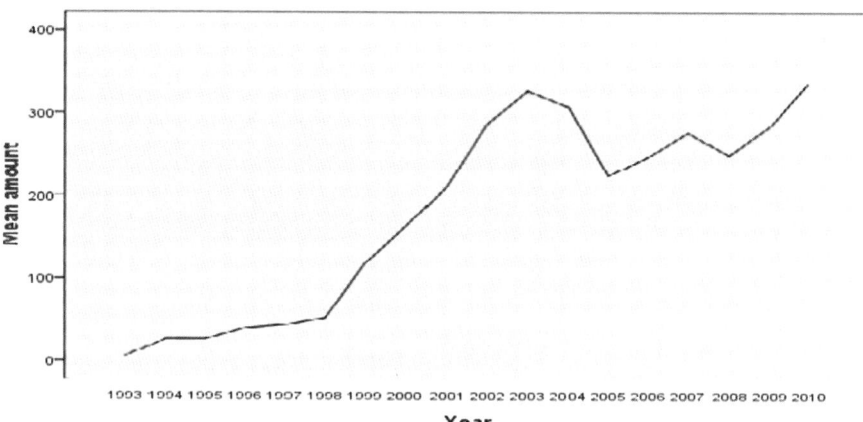

Fig. 10.1 The number of published papers in China containing the keyword "WCU" (1993–2010) (Notes: the numbers come from a search of papers with the keywords of "world-class university" in the database of China National Knowledge Index)

In this case study, two main strategies adopted by the Chinese government are identified: structurally reclassifying the higher education institutions and financially reframing the funding system.

10.3.1   Reclassifying Universities

As previously mentioned, China adopted the Soviet model in the 1950s and thereafter built a redistributive social system. Polanyi (1944) defined the redistributive social system as a structure of social organizations in which goods and services are distributed by central direction from lower-level production units to the center and then back again. This is quite different from a market where buyers and sellers directly engage in exchange.

In order to improve the effectiveness of the redistribution in the field of higher education, the Chinese restructured their comprehensive universities into specialized institutions in the 1950s. Tsinghua University, for instance, which had been a comprehensive university with five colleges (Art, Law, Sciences, Engineering, and Agriculture) and 26 departments, had been transformed into a polytechnic institute mainly producing "red engineers" in 1950s.

At the same time, a hierarchy of higher education institutions was established, in which some of the institutions were affiliated to the functional departments of the state, for instance, the Ministry of Education, Ministry of Machine Building, and Ministry of Metallurgical Industry, while the others were affiliated to provincial government where the institutions were geographically located, thus forming a "strip-block" isolation system (Zha 2009). The ministry-sponsored ("strip")

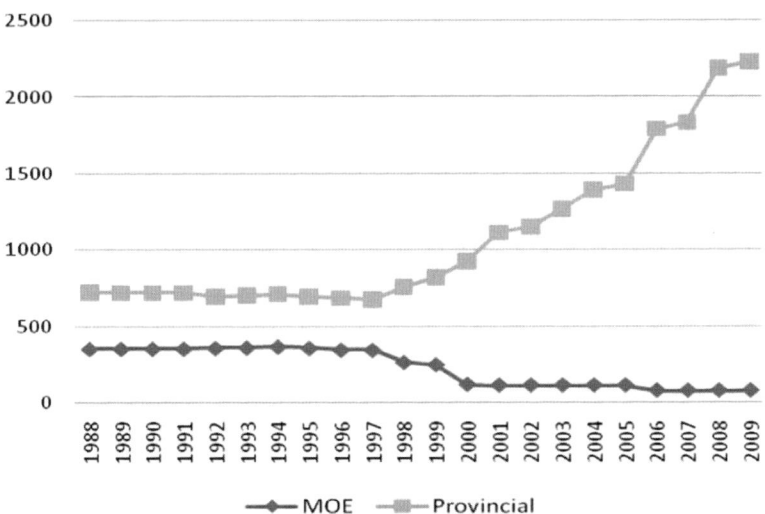

Fig. 10.2 Number of HEIs by affiliation (Ministry of Education vs. provincial government) (Source: China Statistical Yearbook for Education (1989–2010))

institutions were usually of higher status and quality compared to the provincial-supported ("block") ones, as the redistributive system favored the agents at the upper level of power.

In the 1980s, the party reformed the redistributive system. The concept of market was introduced which in turn reorganized the social system (Luo 2007). Consequently, some central ministries that were tied to a planned economy, such as the Ministry of Machine Building and the Ministry of Metallurgical Industry, were dismantled. This made the status of the universities affiliated to them problematic. In 1998, a decision was made jointly by the Party Central and the State Council, stating that ministries other than MOE were not allowed to run higher education institutions. As a result, the number of universities affiliated to provincial government increased rapidly.

Some prestigious universities that were formerly run by ministries, however, would rather choose to be merged into a national elite universities rather than assume a lower status while remain as an independent unit. They knew that higher status in the hierarchy of Chinese higher education meant higher student selectivity, the trademark of an institution of excellence. For instance, the Central Academy of Arts and Design which used to be affiliated with the Ministry of Culture chose to be integrated into Tsinghua University in 1999, and the Beijing Medical University which had been affiliated with the Ministry of Health chose to be merged with Peking University in 2000. As a result, the national elite universities greatly benefited from this reclassification (Fig. 10.2).

Inspired by the benefits from the merger, the primary universities also mobilized resources (in most cases, through their influential alumni) to target desired institutions rather than merely passively accepting those institutions who wanted to merge with them. The merging of Tsinghua University with the Graduate School of the People's Bank of China is a good example. The Graduate School used to be affiliated with the Central Bank of China, (known as the People's Bank of China) and had functioned as the college for training the cadre for the Chinese national financial system. It was revealed in August of 2011 that it had been merged into Tsinghua. Even this was undertaken quietly, it is reported that Tsinghua alumni had played an important role in making it. However, sometimes even despite lobbying, the efforts to merge other institutions were futile. The effort of Tsinghua University to merge Peking Union Medical College (PUMC) in the early twenty-first century is an example. Established in 1906 and developed by various Western missionary organizations, PUMC represented the initial efforts to establish modern medicine in China. In fact, PUMC has a lot of influential alumni both domestically and internationally. They had exerted significant influence in maintaining PUMC as an independent institution. Now, PUMC does not merge with Tsinghua but jointly holds its PhD program with Tsinghua University. The strategy to reclassify universities adopted by Chinese government resulted in a megamerger, which effectively enhanced the competitiveness of Chinese WCU candidate universities.

10.3.2 Reframing the Finance System

Another strategy adopted by the Chinese central government was to reframe the funding system, thus reducing a university's recurrent expenditures while increasingly supporting earmarked grant programs. Examples of such projects are 211 Project (1993), 985 Project (1998), and the Thousand Persons Plan (2008).

The 211 Project is the initial action plan of WCU policy. During the period 1995–2005, known as the period of national 9th five-year plan and 10th five-year plan, the central government, jointly by provincial governments and institutions themselves, invested 36.8 billion RMB in 107 higher education institutions (Inter-Ministry Coordinating Office of "211 Project" 2007).

Unlike the wide range of support from the 211 Project, the 985 Project was very focused in the beginning. The central government provided 1.8 billion RMB for Peking University and Tsinghua University over a period of 3 years. This made it clear that Peking University and Tsinghua University were the only two institutions intentionally selected by the Chinese government to participate in the global competition for the status of WCU. Those universities in the first tier other than Peking University and Tsinghua University became anxious because the 1.8 billion additional funds meant more than money. It also indicated the advantaged status of the concerned universities! After negotiating with the Ministry of Education and involving other significant players such as the provincial/municipal governments, seven other universities were added to the list by 1999, and by 2011, the number of institutions on the list had increased to 39.

Table 10.1 Additional fund received by C9 universities in the 985 Project

Universities	985 Project phaseI (1999–2003)	985 Project phaseII (2004–2010)	985 Project phaseIII (2010–2015)
Peking University	1.8	0.9	4.0
Tsinghua University	1.8	0.9	4.0
Zhejiang University	1.4	0.7	2.64
Nanjing University	1.2	0.6	2.6
Fudan University	1.2	0.6	2.6
Shanghai Jiao Tong University	1.2	0.6	2.6
University of Science and Technology of China	0.9	0.6	1.8
Xi'an Jiao Tong University	0.9	0.6	1.5
Harbin Institute of Technology	1.0	/	/

Unit: billion RMB

The amount of additional funding received through the 985 Project varied among different candidate institutions, due to the variation in the amount that the central government provided for each institution and the variation in the funding capability of the provincial/municipal governments that the institutions belonged to.

Table 10.1 shows the additional funds received by the first nine candidates (also known as C9League) through the 985 Project. A recent Thomson Reuters analysis found that Chinese C9 universities by receiving about 10% of China's R&D expenditures have consistently generated more than 20% of the nation's output of journal articles, and these papers have attracted around 30% of China's total citations (http://www.timeshighereducation.co.uk/story.asp?storyCode=415193&sectioncode=26).

In fact, the 985 Project was launched rather hurriedly. The inside story, as revealed by Xuefei Chen, verified this (Chen 2006), and the changes of the candidate institutions on the list also shed light on it. After the uncertainty of phase II, the 985 Project is now part of the national five-year plans and has become more and more undimmed.

Apart from the project funding coming from higher education, Chinese elite universities have also benefited from the government's increasing investment in R&D. The OECD reported in 2008 that the ratio of GERD (gross expenditure on research and development) to gross domestic product (GDP) in China had increased considerably, from 0.6% in 1995 up to 1.43% in 2006. China's GERD was the third largest worldwide, immediately after the United States and Japan in 2006.

The R&D funds from the government are relatively "easy" to use compared with the subsidy of the 985 Project whose use is limited to hardware. Unlike other types of production, knowledge production relies more on talent than on equipment. The increasing investment by the Chinese government in the field of science and technology has greatly improved the research productivity of Chinese universities. Taking Tsinghua University for instance, 3.6 billion of the total 8 billion RMB in fiscal year 2010 was from research funds. With this "easy" money, professors find it easier to use research assistants, postdoctoral fellows, and elite visiting international scholars as participants in their research.

How did the reframed funding system affect the academic activities in universities? This was illustrated in an interview with a dean of Tsinghua University:

> When the slogan of building WCU came out in 1990s, I laughed at it. We knew our distance (with the world-renowned universities). Becoming one of them? No way. It's another "Great Leap" (doomed to fail) fancied by (someone in) the top. (But) after the 985 Project (was enacted), things changed. First of all, money came in. We are able to recruit new faculty members from the genuine world-class universities, and with the new faculty members joining, we produce papers for international journals. Some (of the papers) are of very good quality... (laugh). Especially after X (a prestigious scholar in the world) started to work with us last year. He brought a team of young scholars from (the universities of) USA. They (the young scholars) all work on cutting-edge studies. Our PhD (students) have real things to do now. (laugh) (The goal of building) a World-class university now? We are more confident.
>
> (Interview conducted on Aug. 16, 2011)

When a policy is accepted and acted upon by deans, the academic life in universities generally undergoes a reformation.

10.4   Implementing WCU Policy: Institutional Strategies

In the following pages, Tsinghua University will be used as a case to be analyzed at the institutional level. This study adopted the perspective of neo-institutionalism to look into how the idea of a WCU was accepted and what strategies were applied in Tsinghua.

Tsinghua University was not selected as the case for analysis because it had produced 280 ministers and nine standing committees at the Politburo for the Republic, including the in-serviced China president and possibly his successor. This was impressive, but not the reason for choosing Tsinghua. The reason why Tsinghua is a valuable case for study is that it is a miniature of the Chinese higher education system.

Established in 1911 and on the site of a former royal garden belonging to a prince, Tsinghua was first a preparatory school for students later sent by the government to study in the United States. It was funded by the Boxer Rebellion indemnity returned by the United States to the Qing Dynasty, on the condition that the fund be used to provide scholarships for the selected Chinese students studying in the United States. This history accounts for the main contradiction in the history of Tsinghua University – on the one hand, it is dependent on the American universities and the dominant Western higher education tradition; on the other hand, it is the place where the Chinese elites had been trained. Many scholars would still argue that this contradiction has not changed much today – more than one-third of the Tsinghua graduates annually choose to pursue graduate studies in Western countries, mainly in the United States. Tsinghua was reported by *Science* (July 11, 2008:185) as the undergraduate alma mater that produces the most PhD's in US universities.

This tension has made Tsinghua the place for the Chinese intellectual elites to reflect on the relationship between modern academic disciplines and Chinese traditional knowledge. In order to incorporate the two, Tsinghua built a Western-like undergraduate college and an Institute of Chinese Study (ICS) in 1925. Three years later, it upgraded to become the National Tsinghua University.

The 1920s started to witness the returning of Tsinghua graduates from the United States. They were young, ambitious, and had the personal experience of studying in the best universities in the West. They felt it was their obligation to upgrade their alma mater Tsinghua into a world-renowned university. Many of them joined the faculty team, and Yiqi Mei, one of those returning, served as the president of university in 1931.

Mei and his cohort adopted strategies to change Tsinghua into a world-class higher education institution. The main strategies included (1) establishing the department autonomy and professor governance; (2) recruiting faculty through international peer review; (3) standardizing the textbooks, library, and labs according to world-class standards; (4) fostering the new function of research by setting up a number of research institutes (in the 1930s, there were only around 20 research institutes in China, while 10 of them were affiliated to Tsinghua University); and (5) actively exchanging faculties with world-renowned universities. Mei's reform focused on three institutional elements that he believed to be crucial for a WCU, namely, academic autonomy, research-intensive, and internationalization. After Mei's presidency in Tsinghua, the university soon entered its "golden age." There is much evidence that "Tsinghua had already been a very international institution in the 1930s" (Wei 2011).

The academic boom came to an end however. The years 1937–1945 witnessed the Sino-Japanese war, which was immediately followed by the Civil War (1946–1949). Mei fled to Taiwan after the Kuomintang (KMT) retreated to Taiwan. The "old" Tsinghua he left behind was restructured in 1950s into a polytechnic university – the "new" Tsinghua.

10.4.1   *Rejuvenating the Vision of WCU*

After the party reformers came to power in the 1980s and the "open" policy became an established national policy, however, the dream of the "old" Tsinghua was reawakened. Tsinghuaers missed the departments and institutes they lost in the 1950s. A number of beautifully written prose about "old" Tsinghua and "old" Tsinghua professors were published. Even the motto of the "old" Tsinghua which comes from an obscure Chinese classic, "Yi Jing" (易经), was reaccepted by the "new" Tsinghua without causing any major ideological inquiry.

> As heaven maintains vigor through movements, a gentle man should constantly strive for self-perfection. As earth's condition is receptive devotion, a gentle man should hold the outer world with great merits.

Once the dream of "old" Tsinghua was awakened, the vision of upgrading Tsinghua into a world-class university became distinct. For Tsinghuaers, it is a desire to rejuvenate their "old" Tsinghua – a comprehensive, research-intensive, and international university. The reason why world-class universities are usually comprehensive was interpreted in one debate at Tsinghua University, which the author witnessed, as indicating the scope of knowledge production of an institution and therefore the opportunity to influence the human knowledge construction.

Although this vision of WCU was met with resistance by the engineering faculties who had emerged in the "new" Tsinghua, the desire to fulfill the vision was very strong, especially that of the former president Dazhong Wang (王大中). A strategy of three steps was formulated by Wang and his vice-presidents: (1) from 1994 to 2002, to upgrade Tsinghua to a comprehensive and research-intensive university; (2) from 2003 to 2011, to rank several disciplines above in the top 10 worldwide; and (3) from 2012 to 2020 (and thereafter), to rank Tsinghua in the top 100 institutions in the world.

10.4.2   Benchmarking Tsinghua with MIT and the Association of American Universities

Organization studies, particularly from the perspective of neo-institutionalism, have argued that an organizational field (a group of organizations) may be highly diverse in the beginning, but they may become similar to one another due to the pressures of obtaining legitimacy. Sociologists DiMaggio and Powell (1983) named these phenomena as isomorphism. They further argued that institutional isomorphism results from three mechanisms: coercive, normative, and mimetic. Coercive isomorphism is driven by two forces: pressure from other organizations on a focal organization to be dependent and pressure on an organization to conform to the cultural expectations of the larger society. Normative isomorphism is a result of professionalization, which involves two processes: (1) members of professions receive similar training (such as that received by physicians, attorneys, and university professors), which socializes them into similar worldviews, and (2) members of professions interact through professional and trade associations, which further diffuses ideas among them. Mimetic isomorphism viewed by DiMaggio and Powell is a response to uncertainty: in the situation that a clear course of action is unavailable, organizational leaders may mimic the peer that they consider successful as they think it is the best response they can make (DiMaggio and Powell 1983).

It is not merely an action of policy borrowing that Tsinghua decided to benchmark AAU in general and MIT in particular. It is rather an effort to obtain legitimacy, by satisfying the cultural expectations held by Western society and following the norms held by the global professional association. To a certain degree, it is mimicry, too. Since the public in China has no idea what a world-class university is and how it should be built, who could deny Tsinghua is a great university if Tsinghua reached or surpassed MIT?

10.4.3 Planning

Planning is a heritage that the Chinese obtained from their experience of the redistributive system in Mao's China. The party reformers, Deng Xiaoping, for instance, believed that planning, like the market, is but one form of governing structures. None is superior to the other. The same idea was held by the Tsinghua leaders.

Planning in Tsinghua is mainly focused on two areas – academic disciplines and faculty recruitment. Tsinghua leaders have rather clear strategies about its disciplines: (1) to resume the liberal arts and social sciences which had been deprived and in fact merged into other institutions in the 1950s. As a result, the School of Humanities and Social Science was established in 1993 after some disciplines had been resumed as research institutes in the 1980s; (2) to build professional schools that have a profound influence on social life, including the School of Economy and Business (1984), the School of Architecture (1988), the School of Law (1995), the School of Public Policy and Management (2000), the School of Medicine (2001), and the School of Journalism and Communication (2002); (3) to set up new disciplines which might have strategic influence on the future of human life. After examining the reference group of AAU, Tsinghua observed that health would become the most important field in human life, after national defense, especially in a time of peace. Therefore, the School of Life Science was established (2008), as were the School of Aerospace (2004) and the School of Environment (2011); (4) to rejuvenate the three pillar disciplines – mathematics, physics, and chemistry; and (5), last but not least, to maintain the strength of engineering that Tsinghua had been celebrated for.

Although the university leaders have a clear plan for the university's development, it is not without faculty resistance, especially from engineering. Since so many new schools had been established in the last few decades, the departments of engineering felt marginalized. The morale of the faculty dropped, and the deans or department heads complained regularly. The great challenges confronting the leaders of Tsinghua University were how to develop the new disciplines while at the same time, retain the strength of the engineering.

Another important field of planning in Tsinghua is faculty recruitment. Under the impact of Mao's radical higher education policy, the faculty recruited by Tsinghua in the 1960s and 1970s were basically from workers-peasants class(工兵学员). Most of them had minimal training in academic disciplines, and they seldom had a masters or higher degree. In the 1990s, Tsinghua started to recruit new faculty members basing on contracts, which greatly enhanced the university's control of

Table 10.2 The number of full professors recruited from outside, 2006–2010

	2006	2007	2008	2009	2010
Full professors recruited from other universities in China	9	7	12	23	9
Full professors recruited from oversea universities (not Chinese nationality)	1	1	5	7	20
Full professors recruited from oversea universities (Chinese nationality)	7	9	13	8	20
Number in total	17	17	30	38	49

faculty recruitment. All faculty recruitment must now be agreed on by the University Committee. As a result, the quality of faculty in Tsinghua has greatly improved. As of August 2011, approximately 75% of the faculty hold doctorate degrees, and 62% are under the age of 45 years. Full professors account for approximately 41% of the faculty.

Although the quality of Tsinghua faculty has been greatly improved, university leaders believe that there still exists a vast gap between Tsinghua and the top world-class universities, especially in terms of the number of great masters, top scholars, and innovative research teams. In order to improve the quality of the first tier faculty, Tsinghua has taken control of the recruitment of full professors. The university reported that since 2005, 55% of the full-professor recruitment quota has come from scholars outside Tsinghua (mainly abroad), while only 45% are university faculty. In fact, the quota from university faculty of 2011 was much lower (Table 10.2).

This strategy, very effectively, renewed the top faculty tier. Most of the faculty recruited in 1960s and 1970s had either retired or been moved to other functional departments, mostly university party organs.

Although this strategy effectively renewed the top faculty tier, it exerted considerable negative effects on the middle-tier faculty. Due to the limited chances for promotion to full professor, young faculty with great potential chose to work in other national universities that could provide them with better opportunities including the title of full professor, research funds, and managerial responsibilities. As a result, the faculty team was weakened, and the so-called innovative research "teams" hardly exist. This has already aroused the attention from the university.

10.4.4 Reforming the Governance

In order to implement the planning, the university reformed the governance framework. As mentioned earlier, contracts had been introduced to recruit new faculty and staff, which greatly enhanced the university's autonomy. Another significant reform concerned the university financing.

When Tsinghua was affiliated to MOE in the redistributive period, it received funding from the allocation of MOE. After market was introduced into higher education system, Tsinghua diversified its funding sources – for example, tuition fees, profits from enterprises affiliated with the university, and donations. This reduced, to a large degree, Tsinghua's dependence on MOE. But the reform of greater significance was the establishment of Tsinghua Holdings Corporation Ltd. Established with a registered capital of $240 million RMB in 2003, Tsinghua Holdings Corporation Ltd, in fact, functions as the management platform for Tsinghua assets. In 2005, Tsinghua Holdings Capital was established as the sole legally qualified investment banking unit under Tsinghua Holdings, managing Tsinghua University's first securities-based fund – Tsinghua Holdings Industry Investment Fund. This fund plays the same role as a university fund does for any private university in the United States, though Tsinghua is a public institution.

With greater control on its personnel and finances, Tsinghua now possesses the organizational autonomy that a WCU experiences.

10.4.5 Outcome

Thanks to its clear vision, good planning, and reformed governance, Tsinghua made good progress in relation to the selected indicators (Yang and Welch 2011).

10.4.5.1 Knowledge Production

Table 10.3 illustrates Tsinghua's publications in the field of science and technology during the period 1996–2009. Tsinghua made remarkable progress, and the publications in 2009 increased more than six times over that of the 1996.

Although the social sciences had been reestablished in Tsinghua for less than two decades, publications in the field ranked above the top 1% globally by June 2011, and its citation has been rapidly grown. Figure 10.3 shows the rate of growth of citations.

The number of Tsinghua's patents has also had significant grown. In 1995, Tsinghua had only 48 patents, but in 2005, it registered 521, which is three times that of MIT in the same year (Gu 2008).

It is reported by the university that Tsinghua holds 11,000 patents, including 9,684 inventions, 6,500 authorized patents (among them 5,069 authorized inventions), 1,800 patent applications, 400 authorized patents abroad, and 828 computer software copyright registration (http://www.tsinghua.edu.cn/publish/then/5993/index.html).

10.4.5.2 Educational Experience for College Students

After introducing the NSSE (National Survey of Student Engagement) instrument into China, Luo and her colleagues compared Tsinghua with its American counterparts (American Universities with Very High Research Activities) in 2009

Table 10.3 The increase of Tsinghua in SCI, EI, and ISTP articles, 1996–2009

	1996	1997	1998	1999	2000	2001	2002	2003	2004	2005	2006	2007	2008	2009
SCI	273	407	424	598	1,054	1,427	1,899	2,212	2,321	2,915	2,866	2,591	2,589	2,758
EI	511	829	576	1,324	1,418	1,449	2,094	2,584	2,299	3,242	3,317	3,393	3,381	3,431
ISTP	238	393	263	372	410	765	1,144	1,303	1,288	1,768	1,579	1,752	1,905	1,377

Source: (Yang and Welch 2012); Brief Statistics of Tsinghua 2010, http://xxbg.cic.tsinghua.edu.cn/oath/detail.jsp?seq=91196&boardid=22
Notes: *SCI* is an abbreviation of Science Citation Index, *EI* is an abbreviation of the Engineering Information Index, *ISTP* is an abbreviation of Index to Scientific & Technological Proceedings

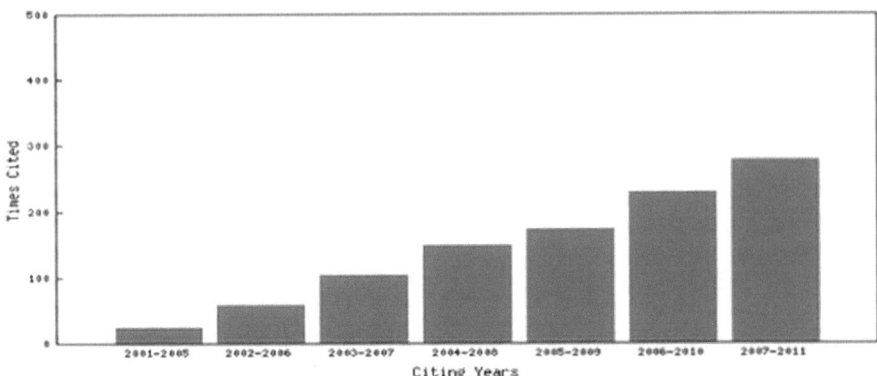

Fig. 10.3 The growth of citations of Tsinghua University in social sciences in general (2001–2011) (Source: Essential Science Indicator (2011) http://news.lib.tsinghua.edu.cn/page.user.article.asp?articleid=904. Notes: SSCI is an abbreviation of Social Science Citation Index)

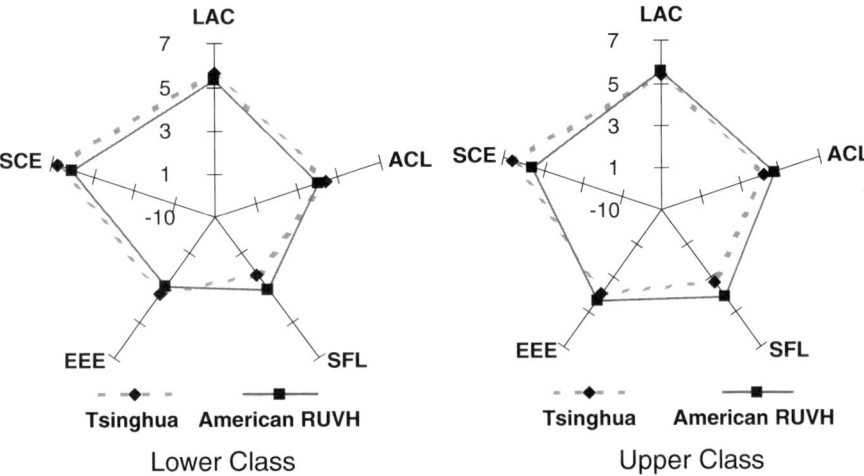

Fig. 10.4 Comparing Tsinghua with American RUVH on five Benchmarks, 2009 (Note: this figure is adapted from the data released in Luo's study (2009))

against five benchmarks: the level of academic challenge, the level of active and collaborative learning, the level of enriching educational experience, the level of student-faculty interaction, and the level of supportive campus environment. Luo's study showed that there were no significant statistical differences on the first three benchmarks between Tsinghua and its American counterparts. For the latter two, Tsinghua's performance was inferior on student-faculty interaction but more supportive on quality of campus environment (Luo et al. 2009). Figure 10.4 indicates the differences.

Because of the clear vision, good planning and sound strategies at both the national and institutional level, Tsinghua University successfully upgraded its faculty quality and academic productivity in only two decades. But is Tsinghua a world-class university now? Reflections are needed in order to answer this question.

10.5   Reflections

Institutions change. The changes occur in quantity and quality. Positive quantitative changes are referred to as institutional improvement; positive qualitative changes are considered institutional innovation. Is a WCU an institutional improvement or an innovation? This is a key question when examining the Chinese experience and trying to interpret it.

The concept of WCU is underdeveloped in terms of theoretical framing. The term "world-class universities" generally refers to a small group of renowned universities which are ranked at the top of the international league tables. This leads to the thinking as if "world-class university" is not a newly emerging form of institution driven by geographic-political restructuring (i.e., "globalization") and the restructuring of human economic production (i.e., "knowledge economy") but a group of existing well-known higher education institutions who bear at the same time the two main properties of high quality and internationalization.

Philip G. Altbach stated in many of his books and lectures that WCUs by nature are research universities in general and based on the American model in particular (Altbach and Balan 2007). Unlike Altbach, who believed the WCU has only one model to follow, Jamil Salmi has argued that world-class higher education institutions could also include those that are neither research-focused nor operating as universities in the strict sense (Salmi 2009). Although they disagree somewhat on how to become a WCU, both Altbach and Salmi have interpreted WCUs in the framework of nation-states, viewing WCU mainly instruments of nation-states to cope with the intense global competition.

Although this is a way to conceptualize WCUs, it is incomplete. Looking at the history of humanity, we may find that while agricultures and industrialization emancipated humans from a dependence on nature for food, the popularization of education (in particular higher education) emancipated humanity from its dependence on social constructions by turning every individual into a potential knowledge producer. Therefore, what the knowledge economy has changed is not only the economy but also the whole of human life. Analyzing world-class universities merely through the technical lens of benchmarks or the lens of nation-state strategy to cope with global competition actually underestimates the importance of WCUs in restructuring our human life. Thus far, the Chinese experience provides at least two points for reflection. The first is about the limitation of the instrumentality of Chinese WCU policy. There is no doubt that the strategies and efforts taken by the party and by state and higher education institutions in China greatly enhanced the global competitiveness of Chinese higher education institutions. But all of these happened when the WCU was deconstructed into observable technical indicators. Without a sense of contributing to an improved human value system, China's efforts to build a WCU would be merely a mimic of other systems, rather than embodying the institutional innovation they desire.

The second point is about the relationship between states and universities. Many scholars have pointed out that the state played a decisive role in China's bid for world-class universities (e.g., Marginson 2011). Yang and Welch believed this, in fact, paralleled the international tide which harnessed universities to economic programs serving national interests rather than preserving the autonomy of universities (Yang and Welch 2011). In paying close attention to Tsinghua's case, however, we detect the opposite. The logic of knowledge production, rather than "serving the country," has dominated the university life of Tsinghua since the WCU policy carried out in Tsinghua. On the one hand, more than two-thirds of the graduates each year choose to either pursue their graduate study in Western countries or work in large global companies, which indicate a weakening of students' faith in constructing their own country. On the other hand, the faculty spend more and more time on getting published in English, anticipating to become "world-class scholars," and thus, quite a number of them have the values and beliefs diverge from those of the state. The Chinese government was trying to ensure that local universities enhance China's competitiveness, but when the knowledge production housed in these universities becomes more and more world class, the elites who used to be defined as national elite might get freed from the framework of nation-states. They produce knowledge that takes part in global circulation. This will in certain ways influence the way of global governance, especially when the knowledge they produce is concerning value system. It seems the relationship between a WCU and the state is much more complicated than what has been previously thought.

Getting back to the question – is Tsinghua a world-class university now? The answer is that it depends. If a world-class university is a university that wins a global competition according to performance indicators, Tsinghua certainly is a runner with full speed surpassing many of his rivals. But if a world-class university is a place where scholars from worldwide gather and produce the knowledge and values to the excellence that our human kind by far can reach, Tsinghua does not fall into the category. In fact, few of the universities ranked above in the world rankings are of the category.

References

Altbach, P. G., & Balan, J. (2007). *World class worldwide: Transforming research universities in Asia and Latin America*. Baltimore: Johns Hopkins University Press.

Bernal, J. D. (1954). *Science in history*. London: Watts.

Chen, X. (2006). Ideal-oriented policing: How 985 project was formulated. *Peking University Educational Review, 4*(1). [in Chinese].

DiMaggio, P., & Powell, W. W. (1983). The iron cage revisited: Institutional isomorphism and collective rationality in organizational fields. *American Sociological Review, 48*(2), 147–160.

Gu, B. L. (2008). Innovation: A way to success for the research university. *Tsinghua Journal of Education, 29*(1), 1–5. [in Chinese].

Hu, S. (1998). *Hu Shi collection (issue11)*. Beijing: Beijing University press.

Inter-Ministry Coordinating Office of "211 Project". (2007). *A report of 211 project: 1995–2005*. Beijing: Higher Education Press. [in Chinese].

Luo, Y. (2006). University ranking as a market guiding system. *Jiang Su Higher Education, 5*. [in Chinese].

Luo, Y. (2007). Socialist state and global capital. *Chinese Society and Education, 1*. [in Chinese].

Luo, Y., Shi, J., & Tu, D. (2009). Report on Tsinghua's undergraduate education 2009. *Tsinghua Journal of Education, 5*. [in Chinese].

Maddison, A. (2001). *The world economy, a millennial perspective*. Paris: OECD.

Marginson, S. (2011). Higher education in East Asia and Singapore: Rise of the confucian model. *Higher Education, 61*, 587–611.

Mervis, J. (2008, July 11). U.S. graduate training: Top Ph.D feeder schools are now Chinese. *Science, 321*(5886), 185.

Morhman, K., Ma, W., & Baker, D. (2008). The research university in transition: The emerging global model. *Higher Education Policy, 21*, 5–7.

Polanyi, K. (1944). *The great transformation*. Boston: Beacon.

Salmi, J. (2009). *The challenge of establishing world-class universities*. Washington, DC: World Bank.

Scott, W. R. (2001). *Institutions and organizations*. London: Sage Publications, Inc.

Wei, W. (2011). The International Perspective of Tsinghua Politics Study in the 1930s. *The Journal of Tsinghua University, 26*(3). [in Chinese].

Yang, R., & Welch, A. (2012). A world-class university in china? The case of Tsinghua. *Higher Education, 63*(5), 645.

Ye, F. (2009). Academic independence, first-class university and graduate education. *Academic Degree and Graduate Education, 4*. [in Chinese].

Yuan, J. (2005). Reexamine the law of the shifts of World Science Centre. *Review of Science Culture, 2*. [in Chinese].

Yuasa, M. (1962). Centre of scientific activity: Its shift from the 16th to the 20th century. *Japanese Studies in the History of Science, 1*, 57–75.

Zha, Q. (2009). Diversification or homogenization: How governments and markets have combined to (re)shape Chinese higher education in its recent massification process. *Higher Education, 58*(1), 41–58.

Chapter 11
The Challenges for Establishing World-Class Universities in Taiwan

Dian-fu Chang

11.1 Introduction

This chapter focuses on how WCUs (world-class universities) have been adopted, interpreted, and institutionalized as a national policy in Taiwan; how leading universities have interpreted and responded to that government policy; and how individual units (departments or professors) have responded to subsequent challenges. This chapter addresses how WCUs have been institutionalized as social systems and have been culturally integrated within Taiwan as well as how WCUs have been institutionalized at the institutional and individual faculty level. In recent years, the world's advanced countries have been providing special funds for university development, such as the UK University Grants Committee, the United States Department of Education with the project fund, Japan, and Germany. Even China has been providing funds to a small number of major universities, such as Beijing University and Tsinghua University, in the form of an annual 600 million RMB (Chinese dollars) and special grants (Chang et al. 2009). The Korean government has provided 1,342,142 million Korean won (equivalent to 1.4 billion US dollars) to promote the 7-year span of the Brain Korea 21 Project (BK21) (Shin 2009). The goal of structural reform of universities in Japan has been to achieve 30 universities (or research fields) of international standing. The California Government Planning Inter-Institution Research Center has provided grants over the last 4 years and gives each center one billion dollars each year. Since 2002, the EU has provided substantial funding (1.3 billion euros) for research projects in nanotechnology (European Commission 2004). In recent years, the development of higher education in Taiwan has been facing international and domestic pressures.

D.-f. Chang (✉)
Institute of Educational Policy and Leadership, Tamkang University, New Taipei, Taiwan
e-mail: dfchang@ncnu.edu.tw

J.C. Shin and B.M. Kehm (eds.), *Institutionalization of World-Class University in Global Competition*, The Changing Academy – The Changing Academic Profession in International Comparative Perspective 6, DOI 10.1007/978-94-007-4975-7_11,
© Springer Science+Business Media Dordrecht 2013

Besides the aforementioned pressure from developed countries, there are domestic problems as follows (Ministry of Education 2004, 2006):

1. The expansion of higher education impacts the allocation of resources. An overemphasis on equal allocation of resources in the past has resulted in a lack of competition that makes it difficult to establish a well-run system of higher education. The excessive dispersal of limited resources has failed to help individual universities establish unique characteristics based on their expertise as well as having a negative impact on academic competitiveness.
2. The quality of education in universities faces new challenges. The rapid development of the higher-education population has outpaced the development of the necessary resources. In fact, the number of private universities and colleges has rapidly increased, but the elementary and secondary schools, child care, aboriginal, disabled and many other basic education needs have received limited resources. The needs of the national university have a crowding out effect, and the lack of resources has resulted in the stagnation of university teaching and an unacceptable level of research quality. It is difficult to improve this situation with the current approach to resource allocation.
3. Universities face insufficient staffing and funding for development. Since the implementation of the public university funding system, the government subsidies for public universities have decreased year by year. Because of the limited number of faculty members, academic departments have too high a student-teacher ratio, and in recent years the ratio of students to full-time teachers has gradually increased.

The Taiwanese government has realized that globalization has intensified the competition among higher-education institutions on a worldwide basis. After Taiwan's admission to the World Trade Organization, overseas universities have been allowed to expand their recruitment of Taiwanese students through educational agencies, distance learning, and two-track or dual-credit systems. In order to enhance the global competitiveness of Taiwanese universities, the government began to call for the pursuit of academic excellence in universities in the late 1990s (Lo and Weng 2005).

11.2 From Academic Excellence Program to Initiative WCU

According to the objectives set out by Executive Yuan in 2004, Taiwanese government was particularly keen on having at least one local university ranked among the top 100 universities in the world within a decade by 2014 and at least 15 key departments or cross-university research centers to be at the top of their disciplines in Asia within in the next 5 years (Lu 2004). The pursuit of academic excellence and a focus on universities' efforts in developing a few selected areas have become the policies adopted by the government in order to improve the quality of university education and achieve its goals. In 1998, the MoE and the National Science

Council (NSC) jointly launched the Program for Promoting Academic Excellence of Universities (Academic Excellence Program), primarily aimed at improving universities' infrastructures and invigorating research (Ministry of Education 2000; Deem et al. 2008). This program supports four research fields, including humanities and social sciences, life sciences, natural sciences, and engineering and the applied sciences.

For humanities and social sciences, the Academic Excellence Program requests that research projects utilize local research materials for arguing against or for elaborating theories from the West. For life sciences, the program stresses the importance of human physiology and the development of biotechnology. For natural sciences, it focuses on atmospheric sciences, material sciences, and earth sciences and expects these disciplines to be recognized internationally for their leading expertise. For engineering and applied sciences, it highlights the importance of the applied studies of networking technologies, wireless communication technologies, and optics and photonics (Ministry of Education 2000; Mok and Chan 2008).

In addition, the MoE and the NSC also formed a panel of eminent local and overseas academics to select research projects for support by the program. In the first round of the Academic Excellence Program, a total of 261 research applications were submitted. After rigorous review, NT$ 4.3 billion was allocated to fund 19 projects, of which three were offered conditionally. The first round of the program was completed in 2004. To further develop a high-quality research culture in Taiwan, the second round of the program was launched in 2000 and finished in 2006. There were 148 research applications in this round, and 12 were granted a total amount of NT$ 2.1 billion. With a rigorous selection process in place, only 6.13% of research applications were selected in the first round of the program, while 8.1% of applications were funded in the second round. The funded rate of humanities and social sciences projects was even lower (i.e., 15.55% for the first round and only 3.29% for the second round of the total funding). Most of the funding went to public institutions, while only two research projects that were jointly submitted by public and private institutions were funded. After reviewing the various rounds of implementation, the government considered the Academic Excellence Program successful in allowing effective integration of resources for fostering cooperation and exchange between outstanding institutions and talented researchers and for boosting research capacity (National Science Council 2005). As a result, the Taiwanese government has become even more committed to investing in certain research areas in order to better place Taiwan on the global academic map.

Another initiative, entitled the *Program for Improving University Fundamental Education* (Fundamental Education Program), under the Academic Excellence Program has been implemented since 2001 to enhance the level of universities' foundations and general studies (Lu 2004). Applications for this program were divided into five groups: humanities and social sciences, life sciences, natural sciences, engineering and applied sciences, and institutional integration. In the first round of the Fundamental Education Program, 112 institutions submitted 432 applications, of which 192 projects from 92 institutions were selected to be funded by the government. In terms of funding, 55.9% of the funding was granted to public institutions, while 44.1% of the fund was allocated to private institutions (Ministry of Education 2004). The MoE plans to allocate NT\$ 1.8 billion for the second round of the program.

11.2.1 National Policy for WCUs

Knowing how to maneuver within the global environment to maximize the benefits of higher education locally is a major challenge facing university systems worldwide (Salmi 2009). In Taiwan, the government has realized that globalization has accelerated competition among universities around the world (Lo and Weng 2005; Lu 2004; Ministry of Education 2006).

The WCUs plan, according to the *Macro Planning Board of Higher Education, Executive Yuan*, is referred to as the *Macro Planning of Higher Education Report* and is intended to provide competitive funding to promote "the development of world-class universities and top research centers plan," ultimately aimed at the development of world-class universities. The project was planned to occur in two phases: the first phase took place in the years 2006–2011, and the second phase will start in 2011 and end in 2015 (Ministry of Education 2009). Grant funding for the relevant purpose allows the universities to move upward and match international practices.

The project needed to achieve the following objectives in the first phase of the implementation timetable from 2006 to 2011 (Ministry of Education 2006):

1. In 10 years, at least one university will become one of the world's top 100 universities. In 15–20 years, that university will become one of the world's top 50 universities, with several research centers in that university having the potential to become some of the world's top-level research centers.
2. At least 10 outstanding fields, departments, or research centers will be among Asia's first-class within 5 years. In 10 years, these will have the potential of becoming among the top 50 in their respective fields globally.
3. The R&D quality of universities will be raised, as will their influence on and visibility in international academic circles.
4. Distinguished foreign teaching and research individuals will be recruited to train students in cutting-edge industries.
5. Substantive exchange and cooperation will be established among transnational academic organizations.

The second phase of the implementation timetable is from 2011 to 2015. In this phase, the project objectives are as follows:

1. Accelerate the internationalization of top universities by expanding the global view of students and attracting international students. The government will provide funds through the project to help universities to set up foreign language teaching programs, to build more international and diverse campuses, and to

accelerate the recruitment of outstanding foreign students. The students can also attend dual-degree programs, foreign student exchange programs, and student-related interactive activities to further explore their international experiences.

2. Enhance the quality of university research and innovation and strengthen the international academic influence and visibility. This includes enhancing basic and applied science in the leading universities, such as cutting-edge nanotechnology research, biomedicine, information technology, and other fields of R&D. It encourages leading academic institutions and private enterprises to further cooperate in the pursuit of research excellence. At the same time, it encourages universities to promote the importance of the emphasis on academic quality by, for example, publishing in leading journals, such as *Nature* and *Science,* will be an important element of improving academic quality, and the number of papers published in leading journals is expected to grow steadily.

3. Actively recruit and nurture talents and strengthen national human resources. Use the project to help the top universities enhance their teaching and research environments; provide the flexibility in teachers' salaries; simplify the procedures for recruiting outstanding scholars; send potential teaching and research staff to study abroad; and help universities to recruit foreign talent, excellent teachers, and research staff to maintain the universities in order to strengthen Taiwan's national human resources.

4. Strengthen industry-university cooperation, promote industrial upgrading, and enhance national competitiveness. Universities with richer technological resources need to integrate other academic institutions and private sector resources to assist the existing industrial upgrades. Looking toward the future, using the results-driven strategy in academic research will lead to the development of new technologies and emerging industries that will further enhance national competitiveness.

5. Respond to social and industrial needs and cultivate top talents. Universities may base their teaching, research capacity, and development strategy in response to the needs of social and industrial development. The second phase of implementation needs to refer to the country's future development requirements of the specialized areas (in terms of key services, six new industries, emerging new industries with smart design) to establish new research centers or to focus research areas. To balance all areas, it needs to develop the country's overall human resources and encourage professors to lead students to engage in technology-related integrated research.

11.2.2 Funding Strategy for WCUs and Top-Level Research Centers

Historically, higher-education institutions were cultural landmarks for their home nations. They educated their own students, trained their own academic staffs, and stored the cultural and local histories of their regions. International pressures, largely the result of global flows of higher-education funding, ideas, students, and staff, have forced institutions to reexamine their missions. These pressures have forced governments, by far the largest funding sources for their higher-education institutions, to reexamine the goals of higher education (Salmi 2009).

By virtue of the already limited resources that were further diminished by the growth in higher education and its pursuit of excellence, the MoE of Taiwan was aware that, instead of assisting all HEIs, they needed to invest extra funding in selected "promising" institutions. Based on this concern, the *Plan to Develop World-class Universities and Top-level Research Centers* was developed based on the suggestions made in the Higher Education Macroscopic Planning Report that was prepared by the Higher Education Macroscopic Planning Committee, which proposed strategies that would raise the level of competitiveness among institutions of higher education (Chang et al. 2009). The purpose of these plans was to assist universities through competitive funding, thus improving their worldwide academic competitiveness. The *Plan to Develop World-class Universities and Top-level Research Centers* is the project with the largest competitive funding.

11.2.3 The Requirements for Institutions

The Ministry of Education (2011) articulated the following four types of performance indicators for the review of the top university plan: (1) academic-oriented, (2) international dimension, (3) industry-university collaboration, and (4) other aspects (selected by the university). In March 2011, the MoE announced that *Towards a Top University Plan* referred to the expected baseline performance indicators for assessment. It is set of guidelines for individual universities or research centers to implement and includes the following:

(a) Establish at least 10 world-class research centers or areas. "World-class" refers to the authoritative journal in the field, the number of published papers in international symposiums in the world's top 10 symposiums, or other selected indicators by universities and approved by the commission of universities.
(b) A 25% increase in the number of full-time faculty members and researchers recruited from abroad (average annual increase is about 5%).
(c) International students in degree programs or the number of exchange students must increase by 100% (average annual increase about 20%).
(d) Full-time faculty members from either domestic or foreign science academies or fellows from an academic society are important and must increase by 200 individuals (i.e., an average increase of 40 individuals per year over 5 years).
(e) In next last 10 years, highly cited papers of HiCi must grow by 50% (average annual growth about 10%).
(f) The number of faculty members in universities or research institutions who go abroad for short-term research or exchange of faculty must grow by 100% (average annual growth about 20%).

Table 11.1 The budget by project phase (2006–2015) (unit: million NT$)

Phase I/year	2006	2007	2008	2009	2010	Total
Budget	100	100	100	100	100	**500**
For WCUs	35–60	35–60	35–60	35–60	35–60	**175–300**
For research centers	40–65	40–65	40–65	40–65	40–65	**200–325**
Phase II/year	2011	2012	2013	2014	2015	Total
Budget	100	100	100	100	100	**500**
For WCUs	35–60	35–60	35–60	35–60	35–60	**175–300**
For research centers	40–65	40–65	40–65	40–65	40–65	**200–325**

Source: The development of world-class universities and top research centers amended plan (97 correction approved version), Ministry of Education 2008, Retrieved May, 5, 2011, from http://www.edu.tw/files/list/B0069/.pdf

(g) The creation of full-degree programs taught in English must grow by 100% (average annual growth about 20%).
(h) Nongovernmental sector of the industry cooperation funds must grow 50% (average annual growth about 10%).
(i) The number of patents in R&D and new varieties of devices in the 5-year total number must increase to 2,000 (average 400).
(j) The proportion of university income from intellectual property rights must grow by 100% (average annual growth about 20%).

11.2.4   Resource Allocation

The Ministry of Education (2008) developed an annual funding forecast for WCUs and top research centers. The current university funding for WCUs is 35–60 billion NT$ (3.5–6.0 billion per year, depending on the number of universities). The leading research centers are funded up to a maximum of 65 billion, depending on current grants for WCUs. For details of resource allocation, see Table 11.1.

Using the list of grants for the top research centers each year with the increases and decreases in funding, the allocation of resources can be viewed as a rough profile. In the first 2 years of the project from 2006 to 2007, a total of 17 universities received grants. For the next 3-year plan, the effectiveness of implementation in the first 2 years determines the resource allocation, and individual universities must reapply for new grants. In the next 3-year plan, there were 11 universities that received new funding for implementing their institutional projects. In addition, there were four universities that also satisfied the review criteria and received key research funding before the end of the plan.

In the first 2 years, selected universities were limited to "key development areas" in accessing most of the funding. The main difference in the second stage of funding is that by allocating block funding, universities were able to focus on their development more flexibly and were more properly able to use relevant funds to upgrade their infrastructure, teaching excellence, and areas of focus.

National Taiwan University and National Chiao Tung University received another NT$100 million each year because of their improved teaching performance and international rankings. Taiwan Normal University received NT$200 million for the excellent performance of its Chinese language program. Three universities took cuts for 100 million, 150 million, and 2 billion because of unclear financial reporting. The amount allocated to the other universities remained unchanged. In the funding plan of this phase, 70% of the funding went to universities of in the northern part of Taiwan, and only 30% of the funding went to universities in the southern part of Taiwan. Some universities were disappointed and have raised the problem of uneven distribution of educational resources by the Ministry of Education.

11.3   Formative Evaluations of Their Impact

The results from and evaluation of the project following implementation have caused some concern among the public. The qualitative indicators that were set for evaluation include the following:

First, assess the adjustment and the strength of the organizational mechanism of the university.

Second, establish an advisory committee to promote the implementation of the WCUs plan.

Third, establish flexible salaries for professors and develop a recruitment plan in terms of their specific measures and performance evaluation for top talents abroad.

Fourth, promote humanities and social science development by promoting specific strategies and increasing funding.

Fifth, strengthen the teacher evaluation mechanism and the reward-elimination mechanism.

Sixth, improve student learning (such as students' participation in research projects, teaching syllabi and online teaching materials, student satisfaction with teaching effectiveness, development of new materials, and standardized tools for assessment).

Seventh, establish measures to encourage teachers to be more engaged in teaching.

Eighth, develop specific strategies to achieve leadership in a related field or the same academic field off campus, and evaluate the effectiveness of these strategies.

Quantitative indicators listed in Table 11.2 are for evaluating the effectiveness of project implementation. The indicators can be grouped into three domains to evaluate effectiveness, namely, the quality of faculty and research results, teaching, and university-industry cooperation.

Table 11.2 Performance indicators and target values for evaluating the results of the developing WCUs and top research centers plan by institutional level

Focusing domains quantitative indicators		Target values	Operational definition
Quality of faculty and research outcomes	1. Ratio of international papers (SCI, SSCI, A, and HCI) increased	Characteristics of universities by years	According to the number of articles over the past 5 years: annual average growth rate (%)
	2. Increase in the number of papers cited	Characteristics of universities by years	According to the average number over the past 10 years: annual growth rate (%)
	3. Number of articles by highly cited papers HiCi	Characteristics of universities by years	According to the average number of articles over the past 10 year: growth rate (%)
	4. Number of editors of internationally journal	Characteristics of universities by years	(Number/number of teachers in the university)%
	5. Number of important international fellows	Characteristics of universities by years	(Number/number of teachers in the university)%
	6. Number of academics domestic and abroad	Characteristics of universities by years	(Number/number of teachers in the university)%
	7. Cumulative major awards domestic and abroad	Characteristics of universities by years	(Number/number of teachers in the university)%
	8. Other	Selected by university	
Teaching	1. Number of undergraduate students enrolled in cross-professional programs	Characteristics of universities by years	(Number of undergraduate students studying in universities)%
	2. Proportion of undergraduate students that pass the European language learning, teaching, and assessment common reference framework (CEF) at the B1 level	Characteristics of universities by years	(Passed number of students/number of undergraduate students in that graduating class)%
	3. Other	Selected by university	

(continued)

Table 11.2 (continued)

Focusing domains quantitative indicators		Target values	Operational definition
University-industry cooperation	1. Number of collaborative projects and amount of funding support	Characteristics of universities by years	According to the average annual growth ratio over the past 3 years
	2. Number of patents	Characteristics of universities by years	According to the average annual growth ratio over the past 3 years
	3. Number of technology transfers and amount of money	Characteristics of universities by years	According to the average annual growth ration over the past 3 years
	4. Other	Selected by university	

Note: For the definition of several growth indicators, please refer to the Ministry of Education's the development of world-class universities and top research centers plan performance indicators and target values defined in the table of the operating line
Source: Towards the total center of University Advancement, National Cheng Kung University, 2011on May 5, retrieved from http://www.ncku.edu.tw/~top/top_web/C/lawmain.htm

11.3.1 Tentative Outputs

Four years after the implementation of the development of world-class universities and top research centers project, the universities have shown significant growth in teaching, research, international, and industry-university cooperation compared with 2005 and 2009 (Ministry of Education 2010b). The universities received 4.4 billion in grants to increase the amount of industry cooperation. The number of enrolled disadvantaged students increased by 160%, the number of international students studying for degrees grew by 41%, and the number of international papers grew by 51%. Table 11.3 shows the evaluation results and the funding changes for 2006 and 2007. Only a few of the universities have been removed or have had funding reduced. However, most grants are going to science- and technology-driven universities. This seems to have created a new imbalance in the campuses.

Using the 10 performance indicators provided by the Ministry of Education, one can review the actual performance of the selected top universities over the past 5 years (2006–2010). For example, indicator 1 refers to the number of published papers in the authoritative journals in a field or in an international symposium needed to reach to the top in the world. Until now, no single university has achieved this goal. Indicator 5 refers to highly cited papers. In the past 10years, highly cited papers in HiCi have increased 50% (average annual growth 10%). So far, both National Taiwan University and National Cheng Kung University have achieved this goal.

As described above, the purpose of the first phase of WCUs project was to enhance the competitiveness of higher education, but it also caused some issues in the implementation processes, as discussed in the following section:

Table 11.3 2006–2007 Evaluation results and the changes of funding (unit: billion NT$)

Universities	2006 Results	2006 Funding	2007 Results	2007 Funding	Change	Remarks
National Taiwan Univ.	Excellent	30	Excellent	30	0	96, No. 1
National Cheng Kung Univ.	Good	17	Excellent	17	0	96, No. 3
National Tsing Hua Univ.	Excellent	12	Excellent	10	2	96, No. 2
National Chiao Tung Univ.	Excellent	9	Excellent	8	1	
National Central Univ.	Excellent	7	Excellent	6	1	
National Sun Yat-Sen Univ.	Good	6	Good	6	0	
National Yang Ming Univ.	Excellent	5	Good	5	0	
National Chung Hsing Univ.	Good	4.5	Good	4	0.5	
National Taiwan Univ. of Science and Technology	Good	2	Good	3	−1	
National Chang Gung Univ.	Excellent	2	Good	3	−1	
National Chengchi Univ.	Good	2	Fair	3	−1	
Yuan Ze Univ.	Good	0.9	Good	3	−2.1	Fuel cells
National Taiwan Ocean Univ.	–	0.9	–	–	–	Aquatic biotechnology
Kaoshiung Medical Univ.	–	0.9	–	–	–	Environmental medicine
Chung Yuan Christian Univ.	–	0.7	–	–	–	

Source: "Development of a flow of international universities and leading research centers program," allocation of funds and description of the situation, the Ministry of Education, Retrieved April 7, 2010, from http://www.edu.tw/high/itemize.aspx?itemize_sn=9959&pages=0&site_content_sn=1238

1. The issue with recruiting outstanding overseas professionals (including students). The universities funded by the project needed to recruit outstanding talent from other countries, and the recruitment numbers have been increasing year by year. The outstanding talent with either a Nobel Prize or a National Academy of Sciences award is also increasing every year. However, the long-term employment for these individuals is only approximately 25% because these recruits need to give up their long-term teaching positions in their home countries. In addition to considering the stability of their salaries, the program also needs to provide better benefits (including for their spouses' jobs, their children's schooling, and other issues), which may attract the brains to come to Taiwan to teach. However,

the current provisions for outstanding talents recruited abroad only provide maximum salaries similar to their home country salaries and cannot offer them more favorable salary. Many universities can only pay for a short-term seminar to recruit outstanding talent. Another issue is the fact that these academics are often a member of an established research team, and the program needs to employ the other team members. The overburden of the expectations of the funding at times results in unsuccessful appointments. Additionally, the process of full-time professor appointments is complex, and the three levels of the review process are resisted by some excellent candidates.

2. University research and resources needed to be integrated. In the first phase of the project, many universities established research centers or areas of focus according to their needs or selected development characteristics. Because this is not guided by policy, the focus of the universities results in research center overlap. The issue is how the selected university strengthen the capacity of resource integration with other universities, academic institutions, and society.

3. Too many evaluations for the granted universities results in focusing on short-term visible results. Currently, the projects are given an annual evaluation that serves as a reference for funding in the next year. However, many research projects or teaching programs are long term. Those universities that are intent on getting better evaluation results tend to allocate the majority of resources and efforts on short-term visible results in their projects rather than concentrate their limited resources on long-term development, which is more desirable. The report from the Control Yuan indicated many problems in phase one of the project. The goal is not clear, the review committee members are inconsistent in focusing research fields, teaching service is neglected, and the review indicators do not consider the characteristics of different disciplines (Ministry of Education 2010a). Because of this, the name of the program will be modified to "establish world-class universities," making the target of the project much clearer.

11.3.2 Rankings

According to various university ranking systems, the WCUs project in Taiwan has improved its ranking over the past 5 years.

11.3.2.1 Shanghai Jiao Tong University Ranking System (ARWU)

The Academic Ranking of World Universities (ARWU) conducted by Shanghai Jiao Tong University ranks world-class university research centers and institutes of higher education. According to its report in 2010, Taiwan has seven universities listed in the top 500. National Taiwan University is the highest ranked university, as it has made substantial progress, mainly due to the significant increase in the number of teachers highly cited in all subject areas. Compared with 2009–2010 rankings, some of those in the list of top universities have improved, but some have dropped backward. For example, the ranking of National Taiwan University in 2009 was 150 and 127 (+23) in 2010. The ranking of National Tsing Hua University on the other hand dropped from 307 in 2009 to 314 (−17) in 2010. The other five universities experienced only minor changes.

11.3.2.2   2010 UK University Ranking System in Asian Countries

According to the 2009 to 2010 Times ranking, the National Taiwan University had in the WCU list, but its ranking fell from 95 to 115, a 20-spot decline. National Tsing Hua University made it onto the list for the first time at 107, Sun Yat-sen University at 163, Chiao Tung University at 181, and National Cheng Kung University progressed from 354 to 281. Comparing these Ministry of Education grant-funded universities, we found that even though National Cheng Kung University was successful in getting funding after National Taiwan University did, its performance was worse than expected (THE 2010).

In 2011, within the top 100 universities in Asia, Taiwan has 11, China has 14, and Japan has 26 universities. According to the survey, Taiwan's 11 are National Taiwan University (No. 21), National Tsing Hua University (No. 31), National Cheng Kung University (No. 32), National Yang Ming University (No. 40), National Jiao tong University (No. 52), National Central University (No. 59), National Taiwan University of Science and Technology (No. 62), National Sun Yat-sen (No. 70), Chang Gung University and Taipei Medical University (tied at No. 89), and National Chung Hsing University (No. 99) (THE 2010).

11.3.3   Quality Evaluation of World University Research Papers

Research papers published is another important indicator used to evaluate the quality and amount of research. Table 11.4 shows the 2007 to 2010 assessment of the quality of university research papers as calculated by the Higher Education Evaluation Center/Foundation (Higher Education Evaluation Center/Foundation 2008, 2009, 2010). The ranking has made progress during this period.

According to the Higher Education Evaluation Center/Foundation ESI (Essential Science Indicators) rankings, National Taiwan University was ranked 54 in the number of global papers and was ranked 165 in citations; National Cheng Kung University was ranked 170 for the number of papers and 362 in citations (Higher Education Evaluation Center/Foundation 2011).

In 2011, 42 universities in Taiwan are on the list created by Essential Science Indicators (ESI) for the medical, science, technology, and agricultural fields. The top three universities with journal papers are National Taiwan University, National Cheng Kung University, and National Chiao Tung University. National Taiwan University, National Cheng Kung University, and National Tsing Hua University

Table 11.4 Research paper quality of Taiwanese university (in the top 500 ranking, 2010)

Universities	2010	2009	2008	2007
National Taiwan Univ.	114	102	141	185
National Cheng Kung Univ.	302	307	328	360
National Tsing Hua Univ.	346	347	366	429
National Chiao Tung Univ.	479	456	463	471
National Chang Gung Univ.	493	479		
National Central Univ.		483		
National Yang Ming Univ.		493	475	

Source: The world's assessment of the quality research papers, Higher Education Evaluation Center/Foundation. Retrieved from http://ranking.heeact.edu.tw/zh-tw/2010/Country/Taiwan; http://ranking.heeact.edu.tw/zh-tw/2009/Country/Taiwan; http://ranking.heeact.edu.tw/zh-tw/2008/Country/Taiwan

are the top three in the number of citations. The top three highly cited papers came from National Taiwan University, National Cheng Kung University, and National Tsing Hua University. Compared to the average number of papers by teachers, the top three universities are National Yang Ming, National Tsing Hua University, and National Chiao Tung University (Higher Education Evaluation Center/Foundation 2011). The statistics data from the Higher Education Evaluation Center/Foundation reveal that despite a large volume of papers coming out of the universities, the low rate of citations indicates the quality of the papers may need to be improved.

11.3.4   The Changes Brought by the WCUs Project

There is a general perception that the pressure of publication and teaching generated by the WCUs project has influenced the quality of life on campuses. Too many reviews of short-term performance have created a new academic culture, which is putting too much emphasis on the publication of journal papers. According to the Ministry of Education statistics, in 2005 (before the implementation of the five-year plan), the 15 top universities had 15 articles published in the journals *Science* or *Nature*. During the years 2006 to 2010, each year only saw 15, 9, 12, 10, and 17 articles published in these journals. Yanhua Wu, the President of National Jiao Tong University, pointed out that papers published in *Science* or *Nature* require a long time and considerable resources to produce (China Times 2011a). The timetable of the WCUs project therefore sets up a new publishing pressure for faculty.

After implementing the WCUs project, we have learned that there is a relationship between the number of papers produced in a university and the scale of a university. Different assessment indicators, university size, the presence of a medical school, and even the proportion of humanities and social sciences in the university also influence the results. However, over focusing on research has led to the teaching activities on too many campuses significantly declining.

In late 2010, academics launched a petition "against only use SSCI and SCI as criteria, and find university spirit back" signed by more than 1,700 scholars (China Times 2011b). The government has overemphasized academic papers in respect to the SSCI and SCI results, resulting in their misuse in Taiwan and resulting in a decrease in the number of books published in the humanities and social sciences. It is also arguable, regardless of the academic atmosphere, that the evaluation criteria for arts and sciences are too similar. There are other side effects which are thought to impact the quality of university teaching.

11.4 Conclusion and Policy Direction

This chapter focuses on how WCUs in Taiwan have been institutionalized as a policy at the governmental level. Using the data collected from the selected universities, the author has explored how WCUs have been institutionalized as social systems and integrated culturally in Taiwan.

Despite the controversial debates over the definitions of a world-class university, the government in Taiwan has adopted a pragmatic approach to the issue. By concentrating resources on a select few, the government believes that it will be able to boost some universities to climb higher in the global university rankings. Despite heated debates among academics in Taiwan, the universities have adopted the strategies discussed above to benchmark the best in the world (Chen and Lo 2007; Ngok and Guo 2007).

The first five-year WCUs plan period finished in 2011. The second five-year plan period has been approved in line with the standards set by the top research centers from April 2011. Changes approved by the top research centers and the Ministry of Education for the 5-year phase II of the WCUs plan include increasing the number of universities selected from 10 to 20. The first grant of the university as the main object of the ways leading research center has shown changed the approved standards. Under the new approved rules, a competitive university may have more than two top centers selected.

The first phase of implementation has provided a basis of excellence in higher education. The next phase of project implementation will be the granting of funds to universities or research centers in key areas as the policy directs. Based on their teaching, research, and development capabilities, universities may decide to redefine their development priorities in response to academic and industrial needs. Besides, to further refer to the country's new requirements for next decade, in terms of key services, six new industries, and emerging industries such as smart products, the selected universities have encouraged to provide new competitive projects for their faculties to follow the developmental needs of the government. In this case, we have knowledge to achieve excellence in higher education is a hard work. To fulfill the dream of establishing WCUs in Taiwan, there is still a long way to go.

References

Chang, D., Wu, C. T., Ching, G. S., & Tang, C. W. (2009). An evaluation of the dynamics of the plan to develop first-class universities and top-level research centers in Taiwan. *Asia Pacific Educational Review, 10*(1), 47–57.

Chen, I. R., & Lo, Y. W. (2007). Critical reflections of the approaches to quality in Taiwan's higher education. *The Journal of Comparative Asian Development, 6*(1), 165–185.

China Times. (2011a). *Five-years-50-billion project first stage only two articles in top journal*. Retrieved May, 2, 2011, from http://tw.rd.yahoo.com/referurl/news/logo/ctnews/SIG=10rtjhpom/ *http:/www.chinatimes.com

China Times. (2011b). *Idea platform-against mass production for SSCI and SCI*. Retrieved May, 12, 2011, from http:/www.chinatimes.com

Deem, R., Mok, K. H., & Lucas, L. (2008). Transforming higher education in whose image? Exploring the concept of the 'world-class' university in Europe and Asia. *Higher Education Policy, 21*, 83–97.

European Commission. (2004). *Looking beyond tomorrow: Scientific research in the European Union* (NA-AB-04-001-EN-C). Retrieved from http://ec.europa.eu/publications/booklets/move/48/index_en.htm

Higher Education Evaluation Center/Foundation. (2008). *The world's assessment of the quality research papers*. Retrieved from http://ranking.heeact.edu.tw/zh-tw/2008/Country/Taiwan

Higher Education Evaluation Center/Foundation. (2009). *The world's assessment of the quality research papers*. Retrieved from http://ranking.heeact.edu.tw/zh-tw/2009/Country/Taiwan

Higher Education Evaluation Center/Foundation. (2010). *The world's assessment of the quality research papers*. Retrieved from http://ranking.heeact.edu.tw/zh-tw/2010/Country/Taiwan

Higher Education Evaluation Center/Foundation. (2011). *ESI agricultural areas of study results*. Retrieved from http://epaper.heeact.edu.tw/images/epaper_heeact_edu_tw/2011_0501_No31/Form_31/form_49-57_04.png

Lo, Y. W., & Weng, F. Y. (2005). Taiwan's responses to globalization: Decentralization and internationalization of higher education. In K. H. Mok & R. James (Eds.), *Globalization and higher education in East Asia* (pp. 137–156). Singapore: Marshall Cavendish Academic.

Lu, M. L. (2004, March 25–26). *The blueprint and competitiveness of Taiwan's higher education*. Paper Presented to cross strait seminar on review and prospect of the policy of University Excellence, Taipei, Taiwan.

Ministry of Education. (2000). *List of projects for the first round of the program for promoting academic excellence of universities*. Taipei: Ministry of Education.

Ministry of Education. (2004). *List of projects for the program for improving university fundamental education*. Taipei: Ministry of Education.

Ministry of Education. (2006). *Plan to develop first-class universities and top-level research centers*. Retrieved form http://www.edu.tw/secretary/itemize_list.aspx?pages=1&site_content_sn=19512

Ministry of Education. (2008). *2008 Educational statistical indicators*. Retrieved from http://english.MoE.gov.tw/lp.asp?ctNode=816&CtUnit=507&BaseDSD=7&mp=1

Ministry of Education. (2009). *Development of world-class universities and top research centers*. Retrieved from http://www.edu.tw/secretary/itemize_list.aspx?pages=1&site_content_sn=19512

Ministry of Education. (2010a). *Responses to the Control Yuan to correct and explain the "50 billion five-year plan" by Ministry of Education*. Retrieved from http://www.edu.tw/news.aspx?news_sn=3352&pages=6&unit_sn=3

Ministry of Education. (2010b). *Toward WCUs project*. Retrieved from http://www.edu.tw/high/itemize_list.aspx?pages=0&site_content_sn=1234

Ministry of Education. (2011). *Annual executive report 2010*. Retrieved from http://www.edu.tw/files/site_content/EDU01/教育部99年度施政效告公告版(1000503).pdf

Mok, K. H., & Chan, Y. (2008). International benchmarking with the best universities: Policy and practice in mainland China and Taiwan. *Higher Education Policy, 21*, 469–486.

National Science Council. (2005). *Yearbook of science and technology.* Taipei: Ministry of Education.

Ngok, K. L., & Guo, W. Q. (2007). The quest for world class universities in China: Critical reflections. *The Journal of Comparative Asian Development, 6*(1), 21–44.

Salmi, J. (2009). *The challenge of establishing world-class university.* Washington, DC: The World Bank.

Shin, J. C. (2009). Building world-class research university: The Brain Korea 21 project. *High Education, 58*, 669–688.

THE. (2010). *The world university of rankings.* Retrieved from http://www.timeshighereducation. co.uk/world-university-rankings/2010-2011/top-200.html

Part IV
WCUs in English Speaking Developing Systems

Chapter 12
Malaysia's World-Class University Ambition: An Assessment

Morshidi Sirat

12.1 Introduction and Context

In this highly globalised era, the ability to create an image and status of products and services in the mind of the public is considered important for highly competitive organisations. Increasingly, universities are drawn into this highly competitive environment, adopting entrepreneurial and market-oriented strategies so as to be ahead of their competitors. With increasing cost of higher education, universities are under constant pressure to provide innovative programme. Thus, higher education is no longer identified as purely public or private goods. There is a need for highly competitive universities to have a commanding position in the global higher education landscape (Marginson 2007). In some countries, governments have backed selected universities in their pursuit for image and status, arguing that by achieving a strategic global positioning, universities will become a magnet for the recruitment of students, particularly international postgraduates. It is argued that such success would inevitably become an important source for national income. In addition, such positioning would also guarantee international and national funding for cutting-edge research and innovation. No less important, these universities would automatically emerge as important nodes for international collaboration and global networks. In this respect, therefore, the 'world-class' label for universities represents a commanding status in the global higher education landscape; it is a dream for many universities in both the mature and emerging higher education systems to be ascribed such a status. Furthermore, the media and international student recruitment agencies, which benefit from a popular system that ranks universities, continue to publicise the image and the benefits arising from this 'world

M. Sirat (✉)
School of Humanities, Universiti Sains Malaysia, Gelugor, Penang, Malaysia
e-mail: morshidi2000@yahoo.com

J.C. Shin and B.M. Kehm (eds.), *Institutionalization of World-Class University in Global Competition*, The Changing Academy – The Changing Academic Profession in International Comparative Perspective 6, DOI 10.1007/978-94-007-4975-7_12,
© Springer Science+Business Media Dordrecht 2013

classness'. For instance, several global university rankings and webometrics, in publishing a list of the so-called WCUs, have attracted the attention of universities in the developing countries into the ranking game.

Arguably, the pursuit of world-class status has led to substantial investment and expenditures (see Salmi 2009) for a small number of universities at the top of the higher education pyramid. For developing countries, with limited resources, scarce talent, and an underdeveloped university governance structure and system, such decisions have resulted in marked structural deficiencies in their national higher education system. In many cases, the national higher education system is not functioning as it should be and problems compound when governments are involved prematurely in seeking to improve the universities' rankings. Noticeably, the higher education system of these countries exhibits various problems relating to access, regional equality, and equity. This situation becomes critical when governments begin to implement plans to identify certain universities as potential candidates for world-class status at the expense of other universities in the system. These few selected universities drain the limited resources available for other regional universities, which have been established for the purpose of increasing access to university education and addressing regional inequity problems. Jamil Salmi (2009) cautions that when governments and their higher education institutions are annually presented with the global university rankings, they should take appropriate steps to upgrade their institutions within the context of their own national higher education system. Jamil Salmi (2009) points out that while most nations want some universities to be regarded as WCUs, only a few can establish a WCU, let alone sustain the resources and results needed to maintain their position. On the basis of Jamil Salmi's observation, the majority of universities in the developing world can continue to dream about achieving this goal, but in all probability it is not within the reach of many. The resources and talented people needed to realise their ambition are beyond what many universities in developing countries have at their disposal. For example, the top 20 universities in the QS World University Rankings have, on average, about 2,500 academic faculty; are able to attract and retain top personnel (high selectivity); and have about US$1b (RM3.07b) endowment and an annual budget of US$2b (RM6.14bil) (Sharifah Hapsah 2011).

There is another way of viewing this scenario. One might consider that 'world class' is not about the standards of the developed countries but more about the standards and aspirations of the developing world, the Muslim world, etc. By segmenting the 'world', universities can operate within their own 'world' (e.g. based on capacity building, social inclusiveness, and sustainable development). This idea of the 'other world is desirable' is currently being promoted by Universiti Sains Malaysia in its effort to introduce an alternative model for the development of higher education. At the close of the international conference on Decolonising Our Universities at Universiti Sains Malaysia in June, 2011, conference participants declared that too many universities in South and Southeast Asia have become mere imitations of western universities, with marginally creative contributions of their own and with little or no organic relationship to their local communities

(Globalhighered 2011). The conference expressed its dislike for the way the process of university rankings evaluates local institutions of learning based on the assumptions of western societies (Globalhighered 2011).

This chapter focuses on how WCUs have been institutionalised on the basis of government policy and how the policy is interpreted and adopted by university management. Data on this issue was collected, through a short self-administered questionnaire distributed to vice chancellors of 20 public universities in Malaysia and a review of their university's websites.

Based on the data collected, we begin with a discussion on the nature of the aspiration to become a WCU, arguing in the process that this aspiration is not confined to universities in the developed countries only. While the more advanced developing countries are becoming image conscious, the trend amongst other developing countries with underdeveloped higher education systems, lack of resources to subscribe to global rankings, and their preoccupation with status-building project are very evident. In the case of Malaysia, the preoccupation with 'world class' or 'world classness' is not confined to higher education and universities. There are coffee outlets claiming to be serving 'world-class coffee', cities with 'world-class' infrastructures, lifestyles which are touted as 'world-class living', and prime ministers considered to have 'world-class stature'. Such is the pervasiveness of the notion of world class. So, what is this 'world class' and what does it mean in the context of the development of universities and higher education? Why is it so catchy?

In addressing the issue of world-class universities, this chapter seeks to answer the following questions:

1. For universities in the developing world, is building a WCU a worthwhile ambition? Why is this world-class idea so prevalent amongst universities and governments despite many other important issues in these countries that need serious and immediate attention? We will argue that seeking world-class status is a misplaced priority for universities in developing countries.
2. Increasingly, national universities, initially established for nation-building ob-jectives, are reorienting themselves to WCU objectives – serving the 'global' as they disengage from the 'local'. Is it a wise move on their part to abandon local knowledge for global participation with possible consequences for a more sustainable national development? In the rush to publish in international refereed journals, research findings of local universities are increasingly inaccessible to the local community where it matters the most.
3. Universities may claim they are 'world class', but in fact this status is ascribed by others, based on global rankings or audit, and after having met a set of predetermined criteria. This status is not something a university can self-proclaim in their publicity materials (Jamil Salmi 2009).
4. When we say 'world class', which 'worlds' are we referring to? It is gen-erally agreed that the standards are based on the developed world, not the developing world. Consequently, universities in the developing countries are

allocating resources to meet developed world standards even though these standards may be inappropriate in the context of their national development. Is it possible to have 'world-class' standards based on other criteria, such as the developing world, which are geared more towards capacity building rather than to status? To redefine world class and its mission against benchmarks that are self-selected rather than selected could be contentious (Campbell 2010; cited in Najua 2008).

These questions will be addressed with reference to the institutionalising of WCUs in Malaysia. Malaysia's *National Higher Education Strategic Plan 2020* has as a goal the establishment of WCUs by 2020. Halfway through the plan, what is the progress to date, what lessons have been learned, and is WCU status a worthwhile ambition for Malaysian universities?

12.2 World Class, World-Class Universities: Putting Ideas into Practice

Rosabeth Moss Kanter in her book *World Class: Thriving Locally in the Global Economy* (1995) discusses the rise of the term 'world class', attributing this phenomenon to one defining characteristic, which is excellence, and this 'excellence' is referred to excellence and high performance in the context of successful industry and businesses in a highly competitive environment. In the context of Kanter's arguments, the measurements for excellence and high performance are highly discernible and quantitative in nature. In the 'business' of the universities, excellence need not be purely quantitative in nature. Publications in tier-one ISI journals are only one of the many criteria considered as a measurement of the performance of universities in the developing world. Other elements include teaching, research, and service to the community. Because of the influence of the WCU arguments, universities are more concerned with the quantitative and measurable aspects of their activities. Normally, these are presented in the form of key performance indicators (KPI). Not many universities have considered measuring performance and excellence in terms of key intangible performance (KIP) such as the impact on the mindset and perceptions of target groups in a community engagement project, for instance. Because KPI is more amenable to measurement and with clear targets/timelines, it is not difficult to convince higher education stakeholders to influence universities to adopt a clear set of KPI in their pursuit of the WCU agenda. Following the trend in the industry and business, excellence and high performance are being adopted at the university level to reflect the status of a university vis-à-vis other universities in the world (obviously in the developed world) through a quantitative lens. Undeniably, WCU is about excellence and high performance (Salmi 2009; Sadlak and Liu 2009; Nian et al. 2011) and with enough resources, appropriate governance, talents, and the right alignment of the strategic factors. Having fulfilled all the conditions mentioned above, WCU would see a further round of excellence and performance in teaching, research, publications, recruitment of talented students and staff, and massive resource endowment. In other words, those that are able to achieve the status of WCU will enjoy benefits that tend to be cumulative over time. Clearly the notion of a WCU is about sustaining the image and status of an institution. It does not say much about how WCUs would improve the well-being of society. In other words, the KIP is a significant omission in the WCU conceptualisation (Universiti Sains Malaysia 2007, 2008).

With the pervasiveness of the concept of 'world class' in relation to WCUs, the whole world looks at WCUs as pinnacles of excellence in higher education, with many playing a pivotal role in the transformation of higher education globally. WCUs are seen as the leaders, and to a great extent, they set the standards for and direction of higher education globally. A. T. Kearney's survey of global cities in 2008 and 2010 (see Kearney 2010) indicates that in all highly ranked global cities, there will be several WCUs. These WCUs are considered as knowledge generators, and more importantly they are the sources of quality human capital. For example, A. T. Kearney reports that Kuala Lumpur, which has excellent infrastructure, was not listed in the global cities table because it lacked world-class universities. Thus, global cities not only set the directions for the global economy but will almost certainly influence development in global higher education too. As a result of A. T. Kearney's findings, governments in developing countries are now beginning to make the connection between global cities and the establishment of WCUs. The establishment of WCUs has become a national priority aimed first at education excellence and second at the development of global cities. It is suggested that the existence of WCUs and the attainment of global cities status would attract internationally mobile students and capital (Kearney 2010).

It is important to note the connections and mutually reinforcing nature of global rankings and WCU status and how these became adopted as policy instruments. Ellen Hazelkorn (2008a) notes this connection in Australia's Campus Review:

> Rankings are the latest weapon in the battle for world-class excellence. They are a manifestation of escalating global competition and the geopolitical search for talent, and are now a driver of that competition and a metaphor for the reputation race. What started out as an innocuous consumer product – aimed at undergraduate domestic students – has become a policy instrument, a management tool, and a transmitter of social, cultural and professional capital for the faculty and students who attend high-ranked institutions...

It is an established fact that world-class status for universities and cities is determined by global rankings and that a WCU status is not what one institution could claim unilaterally (Salmi 2009). In other words, it is a status which is bestowed by others. Notwithstanding the methodological limitations of any ranking exercise as highlighted by Simon Marginson (Globalhighered 2007), it is generally agreed that international league tables show that WCUs, which are the highest ranked universities in the world, are the ones that make significant contributions to the advancement of knowledge through research and that teach with the most innovative curricula and pedagogical methods under the most conducive circumstances. WCUs also make research an integral component of undergraduate teaching and produce outstanding graduates because of their success in intensely competitive learning environment and, more importantly, after graduation. It is these concrete accomplishments and the international reputation associated with them that make these institutions world class (World Bank 2007).

The literature is replete with many examples of global (i.e. western) criteria and standards considered to be universal norms of excellence and high performance, and all aspiring universities have to strive to fulfil these criteria (Hazelkorn 2008b). This provides a starting point for a discussion on which 'worlds' we are referring to (Badat 2010). There is a nascent debate on the need to assess the appropriateness of WCU conceptualisation and its relevance to the Muslim world. This dissenting voice from the developing world is worth noting. If anything, it enriches academic discourses on WCU.

12.3 The Malaysian Case

12.3.1 National Higher Education Strategic Plan 2020

In line with the interest shown in more advanced developing countries, the Malaysian Higher Education Ministry has adopted the WCU concept and framework in its overall strategic planning for the higher education sector (see Ministry of Higher Education 2007). The manner in which the WCU concept has been adopted as a policy statement in the National Higher Education Strategic Plan 2020 (NHESP 2020) and its accompanying Action Plan 2007–2010 is an indicator of national direction and commitments. The NHESP 2020 and the Action Plan 2007–2010, launched in August 2007, set out the role of universities in Malaysia's socio-economic development, with a goal of transforming Malaysia as a hub for higher education excellence by 2020. NHESP 2020 envisions that Malaysia will have a substantial concentration of international students (no less than 100,000) in its higher education institutions by the end of the plan period. The achievement of such an objective is highly dependent on Malaysia's success in developing 'world-class' universities in line with the western standards. Such success reflects the ability of Malaysian universities to compete globally, demonstrating elements of 'excellence' in publications, research, and teaching. Five years after the government announced the plan, it is time to analyse the impact of the strategies for the creation of these prestigious institutions in Malaysia's higher education system. The recent launch of the second Action Plan 2011–2015 of the NHESP 2020 provides an excellent opportunity to reflect on Malaysia's commitment to 'world classness'. Despite the waning interest of many public universities in global rankings, the government has reiterated its WCU aspirations in the National Higher Education Action Plan 2011–2015 (see Ministry of Higher Education 2011). The government is fully committed to selected Malaysia's universities being in the top 100 universities in the world by 2015.

The desire to build WCUs in Malaysia is to propel its economy, which will be based on knowledge and innovation which are assumed to be primarily generated by universities, particularly WCUs or more appropriately world-class research universities. For this reason, the NHESP 2020 has specified that five universities will be upgraded as research universities in the first phase of the NHESP 2020. Malaysia has adopted this policy not because of the need to maintain economic power in the global market but in the interests of international student recruitment, image-building, and the final analysis as a hub for knowledge and innovation.

The official position of the government on establishing WCUs is very clear, but public universities have reacted both for and against this agenda in various ways, as follows:

1. A nonconformist position has been taken by some university vice chancellors. They have raised the issue of which 'world' universities should set the standards that Malaysian universities are obliged to follow. Is it about the standards of the developed world where world class is equated with status and reputation, generating income and publishing high-profile research in English-language ISI journals? Must world class be equated with excellence in the context of country-specific national aspiration and objectives?

2. World class should be interpreted in terms of the developing world realities where universities are playing an important role in nation building. In this context, it is important that research outputs are translated into practical community-level projects. Publication of research findings should not be directed at ISI journals only but also published with a view towards enriching local knowledge, and creating an indigenous technology available to locals in their own languages. International audiences should not be the priority in such publications.

3. Some adopt a conformist position, supporting the push for WCU status based on specified timelines, and with clear KPI, especially publications in top-tier ISI journals.

Table 12.1 presents a list of public universities in Malaysia, with their visions and missions. This table provides some insight into the background of these public universities and the reasons for their position for or against WCUs in the Malaysian context. There is one accelerated programme for excellence (APEX University) and five research universities (including the APEX University) in the national higher education system. This APEX initiative, based on the German model, provides for the government-aided, fast-track transformation of a university to attain world-class status. In the selection process, four universities (USM, UM, UKM, and UPM) were in the final list, and USM was selected as an APEX university in 2008.

12.3.2 Response to WCU (Survey Data)

The following section provides data from the survey, showing how these public universities responded to the questions about WCUs. In response to a question on

Table 12.1 Public universities in Malaysia

No.	Universities	Year of establishment	Categories	Vision	Mission
1	Universiti Malaya (UM)	1962	Research university	To be an internationally renowned institution of higher learning in research, innovation, publication, and teaching	To advance knowledge and learning through quality research and education for the nation and for humanity
2	Universiti Sains Malaysia (USM)	1969	Accelerated programme for excellence (APEX) and research university	Transforming higher education for sustainable tomorrow	USM is a pioneering, trans-disciplinary research-intensive university that empowers future talents and enables the bottom billions to transform their socio-economic well-being
3	Universiti Kebangsaan Malaysia (UKM)	18 May 1970	Research university	UKM is committed to be an institution that moves ahead of society and its era in the development of a dynamic, learned, and morally strong society	The chosen institution that safeguards the sovereignty of the Malay language and internationalising knowledge moulded on a strong sense of the national culture
4	Universiti Putra Malaysia (UPM)	29 October 1971	Research university	To become a university of international repute	To make meaningful contributions towards wealth creation, nation building, and universal human advancement through the exploration and dissemination of knowledge
5	Universiti Teknologi Malaysia (UTM)	1 April 1975	Research university	To be recognised as a world-class centre of academic and technological excellence	To be leader in the development of human capital and innovative technologies that will contribute to the nation's wealth creation

6	Universiti Teknologi MARA (UiTM)	1965	Comprehensive university	To establish UiTM as a premier university of outstanding scholarship and academic excellence capable of providing leadership to *Bumiputeras's* dynamic involvement in all professional fields of world-class standards in order to produce globally competitive graduates of sound ethical standing	To enhance the knowledge and expertise of *Bumiputeras* in all fields of study through professional programmes, research work, and community service based on moral values and professional ethics
7	Universiti Islam Antarabangsa Malaysia (UIAM)	1983	Comprehensive university	Towards actualising the university's vision, IIUM endeavours to produce human capital centred on the Islamic faith, creed, and knowledge	The summary of the mission should read as follows: Integration Islamisation Internationalisation Comprehensive excellence
8	Universiti Malaysia Sabah (UMS)	24 November 1994	Comprehensive university	Universiti Malaysia Sabah strives to be an innovative university of global standing	Universiti Malaysia Sabah strives to achieve academic excellence in various fields by gaining international recognition through learning and teaching, research and publication, social services, and a balanced specialisation of knowledge and personality development of students resulting in high productivity and quality in the context of the society and the nation
9	Universiti Malaysia Sarawak (UNIMAS)	24 December 1992	Comprehensive university	To become an exemplary university of internationally acknowledged stature and a scholarly institution of choice for both students and academics through the pursuit of excellence in teaching, research, and scholarship	To generate, disseminate, and apply knowledge strategically and innovatively to enhance the quality of the nation's culture and prosperity of its people

(continued)

Table 12.1 (continued)

No.	Universities	Year of establishment	Categories	Vision	Mission
10	Universiti Utara Malaysia (UUM)	16 February 1984	Focused university	To become an eminent management university	To be a consistently pre-eminent centre of academic excellence in teaching and learning, research, consultancy, and publication in the field of management and at the same time to bring forth highly competent human capital that is committed to serving in the development of the nation and all humanity
11	Universiti Pendidikan Sultan Idris (UPSI)	1 May 1997	Focused university	To be a prestigious university providing exceptional leadership in education based on the advantage of broad experience and high level of competency in meeting global changes	To generate and foster knowledge through teaching, research, publication, consultancy, and community services to achieve the vision of the nation
12	Universiti Tun Hussein Onn Malaysia (UTHM)	16 September 1993	Focused university	Aspires to pioneer the application of science and technology for universal prosperity	To produce and train competitive professionals and technologists of high ethical values in the global arena through holistic academic programmes, knowledge, and research culture, based on the concept of *Tauhid*
13	Universiti Teknikal Malaysia Melaka (UTeM)	1 December 2000	Focused university	To be one of the world's leading innovative and creative technical universities	To produce highly competent professionals through quality and world-class technical university education based on application-oriented teaching, learning, and research with smart university-industry partnership in line with national aspirations

No	University	Date	Type		
14	Universiti Malaysia Perlis (UNIMAP)	25 July 2001	Focused university	An internationally competitive academic and research institution	To produce a holistic human capital that contributes to the nation's development and industrial competitiveness agenda
15	Universiti Malaysia Terengganu (UMT)	1 February 2007	Focused university	To be an institution that generates, disseminates, and applies innovative knowledge and a catalyst for the development of progressive individuals and sustainable environment	To drive the fields of science, technology, and management of natural resource via the generation of excellent academic and research programme towards the development of individuals who ensure the sustainability of religion, race, and the nation
16	Universiti Malaysia Pahang (UMP)	16 February 2002	Focused university	To be a world-class technological university	We provide high-quality education, research, and services in engineering and technology in a culture of creativity and innovation
17	Universiti Sains Islam Malaysia (USIM)	1 February 2007	Focused university	Fostering academic excellence and an *ummah* able to contribute towards human progress, nation building, and the advancement of the world	To be a leading centre of Islamic studies that utilises advanced approaches and ICT to explore issues for the well-being and harmony of society and Islam
18	Universiti Sultan Zainal Abidin (UniSZA)	26 March 2005	Focused university	Universiti Sultan Zainal Abidin aspires to be a world-class institution of higher learning that produces and shapes talented leaders who are knowledgeable, refined, and noble	Universiti Sultan Zainal Abidin shall enhance and nurture the talent of future leaders in various disciplines through reengineering of knowledge promotion of transparency and openness, instillation of diversity for the benefit of humanity

(continued)

Table 12.1 (continued)

No.	Universities	Year of establishment	Categories	Vision	Mission
19	Universiti Malaysia Kelantan (UMK)	31 March 2006	Focused university	Championing human capital development with entrepreneurial qualities for global prosperity	UMK delivers relevant and excellent academic programmes, research and innovation of high commercial value, and services that fulfil social responsibility, with the goal of raising the level of competitiveness through entrepreneurship. UMK that focuses on the needs of its customers and fulfils the requirements of the educational market through the provision of a conducive environment and through its staff that are knowledgeable, experienced, and committed. The staff also practise professional work culture with participative management and engage in continuous development and improvement
20	Universiti Pertahanan Nasional Malaysia (UPNM)	10 November 2006	Focused university	To be the premier defence university for education, training, and knowledge creation	UPNM is committed to excellence in serving the nation as a premier defence university for leadership and professional development, knowledge dissemination, and application of defence science and technology, as well as policy research

the defining characteristics of a WCU amongst the vice chancellors, a common theme on world class could be described in two words – international recognition and excellence (in teaching, research, and publication). However, based on vice chancellors' responses, approaches adopted in order to achieve such status need not be similar.

UPM, for instance, articulated its views on world class as follows:

The concept of 'world-class' universities echoes the norms and values of the world's dominant research-oriented universities. It centres on academic standards and improvements, the role of higher learning institutions in the society, and the way the academic institutions are accepted at the national and international systems of higher education.

The essence of 'world-class' universities is the combination of great ingredients – the dedication to explore new knowledge frontiers, to master new technologies, and to harvest the abundant riches of diverse cultures, market, and new industries.

Essentially, the characteristics of these 'world-class' universities according to UPM are as follows:

1. Reputation for academic and research excellence
   Academic staff are recognised internationally as leaders in their fields especially in the field of bioscience, tropical agriculture, engineering, information technology, veterinary, forestry, educational studies, and more. Active intellectual and philosophical interactions between academic scholars and students inspire students to excel.
2. Dedicated academic staff
   Most academic staff are well-qualified with advanced degrees from world-recognised universities. Committed academic staff and students work closely together in continuous research and development, earning international achievements and recognition.
3. High-quality and experienced academic support
   State-of-the-art classroom and laboratories; conducive learning environments; excellent student facilities for social, recreational, and sporting activities; a sophisticated IT infrastructure and fibre-optic communications system that facilitates the process of learning and staying on campus; and a spacious and accessible library.
4. World-class programmes
   Academic disciplines that reflect current trends and demands of over 250 fields of study. Currently, UPM offers 53 bachelors, 5 diplomas, and 400 postgraduate programmes at the master and PhD levels.
5. Governance
   The university upholds academic integrity with a commitment to values such as honesty, justice, respect, and responsibility.

According to UKM, a university established to pursue nationalist objectives, a WCU would display the following characteristics:

• Leadership, autonomy, and academic freedom

- Excellent and sought-after academics
- Excellent infrastructure and financial resources
- High-impact research and output
- Student quality and market employability

The transformation goal of UKM is based on a desire to be world class. KPIs are measured for six pillars of excellence comprising of leadership, governance, talent, teaching and learning, research and innovation, and community and industry engagement.

Non-research universities, such as UMK, are more modest in their interpretation of what a WCU entails. UMK views WCUs as institutions which demonstrate the following characteristics:

- Having well-qualified and highly talented staff
- Having niches which are referred to worldwide
- Success rate for admission ≤20% (highly competitive)
- The mover for community development globally
- World player in many aspects

Other non-research but technically focused university, UniMAP, regards WCUs as institutions characterised by:

- Excellence of undergraduate and postgraduate academic programmes
- Excellence of teaching and learning process, equipment, and facilities
- Excellence in research, development, and commercialisation
- Excellence in publication and knowledge dissemination
- Excellence in activities contributing to the cultural, scientific, and civic life of society
- Very high rate of graduate employability

USM, an APEX and research university, provided a contrasting view on the defining characteristics of WCUs. USM considers the concept to be 'deceptive' in that it revolves around one 'world', dominated by the 'west' and ignores Malaysian sociocultural context. USM regards WCUs as institutions which are:

- God-centric
- Heart-centric and transformational
- Have a genuine love for humanity and are people-oriented
- Sincere and futuristic
- Humble and have a willingness to learn from all (not expert or iconic attitudes)

It is worth noting that UiTM, a university with a long history of striving for access and equity in higher education for indigenous groups, has dropped its world-class status ambition in favour of nation building in the context of a highly internationalised higher education. UiTM considers that nation building and national priorities may conflict with the drive for WCU status in the short and medium term.

USM's efforts to delink universities' wider role in society from global rankings have influenced other institutions. UKM, for instance, is now viewing rankings and WCUs in a different light. While this has not yet been adopted as the university's official position, the vice chancellor of UKM, writing in *The Star* (Sunday, 19 June 2011), appears to agree with the UNESCO's Paris meeting on global rankings which stated that:

> ... caution must be exercised in using rankings to influence educational policy and decisions about incentivising higher education as well as allocation of scarce resources at regional, national and institutional levels. There were strong calls urging governments not to initiate policies targeted at creating "world-class" universities as a panacea for success in a global economy.

Other public universities in Malaysia have not articulated this view of WCUs in their mission statements, realising that they have more pressing national and subnational issues to address.

12.3.3 Response to WCU: Mission and Vision Statement

An examination of the websites and documents of universities in Malaysia indicates that the concept 'world class' is an integral part of the vision and mission statement of the following universities:

- Universiti Malaya (UM)
- Universiti Sains Malaysia (USM)
- Universiti Kebangsaan Malaysia (UKM)
- Universiti Putra Malaysia (UPM)
- Universiti Teknologi Malaysia (UTM)
- Universiti Islam Antarabangsa Malaysia (UIAM)
- Universiti Malaysia Sarawak (UNIMAS)
- Universiti Malaysia Sabah (UMS)

World class, as it is being articulated in their mission and vision statements, reflects the qualitative and quantitative aspects of their positioning in the global higher education landscape. Embedded in this articulation is the idea of excellence based on global benchmarking. UPM, UMK, and UniMAP have WCU ambitions in terms of the conventional ways the concept is currently articulated. For instance, in the case of UPM, its mission is 'to make meaningful contributions towards wealth creation, nation building and universal human advancement through the exploration and dissemination of knowledge'. This mission statement suggests that its WCU image is not self-serving but is for the good of the nation.

In line with this vision of becoming 'a university of international repute', UPM has evolved into a multidisciplinary, research-focused university, offering a diverse range of high-quality study programmes which have steadily attracted students from over 60 countries around the globe. UPM is amongst the five Malaysian universities designated as research universities; renowned for their research, development, and commercialisation; and now ranked at the top amongst the most esteemed universities in the region. UPM is today internationally acknowledged for its dedication to creating new frontiers in research.

USM on the other hand describes its mission as prioritising the welfare of the 'bottom billion' in the developing world, centring on the concept of sustainability supported by the seven thrusts of the future, uniqueness, sustainability, humanity, universality, change, and sacrifice (i.e. sincerity). USM's version of world-class ambition is expressed as follows:

> The reform agenda of Universiti Sains Malaysia (USM) under the APEX framework constitutes a radical revision and engagement with the issue of being a world class university. Such a transformation entails engaging with and articulating how USM can truly transform itself and success in a global context that is competitive and often unequal. Redefining excellence in the context of USM's APEX strategy entails rethinking the social, economic, and cultural context of higher education in the Malaysian environment. (Campbell 2010, p. ix)

Generally, universities in Malaysia interpret world class in terms of striving for education and research excellence. The point of reference for excellence is universities in the top tier of the global rankings. In this respect, one Malaysian university, UM, is striving for excellence and aspires to be a WCU through publications in top-tier ISI journals. UM has subsequently adopted the standard western approach and is seeking government resources to pursue WCU status. By contrast, USM has always sought to differentiate itself. It argues that world class should not focus on the standards set by the developed world and suggests that the developing world, and indeed the Islamic world, could work towards WCUs based on the non-western tradition. UM and USM have made it very clear as to how they would proceed to achieve WCU status.

UM's approach is rather conventional, in that its target is status-building and it focuses on research and publications in top-tier ISI journals, on the basis that this has worked well for other world-class universities. Inevitably, UM will need more resources and more talent for this endeavour. USM on the other hand is charting a different course, rejecting western, status-conscious tradition in favour of a capacity-building framework geared towards the social role of universities. USM sees itself as has having a dual status, as both a research-intensive and an APEX (accelerated programme for excellence) university. As a research-intensive university, it has to measure up to the standards of a world-class university, publishing in ISI journals, etc. But as an APEX university, it has an opportunity to experiment with new approaches and frameworks, setting on qualitative targets.

The WCU scenario in Malaysian higher education, as it relates to the case of two contrasting public universities – USM and UM – is an interesting case worth watching closely. When announcing USM as the only university chosen for the accelerated programme for excellence (APEX), the Minister of Higher Education indicated the underlying rationale of this programme in the following comment:

One of the transformational initiatives launched recently involves the APEX initiative which provides for the government-aided, fast-track transformation of a university to attain world-class status within a very short timeframe. It is hoped that this kind of fast-track transformation will push the other universities to adopt a similar stance to achieving world class status. This Accelerated Programme for Excellence (APEX) places the selected institution or institutions at the apex of the HEI pyramid and some of the defining criteria for the APEX status include outstanding leadership, faculties, student body, and infrastructure. APEX universities need to be administered and managed by visionary, versatile, and motivated leaders committed to intellectual and academic advancement. They would need to reflect the excellence they require from their staff and know how to optimise their universities' human resources and assets. They would need to be highly motivated themselves in order to motivate others to heights of excellence (Dzulkifli 2009, p. 8)

USM, representing a dissenting voice in the debate on WCUs in Malaysia, has repeatedly argued that seeking world-class status is diverting the institution's real role and contribution to society. For USM, world class in the developing world context should revolve around two main agenda: (1) prioritising society well-being in that research is conducted for the benefit of society and that research findings are society-relevant and problem-solving in nature and (2) the development of local knowledge and technology should take priority, and publications should be accessible to a broader base of readers. UM on the other hand is willing to take up the challenges of becoming a top 100 university by 2015. A plan was put in place to achieve this WCU status through its high-impact research (HIR-UM) programmes with researchers committed to publishing articles in top-tier ISI journals in their respective fields.

Halfway through the NHESP 2020, public universities in Malaysia are taking divergent routes and adopting varied philosophical stances and interpretations of what it takes to be a WCU. At this juncture of Malaysia's economic development and with many competing priorities, it appears that public universities have the flexibility to chart their own course and directions. In particular, they are using their own resources based on profitable income-generating activities. The government will intervene and realign universities' course of action in specific instances where the government is the main sponsor of programmes and initiatives. While there is an institutionalisation of WCU in terms of policy statements and direction, government has not been pushing the agenda diligently in view of the substantial resources and talent needed to support this project. In the pursuit of WCU status, the government has always reminded universities to be practical and undertaken programmes with a high level of integrity and transparency.

12.4   Conclusion

Although the National Higher Education Strategic Plan 2020 has institutionalised the notion of the WCU in the Malaysian higher education system, the public universities have reacted to it very differently. Based on the survey data and websites analysis, we can categorise Malaysian public universities into four groups: those seeking higher global ranking and desiring to become a WCU, the 'dare to be different' group, the sober and 'down-to-earth' group, and the chameleon group, changing their stance on global rankings and WCU status depending on their performance in the global rankings at a particular time.

In promoting world-class status, the Ministry of Higher Education realises that talent and substantial resources have to be made available to achieve the WCU objective. The Ministry is not oblivious to Jamil Salmi's (2009) requirements for achieving WCU status. The government is allowing universities to set their priorities as they see fit because it is unable to provide sufficient resources for such an effort while reminding the universities they are accountable to the *rakyat* (people) in whatever they do, especially when public funds are involved.

It is worth considering the need to redefine 'world class' in terms of the perspective of the developing world, with nation building and local knowledge being the top priority. However, unless there is a significant shift in how universities and governments in the South (developing, non-western countries) envision their future, standards will continue to be set by the North (developed, western countries) and any other discussion to the contrary is purely academic in nature.

Acknowledgements I am very appreciative of the valuable assistance of Ms Ooi Poh Ling and Ms Siti Maznishah Che Mustafa of the National Higher Education Research Institute (IPPTN) in organising and preparing materials for this chapter.

References

Badat, S. (2010). *Have global university rankings any value for the global South?* Retrieved August 1, 2011, from http://www.isa-sociology.org/universities-in-crisis/?p=421

Campbell, J. (2010). *Understanding reform and the Universiti Sains Malaysia agenda. Discussion and critique.* Penang: Penerbit Universiti Sains Malaysia.

Dzulkifli, A. R. (2009). *In search of a world-class university of tomorrow. The importance of the APEX initiative.* Kuala Lumpur: AKEPT and Oxford Fajar Bakti.

Globalhighered. (2007). *Global university rankings 2007: Interview with Simon Marginson, December 12.* Retrieved August 2, 2011, from http://globalhighered.wordpress.com/2007/12/12/global

Globalhighered. (2011). *Decolonising our universities: Another world is desirable.* Retrieved August 3, 2011, from http://globalhighered.wordpress.com/2011/07/22/. Accessed 3 Aug 2011.

Hazelkorn, E. (2008a, September). *Impact of university rankings: Global excellence vs. local engagement.* Presentation given at the launch workshop for participating regions, OECD/IMHE Reviews of Higher Education in Regional Development 2008–2010, Paris.

Hazelkorn, E. (2008b, May 27). Rising popularity of rankings. *Campus Review,* 6–7.

Kanter, R. M. (1995). *World class: Thriving locally in the global economy.* New York: Free Press.

Kearney, A. T. (2010). *Global cities index.* Retrieved August 3, 2011, from http://www.atkearney.com/index.php/Publications/global-cities-index.html

Marginson, S. (2007). Global position and position taking: The case of Australia. *Journal of International Education,* Spring. Retrieved August 1, 2011, from http://www.international.ac.uk/resources/Global%20Position.pdf

Ministry of Higher Education. (2007). *National higher education strategic plan 2020.* Putrajaya: Ministry of Higher Education.

Ministry of Higher Education. (2011). *National higher education strategic plan 2020. Action plan 2011–2015. Malaysia's global reach.* Putrajaya: Kementerian Pengajian Tinggi.

Najua, I. (2008). USM: Redefining world class. *Prospect Malaysia, 8*, 9–13.

Nian, C. L., Wang, Q., & Cheng, Y. (Eds.). (2011). *Paths to a world-class university. Lessons from practices and experiences.* Rotterdam/Boston/Taipei: Sense Publishers.

Sadlak, J., & Liu, N. C. (Eds.). (2009). *The world-class university as part of a new higher education paradigm: From institutional qualities to systemic excellence.* Bucharest: UNESCO European Centre for Higher Education, Shanghai Jiao Tong University, Cluj University Press.

Salmi, J. (2009). *The challenge of establishing world-class universities.* Washington, DC: The World Bank.

Sharifah Hapsah, S. S. (2011, June 19). Use rankings wisely. *The Star*, Sunday.

Universiti Sains Malaysia. (2007). *Constructing future higher education scenarios.* Pulau Pinang: Penerbit Universiti Sains Malaysia.

Universiti Sains Malaysia. (2008). *Transforming higher education for a sustainable tomorrow.* Pulau Pinang: Penerbit Universiti Sains Malaysia.

World Bank (2007). Malaysia and the knowledge economy. Retrieved September 1, 2012, from http://siteresources.worldbank.org/INTMALAYSIA/Resources/Malaysia-Knowledge-Economy2007.pdf

Chapter 13
Peering Through the Dust of Construction: Singapore's Efforts to Build WCUs

Kong Chong Ho

A diploma from the "right" university is incomparably more valuable than just any old degree. Meritocracy be damned, pedigree counts.

(Brody 2007, p. 122)

13.1 Introduction

East Asian countries are latecomers in the international education, league tables and world-class university formation. This entry was marked by a fundamental restructuring of the university system, particularly top national universities whose task has been the training of the nation's elite. Ishikawa (2009) writes about the painful experience of Japanese universities needing to move away from "long cherished academic traditions that enabled national independence" (p. 7) to face increased competition for reputation and Asia's best students. In this reinvention, Yonezawa (2007) highlights the use of English and the increased challenge from regional competitors as significant pressures for Japanese flagship universities.

Singapore's experience has been just as wide ranging in terms of change, but the restructuring process has been marked by three distinctive features particular to the city state: (a) the shift from being a national university to a WCU is closely tied to the republic's search for international talent both in terms of international students who become young researchers and as skilled labour to augment the workforce as well as well-known researchers to drive basic and applied research; (b) unlike Korea and Japan which have strong industries, Singapore's economic structure is more akin to that of a global city with a well-developed producer and financial services

K.C. Ho (✉)
Faculty of Arts and Social Sciences, Department of Sociology, National University
of Singapore, Singapore, Singapore
e-mail: sochokc@nus.edu.sg

J.C. Shin and B.M. Kehm (eds.), *Institutionalization of World-Class University in Global Competition*, The Changing Academy – The Changing Academic Profession in International Comparative Perspective 6, DOI 10.1007/978-94-007-4975-7_13, © Springer Science+Business Media Dordrecht 2013

sector. This is an important factor when we consider the ecosystem of the university and the potential knowledge spillovers (Audretsch and Feldman 2003) within the system; and lastly, (c) as a city state centred in Southeast rather than East Asia, Singapore's efforts along with its English system of education are attractive to a certain segment of students and professors wishing to gain a foothold in Asia but still able to operate in an international environment.

In this chapter, I argue that these three features have shaped the path development of Singapore's efforts at building WCUs. The search for foreign talent lent a greater urgency as it affected not only the university but also the economy. The global city creates an ecosystem whose features favour business and commerce rather than engineering. And so, while engineering and science research continues to receive high priority, this lacks strong industry participation. And lastly, as a small city state with only a few universities, Singapore was able to be quite nimble in its restructuring effort such that within 10 years (1999–2009), it was able to put in place policies at the national and the institutional levels without much opposition from institutions and segments that were left at a disadvantage.

In developing these points, I will draw upon a survey of international students in four Asian cities to highlight the distinctive characteristics of the Singapore case. This chapter also addresses the most visible impacts arising out of a decade of experimentation. This takes the form of a new institutional structure which places a stronger emphasis on faculty performance as the basis for promotion and tenure as well as salary adjustments. For students, the new system sees more international exposure in terms of student study abroad programmes for undergraduate students and financial support for overseas conferences for graduate students.

13.2   The National Policy Level

To explain the beginnings of the policy which led ultimately to the creation of WCUs in Singapore, we need to look at the relationship between education and the economy. Education policies in the early post-independence period were understandably tied to nation building. Within the context of a multi-ethnic society where each community was responsible for its own education, the policies in the 1960s were tied to the nationalisation of schools and the development of a curriculum which fostered an integration and which was relevant to the needs of the economy. For the latter set of concerns, the strategic decision was for the education system to be in English, since this was perceived to be the international working language. Along with this decision was the push towards science and technology, with a new system of technical schools at the lower secondary level, a system of polytechnics featuring a 3-year diploma programme for 17-year-olds and engineering in the university, with the old Nanyang University being revived as Nanyang Technological University in 1991.[1] This system of education was created to fit an economy where industry was the key sector driving revenue and employment. Within the wider regional context, the period from the 1970s to the 1990s was also the period where industrial production was also moving from Europe and America to East Asia in search of lower costs, implicating Korea, Taiwan, Hong Kong and Singapore in this dynamic.

With the shift towards a world city and its associated strategy of developing producer and consumer services, the focus of human capital development took three routes. Unlike Hong Kong which lost its manufacturing sector, Singapore's stubborn attachment to manufacturing meant that it had to keep its technological edge in order to secure its competitiveness. This meant not just working at the vocational level, a strategy which served the republic well in the 1980s. The technology push required the role of the universities to become a partner of industry in order to maintain a research and development platform which supported the new products research and engineers and research scientists to fuel innovative research. The decade of 2000–2009 saw both the National University of Singapore and the Nanyang Technological University transform into research universities, as a cluster of specialised research institutes (Gopinathan 1999). Most importantly, the Agency for Science, Technology and Research (A*STAR) was formed to spearhead the science and technology research and the development of science parks to attract multinational companies to locate their research facilities in Singapore.

The second route is most evident in the development of business and management studies in Singapore. This included the development of a third smaller specialised management university, as well as the attraction of well-known business schools to host their programmes in Singapore (Olds and Thrift 2005). As Olds and Thrift point out, the development of this institutional system will "expose Singaporean educational institutions to competition (thereby forcing them to upgrade), and to produce (in discursive and institutional senses) a 'global education hub' that would be attractive to students from around the Asia-Pacific region. In theory this cluster of educational institutions would produce and disseminate knowledge at a range of scales, supporting local and foreign firms in Singapore, state institutions in Singapore, and firms and states in the Southeast, East and South Asian regions" (Olds and Thrift 2005, p. 207).

The third route is perhaps the most controversial, and this is the liberalisation of immigration under the banner "foreign talent". After battling the limits of a small workforce (full employment was reached by the mid-1970s) for over a decade, government planners announced in 1989 a relaxation of immigration controls in order to attract foreign talent (Singapore Straits Times, 11 July 1989). In 1991, the Economic Development Board set up an International Manpower Division which

---

[1] According to the NTU website, "Nanyang Technological Institute was established on the same campus (Nanyang University) in 1981 with government funding to educate practice-oriented engineers for the burgeoning Singapore economy". Source: www.ntu.edu.sg/aboutntu/ntuataglance/Pages/Ourhistory.aspx

effectively meant that the board's role of attracting overseas investment to Singapore had been supplemented with the attraction of IT manpower to fill an estimated 1,000 jobs in 1992 (Singapore Business Times, 30 September 1991). This initial specific focus has since been expanded to attract a range of professionals as well as foreign students (Singapore Straits Times, 31 August 1997). At the same time, the menial work of the city has to be done by another group of foreigners as better educated Singaporeans shun these jobs.

The policy to create a hub of higher education institutions drawing in 150,000 international students by 2015 is known as the Global Schoolhouse Project [GSP] (Channel NewsAsia, 16 August 2003). The GSP has a number of significant elements. It is an economic policy because the GSP is created to develop the education sector as a source of revenue and employment and makes a new perception of education as a lucrative market. As a service policy, the Economic Development Board in Singapore plans to "build up the Singapore education brand name" and "develop a vibrant community of tertiary, pre-tertiary and corporate training institutions" so that it can "attract even more students, faculty, researchers and professionals from all over the world" (Today, 16 November 2010).

This policy has both local and foreign elements. Local schools with a good reputation for excellent academic results at the pre-tertiary level have been approved by the Ministry of Education to increase their international student intakes and provide dormitories.[2] The local universities have also seen their international student enrolment increasing. This local effort works in tandem with efforts to attract international tertiary institutes to establish overseas campuses in Singapore. Top foreign universities have also been attracted to set up overseas campuses in Singapore. With 30 years of experience courting multinational companies to Singapore, the government has been able to create a set of incentives for this new group of suitors. For example, according to the *Times of India*, INSEAD received Singapore $10 million for research and land for its Asia campus at one-third the market price (Times of India, March 21 2010). Yet, despite these incentives, the task of establishing overseas campuses has not been an easy one. Sindhu's analysis of two ventures which failed to materialise in Singapore points to the insufficient attention which should have been paid "to the heterogeneous elements that make up networks – the complex human actors and the idiosyncrasies of their communication styles, their personal needs and circumstances... key people failed to embody and translate the global imaginary into globalizing practices and outcomes" (Sidhu 2009, p. 137).

The quality of the GSP is also uneven. As part of the expansion and liberalisation created from this project, a number of organisations concentrate mainly on the adult education market through the teaching fee-paying students. However, Singapore as a brand-name place for further studies has been established on the backs of the world-class institutions it has been able to attract, such as INSEAD, as well as on the growing reputation of its local universities. For example, 10 years ago, Professor

---

[2] See Jason Tan (1998) for a more detailed description of the government's efforts to liberalise the pre-tertiary education sector.

Arnoud De Meyer, then the founding Dean of INSEAD's Asia campus in Singapore, was reported in the local papers for his statement about Singapore's educational institutions demonstrating "satisfactory under-performance or mediocrity" because he was irked at NUS referring to its 89th placing in the Financial Times Top 100 MBA programmes as an "accolade". Professor De Meyer was interviewed in 2010 and said of the climb by NUS and Nanyang Technological University to 35 and 24, respectively, that "they are now among the best, world class" (Straits Times, 3 November 2010).

This climb from 89th position to 35th position in the space of 10 years for the NUS Business School is reflective of the wider sweeping changes experienced by local universities in Singapore, particularly NUS. A significant factor has been the increase in the availability of financial resources. The government increased its spending from Singapore $1.24 billion in 2005 to $2.52 billion in 2010 (Straits Times, 3 November 2010). However, this injection of financial resources would not have achieved the desired results without internal changes to the universities' structure and mission.

13.3   Institutional Level

13.3.1   Mission, Governance and Administrative Systems

> Corporatisation is not a drive towards commercialisation or commoditisation. On the contrary, the highest quality in the world is found in the private universities and what we are doing is borrowing some of these lessons.
>
> (Education Minister Tharman Shanmugaratnam, as cited in Straits Times, 22 November 2005)

The 2000 Ministry of Education report *Fostering Autonomy and Accountability in Universities* was clearly the most significant event in creating the new identity of Singapore universities. As pointed out by Lee and Gopinathan (2008), the committee noted that leading public universities in the world which were referenced in the report had the autonomy to react quickly to the changing conditions of higher education. Having this autonomy[3] was deemed to be necessary for Singapore universities to be competitive with other top universities around the world. Understanding the shape of this autonomy is important. Arising out of this report, the Singapore universities (Nanyang Technology University and Singapore Management University and NUS) had new financial and operational autonomy. Faculties and schools received one-line block grants. Lee and Gopinathan (2008) observed that this new situation "not only strengthens the role of deans of faculties to carry out their management responsibilities in financial matters, but it also aims

---

[3]Both NUS and NTU moved from public universities under the direct control of the Ministry of Education to become non-for-profit companies in 2006, to allow them to operate as private universities (Today, 1 April 2006).

to support and motivate faculties, departments and academic staff members to prioritize academic activities and achieve their desired outcomes" (p. 573).

The financial autonomy also comes with greater responsibility for the university to raise funds. In the years after its corporatisation, there has been active fund raising through the capital market and from donors. Moody's Investors Service has assigned a triple-A rating to NUS SGD $1 billion medium-term note programme (IPR Strategic Information Database, 18 November 2008). As an example for donations, Li Ka-shing donated US$65 million in 2007 to the NUS public policy school with a dollar-for-dollar matching (Agence France Presse, 8 March 2007).

13.3.2   Resource Allocation

Even as Singapore universities have been working harder to raise their own funds, the government has been increasing the education budget. For example, the three universities (NUS, NTU and SMU) received SGD $1.9 billion in 2008 (Business Times, 16 February 2008). In the effort to become WCUs, universities have had to be research intensive. Unlike many other universities in other parts of the world, the university system in Singapore gets its research money directly from the Ministry of Education. Consequently, the increase in university budgets has directly translated into increases in the research spending.

New avenues of research funding were created with the National Research Foundation (NRF) funding being the most significant. These new sources allow researchers from the local universities to access significant funds to conduct a range of research. NRF has also poured money into creating five Research Centres of Excellence (RCEs): Centre for Quantum Technologies, Cancer Research Institute and the Mechanobiology Institute housed in NUS. The RCEs located at Nanyang Technology University are the Earth Observatory of Singapore and the Singapore Centre on Environmental Life Sciences Engineering, affiliated with NUS.

NRF has also funded CREATE, which represents another effort to increase research productivity by housing research centres set up by top universities from around the world. The effort focuses on graduate students and is centred at NUS (Business Times, 29 July 2009). In 2010, there were five research centres in CREATE. The centre anchored by the Technical University of Munich, for example, focuses on the development of the next generation of cars and will involve 150 researchers from TUM, the Hebrew University of Jerusalem, Nanyang University and NUS (Channel NewsAsia, 11 June 2010).

13.3.3   University-Industry Relationships

Alongside the growth of academic research funding available (either through direct funding from the Ministry of Education or the National Research Foundation), there has been an increase in funds available through university-industry collaborations.

This is in large part due to the Singapore government's aim to grow research in a number of strategic areas relevant to the geo-economic Asian context and where Singapore effectively competes. This type of funding includes the S$1 billion life sciences investment fund created in 2000 to encourage co-investments and joint ventures to promote spin-off activities, facilitate technology transfers, strengthen industrial capabilities and commercialise new technologies developed in Singapore (Economist Intelligence Unit, 24 June 2008). Besides tapping into these funds, NUS works directly with A*STAR (Agency for Science, Technology and Research) to develop new applied research. For example, NUS and A*STAR set up a clinical imaging research centre for clinical research and advanced biomedical imaging in humans (Economist Intelligence Unit, 24 June 2008).

Another area of strategic importance is water. General Electric Water and Process Technologies have partnered with NUS to set up the NUS-GE Singapore Water Technology Centre with about 70 researchers to develop and test technologies in key areas like desalination, water reuse, the generation of ultrapure water for the semiconductor industry and chemical analysis of water and waste water (Business Times, 23 June 2009). Professor Michael Saunders of the NUS Environmental Research Institute was quoted as saying that the technologies developed out of this Centre have "exceptional market potential" because "up to 90% of countries (in Asia) do not have adequate technology to provide safe, drinkable water". In the same news article, Barry Halliwell, NUS deputy vice president of research and technology, mentioned that "researchers in this Centre will seek up to $70 million in government funding for their work" (Straits Times, 19 June 2009).

In the process of transformation, NUS has also developed a more efficient infrastructure to support commercialisation efforts. An example of such a change can be seen in the interview with noted NUS academic Ariff Bongso who was the first to isolate stem cells from embryos. According to him, the atmosphere (in the university) was "publish or perish", and so, he rushed to publish but neglected to patent or commercialise his work. As a result, a group of US scientists built on Bongso's research to pioneer the making of stem cell lines in 1998. Bongso points out that Singapore now has the infrastructure to commercialise research. In an interview, he commented, "If I had another discovery today, there'd be the facilities and the know-how for me to patent it. In turn, NUS benefits from the prestige of cutting-edge research such as this, as it brings weight to its ranking among the top 20 universities in the world. I do think the first and most important parameter for that rating is the power of the research of its staff" (Business Times, 27 May 2005).

13.3.4   Faculty Personnel Policy

Universities are in an intense contest to attract the best and brightest. Such competition, moreover, is not just local or regional. It is global, and fiercely so ... The best universities trawl for the best faculty, students, researchers, and partners for collaboration, in a global catchment. (Prime Minister Lee, as cited in Straits Times, 2 July 2005)

> We need to take into account the fact that manpower costs comprises about 70 per cent of our operating costs and the university has to pay internationally competitive salaries to retain and recruit quality academic staff. (NUS President Tan, as cited in Today, 18 February 2006)
>
> In an answer to a question raised in parliament, the Minister of State for Education said in 2006 that in the past five years, about 23 per cent of new academic hires at the three local universities have been Singaporeans, with permanent residents making up another 12 per cent (Straits Times, 15 February 2006).

The three comments made in local newspapers at the same time as NUS was corporatised reflect three new interrelated recruiting realities. The strategy to court talent worldwide is necessary because the best and brightest add significantly to the reputation of the university through their research, publications and research networks. In this context, all tenure-tracked recruitment follows an international search process. Adopting a North American recruitment practice, the university has also instituted policies and financing which allow shortlisted candidates to have campus visits so that both sides know clearly the fit between the candidate and the job.

Secondly, there is a high financial cost involved in recruiting talented individuals. In the wake of corporatisation efforts, NUS raised its fees, and the NUS president remarked in the local media that quality academic staff costs money. Corporatisation has allowed the three local universities the flexibility to offer salaries according to the quality of the candidate, from renowned senior hires to promising young academics. In the physical sciences, the search for talented young hires is boosted by NRF fellowships which provide 5 years of funding for successful candidates to set up their research in Singapore.

And thirdly, statistics show that Singaporean citizens form the minority in new hires at only 23%. A number of consequences stem from this changing staffing profile. Partly because NUS is recruiting better candidates, and also because these candidates are nonlocal professors, the academic geographical mobility will be high as professors move in and out of Singapore. The second effect of a high nonlocal academic segment has been that policy research and civil society participation by academics are affected. In this sense, academic involvement in societal and community development as affairs of Singapore are less addressed by foreign social science professors who are less likely to have a direct stake in Singapore. One attempt at rebalancing the local to foreign ratio has been A*STAR's schemes to allow its returning Singapore scholars a chance to explore careers with NUS and NTU (Business Times, 23 July 2009).

13.4   Implications of Being a Global University Centred in Asia

> A key effort in the last two to three years has been to capitalise on "core competencies" identified through strategic planning exercises, so that the university may be positioned as a "world-class" institution that keeps "good company", collaborating/networking with other institutions of "quality" ... clearly in some ways, a colonial mentality persists in former

Table 13.1 Reason(s) for selecting the university[a] the student is enrolled in

University attribute	NUS	Korea	Taiwan	Japan
Reputation of university	96.6	91.3	91.3	94.5
Latest knowledge and methods	83.8	82.6	85.6	85.5
Reputation for quality and expertise of staff	83.1	83.3	82.3	79.5
Reputation of programme	84.1	64.0	77.0	79.8
Qualifications recognised by employers	88.0	77.7	73.4	78.9
Education in host country language (English in the case of NUS)	81.8	41.0	39.9	26.8
Large number of international students	37.3	33.0	38.0	25.1
University advertises itself strongly	34.0	30.8	33.1	17.8

Note: percentage "agree" = percentage of "important" + "most important"
[a]The universities in Korea, Taiwan and Japan are not revealed to avoid readers making unfair direct comparisons between institutions. The universities in these three countries are top national universities with their own unique strengths

colonies, evident in employment policy, for example, which emphasises brining the best from around the world, often interpreted as the best is West. Yet, at the same time, there is a desire to be locate in the centre as well and a reluctance to remain in the peripheries. (Kong 1999, p. 1525)

NUS goes by the tag line "a leading global university centred in asia", and the changes in the last 10 years have been instituted with this vision in mind. Has NUS, following the wide-sweeping changes which accompanied its corporatisation, reached the status of a world-class university? One way to determine this is from the perception of its international students.[4] The intention here is not to argue that one university is better than the rest. The nine universities in the sample are all highly ranked universities located in major cities in their respective countries. Elsewhere, we have argued that the top universities in East Asia have strengths which are shared with other universities as well as unique strengths (Ho et al. 2011). The intention in this comparison is to highlight particular features in the NUS case.

The majority of international student respondents (80% or higher), all of whom were all studying in top universities in four countries, rated the following attributes most highly: the reputation of the university, the latest knowledge and methods and a reputation for quality and expertise of staff (see Table 13.1). This indicates that

---

[4]The data comes from a survey of students conducted in mid-2009–2010 supported by the Singapore Ministry of Education (The project title is "*Globalising Universities and International Student Mobilities*"; supported by the Academic Research Fund Tier 2 grant [Grant number: MOE 20089-T2-1-101] with Assoc Prof HO Kong Chong of the National University of Singapore as the principal investigator) covering nine national universities in five countries, Singapore, China, Japan, Korea and Taiwan. A common non-random quota sample is designed to replicate the international student population in each of the nine universities along the following dimensions: gender, science versus nonscience enrolment, undergraduate and graduate enrolment. In terms of sending countries, 50% of the sample comes from the top two sending countries, and the other 50% is from the rest of the sending countries. Respondents were asked to complete a 15-min questionnaire which collected data on how they selected the university in which they are enrolled, their adjustment process and their future plans.

Table 13.2 Location attributes influencing student decision to study in host university

City attribute	Singapore	Seoul, Korea	Taipei, Taiwan	Tokyo, Japan
Good job prospects upon graduation	76.2	57.5	52.8	39.0
Safe environment	87.1	70.6	76.6	63.4
Social and recreational facilities	59.4	60.6	64.0	37.3
Global prominence of host city	74.1	58.3	52.8	60.7
Easy to visit home country	69.0	41.6	38.2	32.9

the top universities in this region are perceived by the international student body as having strengths in the quality of teaching and the reputation of its staff.

NUS in Singapore excels among this group of elite universities in using English as the medium of instruction and in the recognition given by employers to their degrees. The widespread use of English is clearly tied to the nature of Singapore as a cosmopolitan city state. This in turn facilitates the degree's currency in the workplace. Given that the survey respondents were international students, it is likely that they are not just thinking about working in the host country and home country but in other countries as well.

The item "good job prospects upon graduation" in Table 13.2 also reflects the currency of a NUS degree. This perception among international students studying in NUS is also strengthened by the existence of the tuition grant and service obligation subsidy scheme for undergraduate and graduate students, respectively. Students opting for lower fees will have to work for a Singapore-registered company for 3 years upon graduation.[5]

Table 13.2 also shows other strengths of Singapore; while Seoul and Taipei fare better for social and recreational facilities, Singapore does particular well in terms of its global prominence and ease to visit home country. These two items are in some sense related through the notion of Singapore as an air-travel hub, which features multiple connections to Asia, where most of Singapore's international students hail from. Both tables show that Singapore's strength lies in its use of English and in its strategic position as a global city in Southeast Asia, both of which are positive features in attracting international students.

While the ability to attract international students remains a key feature in becoming a WCU, another important indicator is research productivity. The corporatisation move which created flexibility in academic salaries, the practice of international hiring and the significant increases in research funding have been the hallmarks of change for NUS. But have these changes led to significant increases in research productivity? According to figures compiled by Wong et al. (2007), the percentage of NUS research publications in referred journals increased from 34.7% in academic year 1996–1997 to 53.1% in academic year 2005–2006. Patent applications have also increased from 52 in 1997 to 124 in 2004. These figures are

---

[5]Source: http://www.nus.edu.sg/registrar/edu/UG/fees.html and https://tgonline.moe.gov.sg/tgis/normal/studentViewServiceObligationSubsidyInfo.action

likely to be even higher if we note that many of the changes have only started gaining momentum in the second half of the decade 2000–2010 during which international staff have settled in, the new research centres are up and running and the generous funding has resulted in projects which are well under way. There is therefore the likelihood of a continued momentum from the initial restructuring process.

13.5   Conclusion

Because East Asia is a newcomer in the international higher education market, the scene is still "dusty with all the new construction". Salmi (2009) mentioned the concentration of talent, abundant resources and appropriate governance as key factors in the creation of WCUs. Singapore universities (as evidenced not just in the National University of Singapore (NUS) but also in the Nanyang Technological University (NTU)) have established these key pillars. They have been corporatised, have put in place recruitment policies which attempt to attract the best international candidates (faculty, researchers and students) and have benefitted from generous pools of state research funds.

While the momentum generated by the changes in the last decade is likely to continue into the next decade for comprehensive research universities like NUS and NTU, Singapore is already diverting some of its resources to experimenting with other models. These include more specialised universities like the Singapore Management University and Singapore University of Technology and Design, as well as a liberal arts college in the form of the Yale-NUS College. The higher education ecosystem has grown more diverse. In the next decade, this may well result in a moderation of growth and change as the dominant universities in Singapore settle more comfortably into their established positions and adjust policies to ensure more sustainable development.

References

Audretsch, D., & Feldman, M. P. (2003). Knowledge spillovers and the geography of innovation. In J. V. Henderson & J. Thisse (Eds.), *Handbook of urban and regional economics: Cities and geography* (pp. 2713–2739). Amsterdam: North Holland Publishing.

Brody, W. R. (2007). College goes global. *Foreign Affairs, 86*(2), 122–133.

Gopinathan, S. (1999). Preparing for the next rung: Economic restructuring and education reform in Singapore. *Journal of Education and Work, 12*(3), 295–308.

Ho, K. C., Ishikawa, M., Ma, S., Sidhu, R., & Satoru, A. (2011). *Globalizing universities and international student mobilities in East Asia*. Paper presented at the Association for Asian Studies, Hawaii.

Ishikawa, M. (2009). University rankings, global models, and emerging hegemony: Critical analysis from Japan. *Journal of Studies in International Education, 13*(2), 159–173.

Kong, L. (1999). Asian higher education and the politics of identity. *Environment and Planning A, 31*(9), 1525–1527.

Lee, M. H., & Gopinathan, S. (2008). University restructuring in Singapore: Amazing or a maze? *Policy Futures in Education, 6*(5), 569–588.

Olds, K., & Thrift, N. (2005). Assembling the "global schoolhouse" in Pacific Asia: The case of Singapore. In P. W. Daniels, K. C. Ho, & T. A. Hutton (Eds.), *Service industries, cities and development trajectories in the Asia-Pacific* (pp. 199–215). London: Routledge.

Salmi, J. (2009). *The challenge of building world-class universities.* Washington, DC: The World Bank.

Sidhu, R. (2009). The 'brand name' research university goes global. *Higher Education, 57*(2), 125–140.

Tan, J. (1998). The marketisation of education in Singapore: Policies and implication. *International Review of Education, 44*(1), 47–63.

Wong, P. K., Ho, Y. P., & Singh, A. (2007). Towards an "entrepreneurial university" model to support knowledge-based economic development: The case of the National University of Singapore. *World Development, 35*(6), 941–958.

Yonezawa, A. (2007). Japanese flagship universities at a crossroads. *Higher Education, 54*(4), 483–499.

News Sources

Agence France Presse. (2007, March 8). Asia's richest man gives windfall to Singapore policy school. *Agence France Presse.*

Business Times. (1991, September 30). EDB starts unit to attract overseas talent. *Business Times.*

Business Times. (2005, May 27). Academics turn business incubators. *Business Times.*

Business Times. (2008, February 16). Education spending up: 3 universities to get $1.9b. *Business Times.*

Business Times. (2009, July 23). New opportunities for A*Star PhD scholars. *Business Times.*

Business Times. (2009, July 29). Work launched for $360 m research hub. *Business Times.*

Channel NewsAsia. (2003, August 16). Singapore launches project to make country a global schoolhouse. *Channel NewsAsia.*

Channel NewsAsia. (2010, June 11). Two more research centres set up under NRF's CREATE programme. *Channel NewsAsia.*

Economist Intelligence Unit. (2008, June 24). Incentives: Industry-specific incentives. *Economist Intelligence Unit.*

IPR Strategic Information Database. (2008, November 18). Moody's assigns first-time rating of AAA to National University of Singapore. *IPR Strategic Information Database.*

Today. (2006, April 1). NUS, NTU go independent. *Today.*

Today. (2006, February 18). NUS fee increase due to rising costs; bulk of it goes towards the hiring of quality teaching staff. *Today.*

Today. (2010, November 16). It'll take more than rules to rule the schoolhouse; what the financial crisis can teach about managing the private education scene. *Today.*

Straits Times. (1989, July 11). S'pore opens door to talent. *Straits Times.*

Straits Times. (1997, August 31). Drawing the best to S'pore. *Straits Times.*

Straits Times. (2005, July 2). PM's challenge to local varsities: Attract top brains. *Straits Times.*

Straits Times. (2005, November 22). 2 challenges ahead in govt push to free up universities. *Straits Times.*

Straits Times. (2006, February 15). Academic hired on merit, not nationality. *Straits Times.*

Straits Times. (2009, June 19). NUS, GE set up water research facility. *Straits Times.*

Straits Times. (2010, November 3). From mediocre to world class. *Straits Times.*

Times of India. (2010, March 21). Harvard Haryana. *The Times of India.*

Chapter 14
Frameworks for Creating Research Universities: The Hong Kong Case

Gerard A. Postiglione and Jisun Jung

14.1 Background

Hong Kong has long been viewed as a trading port driven by a market economy (Tsang 2004). One English medium university sufficed for over 50 years. Mass schooling led to the establishment of a Chinese medium university in 1963. The two universities became training grounds for civil servants, professionals, and urban elites. By 1981, only 2% of the relevant age group gained access to a university place. Access grew to 8% by 1989, when an outflow of professional talent due to upheaval on the Chinese mainland led to a decision to double university places. The number of universities increased to eight by 1997. By 2006, 60% of the 17–20 age cohort had access to postsecondary education, but largely though self-financed community college places. In 2010, Hong Kong had 12 degree-granting institutions. In 2013, the traditional British 3 + 4 + 3 education system was changed to a 3 + 3 + 4 structure (3 years of junior and 3 years of senior secondary education followed by a 4-year university system) (EMB 2005). Competition among institutions of higher education for the best students is intense at times. However, incentives have been introduced to encourage cross-institutional collaboration as a way of strengthening areas of teaching and research (Sutherland 2002).

Knowledge economics and financial retrenchment has shaped policy discourse about higher education. A 2004 report by the University Grants Committee of Hong Kong entitled *To Make a Difference: To Move with the Times* stated:

> Human capital is the single most important asset of Hong Kong. We need home-grown graduates who have a strong sense of belonging, and a strong sense of identity as being a part of Hong Kong. At the same time it is also important to nurture a core of local faculty who

G.A. Postiglione (✉) • J. Jung
Faculty of Education, University of Hong Kong, Pokfulam, Hong Kong SAR, China
e-mail: postiglione@hku.hk; jisun@hku.hk

J.C. Shin and B.M. Kehm (eds.), *Institutionalization of World-Class University in Global Competition*, The Changing Academy – The Changing Academic Profession in International Comparative Perspective 6, DOI 10.1007/978-94-007-4975-7_14, © Springer Science+Business Media Dordrecht 2013

give stability, local character, and cultural and intellectual rootedness to local universities, and engage themselves heavily with the local community. (University Grants Committee 2004).

14.1.1 Economic Drivers

Capitalism remains a sacred part of the Hong Kong's way of life. Mainland China's transition to a market economy has reinforced Hong Kong's economic philosophy and its new effort to link university improvements to the marketplace. Beijing, Shanghai, and Guangzhou compete with Hong Kong to be China's economic powerhouse. Therefore, educational reforms in Hong Kong have taken on a new urgency.

> ... If recently launched educational reforms have the intended effect of producing a more flexible, creative, and skilled workforce, Hong Kong will have a fighting chance to keep its vaunted position as China's international window over a longer time period (Panitchpadki and Clifford 2002).

Since the turn of the Century, Hong Kong has imported a more managerial-entrepreneurial model of higher education. Other drivers affect Hong Kong higher education, such as the transfer of manufacturing to the Chinese mainland and a transition to a knowledge-based service economy. By offering internationally competitive salaries, Hong Kong's universities have been able to recruit top talent from overseas.

14.1.2 National Academic Cooperation

Hong Kong has long been a bridge for sending students overseas for higher education. The first Chinese to study overseas was Yung Wing, who attended the Hong Kong's Morrison Education Society School before earning a degree from Yale University in 1854. (Ting and Pan 2003). The first group sent to America in 1872 included those who attended school in Hong Kong. Dr. Sun Yat-sen, the Father of Modern China, studied in Hawaii and later at the Hong Kong Medical College (later to become the University of Hong Kong). Throughout the rest of the twentieth century, thousands followed, including Nobel laureate Daniel Chee Tsui, a graduate of Hong Kong Pui Ching Middle School. The reform on the Chinese mainland that began in 1978 affected Hong Kong's position as the bridge for China's educational exchange with Western universities. In order to adapt, Hong Kong capitalized on its unique capacity to operate bilingually and biculturally.

The Chinese mainland's economic reforms have strengthened Hong Kong's innovative capacity. Hong Kong shifted from a traditional role of being an academic bridge to being an international hub for higher education services. Finally, Hong Kong has been involved in the Chinese mainland's transition from elite to mass higher education and the Chinese mainland's aspiration for its top universities to achieve world-class status.

Hong Kong benefits greatly from robust university growth on the mainland. The proximity to and unique relationship with mainland universities will become instrumental to enhancing Hong Kong's global competitiveness. China is pushing ahead to create "world-class" universities. As university presidents from around the world visit Beijing and Tsinghua Universities, they cannot help noticing the tremendous sums of money being funneled into modernizing these campuses. They will also hear a great deal about new measures to raise academic quality. Yet, mainland universities need more in the software that characterizes an advanced academic culture focused on research, collaborative work, meritocratic advancement, and top-quality teaching and advisement.

The culture of academic management in Hong Kong's universities has important advantages that go beyond impressive facilities. The University of Hong Kong (UHK) has undergone a major expansion and renovation of its campus to work its 100th anniversary and prepare for its new four year program. But it is in the software of academic culture and traditions—where Hong Kong's top universities have a competitive advantage. These include predominant use of English in higher education instruction and as well as continually raising the standard of Chinese. Academic freedom is well entrenched and has withstood several major challenges in the last two decades. An international faculty has not been sidelined in the day-to-day operation of the universities and compliments the cosmopolitanism of the local staff and their institutions. Transparency is valued and academic staff are involved in planning and key decisions. Working conditions are favorable by international standards, as are academic salaries—despite quickly sliding downward toward the international norms with several cuts in recent years. A performance-based system guides decisions about resources and promotions.

While permanent tenured academic appointments are highly competitive and difficult to obtain in Hong Kong, there is a recognized academic career path and reasonable security of employment. Perhaps most important is the fact that both Hong Kong's universities and its society function according to accepted international standards and have a general commitment to excellence, meritocracy, and an openness to ideas and innovations.

There is a perspective that the main requirement for Hong Kong to maintain its competitive academic system is for society at all levels—including the universities themselves as well as the government and the public—to support the universities and recognize them as a central element of Hong Kong's competitive future. This means both adequate funding as well as attention to maintaining and strengthening Hong Kong's distinctive academic culture. An environment in which the most creative professors can pursue their work is essential. It was pointed out during Steven Hawking's visit that scientists' deference to authority can be a hindrance to scientific breakthroughs. Many mainland Chinese academics are still at the crossroads, stuck between the old traditional bureaucratic control and the new forces of global corporate university culture. But, it will not be that way forever as social change continues in China.

Specific policy initiatives include joint programs of academic cooperation and exchange, internationalization in student recruitment, the continued use of English as language of higher education, an emphasis on academic and professional fields especially relevant to Hong Kong's competitive future, dedication to intellectual freedom that have been a hallmark of higher education in Hong Kong, attracting Hong Kong overseas scientists to return home, continued reform of the school system, an undergraduate curriculum that builds problem-solving skills, commitment to community building, and a research culture that is supported with bold initiatives to sustain a new intellectual environment of discovery and application.

14.1.3 Contexts and Characteristics

It is reasonable to ask how Hong Kong, as special administrative region of China, has more highly ranked research universities than any city in China or elsewhere in the world. There appear to be several determining factors as to why three of its research universities are high in the global rankings, and every one of the other public universities is academically respectable. For example, the Times Higher Education placed the University of Hong Kong (UHK) 34th, the Hong Kong University of Science and Technology (HKUST) 61st, and the Chinese University of Hong Kong (CUHK) 151st in the 2011 global rankings. Meanwhile, Mainland China's Peking and Tsinghua Universities are rank 49th and 71st. The Academic Rankings of World Universities (ARWU) introduced a greater China ranking and has Hong Kong's three top universities at number 3, 5, and 6. In this ARWU ranking, only Tsinghua University in Beijing and Taiwan University in Taipei place higher than UHK, HKUST, and CUHK. In fact, these three are not large by international standards and enroll only 10–20,000 students each. Their sates of establishment are far apart with UHK in 1911, CUHK 52 years and HKUST 90 years later. All are public universities, which although receiving support from government, also charge students a relatively modest amount of tuition. About 80% or more of the undergraduate students are drawn from Hong Kong itself, a tiny region of 1095 km^2 (423 sq. miles).

Nevertheless, there are obvious reasons for success of Hong Kong's universities. Although they were under colonial rule until they become part of the People's Republic of China in 1997, they enjoy more institutional autonomy and academic freedom than almost anywhere else in this part of the world. When the economy is strong, government investment is more generous. However, during economic downturns, academic salaries are cut. Moreover, academics are now expected to take a major role in writing research grants and attracting donations to their universities. Hong Kong's tilt toward a heavy emphasis on research took shape with the approach of the 1990s when the four Asian tigers (Hong Kong, Singapore, South Korea, and Taiwan) were the most dynamic areas of Asia. Even though the Hong Kong government left investment in high tech to the private sector, it was willing to establish a science and technology university as infrastructure for upgrading its economy. This period also corresponded with an era of massification in higher education in many parts of the world. The enlargement of the undergraduate population provided a base for starting to build capacity in its graduate schools and research centers, contributing to a much more diversified system of higher education.

14.2 Three Key Factors: Governance, Internationalism, and Academic Leadership[1]

Governance. Hong Kong's government, through the Research Grants Council and the University Grants Committee, steers the higher education sector by prioritizing funding, setting broad guidelines on performance. Beyond this, the universities are virtually autonomous in other respects and manage their affairs as they see fit. The University of Hong Kong is rooted in the British academic tradition. The Chinese University of Hong Kong, established by the consolidation of New Asia College, Chung Chi College, and United College in 1963, brought traditional American missionary and Chinese traditions into Hong Kong's colonial framework for higher education. The Hong Kong University of Science and Technology added an American research university model and academic governance to the mix, without assaulting the status quo. All three have instituted systems of international governance arrangement standards. This places control by the academics in high regard. However, they also value strong administrative leadership, with an emphasis on fairness and efficiency.

Shared governance seems to work well in Hong Kong, although all three of the universities have somewhat different approaches to it. The universities neither become bogged down in endless academic bickering nor become ruled by autocratic administrators. Academic staff unions are relatively weak. Unlike in the US system, university decisions about tenure and promotion are seldom if ever legally contested in the public courts outside of the university. The differences between the British style University of Hong Kong and the more American-oriented managerial style of the Hong Kong University of Science and Technology have begun to fade as they each have taken a pragmatic view and adopted aspects from each other's governance model.

Internationalism. Hong Kong's internationalism has shifted slowly away from a total focus on the United Kingdom, Australia, and North America to include more academics from the Chinese mainland and a small but increasing number of top academics from every continent. Hong Kong is the Asian headquarters for

---

[1]Parts of this section appear in Chinese within the **Peking University Education Review** (in press).

many multinational companies and is one of the top three (after New York and London) international banking centers. Although its population is 95% Chinese, an international cosmopolitan spirit pervades. Most of the top academics at research universities have overseas doctorates, and many remain mobile and move to academic and administrative posts in overseas universities. The universities place a high value on seeing themselves as international institutions, even though they have grown closer to the Chinese mainland in the past decade and a half.

Nowhere else in Asia can one find better access to international scholarship, including high profile professorial visitors, books, journal publications, and all other forms of open media. There is no censorship of the Internet and no censorship of academic books, even though they may be restricted on the Chinese mainland or elsewhere in Asia. International academic events—forums, seminars, and conferences—on a caliber of anywhere in the world occur on a daily basis. Internationalism is helped along by the universities' maintenance of English as the medium of instruction (although both English and Chinese (the Cantonese dialect but also Mandarin) are used at the Chinese University of Hong Kong to reflect its name and intellectual heritage). This ensures that Hong Kong's universities remain within the mainstream of global science and scholarship. The academic community remains wedded to publishing in international academic journals which are produced in English, although in recent years, Chinese publication has increased as Hong Kong academics have begun to take advantage of the impact won by publishing in the massive academic landscape on the Chinese mainland.

Academic leadership. Without question, the success of Hong Kong's universities rests largely with its academic leadership. Academics are relatively well respected. While no longer the highest-paid academics in the world, salaries compete globally, and Hong Kong is able to recruit some of the best academic minds in the world. The universities ensure that top drawer scholars and scientists, including Nobel laureates, are invited to lecture. Ample support is provided for the professoriate to remain active at international conferences throughout Asia, Australia, Africa, Europe, North and South America. Conditions of academic work—including teaching loads, administrative support, and the availability of research funding, on a competitive basis from local sources—are all globally competitive. Leaders in academic fields play a role in external assessment of research grant applications and in external assessment of all teaching programs and doctoral dissertations. Academic recruitment is done internationally, and promotion and tenure are performance based and quite competitive. This has contributed to the productivity of the professoriate. More recently, Hong Kong has taken advantage of the well of talent among the thousands of young mainland Chinese scholars who studied overseas and have not yet returned to China. Many are recruited to universities in Hong Kong where they can live in a Chinese environment, while at the same time enjoying competitive salaries and working conditions—superior in many cases to what is available on the Chinese mainland. More importantly, Hong Kong offers mainland returnees an atmosphere that has a free flow of information, is less encumbered by bureaucracy, and where academic governance is more participative and transparent. The second international survey of the academic profession revealed that the academic profession in Hong Kong, more than elsewhere, views personnel matters and resource allocations to be largely made on the basis of performance measures.

Faith among the academic profession in Hong Kong has also hinged on the academic caliber of its institutional leaders. Each of the three research universities has ensured that only outstanding academics would be at the helm of their institutions. This has undoubtedly had a great deal to do with the rise of Hong Kong's universities in the international rankings. For example, the last president of the University of Hong Kong is a world-renowned geneticist, and the president of the Chinese University of Hong Kong was awarded a Nobel Prize for his work in fiber optics and current president named "Asian Hero" by the *Time* magazine in recognition of his outstanding contributions fighting SARS. The current president of the Hong Kong University of Science and Technology distinguished himself as a key assistant director of the US National Science Foundation, in charge of the Mathematical and Physical Sciences Directorate. There may be other considerations in the selection of university leaders. However, to sustain its rise in the global rankings, Hong Kong must ensure that the most significant aspects are that the most respected global scholars and scientists are the ones that are in positions of authority at their universities.

14.2.1 The Case of HKUST

The Hong Kong University of Science and Technology (HKUST), founded in 1991, has risen rapidly in the global ranking by attracting top tier academics to the university. This university awards degrees in five schools organized under the academic affairs of the university. The Schools of Science, Engineering, and Business and Management offer undergraduate and postgraduate programs through to the doctorate. The School of Humanities and Social Science provides general education for all undergraduates and enrolls graduate students up to the doctoral level. In 2009, it had about 10,000 students and 500 teaching staff (Table 14.1).

According to Hazelkorn (2009), world-class universities are publicized as a symbol of national pride and used as an indicator of economic dynamism to encourage investment. Altbach (2004) notes the WCU paradox, that "everyone wants one, no one knows what it is, and no one knows how to get one." No direct measure was available to define the superior status of universities in terms of training of graduates, research output, and technology transfers. Nevertheless, the WCUs are said to produce well-qualified graduates who are in high demand on the labor market, conduct leading-edge research published in top scientific journals, and contribute to technical innovations through patents and licenses (Khoon et al. 2005; Niland 2000). Alden and Lin (2004) added the criterion of the university's contribution to society. Gallagher (2011) divides WCU characteristics into inputs and outputs. The inputs include the quality of students they attract, the expertise of academic faculty and administrative staff, the depth of research capability,

Table 14.1 Students and academic staff of HKUST (2009)

	Students			Academic staff		
	Undergraduate	Postgraduate	Total	Regular	Visiting	Total
Science	1,433	509	1,942	102	19	121
Engineering	2,270	1,347	3,617	152	19	171
Business and management	2,149	1,160	3,309	118	15	133
Humanities and social science	N/A	285	285	50	8	58
UG dual degree programs	117	N/A	117			
Total	5,969	3,302	9,271	422	61	483

Source: HKUST website

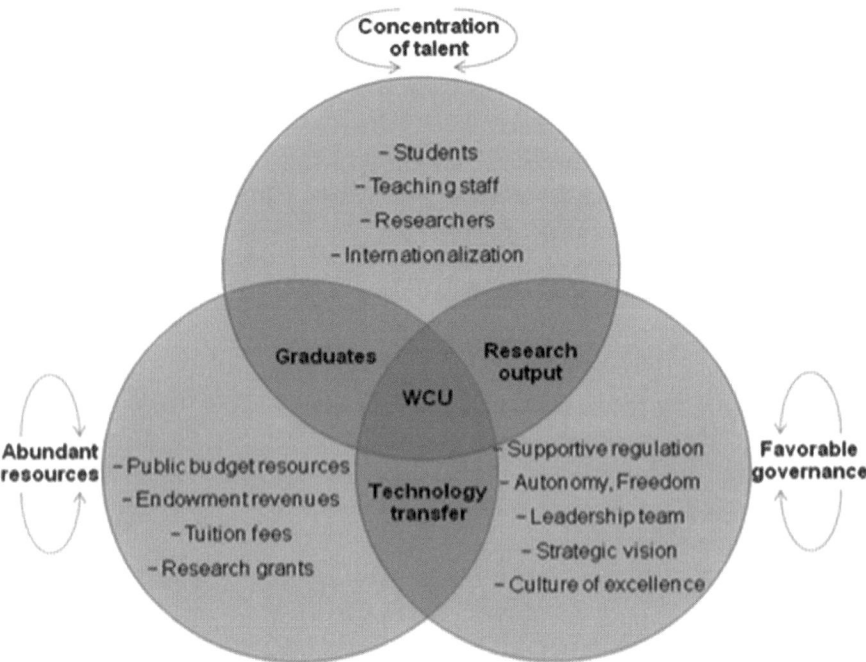

Fig. 14.1 Alignment of key factors (Salmi 2009)

institutional assets, revenue diversity, and costs. Outputs inlcude graduates who take up leadership roles in the professions, business and public service, and high-quality research. Marginson (2011) pointed out the ambiguity of term WCU and suggested Global Research University. GRU experiences three phases: First, institutions build the "capacity" to operate globally. Second, they focus on improving global "connectivity." Third, they do global "activity." In this chapter, the key dimensions of HKUST can be viewed according to Salmi's (2009) categorization (Fig. 14.1).

14.2.1.1 Concentration of Talent

HKUST's most important success factor was the recruitment of outstanding talent. All academic staff had doctorates, and at least 80% had doctorates or had worked at recognized world-ranked universities: Caltech, Imperial, Stanford, Toronto, Cambridge, London, Carnegie-Mellon, Michigan, Chicago, MIT, UC Berkeley, UCLA, Columbia, Northwestern, Cornell, Oxford, Washington, Wisconsin, Harvard, Princeton, Illinois, Purdue, Yale, and UBC. This is not only an indication of quality, but it also represents a wellspring of academic capital that is used to build transnational research collaborations among networks of scholars from similar institutions. HKUST was able to recruit high-quality academic staff for several reasons (Postiglione 2011).

14.2.1.2 Abundant Resources

Like other universities in Hong Kong, HKUST's funding comes from diverse sources—government budget funding for operational expenditures and research, contract research from public organizations and private firms, financial returns generated by endowments and gifts, and tuition fees. Considering that the R&D budget for Hong Kong is only 0.7% of GDP, placing Hong Kong in the 50th position in global rankings for this indicator, the amount of research funds available to HKUST could be considered substantial. In fact, research funding levels have steadily increased (Table 14.2).

As philanthropy continues to grow in Chinese societies, donations will come to play an increasing role in the finance and development of Hong Kong higher education, especially for universities with a long history and thousands of alumni, like the University of Hong Kong. Starting off as the only university in Hong Kong without an alumni sector, HKUST took advantage of the timely rise of Chinese philanthropy. The Hong Kong government facilitated the donation culture by providing matching grants to donations made to universities. The following donations were publicized when given to HKUST: Sino Group $20 million, Kerry Group $20 million, Shun Hing Group $10 million, Shui On Group $25 million, and Hang Lung Group $20 million. By agreement with the donors, the donation amounts from the following donors were not disclosed: Hang Seng Bank, Hysan Trust Fund, and Li Wing Tat family. There were also donations of equipment from IBM and JEOL. All of these donations quoted above were made during HKUST's early development stage. During its 10th anniversary, HKUST noted that it received substantial contributions from 18 foundations and 19 corporations, as well as 7 individual and family donors (Table 14.2).

Top universities show the success of their faculty in competing for government research funding. If the number of grants per academic staff is calculated, HKUST has a higher success rate on competition for government research grants than other universities.

Table 14.2 HKUST Research Funding by source 2001–2010 in HK$ Millions (%)

	2001	2002	2003	2004	2005	2006	2007	2008	2009	2010
Block grant	3.9 (1.6)	6.0 (3.5)	16.9 (5.5)	23.1 (11.3)	18.1 (7.7)	14.3 (6.5)	25.1 (9.9)	73.4 (27.8)	77.2 (20.3)	52.7 (16.2)
Other UGC grants	0.6 (0.2)	20.3 (11.8)	17.3 (5.7)	25.7 (12.6)	18.1 (7.7)	3.3 (1.5)	18.3 (7.2)	10.4 (3.9)	73.3 (19.3)	16 (4.9)
RGC direct	8.3 (3.3)	8.7 (5.1)	9.7 (3.2)	10.0 (4.9)	8.6 (3.7)	7.8 (3.6)	6.4 (2.5)	8.9 (3.4)	7.5 (2.0)	7 (2.2)
Other RGC grants	95.2 (38.1)	94.0 (54.7)	114.0 (37.4)	103.7 (50.7)	98.6 (41.9)	96.1 (44.0)	116.6 (46.1)	114.8 (43.5)	108.7 (28.7)	133.3 (41.0)
Other sources	141.8 (56.8)	42.8 (24.9)	146.8 (48.2)	42.1 (20.6)	91.9 (39.1)	96.9 (44.3)	86.6 (34.2)	56.6 (21.4)	112.8 (29.7)	116 (35.7)
Total	249.8 (100.0)	171.7 (100.0)	304.8 (100.0)	204.6 (100.0)	235.3 (100.0)	218.5 (100.0)	253.1 (100.0)	264.0 (100.0)	379.4 (100.0)	325 (100.0)
Wage amount project HK$'000	589	436	643	433	567	533	594	650	795	713

Source: UGC(2001–2010) Annual Statistics, Research Projects, http://cdcf.UGC.EDU.hk/cdcf/STATINDEX.DO?lANGUAGES=EN.
Note: Figures may not add up to the corresponding totals due to rounding.

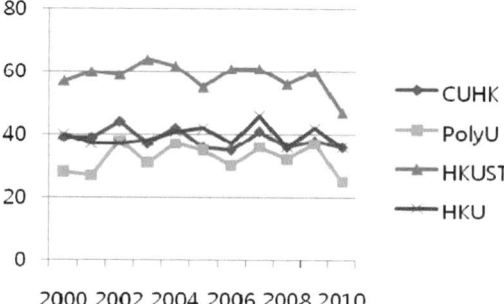

Fig. 14.2 Number of applications supported (success rate, %) (Note: *CUHK* The Chinese University of Hong Kong, *Poly U* The Hong Kong Polytechnic University, *HKUST* The Hong Kong University of Science & Technology, and *HKU* The University of Hong Kong). Source: http//www.uge.EDU.HK/eng/Rgc/RESULT/gRF/gRF.htm

14.2.1.3 Favorable Governance

Strategic Vision and Goals

To be able to develop an appropriate vision for the future of the university and to implement this vision in an effective manner, the leaders needs to understand the core agenda of the institution and be able to apply the vision with the necessary operational skills. Vision setting will consist of delineating the main areas where the institution wishes and has the potential to operate at the forefront (Salmi 2009).

Before HKUST, Hong Kong had functioned with two elite universities, one English language medium and one Chinese language medium. A third university had to be justified more than on the basis of student demand. HKUST espoused the maxim "create, don't replicate" and emphasized that it was "designed to be different." These twin maxims had the effect of emphasizing the importance of being unique at a time when Hong Kong still viewed the universities as elite institutions. Moreover, HKUST professes to become a "leading force in higher education," "a global academic leader," "an agent of change," and "a catalyst for significant progress in science and technology research and education in Hong Kong, and the Mainland." This coincides with Salmi's assertion that a world-class research university "should be based on a forward looking vision that is genuinely innovative" (2009).

External Governance

If a new research university is to be established and nested within a particular model of higher education, and the system provides enough autonomy to permit it to develop its particular edge over other long established institutions of the system by innovating in its governance or academic structure in accordance with a unique vision, this is a potentially valuable advantage. It also represents a systematic way to speed up the process of introducing reforms in other top institutions, whose ethos and long history prevent any radical changes that would be risky to the identity and long established brand of the university.

The factor contributing to HKUST's innovative character was the highly autonomous nature of higher education in Hong Kong. Although HKUST has been a public institution from the start, it is autonomous in most respects. It can innovate without having to receive approval by government or the UGC, and it is not required to adhere to conventions followed by the other two government universities, although it may be in its interest to adhere to conventions concerning recruitment of students. In fact, the University of Hong Kong and Chinese University of Hong Kong had operated differently, one with a 3- and the other with a 4-year bachelor degree program for many years, although they eventually standardized in order to lighten the examination pressure on secondary school students who had been taking two rather than one university entrance examination.

Internal Governance

A key innovation of HKUST that contributes to its maxim "be unique and not duplicate" is the manner in which administrators are chosen (Woo 2006). All deans would be appointed rather than, as was the case in the other universities of Hong Kong, be selected or elected from within a school or faculty. While this is the modus operandi at top American universities, it is innovative within the context of Hong Kong. At the time, Hong Kong had a system that adhered closely to the British model of higher education.

HKUST was being established during the sunset years of the British administration and at a time when the United States and Mainland China were Hong Kong's major trading partners. Not only were most major universities in the world located in the United States, but the higher education system in Mainland China operated more closely to the American model of higher education, and most of China's prospective academics who studied overseas did so in the United States. This gave HKUST a tremendous advantage. In short, to be unique, HKUST merely had to adapt innovations from the American university system. British higher education was closely guarded and protected, creating inertia to change. Thus, the timing of its establishment, something that may be difficult to duplicate elsewhere, mattered a great deal to its rapid rise.

Collaboration and Partnership

HKUST's collaborations, partnerships, and internationalization have contributed to its success (Ji 2009). Under the Hong Kong Area of Excellence scheme in research, HKUST has collaborative project with other leading universities in Hong Kong in the following areas: Chinese Medicine: Research and Further Development (with

CUHK), Institute of Molecular Technology for Drug Discovery (with HKU), Centre for Marine Environmental Research and Innovation Technology (with CUHK), Developmental Genomics and Skeletal Research (with HKU), and Control of Pandemic and Inter-Pandemic Influenza (with HKU).

HKUST has a Research and Development Corporation (RDC) for partnerships and knowledge transfers with industry. RDC partnerships and other HKUST academic partnerships include but extend far beyond Hong Kong itself. For example, HKUST, Peking University, and the Shenzhen Municipal government established a tripartite cooperative institution that engages in production, study, and research. It helps to commercialize high-tech research products. With an $800M donation, HKUST established a Nansha Graduate School in Guangdong Province to promote scientific cooperation between Hong Kong and the Chinese mainland. HKUST also has a partnership in Beijing's financial district under a tripartite agreement to establish an International Financial Education and Training Center in Beijing with Beijing Financial Street Holding Co., Ltd. and Beijing International Financial Center (Liu and Zweig 2009).

14.3 Building World-Class Universities: Government Frameworks

Research universities play a critical role in training the professional, high-level specialists, scientists, and researchers needed by the economy and in generating new knowledge in support of national innovation system (World Bank 2002). Therefore, many governments are trying to make sure that top universities are actually operating at the cutting edge of intellectual and scientific development. Policy makers and university leaders search for strategies and pathways, often borrowed, for establishing such universities and identify the challenges, costs, and risks. They have developed diverse strategies, some innovative and progressive, others copying policies elsewhere, whether relevant or not. In the case of Hong Kong's autonomous universities, becoming WCUs could not be accomplished without a favorable policy environment to permit individual institutions with respected academic leaders, clear mission and goals, strategic planning, and supportive internal environment for academic staff development to translate the institutional vision into concrete targets and programs.

14.3.1 Establishment of WCUs

Salmi (2009), according to governments have to consider upgrading a small number of existing universities that have the potential to excel, merge, and consolidate existing institutions or establishing new ones. In the Hong Kong case, both existing and new institutions were supported. Rather than using a conventional strategy of concentrating resources in one or more already established flagship institutions, Hong Kong used a strategy for creating research universities in which universities complement one another and thereby strengthen the entire system's research capacity.

14.3.2 Specific-Purpose Program

Some Asian governments have launched initiatives such as COE Program (Japan), 211 and 985 programs (China), and Brain Korea 21(South Korea). In order to provide incentives for elite institutions to focus on research excellence, governments may provide specific funds. This approach is more likely to produce differential outcomes when allocations for different funding streams, whether reward-based or improvement-based, are limited to a few rather than shared among all institutions.

It is somewhat remarkable that Hong Kong has not launched any official government policy or initiative strategy to establish representative world-class research universities. However, government has increased funding for research at a continual pace and has successfully employed a competitive-based allocation system among the universities. It was not until 1991 that the government accepted the advice of the UGC to establish a Research Grants Council (RGC) with annual funding of $100 million. Since then, research finding has grown considerably. A significant amount is identified by universities from UGC/RGC funds for research (approximately $4.5 billion per year), and the RGC now disburses about $750 million per annum for research projects. The Innovation and Technology Fund of the government is projected to spend $ 1.0 billion on R&D in 2010/2011, having been spending from $400 million to $800 million per year in the recent past (UGC 2010a).

14.3.3 Performance-Based Funding

Hong Kong's performance-based funding approach reflects a view that institutions should be funded, not for what they are, but for what they do. They are typically related to a set of quantitative indicators measured over intervals of time, and funding flows in accordance with improvements in the measures. They may be used to encourage some institutions to expand their level of activity in particular areas. Their effectiveness in promoting differentiation depends on clarity of purpose and the selections of indicators.

In case of Hong Kong, with the increase of funding to RGC from the Research Endowment Fund, it is inevitable that its mode of functioning and organization will change. The RGC is rising to the challenge with the Theme-based Research Scheme and the Public Policy Research Initiative. The UGC's view is that this mode will reassure institutions with different roles and strengths that their needs are being properly addressed and this mode will also permit them to differentiate themselves more effectively (UGC 2010a). At present, the RGC's work is assisted by four specialist subject panels, responsible for Physical Sciences, Engineering, Biology and Medicine, and Humanities, Social Sciences, and Business Studies.

14.3.4 Quality Assurance

Quality assessment is concerned with outcomes and how good they are. In terms of research, assessments may affect eligibility for funding of doctoral students or participation in particular programs. In spite of small size of Hong Kong higher education, there are three different bodies (HKCAAVQ, Joint Quality Review Committee, and the Quality Assurance Council) responsible for the quality assurance of different higher education institutional providers. UGC is trying to integrate three bodies to make single system for quality assurance, and in the process increase transparency so as to permit better-informed choices by consumers (UGC 2010a).

14.4 Conclusion: Concerns About the Asian Race to Build WCUs

The competition for world-class status in some countries has fused national and institutional priorities and transformed global rankings from a benchmarking tool into a strategic instrument.

The endeavor to build WCUs can have some positive benefits by helping universities identify targets and actions and monitor peer performance and public comment (Hazelkorn 2009). The flipside—the tendency toward gaming the system is far less positive (Ishikawa 2009). By doing so, the distinctiveness of individual institutions becomes submerged as the game becomes one of attaining a standardized set of characteristics that are said to characterize WCUs (Cohen and March 1974; Reale and Seeber 2011).

Few societies or institutions can afford the level of investment required for WCUs without sacrificing other social and economic objectives such as widening access, institutional diversity community partnerships, cross-institutional collaboration, and resource sharing and knowledge transfer (Usher and Savino 2006; Hazelkorn 2008a). Therefore, asian WCUs may tend to inflate the academic "arms race" as the WCU quest pulls in more and more countries. The downside effect of this competitive pursuit of academic prestige can end up being a costly, zero-sum game in which resources, including administrative and faculty attention, gets diverted away from the collective action necessary to improve student learning. Indeed, most input indicators have an irrelevant or very small effect on student's learning. How much students grow or change has only an inconsistent or trivial relationship with such input measures as educational expenditures per student, student/faculty ratios, faculty salaries, percentage of faculty with highest degree in their field, research productivity, size of library, admission selectivity, or prestige rankings (Dill 2006).

For the Hong Kong case, societal context and institutional autonomy matter as much as government policy. Universities are able to capitalize on knowledge about local, national, regional, and global changes. While government plays a macro steering role in terms of overall finance and alignment with other sectors of growth in economy and society, it does not institute specific policies driven by global university rankings. Universities can introduce initiatives without consulting government. Unlike the Chinese mainland where special note was taken of the nominal position of their universities when the global university ranking scales became popular at the tail end of the twentieth century, Hong Kong's top three research universities were more concerned with maintaining their high ranks rather than instituting major reforms to jack up their global standings.

The case of the oldest and newest research universities (HKU and HKUST) provides examples of how universities with highly differentiated academic cultures and formats of governance can operate within a system of public universities, avoid unhelpful standardization of operating procedures, and continue to excel on the basis of their unique characteristics without assaulting each other's academic traditions, all the while learning from each other and adapting useful innovations. Likewise for the Chinese University of Hong Kong which has a unique tradition of maintaining Chinese language medium instruction for a significant amount of its curriculum, yet, it remains integrated into the global academy where English scientific journals lead the advancement of knowledge. CUHK plays a key role in helping to lead thinking about how Hong Kong Chinese academic culture resonates with national academic culture.

The case of HKUST is particularly valuable because it demonstrated that in broad terms, vision was as important as finance and in recruitment of top talent, national sentiment was as important as salaries. The leadership of the new institution was not only able to identify the advantageous conditions that existed at the time but to take advantage of them in ways that were highly effective. In HKUST's case, drive and commitment cannot be discounted as key factors. It situated itself within an almost alien academic culture without assaulting the host academic ethos. British and American academic traditions discovered grounds for integration like nowhere else in the world.

References

Alden, J., & Lin, G. (2004). *Benchmarking the characteristics of a world-class university: Developing an international strategy at university level*. London: Leadership Foundation for Higher Education.
Altbach, P. G. (2004). The costs and benefits of a World-Class Universities. *Academe, 90*. In http://www.aaup.org/AAUP/pubsres/academe/2004/JF/Feat/altb.htm.

Altbach, P. G., & Postigline, G. A. (in press). The Hong Kong academic advantage. Peking University Education Review.

Altbach, P. G., & Salmi, J. (2011). *The road to academic excellence: The making of world-class research universities.* Washington, DC: The World Bank.

Cohen, M. D., & March, J. G. (1974). *Leadership and ambiguity.* New York: McGraw-Hill.

Dill, D. D. (2006). *Convergence and diversity: The role and influence of university rankings.* Keynote address presented at the CHER 19th annual research conference. Germany.

Education and Manpower Branch (EMB). (2005). *The new academic structure for senior secondary education and higher education: Action plan for investing in the future of Hong Kong.* Hong Kong Government Printer.

Gallagher, M. (2011). The role of elite universities in national higher education and research systems, and the challenges of prosecuting the case for concentrating public investment in their development in Australia. In N. C. Liu et al. (Eds.), *Paths to a world-class university: Lessons from practices and experiences* (pp. 3–27). Rotterdam: Sense Publishers.

Hazelkorn, E. (2008a). Learning to live with league tables and ranking: The experience of institutional leaders. *Higher Education policy, 21,* 193–215.

Hazelkorn, E. (2009). Attitudes to rankings: Comparing German, Australian and Japanese experience. In S.Kaur, M.Sirat, & W. G. Tierney (Eds.), *Addressing critical issues on quality assurance and university rankings in higher education in the Asia Pacific.*

Ishikawa, M. (2009). University rankings, global models and emerging hegemony. *Journal of Studies in International Education, 20*(10), 1–15.

Khoon, K. A., Shukor, R., Hussan, O., Saleh, Z., Hamzah, A., & Ismail, R. (2005). *College Student Journal.* In http://findarticles.com/p/articles/mi_m0FCR/is_4_39/ai_n16123684/.

Liu, A., & Zweig, D. (2009). *Training a new generation of Mainland students: The role of Hong Kong,* manuscript.

Marginson, S. (2011). Global perspectives and strategies of Asia-Pacific research universities. In N. C. Liu et al. (Eds.), *Paths to a world-class university: Lessons from practices and experiences* (pp. 3–27). Rotterdam: Sense Publishers.

Niland, J. (2000, February 3). The challenge of building World-class universities in the Asian Region. *ON LINE Opinion.* Retrieved April 10, 2006, from http://www.onlineopinion.com.au/view.asp?article=997.

Panitchpadki, S., & Clifford, M. L. (2002). *China and WTO: Changing China and changing world trade.* Singapore: Wiley.

Postiglione, G. A. (2011) The Rise of Research Universities in Altbach, P. A. and Salmi, J., *The Road to Academic Excellence*, Washington, DC. The World Bank.

Reale, E., & Seeber, M. (2011). Organization response to institutional pressures in higher education: The importance role of the disciplines. *Higher Education, 61,* 1–22.

Salmi, J. (2009). *The challenge of establishing world-class universities.* Washington, DC: The World Bank.

Shuoming, Ji. (2009). Taking aim at Hong Kong's Science and Technology: Fuse China with industrial power. *Chinese Weekly,* (May 24) 24–31.

Sutherland, S. (2002). *Higher education in Hong Kong.* Hong Kong: Research Grant Council.

Ting, J. S. P., & Pan, Z. (2003) Boundless learning: Foreign educated students of Modern China (Hong Kong: Hong Kong Museum of History).

Tsang, S. (2004). *A modern history of Hong Kong.* London: I. B. Tauris.

University Grants Committee (2004). To make a difference to move with the times, Hong Kong: Universities Grants Committee, January.

University Grants Committee (UGC). (2010a). *Aspiration for the higher education system in Hong Kong: Report of the University Grants Committee.*

University Grants Committee (UGC). (2010b). *Report of a quality audit of The Hong Kong University of Science and Technology.* Quality Assurance Council.

Usher, A., & Savino, M. (2006). *A world of difference: A global survey of university league tables* (Canadian education report series). Toronto: Educational Policy Institute.

Woo, C. W. (2006) Jointly creating the Hong Kong University of Science and Technology. Hong Kong: Commercial Press.

World Bank. (2002). *Constructing knowledge societies: New challenges for tertiary education.* Washington, DC: World Bank. Retrieved December 2, 2008, from http://go.worldbank.org/N2QADMBNIO.

Part V
Conclusion

Chapter 15
Universalizing the University in a World Society

Francisco O. Ramirez and John W. Meyer

15.1 Introduction

With rapid recent globalization, higher education has come to be seen as a central focus and source of national development. The university is key to knowledge production and transmission, and knowledge is a core component and source of the knowledge society or economy. This is a sort of society in which many elements distant from the production economy make up dominant components of measured national economic success. And most of these elements derive their value not from demonstrated functional utility for the production economy but from the certificated value they derive from the educational system: professional roles, resting on such certificates, are central. The changes involved make higher education and its expansion and improvement main foci of national policy and make educational competitions within and between national societies core elements of successful participation in global progress. These changes call for better university organization and more professionalized management. In this chapter, we review the situation as it is described in the literature, covering a variety of national policy systems.

The studies in this book report on a higher educational world with a remarkably high level of convergence. The chapters – and the participants in the educational development on which they report – share a common language, with apparently consensual meanings of abstract terms: university, teaching, research, national needs, national development, knowledge society, science, world-class university, university rankings, the American research university, and so on. Partly, the consensus arises

F.O. Ramirez (✉) • J.W. Meyer
School of Education, Stanford University, Stanford, CA, USA
e-mail: ramirez@stanford.edu; meyer@stanford.edu

J.C. Shin and B.M. Kehm (eds.), *Institutionalization of World-Class University in Global Competition*, The Changing Academy – The Changing Academic Profession in International Comparative Perspective 6, DOI 10.1007/978-94-007-4975-7_15,
© Springer Science+Business Media Dordrecht 2013

from professionalization and a good deal of interaction among the authors and with the editors. But it clearly goes far beyond that, and around the world, schooled persons could follow the discussions here.

In fact, the discourse involved is simultaneously global but also reflective of local instantiations in a great many countries. This sort of globalization is characteristic, now, of social organizational phenomena in many social sectors (e.g., Drori et al. 2006). Roland Robertson (1992) used the term "glocalization" to describe the general phenomena – Kehm (Chap. 6) and Marginson (Chap. 5) call it "glonacal." University people, and the elites that manage and monitor the universities, everywhere have frames of reference with a great deal of global commonality. They can routinely discuss an abstraction such as a "world-class university," with the confidence that this entity could in principle be found or created anywhere, with rather homogeneous meanings and functions. And thus, it is clear that particular local institutions can be accredited or rated in terms of globally common systems of ranking and classification, just as organizations everywhere can be rated on the same scales of transparency, environmental protection, respect for human rights, or corporate social responsibility in general (Drori et al. 2006). Within the educational domain, student achievement in many different subjects can be assessed and compared on the same PISA or IEA scales (Baker and LeTendre 2005). Similarly, nation-states can be compared on a host of dimensions related to human welfare, environmental status, educational development, and so on. With the collapse of Communism (and its conception of a net material product), all countries can have a gross domestic product rated on the same dimension (though there are several alternative conception of how to integrate the separate currencies).

The ranking, rating, and classification of universities in common evaluation frames are now given great importance across the widest range of national societies. Public policies to improve university status in global terms, and on global standards, now seem to be urgent functional requirements for proper national development. The struggles of universities for self-improvement and betterment are seen, not as private competitions in a zero-sum status system but as efforts at more general collective national goods. These struggles are often imagined as efforts to reinvent higher education, efforts that call for better organization and professionalized management.

In short, everywhere one travels in our world, one finds national elites eager to improve their universities in global, not national, terms. And, one finds university leaders acutely conscious of their status in a global system and driven to improve it. Lastly, one also finds consultants interacting with university leaders and national elites to help create world-class universities.

It was not always so and is clearly a property of very recent decades, as the chapters in this book uniformly establish. In this chapter, we step back to try to understand how the whole new system has come into being on a global scale. We start by considering the world of higher education in previous periods, when very different conceptions and evaluations were dominant. Then we discuss what has changed and how the dimensions of the world described by the chapters of this book have been produced.

15.2 The Universalism of the University

As its name implies, the university has had since its Western medieval origins, along with its specific mundane location, a claim to universality (Rashdall 1936). Its essence, indeed, has always been to bring knowledge understood to be universal down into the specific locale of a city, a state, or later a national state (Riddle 1990, 1993). Timeless and placeless theological knowledge was most central, followed by canon and civil law understood as somewhat more historical in construction. The less certain and eternal universals of the mundane world in medicine and philosophy followed in the academic procession. But in all cases, the special knowledge that entered the university has always had clearly universalistic claims (Frank and Meyer 2007).

In the medieval period, as now, university status depended on the assessments of others, so ranking and rating were crucial. Charters from popes and emperors, and later national states, were important. But so was the good opinion of others: were one's certificates accepted by the colleagues at the great centers in Paris, Oxford, or Bologna (Clark 2006)? Criteria were vague – was an "incomplete" university lacking a law faculty really a university? And because the university concept had claimed its universality, much competition was constructed for preference and antiquity among the major university centers: rankings and ratings have a very old history, along with conflicts over them.

Thus, throughout its history, the university could readily be compared with others in schemes of assessment. A century ago, the Scientific American could publish quantified assessments, and Western Reserve University President Thwing (1911) could write a genial book reviewing and comparing 20 universities in 19 countries, apparently after having visited and examined almost all of them.

In all such assessments, prestige was involved – the standing of the university in a scheme of high virtue. The prestige of a country could be involved too, if its university carried proper high cultural value. In reality, diffuse cultural values, more than instrumental aims and efficacy, were at issue. For instrumental purposes, even a cathedral (which could help protect foreign merchants) was more valuable than a university. This situation changed dramatically in the production of our world and the world depicted in the chapters of this book.

15.3 The Modernist View

By the mid-twentieth century, the university model had spread throughout the developed, and much of the developing, world (Riddle 1990). Enrollments and counts of institutions had spread substantially, especially after the Enlightenment. At this point, universities were almost all firmly located within a national society, typically under some sort of regulation from a national state. But they could, as always, be subject to common definitions and compared with each other. Thus, directories could attempt to list, with some standardized information, all the universities in the world or in regions of it (e.g., The World of Learning). To be sure, variations among systems were recognized (and became the central focus of, e.g., Clark 1983, whose discussion lies in the background of Marginson's Chap. 5), so that one could speak of the German, English, French, or American university (Flexner 1930). The differences among these models, however, were principally organizational in character – they dealt much less with the core knowledge base, and chemistry in Germany was pretty much also chemistry in France or the United States (see Fourcade (2009) for some substantive variations in the field of economics). University models, thus, varied in how the institutions were organizationally linked to society, not mainly in the substantive content of the teaching and research undertaken within universities. Indeed, in the chapters of this book, attention to the substantive topics of research and instruction in universities is quite limited, aside from the overwhelming stress on the importance of science and technology in global competitions. Yan Luo, in Chap. 10, and Kong Chung Ho, in Chap. 13, are in some measure exceptional here and give some attention to matters of substance over and above organizational form.

Historically, the knowledge involved had cultural or prestige value more than instrumental use in society itself. For the individual too, university education carried markers of prestige more than the capacities for enhanced production. The old professions supported by the university – theology, law, and medicine – were seen as carrying more religious and cultural than instrumental (or especially economic) values. In the post-Enlightenment or modern period, practical concerns had penetrated the sacred halls, particularly in radical countries like France, the United States, or later the Soviet Union. But for the most part, the university was a prestige item, and really useful training was produced elsewhere, in apprenticeships, practical experience, specialized technical schools (like the grandes ecoles), or vocational training (Frank and Meyer 2007).

There were, thus, good reasons to be skeptical about whether university expansion was in the public good or whether it was a publically admirable private good. Perhaps the game was not worth the candle, and both societies and the individuals in them should constrain their desires for instrumentally empty prestige values. A 1931 paper of the Federation of German Industries (as reported in the New York Times by Jedell) warns of the costs of overeducation: " . . . a sterile, educated proletariat is being produced . . . while millions are wasted on its training . . . graduates . . . have not chosen their callings from any native endowment . . . but from an erroneous belief that their diploma would help them more readily to develop an income. The responsibility, therefore, rests chiefly upon the parents who without informing themselves in authoritative quarters about economic prospects and possibilities, deem it their duty to make advanced studies possible for their sons and daughters . . . This evil . . . is directly connected with the distorted value placed in Germany on going through the higher schools that are feeders to the university."

This perspective now seems extreme and is entirely foreign to the analysts of the chapters of this book and to the policy worlds they depict. But versions of this view were central and widely shared doctrines among theorists and researchers on higher education a half century ago. The story line was that the prestige linked to higher education, and the gratuitous educational requirements for occupational success, was driving an irrational, arbitrary, expensive, and inflationary educational expansion. Titles tell a good deal: Collins' *The Credential Society* (1979), Berg's *The Great Training Robbery* (1970), Freeman's *The Overeducated American* (1976), Illich's *Deschooling Society* (1971), Dore's *Diploma Disease* (1975), and Boudon's *Education, Opportunity, and Social Inequality* (1974). These often-sophisticated and sometimes mathematicized analyses spelled out the inflationary dynamics involved as status groups and individuals competed for educationally based preferment (see summaries in Rubinson and Fuller 1992; Rubinson and Browne 1994).

In all these accounts, the state played an important role, but one diametrically opposed to that depicted in the chapters of this book. It was clear that traditional European states had exercised their powers to block much putatively irrational expansion of the universities and had managed to control the higher educational system so that it simply met the needs of a slowly changing occupational order (Ben-David and Zloczower 1962; Collins 1971). The Western theorists were less likely to celebrate very similar state-driven constraints on educational expansion put forward in the Communist world (Lenhardt and Stock 2000; Baker et al. 2004). But the state elites of that world shared the view that higher education should simply meet the core needs of a very material and functional national society and that overeducation would be destabilizing and counterproductive. Student protest movements in the sixties and seventies were often imagined as evidence of the destabilizing effects of too much higher education, evidence to the contrary notwithstanding (Ramirez et al. 1973).

The problem case, and instance of uncontrolled inflation, was the United States – after World War II the only power really left standing. Famous for the absence of legitimate national state power and authority in educational matters, there was no power capable of blocking the competitive pressures of parents and children eager to outdo their neighbors. And given that educational certificates were routes to success in an expanding array of valued occupations in the stratification system – a situation tacitly explained in the prevailing theories as somehow functional in character – educational inflation was a natural product. And it was dramatically visible in the United States, with its long history of early educational expansion at all levels (Rubinson 1986).

The modern logic of the postwar period was quite clear. Economic, political, and social development were clearly needed – especially in the newly independent countries that might otherwise be susceptible to radical solutions. Education could fit people into the expanding modern economies and societies, and expanding mass education could clearly eliminate some bottlenecks. But the point was functional and built on a functionalist analysis of developing nation-states. Education should fit people into a social (and perhaps especially economic) structure, and as this structure expands, education had to expand. The idea that education might actually drive the whole development program had no pride of place: the main fear was that traditional and conservative societies would be too much inclined to keep their children home, rather than pushing them into roles as cogs in the machinery of progress. Philip Foster's well-known work (1965) illustrated how villagers would be likely to block educational expansion by thwarting the growth of more technical and vocational forms of schooling.

In the modern vision of half century ago, educational expansion was clearly needed to fit in with growing economies. But the main emphases were on the expansion of primary education (especially to create citizens) and even more secondary education (to create citizens but especially effective and committed workers). Thus, a most important document in the period – Harbison and Myers' Education, Manpower, and Economic Growth (1964) – was a massive and successful celebration of the virtues of expanded secondary schooling. It had worldwide impact as ideology, despite its strikingly limited evidentiary base. The commitment to development, and to education as a means for national development, was substantially a matter of faith (and set against an alternative Communist faith).

From this point of view, higher educational expansion was a dubious good. It was more likely to result from status competitions, as both states and individuals competed for prestige. Individuals would compete for enhanced stratificational positions. Nation-state elites would compete for symbols of status – universities, along with airlines, flags, songs, and presidential palaces. None of it made much sense in terms of real economic, political, and social development, and the apparent inefficiencies involved were striking. Worse, higher education could be counterproductive, as it reflected and reinforced a revolution of rising expectations (e.g., Huntington 1968): despite a complete absence of relevant evidence, it was doctrine that having large numbers of unemployed college graduates was destabilizing for a slowly developing social order.

A detailed analysis of international, national, and academic ideologies for the period has not been done. But it is obvious that the weight of world opinion ran against any explosive expansion of higher education, while it celebrated rapid expansions at lower levels of education. For decades this was World Bank doctrine. Higher educational expansion happened anyway and at growth rates exceeding those of lower educational levels (Schofer and Meyer 2005). Countries created universities at a great rate, and parents set their children – very much including female children – to them (Bradley and Ramirez 1996; Ramirez and Wotipka 2001). More universities were established after World War II than throughout earlier human history. It is important to understand why we find this global trend, often seen as irrational and counterproductive in an earlier era.

By the time we come to our own period, as reflected in the chapters of this book, the old concerns have disappeared. The authors here generally maintain something of a distant and academic posture toward national policies for pell-mell expansion and for global competition: they certainly see the modern system as targeted on prestige competitions as much immediate socioeconomic functions. But they describe a world in which there are few legitimated reasons to be careful about educational expansion, or about spending the odd billion to make a central national university more prestigious (but see Cremonini et al. in Chap. 7). No one fears that we are now in a world in which there is indeed "no salvation outside higher education" (Shils 1971).

The old conservative voices criticizing educational expansion as productive of anomie, as in the German example quoted above, are mostly stilled. So are the mainline liberal voices that dominated the literature in the 1950s and 1960s, seeing higher educational expansion as inefficient and inflationary. And so are the voices on the old left – dominant in the Communist world, and overwhelming in Maoist China, but clearly extant more broadly – that saw educational expansion as false consciousness on a massive scale and destructive of the coherence and power of the working class and its party. The earlier and intense "Red versus Expert" debates have waned: higher education is now widely regarded as the cat that, regardless of its color, can catch mice.

15.4 Sources of the Postmodern Model

A set of interrelated changes, on a global scale, lie behind the dramatic shift from models in which higher educational expansion is a suspect good reflecting prestige more than functionality to the models central to the chapters of this book. The changes involved are referred to casually in the chapters here – they lie at the background of the policy worlds under review. We can focus on them here:

1. First, as the chapters here quite uniformly recognize, there were the actualities and perceptions of dramatically increased globalization – cultural, political, but especially economic interdependence on a grand scale. Progress, it became clear, must occur in a global, not an autonomous national, context. Positively, this encouraged the expansion of a more globally validated rationalized knowledge system. Negatively, it discouraged the modern functionalism that envisioned education staffing national "needs" in a slowly developing national occupational system – occupations, stratification, and competition would henceforth occur on a more global level (Rosenmund 2006). And in the relatively open system of global society, more education became an unqualified good, rather than a source of local anomie. Awareness of the matter may have been especially intense in old Europe. Essentially all the chapters of this book portray national policies rooted in competition in global society. Sometimes the competition is a direct one for global educational prestige and authority (e.g., Sirat in Chap. 12, on Malaysia). Sometimes it is more indirect, reflecting the importance of education in competitions that are economic and technological.
2. Second, there was a rapid expansion, worldwide, of the scientific and social scientific analysis of reality and of the authority of such analyses (Drori et al. 2003). The institutions involved expanded everywhere, in many respects partly substituting at the global level for authorities missing from a stateless world order (e.g., Haas 1992). The charisma of older knowledge institutions, linked to nation-states declining in cultural centrality, was replaced by modern forms of rationalized expertise. And these modern forms expanded to cover more topics, in more places, with more penetration into the formerly local and parochial

(Frank and Gabler 2006). Naturally, this change made the university a much more central institution as a locus of scientific authority – more a creator of the rationalized and functional society than a servant of it.

The university came to be seen as a source of all sorts of new products (computer games) but even more of all sorts of new services (e.g., the various new therapies, new forms of organizational rationality like planning and leadership). The university becomes the main source of theories of management science, and not surprisingly, the university is increasingly rationalized around principles, policies, and procedures that celebrate sound management (Ramirez 2006b, 2010).

3. Third, there was a dramatic expansion in the perceived status of the individual human person, celebrated in a great explosion of international norms – rapidly adopted by almost all national states – about the rights and powers of this person (Elliott 2007; Elliott and Boli 2008). This human person was seen as entitled on increasing number of dimensions, with educational, health, religious, and personal expression rights. And most aspects of the person were recognized (with explicit statements of the rights of women, gays, children, indigenous people, and so on). But most important for our purposes here, the perceived legitimate capacities of people were greatly expanded. People were empowered to act, with increasingly naturalized rights to economic, social, religious, cultural, and political action. History, with this liberal and neoliberal expansion (often commented on in the chapters here), was henceforth to be produced by individual choices, not the purposes of the old corporate groups (especially national states). Both human capital ideas and human rights emphases reflect the growing centrality of the individual person in the wider world (Ramirez 2006a).

In a global society in which progress rests on the capacities of individual persons, rather than cultural traditions or histories or structures, it makes eminent sense to focus social effort on the expansion and disciplining of these individuals in an educational system. At the bottom of society, empowered human persons everywhere now require massive amounts of compulsory mass education. At the top, the university becomes a fountainhead of progress.

15.5 The Postmodern Model: The Knowledge Society

The central change producing the global higher educational system described and analyzed here, along with its national-level instantiations, lies in the conception of the "society" to which the university has always been linked. At one time, this society was Christendom (all recognized universities, in practice, were to be found in Western Christendom and cognitively linked this order to a shared cosmos).

In the modern period, society generally meant national societies – distinct and competing sacralized entities within the common cosmos – and the university provided universal knowledge sustaining a concrete nation and state. As the period wore on, society was increasingly seen in terms of a development scheme built around modern notions of social, political, and especially economic life. Development and modernization involved the creation of a set of interdependent institutions to which education was to make a functional contribution. The ideologies involved had something of a realist character and treated economic development as central. "Economic" meant chiefly material production – explicitly so in the Communist version. But in the West, "economic" increasingly meant something more abstract – reflected in statistics like the gross national product per capita, rather than tons of steel, miles of railroad track, or bushels of wheat. Nevertheless, the imagery involved was still rooted in earlier materialist notions. So education's contribution might be evaluated as improved labor quality, as in human capital conceptions.

But a conceptual shift was going on, captured in Daniel Bell's (1976) "The Coming of Post-Industrial Society." Analyses of the modern "economy" were dramatically clear that economic "value," now seen in abstract money rather than concrete automobiles, was increasingly located in something called the "service sector" (e.g., Kerr et al. 1960). A product could still be imagined. For one thing, this service sector could be seen as enhancing material production. For another, one could envision the service sector has having products in its own right – education or health or social order or financial advice – assessable in market terms. But of course, these sorts of products lack the clear market visibility of the loaf of bread or gallon of gasoline.

Indeed, often the only way to be clear about the value of service activity was to define it in terms of the credentials – usually educational – of the producers of the activity. A doctor should be paid even if the patient dies, a teacher even without much learning produced, and a civil servant even if the paperwork is of no use. Thus, the value (and thus stratification) system of the whole Western world, as assessed in monetary terms, tended to shift toward making educational credentials quite central.

Further, if education came to be central in the product of extant goods and especially services, it also became even more central to a new postmodern theory of progress. If educational credentials became the basis on which current production (e.g., of a manager with an MBA) could be assessed, the expansion of educational credentials could create and legitimate new forms of value assessed as productive (e.g., a human relations manager, an educational planner, or an environmental engineer).

We have, then, the rise of the knowledge society – built around monetarized notions of value far removed from the exchange of instrumentally useful commodities on markets and closely linked to the educational system. And higher education, rather than primary or secondary education, becomes central. The university produces the knowledge and then defines the knowledge as valuable. And it produces the producer of this often barely visible knowledge in action – teaching. Teaching, we now call it, and research are both central to GDP and its growth. Unsurprisingly, the university that lays such golden eggs, instead of being an expensive prestige good of dubious (perhaps negative) instrumental value, becomes a central totem of the mystery of progress.

Thus, with the rise of the knowledge society, expanded and improved universities become foci of policy everywhere. And the great world centers actively encourage it. The World Bank's report on higher education in the Third World (2000) shows none of the older concern about irrational status competitions and displays anxiety only about whether universities in the periphery can expand enough with enough quality to make progress happen. This report is a major reversal of its earlier stance regarding investment in higher education and tertiary enrollment growth. In dozens of policy documents, the OECD demands that countries invest more in scientific research if they wish to compete in the global economy. Moreover, the improvement of the university has become the goal of much policy discourse with a strong emphasis on better and more flexible organization and more professionalized management (Ramirez 2006b). In practice, professionalized management has meant more university administrators and staff with more educational credentials, often consulting with experts with at least equally impressive credentials. Thus, the universalization of the university has involved both its worldwide expansion but also universal standards for assessing its quality and, presumably, its contribution to national and world progress.

A consequence of the postmodern rise of the knowledge society is that it becomes difficult to give substance to the notions of value, production, and progress that are involved. As noted above, the substance of research and instruction is not the focus of the chapters here, or of the policy worlds on which they report. The categories of the medieval world – theology, law, medicine, and philosophy – are long gone but so for the most part are the modern stand-alone fields of knowledge, like economics or physics. Kong Chong Ho's Chap. 13, on Singapore, stands out, referring concretely to topics like quantum technologies, cancer research, an earth observatory, clinical imaging, desalination, water technology, or nanotechnology. Interdisciplinary problem-solving ventures within the university are much in vogue, often contrasted to disciplinary silos. Even in the social sciences, these interdisciplinary efforts are hailed in institutes designed to combat poverty or promote well-being.

The main exception here is the overwhelming emphasis, in the national policies described here, on science and technology as foci of progress. Sometimes science includes social science, and sometimes, national emphases note the importance of the humanities – as in the Malaysian case in Chap. 12 – but this is quite rare. The global world is a rationalized place, and the knowledge emphasized in it is similarly highly rationalized: that is why it belongs in the university (Frank and Meyer 2007).

15.6   World-Class Universities

We arrive at an understanding of why much policy attention, in the current world, goes to higher education, and its expansion and improvement. The chapters of this book dramatically illustrate the point. The world is a very interdependent place; rationalized knowledge is everywhere the same and is central to progress, and individuals are the core units of a world society and the carriers of effective action. Social success of individuals, organizations, and national societies rests critically on the human component, and social improvement rests on the improvement of this human component. Schooling is central, and higher education – producer of both the personnel and the knowledge for the knowledge society – is most central.

So around the world, policy elites support, rather than resist, all sorts of pressures to expand university education and to organize it around a world knowledge system rather than any parochial local one. Curricula everywhere tend to reflect world standards and to evolve along with these standards (Frank and Meyer 2007; Frank and Gabler 2006). And, in the global knowledge society, the whole higher educational system is envisioned as a source of progress.

As Frank and Gabler (2006) make clear, the focus of expansion in the current period is on the natural and social sciences, rather than on the humanities that reflect older national and civilizational cultures. And in the chapters of this book, the depicted goals of educational policy typically focus on scientific and technical improvements: the humanities are rarely emphasized at all.

If the university's cultural claims have always been to bring universal knowledge down into local society, and thus have had globalized qualities, the postmodern shift to globalized notions of a world knowledge society and value system greatly intensifies expanded efforts at universalization. The chapters of this book display many dimensions of these efforts.

First, there is the rise of the concept "world-class university" itself. This implies global recognition and global significance. So indicators like the presence of international students and faculty increase in importance, so do measures of international recognition – citations, international publications, rankings, and ratings.

Second, especially in the developing world, there is a concern about upgrading universities that might not be entirely first-class operations. Rankings are important but also indicators of membership in the latent class involved. Rationalized "accounting for excellence" exercises diffuse worldwide (Ramirez 2010).

Third, at the emergent global level, direct concerns about prestige – at both university and national levels – arise, in some ways reflecting the old processes so heavily criticized a half century ago. In the same way that the sprawling modern occupational system – often lacking direct measures of productivity – rests on educational credentials, educational systems have the same dependencies and for the same reasons. Research showing the actual social benefits of higher educational expansion is conspicuous for its weakness or absence: it has been very difficult to find positive effects of higher educational enrollments (or quality) on growth in the GDP/capita, for instance (e.g., Benavot 1992; Chabbott and Ramirez 2000), and defenses of the virtues of much investment in higher education often rely on very qualitative examples in a highly irrational way made famous by Kahneman and Tversky (1979) and others.

Concretely, it is hard to imagine any research findings that would validate economically sociopolitical decisions to concentrate investments on two or three Harvards rather than distributing them more widely among many – a point made by Shin in Chap. 2 and by Cremonini and colleagues in Chap. 7, who also notice that researchers do not seem to be looking at the issue. Vague reasoning about the virtues of interactive synergistic effects is required – evidence is unlikely to help. Further vague reasoning can argue that having Harvards can create top-down diffusion, or demonstration effects. Again, evidence is unlikely to help – and few researchers seem even to be looking for it.

So the old prestige competitions arise in full force, now at the global level. And of course, absence of a strong world state, there is nothing to stop them, exactly as theorized by Ben-David and Zlockzower (1962) and by Collins (1979, 1971). Universities compete – within countries but now also at the global level – with the positive supports from their national Ministries. And the Ministries compete too, acutely aware of how many universities they have in the top 100 of some rating scheme.

15.7   Criteria, Ratings, and Strategies

The notion of the world-class university has, obviously, taken hold in the real world and historically evolves over time. It thus becomes problematic to attempt a formalized academic definition (but see Shin, in Chap. 2). And in most of the chapters here, little definitional effort is made, and authors rely on the emergent common sense understandings of the current global system.

In this system, many interrelated dimensions are involved. All the dimensions are seen as having a good side and a bad side – there are few trade-offs or ambiguities. It is good to produce more research, to be heavily cited, and to publish in prestigious and international fora. It is good to have courses and programs in the international lingua franca. It is good to have international students and professors. It is good to be strong in fields like science, engineering, and social science.

And, of course, it is good to have many resources. As noted above, it is difficult to show the positive effects of higher education on society, so there is a strong tendency to substitute measures of cost for invisible measures of benefit. It is thus clearly good to be expensive – to have a big research budget, expensive facilities, and so on. In the same way, it is good to have as intake the best students and professors and in this more subtle way to be more expensive. The more social resources a university can use up, the better, in this scheme.

All these dimensions are pulled together in the available global ranking systems, which are attended to by the authors here and by the policy elites they study. The ranking systems vary on which indicators they emphasize. But their authors clearly know that they are creating measures for an unmeasured variable that actually exists in the real world. That is, university prestige and reputation is the institutionalized gold standard. So, if one is to create a new measure, it had better have Harvard at the top, or nobody will pay attention. The measure-builder can monkey around a bit – as with British tendencies to raise domestic ratings by counting internationalization quite heavily – but not too far.

In the same way, national and university strategies to achieve greatness vary less than one might expect. They are driven by the existence of a real (or anyway institutionalized) value system. In the current period, this famously puts "the American research university" at the top (see the chapters in Rhoten and Calhoun 2011), and so strategies to move in other directions – say to create versions of grande ecoles – are likely to fail. All the chapters in this book report policy models and organizational efforts, reflecting the character and context of the American research universities. Interestingly, when the authors here do venture definitional statements, these cover broader and somewhat different terrains: they sometimes emphasize that a good university ought to contribute to local and national and world society, ought to help solve problems at all levels, ought to produce demonstrably good educational consequences, and so on. Such matters, of course, are distant from the available rating schemes but also from the actual policy emphases reported here: as a practical matter, global ratings rooted in global standards unrelated to the actual social problems of the world are what matters.

Heyneman and Lee, in Chap. 4, pull together the macrolevel contextual factors that are involved in this stratification system. Naturally, they celebrate the hegemonic American forms, treating these as functional requirements for world-class universities anywhere. This makes sense in the current system but might have seemed very odd in another period (e.g., around 1900, when German universities, by no means highly ranking on Heyneman's criteria, were dominant).

Familiar American paradigms are made central. These stress the university as a decision-making organizational actor (Kruecken and Meier 2006), an open communication and competition system, a focus on high productivity and to its assessment, and so on. The same themes appear in almost all the national policy systems described in the chapters here. There is a good deal of circularity here: if the universities in the hegemonic United States are seen as at the top, of course American organizational and political principles will be seen as essential criteria for world-class status. Meanwhile, ironically, American scholars fear that the American advantage in higher education is withering (Douglass 2009). In the spirit of "A Nation at Risk," we now have "A Gathering Storm" as a metaphor for the rise of competition in the sphere of higher education. The fear, of course, is based on the assumption of a strong link between higher education expansion and quality and economic and social development.

But in contrast to models that place the decision-making (but accountable) university organization at the center of the evolution of the world-class university (as the abstract ideas of Shin in Chap. 2, or Heyneman and Lee in Chap. 4), the empirical chapters of this book place the national state and its elites at the center of the core processes involved. In Germany and France, just as in the Asian cases emphasized by Marginson in Chap. 5, national decision-making was central. Sometimes it is the nation-state worried about competing with the rising neighbors (Chang on Taiwan in Chap. 11, Yonezawa on Japan in Chap. 8). Sometimes it is a more abstract concern with prestige (Sirat, Malaysia, Chap. 12). And sometimes it is a concrete concern with development needs, as in the chapter on Singapore. But in this book, there are no cases in which universities on their own rose to the top of the heap.

Of course, this is true of the famous American model too, in good part. The great American state universities were created in this way. The fact that six of Shanghai's top hundred universities are parts of the University of California system results rather directly from the well-known plan of officials of the State of California to stratify higher education and pour resources into the top end of the system. Similar decisions at the national level were instrumental in the rise to dominance of the nation's elite private universities. Stanford's rise in the postwar period, for instance, was massively facilitated by the decision of a central national foundation that America needed more elite universities (Lowen 1997).

15.8   Conclusion

Conceptions of the world-class university are quite highly standardized and have spread around the world. They reflect expanded notions of universalized knowledge, heavy with science and social scientific analyses. They reflect more globalized conceptions of the uses of this knowledge and the mobility of the people who will produce and use it. Finally, they reflect notions of a high level of quality, so that the participants in a world-class university can properly compete in a global communication and stratification system.

So countries and universities compete for entrance into the newly evolving category. University prestige, obviously, is involved, so is national prestige. The prestige competitions are intensified because the global society – like the earlier American society, which in some ways it models – has a stateless quality. There is no global public body that can define and certify membership in the appropriate world-class category – it must be done through competitive mechanisms.

But beyond prestige, the rise of postmodern conceptions of value – the knowledge society in which many forms of educational certified status count just as much as bushels of potatoes, or tons of steel – makes the university and its teaching and research convincingly appear to be productive for progress now defined much more abstractly than in the past. The university generates new conceptions of value and also produces the values newly defined. This is the case with respect to student output but also as regards university organization and management. A proliferation of international conferences focuses on the need to cope with the challenges of globalization via rethinking higher education to make universities more transparent, more accountable, more innovative, and more competitive. Universalized standards of assessment emerge and justify world, regional, and national rankings. The resultant competitions within and between countries have qualities that would a few decades ago have been taken as indicators of rampant inflationary processes.

Universalizing the university is a common thread throughout this book and indeed throughout policy discussions regarding higher education everywhere. Thus, the old and much criticized inflationary cycle is put in place, and competitions – for students, professors, enrollment rates, publication rates, and so on – are set in motion, obviously leading to expanded individual, organizational, and national investments. In the old days, this might have been criticized. But in the brave new world, a new set of assumptions prevail and legitimate the competitions involved. The new assumptions foster ideas about a knowledge society and economy, in which all sorts of education-produced goods are counted as equal to the old necessities of life. The educational competitions, thus, can constantly produce new, though often barely visible, legitimated goods. Therefore, these competitions need not be seen as wasteful destructions of value but rather as producers of valued progress.

References

Baker, D., & LeTendre, G. K. (2005). *National differences, global similarities: World culture and the future of schooling*. Stanford: Stanford University Press.

Baker, D. P., Koehler, H., & Stock, M. (2004). *Socialist ideology and the contraction of higher education: Institutional consequences of state manpower and education planning in the former East Germany*. Berlin: Max Planck Institute for Human Development.

Bell, D. (1976). *The coming of post-industrial society: A venture in social forecasting*. New York: Basic Books.

Benavot, A. (1992). Educational expansion and economic growth in the modern world, 1913–1985. In B. Fuller & R. Rubinson (Eds.), *The political construction of education: The state, school expansion, and economic change* (pp. 117–134). New York: Praeger.

Ben-David, J., & Zloczower, A. (1962). Universities and academic systems in modern societies. *European Journal of Sociology, 3*, 45–85.

Berg, I. (1970). *Education and jobs: The great training robbery*. New York: Praeger.

Boudon, R. (1974). *Education, opportunity, and social inequality: Changing prospects in western society*. New York: Wiley.

Bradley, K., & Ramirez, F. (1996). World polity and gender parity: Women's share of higher education, 1965–1985. *Research in Sociology of Education and Socialization, 11*, 63–91.

Chabbott, C., & Ramirez, F. (2000). Development and education. In M. Hallinan (Ed.), *Handbook of sociology of education* (pp. 163–187). New York: Plenum.

Clark, B. R. (1983). *The higher education system: Academic organization in cross-national perspective*. Berkeley: University of California Press.

Clark, W. (2006). *Academic charisma and the origins of the research university*. Chicago: University of Chicago Press.

Collins, R. (1971). Functional and conflict theories of educational stratification. *American Sociological Review, 36*(6), 1002–1019.

Collins, R. (1979). *The credential society: An historical sociology of education and stratification*. New York: Academic.

Dore, R. P. (1975). *The diploma disease: Education, qualification and development*. Berkeley: University of California Press.

Douglass, J. (2009). Treading water: What happened to America's higher education advantage. In J. A. Douglass, C. J. King, & I. Feller (Eds.), *Globalization's muse. Universities and higher education systems in a changing world* (pp. 165–186). Berkeley: University of California/Public Policy Press.

Drori, G., Meyer, J., Ramirez, F., & Schofer, E. (2003). *Science in the modern world polity: Institutionalization and globalization*. Stanford: Stanford University Press.

Drori, G., Meyer, J., & Hwang, H. (Eds.). (2006). *Globalization and organization*. Oxford: Oxford University Press.

Elliott, M. (2007). Human rights and the triumph of the individual in world culture. *Cultural Sociology, 1*(3), 343–363.

Elliott, M., & Boli, J. (2008). *Human rights instruments and human rights institutionalization, 1863–2003*. Budapest: World Congress of the International Institute of Sociology.

Flexner, A. (1930). *Universities: American, English, German*. New York: Oxford University Press.

Foster, P. J. (1965). *Education and social change in Ghana*. Chicago: University of Chicago Press.

Fourcade, M. (2009). *Economists and societies: Discipline and profession in the United States, Britain, and France, 1890s to 1990s*. Princeton: Princeton University Press.

Frank, D., & Gabler, J. (2006). *Reconstructing the university: Worldwide changes in academic emphases over the twentieth century*. Stanford: Stanford University Press.

Frank, D., & Meyer, J. (2007). University expansion and the knowledge society. *Theory and Society, 36*(2007), 287–311.

Freeman, R. (1976). *The overeducated American*. New York: Academic.

Haas, P. M. (1992). Epistemic communities and international policy coordination. *International Organization, 46*(1), 1–35.

Harbison, F., & Myers, C. (1964). *Education, manpower, and economic growth: Strategies of human resource development*. New York: McGraw-Hill.

Huntington, S. P. (1968). *Political order in changing societies*. New Haven: Yale University Press.

Illich, I. (1971). *Deschooling society*. New York: Harrow Books.

Jedell, H. (1931, November 1). Warns Germany on overeducation: Sees economic waste. *New York Times*, p. 56.

Kahneman, D., & Tversky, A. (1979). Prospect theory. *Econometrica, 47*, 263–291.

Kerr, C., Dunlop, J., Harbison, F., & Myers, C. (1960). *Industrialism and industrial man; the problems of labor and management in economic growth*. Cambridge: Harvard University Press.

Kruecken, G., & Meier, F. (2006). Turning the university into an organized actor. In G. Drori, J. Meyer, & H. Hwang (Eds.), *Globalization and organization* (pp. 241–257). Oxford: Oxford University Press.

Lenhardt, G., & Stock, M. (2000). Hochschulentwicklung und Bürgerrechte in der BRD und der DDR. *Kölner Zeitschrift für Soziologie und Sozialpsychologie, 52*, 520–540.

Lowen, R. (1997). *Creating the cold war university: The transformation of Stanford*. Berkeley: University of California Press.

Ramirez, F. (2006a). From citizen to person; rethinking education as incorporation. In D. Baker & A. Wiseman (Eds.), *The impact of comparative education research on neo-institutional theory* (pp. 367–388). Oxford: Elsevier Science.

Ramirez, F. (2006b). The rationalization of universities. In M.-L. Djelic & K. Shalin-Andersson (Eds.), *Transnational governance: Institutional dynamics of regulation* (pp. 224–245). Cambridge: Cambridge University Press.

Ramirez, F. (2010). Accounting for excellence: Transforming universities into organizational actors. In V. Rust, L. Portnoi, & S. Bagely (Eds.), *Higher education, policy, and the global competition phenomenon* (pp. 54–75). New York: Palgrave.

Ramirez, F., & Wotipka, C. (2001). Slowly but surely? The global expansion of women's participation in science and engineering fields of study, 1972–1992. *Sociology of Education, 74*, 231–251.

Ramirez, F., Rubinson, R., & Meyer, J. (1973). *National educational expansion and political Development: Causal Interrelationships, 1950-70* (With R. Rubinson & J. Meyer). SEADAG Papers on Education and National Development. Asia Society.

Rashdall, H. (1936). *The Universities of Europe in the middle ages* (F. M. Powicke & A. B. Emden, Ed., 1895, 2nd ed.). Oxford: Oxford University Press.

Rhoten, D., & Calhoun, C. (2011). *Knowledge matters: The public mission of the research university*. New York: Columbia University Press.

Riddle, P. (1990). *University and state: Political competition and the rise of universities, 1200–1985*. Ph.D. dissertation, School of Education, Stanford University, Stanford, CA.

Riddle, P. (1993). Political authority and university formation in Europe, 1200–1800. *Sociological Perspectives, 36*, 45–62.

Robertson, R. (1992). *Globalization: Social theory and global culture* (p. 1992). London: Sage.

Rosenmund, M. (2006). The current discourse on curriculum change. In A. Benavot & C. Braslavsky (Eds.), *School curricula for global citizenship* (pp. 173–194). Hong Kong: Comparative Education Research Center, University of Hong Kong/Springer.

Rubinson, R. (1986). Class formation, politics, and institutions: Schooling in the United States. *American Journal of Sociology, 92*, 519–548.

Rubinson, R., & Browne, I. (1994). Education and the economy. In N. Smelser & R. Swedberg (Eds.), *The handbook of economic sociology*. Princeton: Princeton University Press.

Rubinson, R., & Fuller, B. (1992). When does school expansion drive economic change and the class structure? In B. Fuller & R. Rubinson (Eds.), *The political construction of education*. New York: Praeger.

Schofer, E., & Meyer, J. (2005). The world-wide expansion of higher education in the twentieth century. *American Sociological Review, 70*(6), 898–920.

Shils, E. (1971). No salvation outside higher education. *Minerva, 9*(3), 313–321.

The World Bank. (2000). *Higher education in developing countries: Peril and promise*. Washington, DC: World Bank Institute Press.

Thwing, C. (1911). *Universities of the world*. New York: Macmillan.

World of Learning. Multiple years. London: Allen and Unwin.

Chapter 16
The World-Class University Across Higher Education Systems: Similarities, Differences, and Challenges

Jung Cheol Shin and Barbara M. Kehm

16.1 Introduction

In his chapter, Shin set out to define the term "world-class university" from a broader perspective (world-class, national-class, and local-class) in order to better understand the concept of world-class university in higher education systems. According to the conceptual approach, there is only a small number of "world-class" universities. Most of them are located in higher education systems of economically advanced countries. The emerging top-ranking universities in other countries are not in the world-class category, although their universities are very competitive in research productivity. This suggests that world-class universities are not established in a short time, which is disappointing to policymakers and university leaders in the developing higher education systems. Some research-productive universities in developing or recently developed countries may be top-ranked in global rankings, but the ranking status does not always mean that the university is considered a world-class university. This points to the fact that the status of a world-class university is not only related to hard indicators but also to the softer indicator of reputation which takes time to build up. As Hazelkorn (2011: 21) put it: "Rankings are a symptom but also an acceleration of the 'reputation race.'"

This book has paid attention to the development of higher education systems as well as other contextual factors in discussing a world-class university. On the one hand, the different contexts in each country explain how the initiatives to establish a world-class university differ even though the goal is similar across countries. On

J.C. Shin (✉)
Department of Education, Seoul National University, Seoul, Republic of (South Korea)
e-mail: jcs6205@snu.ac.kr

B.M. Kehm
International Centre for Higher Education Research, Kassel University, Kassel, Germany
e-mail: kehm@incher.uni-kassel.de

J.C. Shin and B.M. Kehm (eds.), *Institutionalization of World-Class University in Global Competition*, The Changing Academy – The Changing Academic Profession in International Comparative Perspective 6, DOI 10.1007/978-94-007-4975-7_16,
© Springer Science+Business Media Dordrecht 2013

the other hand, there are similarities between countries in such initiatives despite differing contexts. The similarities are found in the design and implementation of the world-class initiatives. Through such similarities across universities and countries, contemporary higher education is becoming homogenized, especially in the countries where the drive for establishing a world-class university is strong as institutionalists argue (e.g., Meyer and Rowan 1977). Through these homogenization processes, contemporary higher education loses its diversity and focuses exclusively on research productivity which is unhealthy both for society as well as higher education.

It is timely therefore to discuss world-class university initiatives from a skeptical perspective. While this may be biased or may wrongly predict the future development of a world-class university, we are sure that policymakers and academic researchers who are working closely with policymakers at national or institutional levels will identify implications to be considered.

16.2 Similarities and Differences Across Higher Education Systems

16.2.1 Why a World-Class University?

Although there have been globally competitive research universities in advanced countries such as the USA, the UK, and Japan for some time, serious policy discussions about a world-class university started in the mid-1990s when China launched a program to foster the development and reputation of 100 key universities to become globally competitive in the twenty-first century. Following this, China launched a new program in May 1998 (985 project) to support a more select group of altogether 39 universities to become a new elite group. Its neighboring countries Taiwan and Korea adopted similar programs based on the Chinese initiatives in 1998 and 1999, respectively. Among these northeastern Asian countries, there is a sense of chasing and being chased. China is becoming a global economic power and chasing Korea and Taiwan. Both Korea and Taiwan began to respond to the Chinese initiatives to sustain their economic status in the global economy and began to chase Japan and other advanced economies. Finally, Japan joined the world-class university initiatives in 2002 in an effort to become more globally competitive as well.

Stimulated by these initiatives and the rapid growth in global knowledge production, European countries, now also feeling "chased," joined the race for establishing world-class universities. Germany adopted the Excellence Initiative in 2004, followed by France in 2006. Although both countries have long history of higher education development within a developed economy, they have a lower participation rate in higher education among the relevant age cohort compared to the USA and Japan as well as compared to recently emerging higher education markets such as

Korea and Taiwan. Furthermore, the continental European countries are behind the Anglo-American countries in terms of the competition for bibliometric research productivity, not least due to the fact that the domestic language is not English.

Because of the quantified bibliometric measures, historically rooted advanced higher education systems are experiencing structural changes. The impact is higher in the advanced European countries than in the developing higher education systems (e.g., Korea, China, Taiwan, Singapore, Hong Kong) because their systems are firmly rooted in their society and national culture, and it is not easy to change them. Also, the language barrier is a serious concern. The advanced systems had well-developed research centers in their regions and did not have to study in Anglo-American universities to become internationalized. In contrast, the developing higher education systems such as Korea, Taiwan, and China found it relatively easy to transform their systems to adopt Anglo-American systems. This is easier for the developing countries that are small in size and have a British colonial background, such as Singapore and Hong Kong SAR. Malaysia has also benefitted from their use of English.

The rapid dissemination of the idea of world-class universities is related to the global economy and its ideological basis in neoliberalism which spread in the 1990s. The world-class university initiatives were adopted by many countries after the mid-2000s when the global rankings emerged. Now, most higher education systems including those in the Middle-East, Africa, and Latin America as well as in the East Asian countries have some form of world-class university initiative. With the increase of these initiatives, neoliberal parties in Asia and Europe are the main actors in the race for world-class universities and competition-based higher education reforms. Furthermore, international organizations such as the World Bank and the OECD have been leading the world-class university discussion through the funding and hosting of international events. The involvement of these international organizations in the discussions about world-class universities legitimizes world-class university initiatives even in economically underdeveloped countries.

16.2.2   Similarities and Differences

The nine case studies in this book have similarities in terms of policy design and implementation. The similarities can be found mainly in their approach to building a world-class university. First of all, most of the countries selected a small number of universities in order to bring them up to world-class status. This strategy produces mission differentiations between universities in the respective higher education systems. This is quite innovative in countries with a strong German university tradition because these countries perceive all universities to be research universities. Higher education institutions focusing mainly on teaching and without an explicit research mission are called differently in these countries, for example, polytechnic, college, or university of applied sciences. This strategy was adopted in the developing systems (Korea, China, Taiwan, and Malaysia) as well as in the advanced higher education systems (Germany, France, and Japan). The exceptions are Singapore and Hong Kong where the systems are small.

Second, these countries adopted governance reforms to provide flexibility for their universities and to develop them into actors on markets. In particular, the state withdrew from detailed regulation thus giving universities more autonomy. In some countries, universities were endowed with corporate status. In most cases, the governance reforms were initiated to develop higher education institutions into organizations which entailed five distinctive shifts: first, a reduction of detailed state regulation; second, a reduction of the decision-making power of collegial academic bodies within the institutions; third, an increase in the power of the central level management; fourth, an increase in external stakeholder guidance through the introduction of boards; and fifth, an increase in competition and market pressures (cf. De Boer et al. 2007). As a result, universities became more sensitive to market demands and were required to be more active in generating external resources.

Third, these countries are actively engaged in enhancing their global ranking status. The non-English-speaking developing countries (Korea, China, and Taiwan) are encouraging their professors to teach courses in English as are the English-speaking developing countries (Singapore and Hong Kong). In addition, even the English-speaking developing countries (Malaysia, Singapore, and Hong Kong SAR) are seeking to attract more talented international professors and students from abroad.

Fourth, these countries reformed their academic staff systems in order to hire more research-competitive faculty and to motivate their research activities. They also increased their requirements for promotion. In most of the research-competitive universities in the seven Asian countries, publishing in international journals is one of the official or semiofficial requirements for hiring and promotion. These countries are also adopting financial incentive systems for research-productive professors.

What is more, the policy approaches for establishing world-class universities are similar because of the shared technical dimensions of world-class university initiatives as reflected in policy design and implementation at the institutional as well as at the governmental level. In their selection processes, many countries applied a similar protocol: evaluation, funding decisions, midterm evaluation, etc. This protocol is the norm in research funding decisions in many countries and has been considered as "fair" when there are many competitors for a limited number of opportunities. The protocol has been applied for resource allocation in other education projects.

Second, bibliometric data have been widely used as a measure of a world-class university by policymakers and university leaders as well as by global rankers. Evaluators use bibliometric data because they can compare and evaluate a university, a department, and individual professors. Although bibliometric data do not make sense in some disciplines especially the soft disciplines (arts and humanities and social sciences), such data have been widely used in government funding decisions and evaluations. The wide use of bibliometric data results in the standardization of scholastic productivity by measureable indicators. Quite often, funding agencies and evaluators request standardized indicators (e.g., h-index, g-index) as well as the number of publications and citations. As a result, higher education systems are becoming similar across universities, disciplines, and countries.

Nevertheless, there are some notable differences in the approach of the various countries, depending on their history of higher education and their educational and economic context. The advanced systems (Germany, France, and Japan) focus on upgrading research capacity. These countries have research centers within as well as outside universities with high-quality research capability. Their main goal is to upgrade their research competiveness and achieve synergy through the reorganization of their existing research infrastructure. The German and Japanese governments sought to upgrade research capacity through funding selective universities, while the French government focused on integration and collaboration between universities, research institutes, and the private sector to produce synergy and to move their universities up in the global rankings.

In contrast, the developing countries focus on incubating research centers because their research infrastructure is in its infancy compared to the advanced systems. English-speaking developing countries (Singapore and Hong Kong SAR) attempted to accomplish their goals through attracting talented foreign professors as well as investing in research and development. Their research performance in the global knowledge production market is remarkable, and the rapid growth of these universities is impressive. This strategy was not adopted in other developing systems (Korea, Taiwan, China, and Malaysia) because it is not easy to implement in non-English-speaking countries (Korea, Taiwan) or economically less developed countries (e.g., Malaysia). China has adopted both strategies for selecting universities and accomplished its goals in a relatively short time because China could attract talented Chinese scientists from top-ranking universities in other countries, especially in the USA.

Non-English-speaking developing countries sought to enhance their research productivity through mission differentiation and research capacity incubation. This strategy was also successful in Korea and Taiwan where research productivity increased dramatically during the last decade. Both countries developed a project-based research funding program to build a competitive world-class university. Unlike the Chinese approach, the two countries did not select some universities for support but selected research teams (or consortiums). This is because an institution-based approach is quite difficult in countries where all universities are regarded as research universities. The German and Japanese initiatives were undertaken in a similar fashion.

The similarities and differences between the different higher education systems in the institutionalization of a world-class university are presented in Fig. 16.1.

16.3 Challenges

The policy initiatives by governments and the strategic responses by universities and academics pose challenges to contemporary higher education. As leading research universities enter the ranking game and their followers are confronted

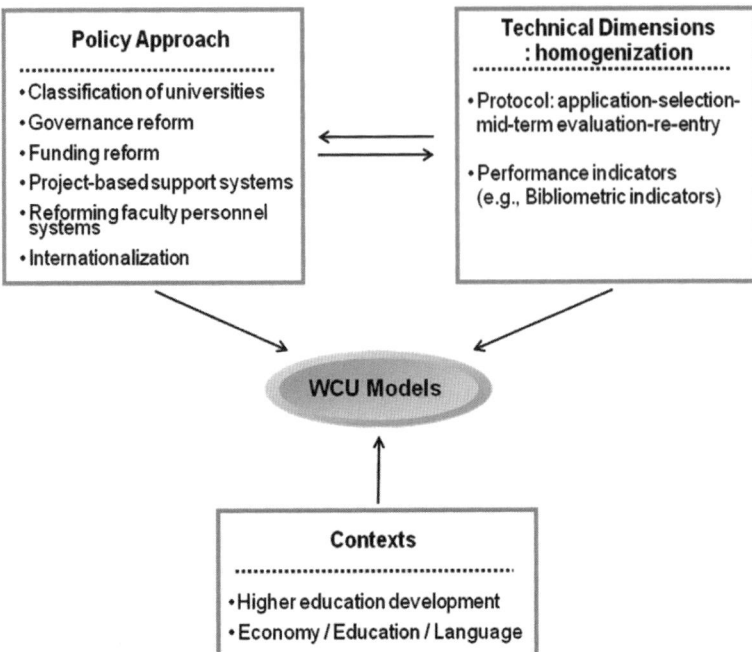

Fig. 16.1 Similarities and differences in institutionalization of WCU

with an identity crisis, all universities have to realign their functions to focus on research and internationalization. Often, student tuition fees are increased to support this new focus. A fundamental question for higher education is how mass higher education can coexist with excellence initiatives based on high selectivity. This section discusses the concept of world-class university in relation to mass higher education, the issue of research and its social contribution, the issue of aligning focus between global, national, and local dimensions, and finally ethical dimensions of world-class university.

16.3.1   World-Class University and Massification

The world-class university is more closely related to research and graduate education, while mass higher education is more oriented toward teaching and undergraduate education. Can both orientations coexist in a university? A similar question is whether teaching and research can coexist in a university. In theory, research can be a source for teaching, and professors sometimes find their research ideas in their teaching. However, in reality the close relationship between teaching and research is not the norm in all countries. Both may be in conflict (Shin 2011a). In the USA, research-productive professors in many top-ranking universities teach only graduate courses, and teaching-focused professors are in charge of undergraduate courses. In some countries, the government is deeply involved in this division of labor through its funding policy (Leistyte et al. 2009; Schimank and Winnes 2000). Despite this trend, teaching – including undergraduate teaching – and research continue to be equal duties of professors in most continental European countries.

Still, with massification, higher education looks like an extended version of secondary education (Shin and Harman 2009) in most Anglo-American countries. Undergraduate courses are oriented more toward the liberal arts than subject-specific knowledge, college professors teach many courses like high school teachers, and the college classroom resembles high school. Advanced placement courses in US high schools and the Grandes Ecoles preparation courses in France are college courses taught in high schools. Thus, the upper secondary high school classroom has some similarity to the undergraduate classroom.

Separating undergraduate from graduate education has several benefits. Graduate education is high cost compared to undergraduate education (Bloom 1983; Smith 1992). In their tuition decisions, however, universities do not pay much attention to the fact that the high costs were caused by research and graduate education; as a result, universities tend to put the financial burden on their undergraduate students (Shin 2011a). In many universities, there are more undergraduate students than graduate students. However, the tuition policy of these universities does not differentiate between undergraduate and graduate students. As a consequence, universities levy charges on undergraduate students that go to support graduate students. Although governments support graduate education and research through providing support for research and development (R&D), undergraduate students pay a share of the costs for graduate education. Consequently, differentiating undergraduate education from graduate education may become an issue in the discussion of a world-class university.

16.3.2 Knowledge Production and Its Social Contribution

We assume that knowledge production contributes to national and social development. Without that assumption, no government might invest in it. On a global scale, we have seen the emergence of knowledge societies which means that increasing knowledge rather than consumer goods or services determines the wealth and well-being of a given nation. Producing new knowledge and disseminating existing knowledge to ever more people is therefore deemed an important part of every society. In this setting, world-class universities not only become a symbol for the most advanced and most competitive knowledge-producing institutions but also for the nation's wealth and global competitiveness in which they are located.

Of course new knowledge is not exclusively produced in universities. Because cutting-edge research in many cases tends to be expensive, governments have tried to pool resources in order to achieve more efficiency and effectiveness. Dill and van Vught (2010) have addressed this issue by analyzing national innovation frameworks, and Etzkowiz and Leydesdorff (1997) have coined the term of triple helix which emphasizes the knowledge production process as a form of collaboration between university, industry, and government in order to maximize its utility for society.

However, not all kinds of knowledge production lend themselves for direct utilization and application. This has led to crises of legitimacy in some subjects and disciplines which were confronted with the question of how much they contribute to the well-being of society and the economy. Of course, it is easier to measure such a contribution when looking at knowledge produced in engineering or natural sciences. The contribution of the social sciences and humanities to societal problems is more difficult to measure. But social cohesion, culture, identity, and education to name but a few of the contributions to society by the social sciences and the humanities are important elements for social stability and order which are needed in order to uphold a process of knowledge production at all. The better educated the members of a given society are, the higher the standard of living overall.

These are elements that typical ranking indicators to determine world-class status of universities do not take into account. They dominantly focus on the number of publications and citations. The purely quantitative measures lose their validity when it comes to the question how much the knowledge which is being produced contributes to the wealth, the well-being, and the social order and stability of a given society and economy. We argue here that all universities, and especially world-class universities, should focus more on these aspects.

16.3.3   Global, National, or Local Focus

Another issue that a world-class university should address is the priority of a global, national, or local orientation. Being world-class seems to imply a global orientation as such because the competition for this status is organized by global rankings. But is there any global division of labor between universities? One assumes a world-class university contributes to global issues, while national or local universities address national or regional issues. This question is related to the identity of a world-class university. Although we call them "world-class" universities, most focus on national issues because the majority of their funds come from the state. A world-class university is based on global ranking, but most top-ranked universities are seeking to align their focus on national as well as global issues. In addition, from the local perspective, a world-class university is expected to contribute to its community too. A world-class university is therefore confronted with complex expectations: competing on the global stage, pursuing national priorities, and dealing with local needs.

Leading universities worldwide are expected to address human and social problems. That is why we call a globally leading university a world-class university. There are many common problems that humankind is confronted with. We need scientific knowledge to solve many problems – we continue to suffer with unknown diseases, confront environmental problems, struggle to develop energy-efficient transportation, and solve food shortages. In addition, we need to develop better social systems and to live in better social environments. We expect the leading universities to focus on these common global issues.

From a national point of view, a government expects a world-class university to contribute to national competitiveness because the government is actively involved in developing the world-class university as part of its national innovation system (e.g., Sidhu et al. 2011; Yang and Welch 2011). That is why governments facilitate and support world-class universities. This perspective has been emphasized in national innovation systems. A world-class university is a part of a policy effort to establish national innovation systems. This policy approach has been followed in many countries, in both developed as well as developing countries.

As well as global and national perspectives, local demands are also relevant to a world-class university. The local economy is often associated with the universities in this area. The idea of a national innovation park is related to the demands for economic development, and it is also highly associated with the local economy. For example, one cannot imagine Silicon Valley without Stanford and UC Berkeley in the local area. Local communities expect the world-class university in their area to contribute to the community. They expect faculty involvement in local affairs, they expect to use the university facility, and they expect a world-class university to contribute to the local economy in various ways.

16.3.4 Ethical Dimension of World-Class University

The WCU requires a concentration of public funding in selected universities. This raises the issue of equality between universities and between students in the universities. People should benefit equally from public money. If one student in a world-class university benefits more than a student in a non-WCU, this may counter the general principle of the public use of tax. A world-class university should prove its contribution to the society as the basis for using more public funding than other types of universities. However, most world-class universities assign priority on their own benefits rather than to the social development in their national and local communities. In addition, these universities are actively involved in income-generating activities in order to be able to compete with universities which are in the same league as they are. This income generation may be in conflict with their need to provide value for society.

Many academics and institutional leaders support the move to a world-class university even though they feel such a university is not the optimal direction for their university or for their society. As discussed, the world-class university is not superior to national-class or local-class universities. It is an issue of mission focus rather than believing one type of university is better than the others. In reality, however, many universities are seeking to be world-class. This raises the question of whether it is ethical to move toward being a world-class university despite the doubt of whether that is the right direction. The research literature has described this phenomenon as mimetic or even coercive isomorphism (e.g., Powell and DiMaggio 1991). Mimetic (i.e., imitation) or coercive (i.e., forced) isomorphism indicates the push all organizations, including universities, experience in competitive environments. Any university wants to be as good or even better than that university which it considers to be its competitor or which is more successful. In rankings and league tables, universities compare themselves with each other by looking at the respective positions on the scale. Those universities higher up on the scale are imitated by those lower down on the scale in order to move up. In some countries, for example, in China, the government selects certain universities, provides them with additional funding and other forms of support, and expects them to move up on the ranking scales. These universities are thus coerced into competing and becoming more successful. In the process, such universities raise faculty salaries to attract research-productive professors and tend to raise student tuition to cover the costs. As a result, students pay a share of the costs involved in building a world-class university (Shin 2011b). Should students pay such costs?

Ethical issues can emerge in this global competition between leading universities. There are many unethical ways to enhance research performance. For example, plagiarism is an ethical issue in academic research. Co-opting other academics' research ideas is also reported at times. In Europe as well as in some Middle Eastern countries, the practice of some universities to "buy in" so-called star researchers on 5- or 10-% contracts in order to boost their positions in rankings has also acquired a somewhat unethical taste.

16.4 Conclusion: The Future of World-Class University

Can a world-class university be sustainable in the future? The answer depends on whether a WCU is a short-term phenomenon or long-term trend in higher education. There is a long-standing rivalry between some universities, for example, between Ivy League universities in the USA, and across borders, for example, between French Grandes Écoles and Oxford and Cambridge in the UK. This competition has contributed to academic development and has led to many positive effects. Possibly the current global competition among WCUs may provide similar benefits.

A meritocracy exists in many WCUs, especially in developing countries. Academic culture is being transformed into an open culture, universities are becoming closely associated with economic development through knowledge production, and WCUs promote a division of labor between higher education institutions. But we can also note that serious competition between universities produces dysfunctions within academic society. Plagiarism can become an issue in the competition to be seen as research productive. The race to become a WCU may lead to sacrificing education and community service, as well as the need to levy additional charges from undergraduate students.

Nevertheless, many potential WCUs are preparing to get on the top-ranking lists. International organizations such as the World Bank, OECD, and UNESCO are actively involved in discussions about the establishment of WCUs worldwide through providing research funding or hosting international conferences. Increased collaboration may accelerate the trend and may produce a general model of a WCU. Once the WCU is embedded as a part of the global market for higher education and its links to the global knowledge economy, it will have a strong tie to that economy. The strong tie between a WCU and the knowledge economy may be true for many developing countries as well as for developed countries. It looks like a competition of nations rather than the production of academic league tables. In developed countries, the WCU is a key component of the economic system. However, once it is embedded in the global economy, it may not be easy to detach from it. Governments may invest creating and supporting WCUs, highly productive research professors may join a WCU, and talented students may apply for admission.

Once a university is in the WCU competition, it may be bound by global rules. If we cannot escape the long-term trend toward WCUs, our task as higher education researchers may lie in critically analyzing the development. If WCUs are – like rankings – a phenomenon that is here to stay, policymakers need to become aware of the necessity for a diversified higher education system in which the non-WCU universities equally need the support and a sense of being valuable and valued institutions in their given society without being downgraded to "second class." Diversified models for higher education institutions should be discussed and studied in academic circles.

References

Bloom, A. M. (1983). Differential instructional productivity indices. *Research in Higher Education, 18*(2), 179–193.

De Boer, H., Enders, J., & Schimank, U. (2007). On the way towards New public management? The governance of university systems in England, the Netherlands, Austria, and Germany. In D. Jansen (Ed.), *New forms of governance in research organizations. Disciplinary approaches, interfaces and integration* (pp. 137–152). Dordrecht: Springer.

Dill, D., & Van Vught, F. A. (2010). *National innovation and the academic research enterprise: Public policy in global perspective*. Baltimore: Johns Hopkins University Press.

Etzkowitz, H., & Leydesdorff, L. (1997). *Universities and the global knowledge economy: A triple helix of university-industry-government relations*. London: Francis Pinter.

Hazelkorn, E. (2011). *Rankings and the reshaping of higher education. The battle for world-class excellence*. Basingstoke: Palgrave Macmillan.

Leistyte, L., Enders, J., & Boer, H. (2009). The balance between teaching and research in Dutch and English universities in the context of university governance reforms. *Higher Education, 57*(4), 509–531.

Meyer, J. W., & Rowan, B. (1977). Institutionalized organizations: Formal structure as myth and ceremony. *American Journal of Sociology, 83*(2), 340–363.

Powell, W., & DiMaggio, P. J. (Eds.). (1991). *The new institutionalism in organizational analysis*. Chicago: University of Chicago Press.

Schimank, U., & Winnes, M. (2000). Beyond Humboldt? The relationship between teaching and research in European university systems. *Science & Public Policy, 27*(6), 397–408.

Shin, J. C. (2011a). Teaching and research nexuses in a research university in South Korea. *Studies in Higher Education, 36*(5), 485–503.

Shin, J. C. (2011b, June). *The costs of world-class university: Who pays?* The paper presented at 24th conference of Consortium for Higher Education Researchers, Iceland.

Shin, J. C., & Harman, G. (2009). New challenges for higher education: Asia-Pacific and global perspectives. *Asia Pacific Education Review, 10*(1), 1–13.

Sidhu, R., Ho, K. C., & Yeoh, B. (2011). Emerging education hubs: The case of Singapore. *Higher Education, 61*(1), 23–40.

Smith, T. S. (1992). Discipline cost indices and their applications. *Research in Higher Education, 33*(1), 59–70.

Yang, Y., & Welch, A. (2011). A world-class university in China? The case of Tsinghua. *Higher Education*. doi:10.1007/s10734-011-9465-4.

Author Bios

Editors

Jung Cheol Shin

(Associate Professor, Department of Education, Seoul National University)
Dr. Shin is an associate professor at Seoul National University. He served for the Korea Ministry of Education about 18 years. His research interests are higher education policy, knowledge production and social development, academic profession, and quality assurance. His researches have been published in international journals *Higher Education*, *Review of Higher Education*, *Studies in Higher Education*, *Scientometrics*, *Education Policy Analysis Archive*, and *Asia Pacific Education Review*. He is the executive editor of *Asia Pacific Education Review,* the Review Editor of *Higher Education,* and a board member of *Tertiary Education and Management*. He has been invited as guest speakers by leading research universities in many countries including the USA, Japan, China, Australia, Mexico, and Taiwan. Currently, he is leading 10 years research project on knowledge production and social development with Prof. Loet Leydesdorff of University of Amsterdam funded by National Research Foundation of Korea.

Barbara M. Kehm

(Professor, International Centre for Higher Education Research, Kassel University)
Dr. Kehm is a professor of higher education research and managing director of the International Centre for Higher Education Research. Her main research interests are in the area of internationalization in higher education and new forms of governance. She has published more than 20 books and over 200 articles and book chapters on a broad range of topics in higher education research. She is a member of the editorial board of four international journals in the field. She is currently the secretary of the Consortium of Higher Education Researchers (CHER) and was chairperson of the German Association of Higher Education Researchers and member of the Executive Board of EAIR. In March 2011, she was appointed a member of the newly

J.C. Shin and B.M. Kehm (eds.), *Institutionalization of World-Class University*
in Global Competition, The Changing Academy – The Changing Academic Profession
in International Comparative Perspective 6, DOI 10.1007/978-94-007-4975-7,
© Springer Science+Business Media Dordrecht 2013

established international advisory board of the University of Helsinki in Finland. Dr. Kehm has provided her expertise in a number of countries, among them the Emirate of Oman, Syria, and China. Recent publications include Kehm, Barbara M., Huisman, Jeroen, Stensaker, Bjorn (Eds.): The European Higher Education Area: Perspectives on a Moving Target. Rotterdam: Sense 2009 and Kehm, Barbara M., Stensaker, Bjorn (Eds.): University Rankings, Diversity, and the New Landscape of Higher Education. Rotterdam, Taipei: Sense Publishers 2009.

Chapter Authors (by chapter)

Wanhua Ma
(Professor, Graduate School of Education, Peking University)
Dr. Ma, Wan-hua is a professor/director of the Center for International Higher Education, Graduate School of Education at Peking University. She got both her master and Ph.D. degrees at Cornell University, USA, in the 1990s. She began to work at Peking University in 1997. Since then, she has been invited as visiting scholars and professors to many universities. In 2003, she was invited as a visiting professor at UC Berkeley, teaching an undergraduate course on economic reform and education change in China. In 2004/2005, she also served as education consultant for East-west Center at Hawaii University. In 2005/2006, she was selected as Fulbright New Century Scholar, carrying out a research project on the formation of global research universities. In 2007, she was nominated as Erasmus Mundus professor to Finland and Norway. In 2008, she got the DAAD fellowship to visit Kassel University, Germany. And in 2009/10, she worked as education consultant for the World Bank. Besides, she has participated many international research projects sponsored by Ford Foundation, UNESCO, UNDP, and other organizations. She has published extensively on reforms of Chinese higher education, American research universities, and regional higher education development both in English and in Chinese. Her current research focuses on higher education internationalization, the development of global research universities, and Chinese higher education reform.

Stephen P. Heyneman
(Professor, Peabody College of Education, Vanderbilt University)
Stephen P. Heyneman received his Ph.D. in comparative education from the University of Chicago in 1976. He served the World Bank for 22 years. Between 1976 and 1984, he helped research education quality and design policies to support educational effectiveness. Between 1984 and 1989, he was in charge of external training for senior officials worldwide in education policy. And between 1989 and 1998, he was responsible for education policy and lending strategy, first for the Middle East and North Africa and later for the 27 countries of Europe and Central Asia. In July 2000, he was appointed professor of International Education Policy at Vanderbilt University. Current interests include the effect of higher education on social cohesion, the international trade in education services, and the economic and social cost to higher education corruption.

Jeongwoo Lee

(Ph.D. Student, Peabody College of Education, Vanderbilt University)
Jeongwoo Lee is a Ph.D. student in International Education Policy and Management at Peabody College, Vanderbilt University. Current research interests lie in, but are not limited to, three areas of focus: education for social cohesion, the contribution of education to poverty alleviation and economic development, and access and equity in higher education.

Simon Marginson

(Professor, Center for the Study of Higher Education, University of Melbourne)
Dr. Marginson is a professor of Higher Education at the University of Melbourne, in the Centre for the Study of Higher Education. A Ph.D. graduate from the same university (1996), his work focuses on higher education systems and policy, especially international and global aspects. Dr. Marginson has won three American awards for scholarly publication and in 2011, became a coordinating editor of *Higher Education*. Current research concerns the global strategies of research universities in the Asia-Pacific (20 cases), relations between public and private sector research organizations (Australia, Netherlands, and Korea), and the contribution of universities to path-breaking creativity. Recent books include *International Student Security* with Chris Nyland, Erlenawati Sawir, and Helen Forbes-Mewett (2010), *Higher Education in the Asia-Pacific*, with Sarjit Kaur and Erlenawati Sawir (2011), and *Handbook on Globalization and Higher Education*, with Roger King and Rajani Naidoo (2011). Four of Dr. Marginson's books have been translated in China.

Leon Cremonini

(Researcher, Center for Higher Education Policy Studies, University of Twente)
Leon Cremonini is a researcher at the Center for Higher Education Policy Studies (CHEPS) since 2006. He graduated in International Political Science from the University of Bologna, Italy, in 2000. Over the last decade, Leon worked both in Europe and at the RAND Corporation in the United States. His interests concentrate on the internationalization of higher education, quality assessment at the institutional and program level, and on the study of university and program rankings. He presented papers and published on these topics and has been involved in a number of international projects concerned with the development of quality assurance and accreditation systems in several countries in Africa, the Middle East, and Southeast Asia.

Paul Benneworth

(Senior Researcher, Center for Higher Education Policy Studies, University of Twente)
Paul Benneworth is a senior researcher at the Center for Higher Education Policy Studies at the University of Twente in the Netherlands. His research concerns the relationships between universities and society, particularly in the fields of business, community, and regional engagement. From 2010 to 2012, he was the project leader of the European Science Foundation-funded project Measuring the Value of Arts

and Humanities Research, part of the Humanities in the European Research Area ERA-NET program.

Hugh Dauncey
(Professor, Department of French Studies, Newcastle University)
Dr. Dauncey teaches and researches in the department of French Studies, Newcastle University, GB. Before working at Newcastle University, he worked in France at the ESCAE Bordeaux and the Université Paris VII. He is an associate researcher at the CNRS-Université Paris I Sorbonne Georges-Friedmann Research Centre. His research interests center on French public policy in a range of fields, but he focuses principally on cultural policy of all kinds and France's "exceptionalism" in terms of state attitudes toward France's place in a globalized world. For a number of years, he has taught modules on the French education system which focus particularly on how "republican values" are translated into practice in the context of higher education and research. In 2003, he was appointed Chevalier dans l'Ordre des Palmes académiques in recognition of "services to French culture."

Don F. Westerheijden
(Senior Research Associate, Center for Higher Education Policy Studies, University of Twente)
Dr. Westerheijden graduated from the Faculty of Public Administration and Public Policy at the University of Twente in 1984 and subsequently completed his dissertation there, on political and bureaucratic decision-making, in 1988. Since then, he has worked as senior research associate at the Center for Higher Education Policy Studies (CHEPS) of that university, where he coordinates research related to quality management and he is involved in the coordination of Ph.D. students. He has edited and contributed to books on quality assessment in higher education and produced a large number of articles on the topic. He is a member of the editorial boards of three journals related to quality in higher education. In addition, he is a member of the expert panel of Studychoice.nl, the Dutch national website for comparative study program information. His research interests include institutional and systematic impacts of internal and external evaluation of quality (of education, of research, and of institutions) in Europe, among other things focusing on the Bologna process, student information systems and other "rankings," and methodological issues of policy evaluation, case study, and comparative research. Don is involved in a number of projects for education ministries, higher education agencies, and higher education institutions across Europe, Asia (Hong Kong, Vietnam, SEAMEO), the United States (Ford Foundation), and Southern Africa (Mozambique).

Akiyoshi Yonezawa
(Associate Professor, Graduate School of International Development, Nagoya University)
Dr. Yonezawa is an associate professor at the Graduate School of International Development (GSID), Nagoya University. With sociological background, he is mainly researching on the comparative higher education policies, especially focusing on world-class universities, quality assurance of higher education, and public-private

relationship of higher education. Before moving to Nagoya University in October 2010, he has worked at National Institution for Academic Degrees and University Evaluation (NIAD-UE), Tohoku University, Hiroshima University, OECD, and the University of Tokyo. His recent articles are Learning Outcomes and Quality Assurance: Challenges for Japanese Higher Education, Evaluation in Higher Education (2009), Japanese University Leaders' Perceptions of Internationalization: The Role of Government in Review and Support (2009), and The Internationalization of Japanese Higher Education: Policy Debates and Realities (2011).

Yong Suk Jang
(Associate Professor, Public Administration, Yonsei University)
Dr. Jang is an associate professor of Public Administration at Yonsei University. He received his Ph.D. in sociology from Stanford University and taught at the University of Utah (2001–2004) and Korea University (2004–2008). His current research interests include macro-comparative analyses of nation-states and organizations, governance, and neo-institutionalism. Recent publications include Classics of Organization Theory, 7th ed. (Wadsworth Cengage Learning) and articles in Administrative Science Quarterly, Asian Business and Management, Sociological Perspectives, International Sociology, International Journal of Comparative Sociology, Development and Society, The Journal of Educational Administration, Journal of Korean Association for Policy Studies, Review of International Area Studies, and Quarterly Journal of Labor Policy, Human Resource Management Review, and Korean Journal of Sociology.

Yan Luo
(Associate Professor, Institute of Education, Tsinghua University)
Dr. Luo Yan is an associate professor and the vice-director of Education Policy and Administration of the Institute of Education, Tsinghua University of China. She got her bachelor's and master's degree in education from Beijing Normal University and Ph.D. in sociology from the University of Hong Kong. From 2007 to 2008, she worked in the Center of Educational Evaluation and Policy (CEEP) of Indiana University (Bloomington), helping to design an international comparable and culturally adapted version of NSSE survey. With the instrument NSSE-China and working with her colleagues in Tsinghua, she successfully conducted 2 year-round surveying across China. She published a lot of papers on institutional analysis of Chinese higher education and strategies for institutional improvement, in the theoretical perspective of sociological neo-institutionalism. Seconded by Chinese Ministry of Education, she is now working in the section of Higher Education of UNESCO Headquarter.

Dian-fu Chang
(Professor, Graduate Institute of Educational Policy and Leadership, Tamkang University, Taiwan)
Dr. Chang is a professor of Graduate Institute of Educational Policy and Leadership, Tamkang University. Prior to this position, he worked in two different universities.

The first one is as a professor of Graduate School of Education in National Cheng Chi University, Taipei City. The later one is as a professor and dean of College of Education, National Chi Nan University. He holds a doctorate in education from Teachers College, Columbia University. His research centers on higher education and educational policy issues in national and international levels. He has over 20 years' experience in higher education—including teaching, research, and policy work with the government of Taiwan. He has been invited as guest speakers by leading better teaching and learning for university students or adults in China, Japan, and annual conference of Taiwan Educational Policy and Evaluation Society. His most recent efforts has focused on the 2 years integrated projects on ASEAN 10 plus 3 countries to discuss the higher education issues and compare their different development experiences funded by National Science Council of Taiwan.

Morshidi Sirat
(Deputy Director-General, Ministry of Higher Education, Malaysia and Professor, School of Humanities, Universiti Sains Malaysia, Penang)
Professor Morshidi is Deputy Director-General, Department of Higher Education (Public Sector), Ministry of Higher Education, Malaysia. Between April 2002 and Feb 2011, Morshidi was the director of the National Higher Education Research Institute Malaysia (IPPTN), and during this period, he specialized in higher education policy research. Morshidi has published widely in higher education related journals and authored/coauthored 20 books and monographs on higher education. Morshidi is also active in international research collaboration with organizations such as OECD/IMHE, the World Bank, UNESCO, the ADB, SEAMEO-RIHED, and International Institute for Educational Planning, Paris. Recently, Morshidi has just completed a 3-year research project on *Ideopolis Kuala Lumpur* (a city based on knowledge and innovation).

Kong Chong Ho
(Associate Professor, Faculty of Arts and Social Sciences, National University of Singapore)
K. C. HO is associate professor of Sociology and vice dean (Research) at the Faculty of Arts and Social Sciences, National University of Singapore. Trained as an urban sociologist at the University of Chicago, Dr Ho's research interests are in the political economy of cities, migration, higher education, youth, and leisure. Dr Ho is board member of Research Committee 21 (Sociology of Urban and Regional, International Sociological Association) and an editorial board member of Pacific Affairs. His recent publications include Ho, K.C. Ang, I, and Ho, K.W. (2011), Youth.sg: State of Youth in Singapore (National Youth Council), Sidhu, R. & Ho, K.C. & Yeoh, B. (2011). The Global Schoolhouse: Governing Singapore's Knowledge Economy Aspirations In Higher Education in the Asia Pacific. Springer Marginson, S. ; Kaur, S. ; & Sawir, E. (Eds.). Springer, Dordrecht; and Sidhu, R. & Ho, K.C. & Yeoh, B. (2011). "Emerging Education Hubs: The Case of Singapore." *Higher Education.* He is the lead researcher in a comparative project "Globalizing

Universities and International Student Mobilities in East Asia," involving leading universities in China, Japan, Korea, Taiwan, and Singapore.

Gerard A. Postiglione
(Professor, Faculty of Education, University of Hong Kong)

Dr. Postiglione is professor and head, Division of Policy, Administration, and Social Sciences, Faculty of Education, University of Hong Kong. He published over 100 journal articles and book chapters and 10 books. He edits the journal, *Chinese Education and Society*, and four book series. His latest book is *Crossing Borders in East Asian Higher Education*. He was a researcher/consultant/trainer for Asian Development Bank, Institute of International Education, United Nations Development Programme, World Bank, Carnegie Foundation for the Advancement of Teaching, and the Ford Foundation. He was invited to address China's Ministry of Education, the American Council on Education, White House Fellows, Office of the Secretary of Education, and UNESCO and was brought to 20 countries to speak on educational reform. He has appeared on CNN and is quoted in the *New York Times, International Herald Tribune, BusinessWeek* and *Newsweek*. He held sabbatical appointments at Yale University, Peking University, Johns Hopkins University, Stanford University, and Columbia University.

Jisun Jung
(Postdoctoral Fellow, Faculty of Education, University of Hong Kong)

Dr. Jisun Jung is a postdoctoral fellow in the Faculty of Education at the University of Hong Kong. She received her Ph.D. from Seoul National University, Korea. She is involved in the international comparative research project "The Changing Academic Profession." Her current research focuses on research productivity of academics, academic career development, and university ranking.

Francisco O. Ramirez
(Professor of Education, Stanford University)

Francisco O. Ramirez is professor of Education and Sociology (by courtesy) and associate dean for Faculty Affairs in the School of Education at Stanford University. His ongoing research interests focus on the rise of a global human rights regime and its transformation to human rights education, the changing status of women as citizens and persons, and the influence of templates of excellence in higher education on universities worldwide. Recent publications may be found in Social Forces, Sociology of Education, Comparative Education Review, among others. Ramirez has been an invited fellow at the Center for the Advanced Studies of the Behavioral Sciences. His most recent keynote address was at the Hong Kong Sociological Association.

John W. Meyer
(Professor of Sociology, Emeritus; Professor of Education)

John W. Meyer is professor of Sociology (and, by courtesy, Education), emeritus, at Stanford. He has contributed to organizational theory, comparative education, and the sociology of education, developing sociological institutional theory. Since the 1970s, he has studied the impact of global society on national states and societies (some papers are collected in Weltkultur: Wie die westlichen Prinzipien die Welt durchdringen, Suhrkamp, 2005; a more extensive set is in G. Kruecken and G. Drori, eds.: World Society: The Writings of John W. Meyer, Oxford 2009). In 2003, he completed a collaborative study of worldwide science and its national effects (Drori, et al., Science in the Modern World Polity, Stanford). A more recent collaborative project is on the impact of globalization on organizational structures (Drori et al., eds., Globalization and Organization, Oxford 2006). He now studies the world human rights regime and world curricula in mass and higher education. He has honorary doctorates from the Stockholm School of Economics and the Universities of Bielefeld and Lucerne and received American Sociological Association's awards for lifetime contributions to the sociology of education and to the study of globalization.

Index

Printed by Printforce, the Netherlands